# TANTRA

## ENLIGHTENMENT
## TO REVOLUTION

# TANTRA

## ENLIGHTENMENT TO REVOLUTION

IMMA RAMOS

Thames & Hudson   The British Museum

**Front cover:** Detail of fig. 134, Kali, Krishnanagar, Bengal, India, late 19th century, painted and gilded clay, British Museum 1894,0216.10
**Back cover:** Fig. 71, A woman visiting two Nath yoginis, northern India, mid-18th century, gouache on paper, British Museum 1913,1218,0.10
**Frontispiece:** Detail of fig. 98, *thangka* showing Chakrasamvara in union with Vajrayogini, Tibet, 18th century, painted silk, British Museum 1957,0413,0.1

*Tantra: enlightenment to revolution*
Supported by

This publication accompanies the exhibition *Tantra: enlightenment to revolution* at the British Museum from 23 April to 26 July 2020.

This exhibition has been made possible by the provision of insurance through the Government Indemnity Scheme. The British Museum would like to thank the Department for Digital, Culture, Media and Sport, and Arts Council England for providing and arranging this indemnity.

First published in the United Kingdom in 2020 by Thames & Hudson Ltd, in collaboration with the British Museum.

*Tantra: enlightenment to revolution* © 2020 The Trustees of the British Museum/ Thames & Hudson Ltd, London

Text © 2020 The Trustees of the British Museum
Images © 2020 The Trustees of the British Museum, courtesy of the British Museum's Department of Photography and Imaging, unless otherwise stated on pp. 310–11

Design © 2020 Thames & Hudson Ltd, London
Designed by Peter Dawson and Amy Shortis at gradedesign.com

British Library Cataloguing-in-Publication Data
A catalogue record for this book is available from the British Library

ISBN 978-0-500-48062-5

Printed and bound in Italy by Printer Trento SrL

The papers used in this book are natural, renewable and recyclable products and the manufacturing processes are expected to conform to the environmental regulations of the country of origin.

Thames & Hudson Ltd, 181A High Holborn, London WC1V 7QX

To find out about all our publications, please visit **www.thamesandhudson.com**. There you can subscribe to our e-newsletter, browse or download our current catalogue, and buy any titles that are in print.

For more information about the Museum and its collection, please visit **britishmuseum.org**.

# CONTENTS

# SUPPORTER'S FOREWORD

The Bagri Foundation is particularly excited to be lead supporter of the exhibition *Tantra: enlightenment to revolution* at the British Museum. Tantra is a belief system that remains greatly misunderstood. The last exhibition on the subject, held in 1971 at the Hayward Gallery and simply called 'Tantra', broached this complex tradition through the now popularized lens of ecstasy and eroticism. It is now time to move beyond this view, and to explore the wider, lesser-known philosophies of Tantra and their impact throughout history.

We celebrate the importance of this exhibition, which goes beyond the populist images of Tantra to focus on the fundamentals of its spiritual practice as well as its complexities and evolution, and the multiple cross-over points of Tantra with major world religions. Congratulations are due to the Director, Hartwig Fischer, and the exhibition curator Dr Imma Ramos at the British Museum, who have bravely addressed the depth and breadth of this subject, which, without scholarly attention, is not so easily translated to the wider global stage.

Our endeavour is to contribute to global discourse by sharing knowledge and expertise about cultures across Asia. With a keen interest in Tantric art and its principles – its ability to inspire spiritual awakening and its quest for universal truth – and at a moment when it is vital to find points of connection, we are very pleased to support this exciting and timely exhibition.

Dr Alka Bagri
Trustee, Bagri Foundation

# DIRECTOR'S FOREWORD

From around the 6th century CE the philosophies and practices of Tantra spread across India. The movement's beliefs, outlined in texts named *Tantras*, promised accelerated spiritual enlightenment as well as worldly and supernatural powers, achievable through rituals designed to awaken a person's inner divinity. Tantra had widespread appeal across multiple levels of society and elements of it can be found across Asia's diverse cultures.

This publication and its accompanying exhibition trace the history of Tantra, from its origins, major beliefs, artistic expressions and royal patronage in India, to its spread across Asia, and finally to its redefinition from the 19th century until today in India and the West. It presents masterpieces of sculpture and painting, as well as ritual implements, illuminating Tantra's intimate relationship with Hinduism and Buddhism.

Tantra has been the subject of great fascination for centuries. However, it has often been misunderstood, particularly in the West where it is interpreted as a hedonistic guide to sex. Although the erotic plays an important role in Tantra, it should be understood as part of a broader philosophy of ritual transgression. Many Tantric texts describe ceremonies that deliberately subverted existing social and religious norms – for example, engagement with the taboo, such as human remains, bodily fluids and intoxicants. Tantra challenged distinctions between opposites by teaching that all material reality is sacred, including the 'forbidden', which could be ritually harnessed. This publication includes images and descriptions of practices that are often macabre and erotically charged, challenging us to question our assumptions about the nature of the divine.

The British Museum has one of the most comprehensive collections of Tantric material in the world and is in a unique position to present a history of Tantra through objects that challenge assumptions about it in stimulating ways. This is the first in-depth study of the Museum's collection and the first historical exploration of Tantric visual culture, from its origins in India to its reimagining in the West.

While most objects are drawn from the Museum's own collection, significant loans are also included from the National Museum, New Delhi, Trustees of the Chester Beatty Library, the Metropolitan Museum of Art, the Rubin Museum of Art, Cambridge University Library, the British Library, National Trust, Hauser & Wirth, Bradford Museum and Galleries, Richard Saltoun Gallery and the Wellcome Collection. We are most grateful to all generous lenders.

The British Museum also extends its warmest thanks to the Bagri Foundation, the lead supporter of *Tantra: enlightenment to revolution*.

Hartwig Fischer
Director, British Museum

# PRELUDE

Crowning the top of a hill on the bank of the Brahmaputra river in north-
east India, the temple of Kamakhya in Assam is regarded as the most
revered site of goddess worship in South Asia (figs. 1, 2). Dating back to at
least the 8th century CE, Kamakhya is described in early textual sources as
a centre of Tantra, a philosophy that affirmed the world as a manifestation
of Shakti, divine feminine power.[1] The ritual practices that are still conducted
in and around the temple today reveal some of Tantra's enduring core
beliefs. Pilgrims descending into its inner sanctum or *garbhagriha* ('womb-
chamber'), a dark and cave-like space, encounter a fissure in a large rock,
which is venerated by devotees of Shakti as the *yoni* or vulva of the goddess,
and has made the temple famous as a Seat of Power (Shakti Pitha).
According to the Tantric worldview, Shakti pervades the material world
and can be ritually channelled and internalized to reach a spiritually
enlightened state, and to cultivate worldly success and even supernatural
abilities along the way.

Every summer at Kamakhya, the Ambuvachi Mela ('issuing forth
of rain festival') celebrates the goddess's annual menstrual flow, which
is believed to nourish the earth.[2] The four-day festival takes place every
June–July, during the monsoon season, and is closely connected to
the agricultural cycle. During this time of the year the water from an
underground spring runs red with iron oxide from the soil, trickling over

**Fig. 1**
**Pilgrimage souvenir**
**representing Kamakhya**
**temple crowning**
**Nilachal Hill**
Guwahati, Assam, India
2004
Chromolithographic print,
18.5 × 24.6 cm
British Museum 2005,0509,0.13
Donated by K. K. Maheshwari

**Fig. 2**
**Kamakhya temple**
Guwahati, Assam, India
2008

the *yoni* in the temple's inner sanctum so that it appears as if the goddess is menstruating.[3] According to orthodox Hindu belief, menstrual blood is considered highly polluting and therefore dangerous, but at Kamakhya it is channelled for its auspiciousness and potency.[4] Tantra not only validates and affirms all aspects of the female body, regarded as a vessel of Shakti, but also challenges cultural distinctions between purity and impurity. By engaging with the transgressive and the taboo (either literally or symbolically), the repressed powers of traditionally forbidden practices and substances can be harnessed. At Kamakhya, reddened pieces of cloth wrapped around the *yoni* are sought after by pilgrims and prized for their talismanic, protective and life-giving properties. The power of the *yoni* and its menstrual fluids are viscerally conveyed to visitors by a sculpture depicting a squatting figure of a goddess displaying her vulva (fig. 3).

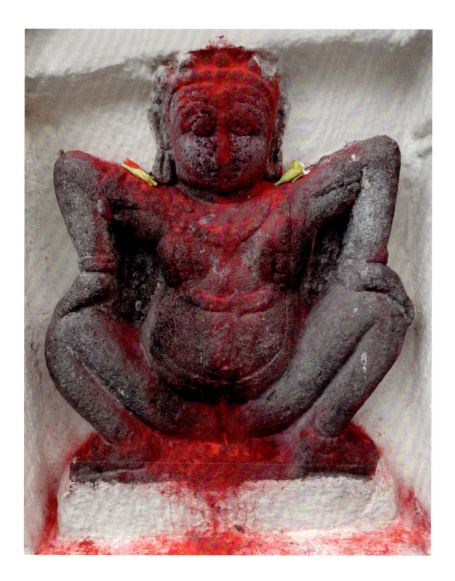

Devotees regularly anoint her pudendum with red pigment or *sindoor* to receive her blessing as an embodiment of fertility and creative power.[5]

There are numerous representations of goddesses in and around the Kamakhya temple site. All are understood as manifestations of Shakti, their characteristics reflecting a uniquely Tantric tension between the destructive and the maternal. One depicts the skeletal goddess Chamunda, clutching a skull-cup filled with blood to satiate her ravenous hunger (fig. 4). She is seated on a human corpse, evoking the world of the cremation ground. In one of her other four hands she carries a sword of wisdom with which she destroys not only demons (*asuras*) on the cosmic battlefield but also the devotee's ego, symbolized by the corpse as well as the garland of decapitated heads around her neck. Her violent appearance, while inspiring awe and fear, also conveys compassion and her desire to assist followers on their path towards enlightenment by releasing them from ignorance. Pilgrims at the temple regularly leave her offerings of flowers.

Tantra transformed South Asia's major religions, and today elements of it can be found across Asia's diverse cultures. However, it remains largely

**Fig. 4**
**Sculpture of the goddess
Chamunda**
Kamakhya site, Guwahati,
Assam, India
*c.* 10th century
Granite adorned with *sindoor*

misunderstood in the West, where it is equated with sex. The popular 'Tantra' festivals that take place in 21st-century North America and Europe feature playgrounds of flesh and free love conjured by the burgeoning corporate Wellness industry. Workshops tackle a moveable feast of topics, from the 'Art of Tantric Massage' and 'Multi-Orgasmic Men and Women' to 'Sexercises' and 'Igniting the Fifteen Chakras to the Sublime'. The only thing more slippery than a Tantric Massage demonstration is how the category of 'Tantra' itself is being sold: as an all-encompassing spiritual fix, synonymous with heteronormative sexual pleasure. The plethora of hedonistic offerings is not unusual, however. Tantra has been misunderstood as a 'cult of ecstasy' in the West since the early 19th century, when Christian missionaries, Orientalist scholars and colonial officials wrote the first detailed interpretations of a diverse range of texts, rituals and traditions in India and monolithically classified them as 'Tantric', often reductively dismissing them as promoting orgiastic and degenerate behaviour. This overwhelmingly negative colonial-era view would give way in the 20th century to a reappraisal of Tantra in the West, emphasizing its apparent expression of countercultural free love.

# INTRODUCTION

The Sanskrit word *Tantra* refers to a type of instructional religious text, system or doctrine that originated around the 6th century CE in India. The name derives from the verbal root *tan*, meaning 'to weave', 'extend' or 'compose'; the wider tradition of Tantra 'wove' together various rituals and practices propounding *Tantrashastra* ('the teachings of the *Tantras*'), which were presented as the divine revelations of gods and goddesses. Many of the ideas and deities described in the *Tantras* were present around a century before, judging by surviving archaeological and sculptural evidence.[1] The geographical origins of this tradition are unclear but eastern India (Bengal and Assam) and the north-west (Kashmir) were important early centres where *Tantras* were composed, most of them from the 8th century onwards.

The majority of the *Tantras* and Tantra-related texts focus on the most effective ritual practices (*sadhanas*) for achieving spiritual enlightenment alongside worldly and supernatural powers.[2] These rituals, which guide the practitioner in sacralizing the body, are considered highly dangerous if carried out incorrectly and therefore require initiation and guidance from a Tantric teacher or guru. Tantra did not constitute an independent religion but was rather a movement that infiltrated and transformed South Asia's mainstream religious traditions, especially Hinduism and Buddhism. Part of the success of Tantra lay in its ritual transgression of the orthodox codes of conduct prescribed by these dominant traditions.

Tantra presented an alternative *dharma* ('path of action' or 'duty') to the prevalent Hindu one at the time. Hinduism itself is made up of a vast range of different beliefs, practices and scriptures.[3] Many of its traditions emerged out of the divinely revealed *Vedas* (literally 'knowledge'; a body of texts composed *c.* 1500–500 BCE) and its later sacred Vedic texts including the *Puranas* ('old' or 'ancient', composed from around 300 CE). The *Vedas* include liturgical hymns and guidance for Brahmins (priests) on how to deliver them ritually, including through fire offerings to gods (*homa*). Only Brahmins had the authority to use the *Vedas* in rituals, hence the oft-used scholarly term 'Brahmanical' to describe orthodox Hinduism.[4] The *Puranas* were dedicated to the devotional worship and mythologizing of deities, especially the gods Vishnu (preserver of the universe), Shiva (destroyer of the universe) and Shakti, also referred to as Mahadevi or Great Goddess (the universe's all-pervasive force). The rise of Tantra coincided with the rise of three major traditions within Hinduism, each revering one of these deities as the supreme manifestation of the divine: Vaishnavism (centring on Vishnu), Shaivism (centring on Shiva) and Shaktism (centring on Shakti). Tantric teachings first arose among nonconformist devotees of Shiva and Shakti.[5]

By the 7th century Buddhism had drawn on and creatively adapted Tantric ideas. Buddhism was based on the teachings of Gautama Buddha (5th century BCE) who taught that suffering is a part of everyday life, that the root of suffering is craving, and that happiness lies in liberating the self from the ties of attachment to this world. After the Buddha's death, communities of monks and nuns continued to promote the Buddha's message, but new schools of thought developed that approached the teachings in different ways. One of the first, which remained closest to the early Buddhist scriptures, was the Theravada ('Teaching of the Elders') tradition, revolving around the attainment of spiritual liberation through one's own efforts. Between around 150 BCE and 100 CE a new tradition emerged, known as the Mahayana ('Great Vehicle'), which emphasized the cultivation of compassion and devotion to a number of Buddhist deities and Bodhisattvas (enlightened saviour beings). The Tantric tradition, known as the Vajrayana ('Thunderbolt Vehicle') in Buddhist circles, retained the core philosophical teachings of Gautama Buddha and the Mahayana path but promised infinitely more powerful, practical methods for attaining the same goal – that of enlightenment.[6] While the Hindu *Tantras* were understood as the original teachings of Shiva and Shakti and were often framed as dialogues between the deities, the Buddhist *Tantras* had their own equivalent divine narrators.

Tantra quickly spread across the subcontinent and became a mainstream, pan-Indian movement by about the 9th–10th centuries, transforming and 'Tantricizing' Hinduism and Buddhism. Tantric forms of Buddhism would go on to spread across South, South East, East and Central Asia via travelling pilgrims, monks, teachers and merchants.

## THE PATH OF POWER

Between the 9th and 6th centuries BCE the concept of *samsara*, the idea that beings are cyclically reincarnated into the world, developed in India.[7] Ancient Hindu and Buddhist ascetics advocated certain practices, including renunciation, austerity, meditation and yoga, in order to release themselves from this cycle and achieve spiritual enlightenment. Enlightenment was understood in different ways. *Moksha* (liberation) from the Hindu perspective suggests a release from this world, conceived as an illusion (*maya*), through the realization of one's unity with Brahman, the transcendent principle binding the universe. *Nirvana* ('blowing out') from the Buddhist perspective implies a complete extinction of the self. In contrast, the Tantric view asserted that the world is not illusory but real – that one does not need to negate this world or escape from it in order to reach a state of *moksha* or *nirvana*. Not only is the world real, it is also understood as the concrete manifestation of divine power; only the limitations of the mind prevent recognition of this fact. Rather than attempting to transcend this fluid, power-charged world, a Tantrika (Tantric practitioner) can sublimate it and magically transform reality itself. The Tantrika achieves this realization and channels this power by identifying with and internalizing one of the many all-knowing, all-powerful Tantric gods.

This approach to divinity contrasted with mainstream Hindu and Buddhist ones, which generally treated gods as external forces to be worshipped. Moreover, while the benevolent and peaceful qualities of deities tended to be emphasized in orthodox contexts, Tantra introduced and promoted a multitude of deities who were uniquely ferocious and sexually charged, drawing on Indian models of demons and converting them into agents of spiritual transformation. As described in Tantric texts, these deities could be internalized and appeased via a range of mental and bodily practices, including through visualization and Tantric forms of yoga. Indeed, the Tantric perception of the body marked a dynamic shift in attitudes towards corporeality. Rather than viewing it as a flawed, decaying carrier of unclean substances and as an impediment to spiritual liberation as in orthodox Hindu and Buddhist traditions, Tantric teachings focused on the body as the ultimate instrument for self-deification, and regarded it as a microcosmic mirror of the universe. Tantric mental practices involved visualizations of deities, using material aids such as paintings and sculptures as well as symbolic, geometric diagrams (*yantras* and mandalas). Sanskrit syllables embodying the nature of a god or goddess (mantras) could also be ritually used as tools to invoke their presence.

Ritual instructions for self-divination are preserved in some of the earliest surviving Tantric palm-leaf manuscripts in Sanskrit from Nepal. A 14th/15th-century copy of the Tantric Hindu *Yoginihridaya* (*Heart of the Yogini*), originally composed in the 10th/11th century, consists of a dialogue between the goddess Tripurasundari and the god Bhairava (fig. 5). One folio begins with a benediction to the goddess and proceeds to outline a ritual called *nyasa* ('placing' or 'marking') for internalizing her power. This involves pronouncing mantras and touching different parts of the body, including the 'shoulder, the extremity of the hand, the hip, and the toes and (…) on the base and the back of the head'.[8] The absorption of the essence of the mantras must be visualized to achieve self-deification and an adoption of Tripurasundari's cosmic form. According to the text, *nyasa* 'purifies the body, and is supreme'.[9] Mantras play a fundamental role as 'power-words' in Tantric practice, and are transmitted from guru to disciple after initiation (*diksha*).[10]

While the orthodox Hindu and Buddhist paths conceived of *moksha* and *nirvana* as ideal yet remote goals that could be realized only gradually, over many lifetimes, advanced Tantric rituals passed down from guru to disciple were believed to be so powerful that they could offer a fast-track to enlightenment within a single lifetime. Another key characteristic of Tantra was that enlightenment was not the only goal. Tantric texts emphasize the importance of cultivating worldly and supernatural powers or attainments (*siddhis*), no longer considered obstacles to spiritual release as they had been viewed traditionally. If the Tantric world was one of limitless sacred power

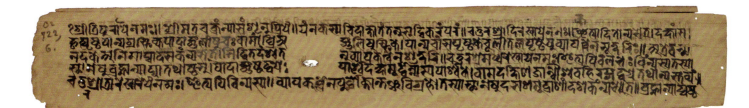

**Fig. 5**

**Folio from the *Yoginihridaya***

Nepal

14th–15th century

Palm leaf, 5 × 32.8 cm

Cambridge University Library

MS Or.722.6 (fol. 1v)

that could be channelled through the body and mind, then this fluid energy could be harnessed, mastered and manipulated to empower the Tantrika. The *siddhis* desired by the Tantrika might include longevity, prosperity, political gain, defence against malevolent forces, the conquering of obstacles, or even powers of flight and invisibility. This binding of liberation- and power-seeking, and the idea that it was unnecessary to live a renunciant, ascetic life free from worldly concerns in order to achieve a higher state of consciousness, was key to Tantra's success among lay non-celibate householders in medieval India. The notion that one could achieve enlightenment in this earthly realm quickly, and also attain powers along the way, was attractive to many.[11]

With great power came the possibility of inevitable dangers and difficulties along the Tantric path. Tantrikas were even described as heroes (*viras*) because of the risks and challenges they faced in striving to achieve their aims. The most notorious risk came through the ritual use of traditionally taboo substances that were believed to violate socio-religious purity strictures according to Brahmanical texts such as the *Dharma Sutras* (composed sometime between the 3rd century BCE and 1st century CE). Within the Hindu Tantric tradition, articulated in texts including the *Bhairava Tantras* and *Vidyapitha Tantras* (6th–7th centuries), these became known as the 'Five Ms' (*panchamakara*): wine (*madya*), fish (*matsya*), meat (*mamsa*), sexual fluids generated from ritual intercourse (*maithuna*) and parched grain (*mudra*). The equivalent Buddhist Tantric texts (including the *Mahayoga Tantras* and *Yogini Tantras*, 8th–10th centuries) also included the five Tantric ambrosias or *panchamrita* (urine, excrement, semen, menstrual blood, brains) and the five Tantric meats or *panchamamsa* (human flesh, beef, horse, dog and elephant). In both Hindu and Buddhist Tantric texts such substances were described as being ritually consumed or offered to deities. According to orthodox Hinduism, engaging with the 'polluted' or the intrinsically repulsive could contaminate and corrupt one's very being. Tantric texts, however, philosophically challenged these distinctions between purity and impurity as artificial constructs. The affirmation that all was sacred in the material world, including the 'forbidden', eradicated such distinctions in the mind of the Tantrika when a 'god's-eye view' was adopted. As the *Guhyasamaja Tantra* (*c*. 8th century) stated: 'the wise man who does not discriminate achieves Buddhahood [enlightenment]'.[12]

A 12th-century Nepalese copy of the Tantric Buddhist *Vajramrita Tantra* (*Nectar of the Thunderbolt Tantra*) (fig. 6), a text originally composed in the 9th/10th century, is based on a conversation between the Buddha and the

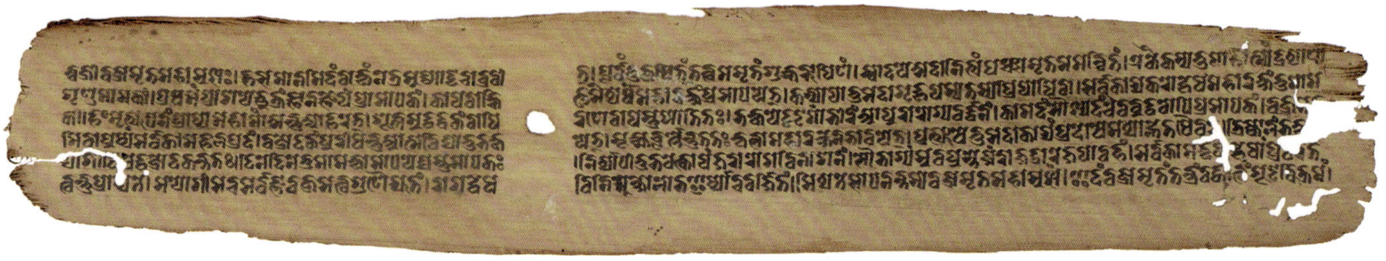

Fig. 6
**Folio from the** *Vajramrita*
*Tantra*
Nepal
1162 CE
Palm leaf, 5 × 31 cm
Cambridge University Library
MS Or.158.1 (fol. 12r)

goddess Mamaki. One folio describes the benefits that come from the ritual ingestion of the five ambrosias: 'eating these substances involves an increase of life and health; it confers pleasure as well as the awakening of the Buddhas'.[13] According to the text, the Tantrika should mix the substances and consume them three times a day, until their body becomes 'free from sickness and old age' and 'endowed with the qualities of [a god], free from attachment and aversion, and free from covetousness and envy'.[14]

From this perspective, urine, excrement, semen, menstrual blood and brains could be transformed into receptacles of the divine. By ingesting taboo substances, offering them to deities and interacting with powerful and potentially destructive forces, the Tantrika could stimulate an inner breakthrough. Rather than suppressing emotional obstacles to enlightenment, such as disgust, fear and desire, the practitioner would confront and harness their power, ritually engaging with them in order, ultimately, to transcend them.

Many images of Tantric deities articulate this concept by depicting them in sexual union and/or covered in human remains. Such an approach naturally led to the shattering of other conventional 'dualisms', projected by the ego-mind, which resulted in inhibiting misperceptions of reality. These included distinctions between oneself/others, masculine/feminine, sacred/profane, pure/impure and permanent/impermanent. The 8th-century *Panchakrama* (*Five Stages*) by the Indian Tantric Buddhist master Nagarjuna distils this point succinctly:

> Defilement and purification –
> Knowing them from the perspective of ultimate reality
> The one who knows [them as] one thing
> Knows communion (…)
> As oneself, so an enemy (…)
> As one's mother, so a whore, (…)
> As urine, so wine.
> As food, so shit.
> As sweet-smelling camphor, so the stench from the ritually-impure
> As words of praise, so revolting words (…)
> As pleasure, so pain.[15]

Since the potential hazards of these practices were great and detachment and discipline were key, Tantric teachings were initiatory, accessible only via an experienced guru. For this reason, Tantric texts and objects often employ highly esoteric, ambiguous and metaphorical language to ensure that only advanced Tantrikas, under the guidance of their guru, could navigate and plumb their true meanings and depths. As a result, the interpretation of the *Tantras* remains a dynamic, often hotly debated subject, particularly regarding whether their transgressive instructions, which can be both sexual and stomach-turning, should be read literally or symbolically.[16] This ambiguity allowed for multiple readings and inspired many commentaries as well as related expressions in the visual arts.

The tension is partly resolved, or at least explained, by the distinction between the 'left-hand path' (*vamachara*), which interprets the instructions of Tantric texts literally, and the 'right-hand path' (*dakshinachara*), which interprets them symbolically, through visualization techniques and by using substitutes (such as milk and flowers) for taboo substances or acts. This 'softening' or 'sanitizing' of Tantra made the movement more acceptable among popular and even monastic, celibate audiences, ensuring its mainstream dissemination while simultaneously respecting the greater power promised by the 'left-hand path'.[17] Whether or not the transgressive elements of Tantric texts are taken literally (and the lines were frequently blurry), both approaches tap into the same wellspring of symbolic vocabulary. In the case of sexual rites (*maithuna*), for example, the union of Tantric deities is visualized, sacralizing and empowering the body of the practitioner. In the Hindu *Tantras* the deities envisaged in union are usually Shiva and Shakti, representing pure consciousness (*purusha*) and creative force (*prakriti*), respectively. In the Buddhist *Tantras* the goddesses represent wisdom (*prajna*) while their male counterparts represent compassion (*karuna*). If the Tantrika is a celibate monk or nun, the divine sexual rite may be imagined as a symbolic, internal union using visualization exercises; or it may be re-enacted physically by a non-celibate couple visualizing each other as embodiments of the deities. Some Tantric texts recommend going even further and performing sexual rites with a 'taboo' partner such as a socially outcast individual, to violate and overturn orthopraxy entirely.[18]

In the *Vajramrita Tantra* (fig. 7), Mamaki asks the Buddha how to access the nectar (*amrita*) of the thunderbolt (*vajra*), which is understood as both a nectar of immortality and as creative seminal fluid. The Buddha tells the goddess that it can be accessed through pleasure, including sexual union, if both partners have internalized the deities: 'the nectar of the *vajra* is produced by the unions of *vajra* [a metaphor for the phallus] and lotus [a metaphor for the vulva]. (…) the male practitioner [representing the god] should kiss the lotus, whereas the female partner [representing the goddess] should kiss the *vajra*. The aim of the unions of *vajra* and lotus is to produce the nectar [seminal fluid]'.[19] The text instructs the reader to keep its teachings secret, revealing them only to an initiate who 'desires the

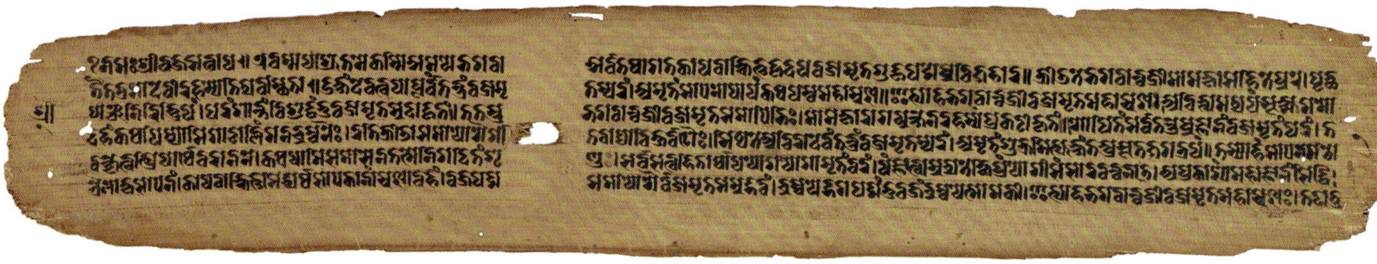

**Fig. 7**
**Folio from the *Vajramrita***
***Tantra***
Nepal
1162 CE
Palm leaf, 5 × 31 cm
Cambridge University Library
MS Or.158.1 (fol. 1v)

supreme awakening'.[20] While the Buddha's teachings, according to scriptures composed shortly after his death, centred on a critique of desire as the root of attachment, Tantric Buddhist texts turned this idea on its head by suggesting that desire without attachment was not only possible but also fundamental to shattering false dualisms and achieving ultimate Buddhahood.

Many Tantric texts included passages of a sexual nature similar to those in the *Vajramrita Tantra*, employing layered, metaphorical terms and erotic imagery (from *amrita* to *vajra*), that could be read on literal or symbolic levels. When some of the earliest translations of these texts into English were carried out during the British colonial period in India, their contents were reductively interpreted and misunderstood, which went on to inform current misunderstandings of Tantra in the West as an orgiastic cult of ecstasy.

## WHO WERE THE TANTRIKAS?

Who were the original Tantrikas and who wrote the *Tantras*? In principle, Tantric initiation was open to people from all social backgrounds. This was one of the key ways in which Tantra challenged the hierarchical social order within orthodox or Brahmanical Hinduism, which divided people into four classes (*varnas*) by birth. Each *varna* had to conform to prescribed roles and rules of behaviour: the Brahmins (priests and teachers), Kshatriyas (warriors and rulers), Vaishyas (farmers, traders and merchants) and Shudras (labourers). Only the first three were permitted to hear the sacred *Vedas*. There was an excluded fifth *varna*, or *avarna* (literally *varna*-less or outcasts), members of which were prohibited from participating in Vedic ritual altogether and deemed the polluted class because their roles involved contact with impurities through street sweeping, latrine cleaning and the handling of cadavers. Tantra, on the other hand, offered the possibility of initiation and greater ritual participation for Shudras and outcasts, as well as for women, who were excluded from Vedic initiation, although the extent to which this was achieved in practice is uncertain and unquantifiable.[21] According to the *c.* 7th-century *Svacchanda Tantra*: 'All those who have been initiated (…) are of equal nature. (…) Once a person has taken up this Tantric system he may never mention his former caste. (…) if he aspires to the highest *siddhi* [attainment or power] he must make no [such] discriminatory distinctions. (…) it is [only] through [this] freedom from discrimination that one will certainly attain both *siddhi* and liberation.'[22]

The *Tantras* are believed to have originated among ascetic groups living on the margins of society, in cremation and charnel grounds (*shmashana*). According to Hindu belief, cremation is the final rite in the course of an individual's existence, ceremonially affirming non-attachment to the body. In Buddhism, similarly, the corpse is cremated, though sometimes it is exposed for the benefit of carrion-eating animals. As a threshold where transition from life to death regularly takes place, the *shmashana* is a space offering unparalleled access to the spirit world and the beings that inhabit it. It was also regarded as a polluted and, therefore, inherently potent environment because of its association with death, decaying corpses and carrion-eating animals. Legends circulated about the so-called Kapalikas ('skull-bearers') who emulated the violent Tantric deity Bhairava by smearing ashes over their bodies, carrying a human cranial cup (*kapala*) as an alms bowl and consuming and making offerings of taboo substances.[23] The cremation and charnel grounds they inhabited became recurring motifs in Tantric texts and imagery as the favourite haunts of ferocious deities and therefore ideal sites for carrying out Tantric rites, especially at night. Because they were also regarded as frightening spaces inhabited by ghosts and demonic spirits, these funerary settings encouraged practitioners to confront any limiting fears, including those linked to self-attachment, which were overcome to make way for a new divine identity.

The use of a human skull as an eating and drinking vessel was also a recurring motif. As an instrument of fierce Tantric deities the skull-cup is often shown overflowing with blood and entrails, symbolic of negative forces and states of mind, such as greed and ignorance, which the deities cut up and dissolve. Mortal Hindu and Buddhist Tantrikas used *kapalas* in ritual contexts not only as 'power-objects' but also to signify their transcendence of both aversion and attachment. Although this image of the transgressive, charnel-ground-dwelling Tantrika (and especially the skull-bearing Kapalika) became iconic in Tantric traditions, the elaboration of Tantric doctrine, and its codification and propagation in textual form, owed more to transregional networks of Hindu and Buddhist monastic centres inhabited by scholars (*pandits*) well-versed in the liturgical language of Sanskrit. While the movement's early practitioners may have been marginalized 'underground' figures, its mainstream acceptance was certainly a result of its adoption by the elites.[24] Royal and aristocratic patronage of Tantric gurus and monumental public Tantric temples, sculptures and paintings played a major role in the promotion of Tantra. This was especially the case between the 7th and 12th centuries, after the breakdown of the Gupta and Vakataka dynasties (*c.* 550 CE) decentralized the politics of the Indian subcontinent, giving rise to multiple feudal kingdoms with shifting boundaries. Many of these kingdoms' rulers, facing constant precariousness and uncertainty, were drawn to Tantra's promises of worldly and supernatural power.

## THE ROLE OF WOMEN

Power is central to Tantra – a power described and visualized as feminine, resulting in the centrality of goddesses within the movement and inspiring the dramatic rise of goddess worship (Shaktism) in medieval India. The goddesses venerated by Tantrikas directly confronted traditional models of womanhood as passive and docile in their intertwining of violent and erotic power. According to many Tantric texts, the veneration of goddesses should carry over into the veneration of mortal women as natural embodiments and transmitters of Shakti. This marked a dramatic departure from previous orthodox Hindu and Buddhist teachings regarding the status of women.[25] For example, according to the Brahmanical *Manava Dharma Shastra* (*Code of Manu*), a text on Hindu conduct composed sometime between the 2nd century BCE and 3rd century CE, women should remain submissive towards and dependent upon men, who in turn must guard against women's wild temperaments:

> In childhood a female must be subject to her father, in youth to her husband, and when her lord is dead to her sons; a woman must never be independent. (…) Because of their passion for men, their mutable temper, and their natural heartlessness, they become disloyal towards their husbands (…). Knowing their disposition, (…) [every] man should most strenuously exert himself to guard them.[26]

Although Gautama Buddha insisted that anyone could achieve enlightenment regardless of gender or social background, early Mahayana texts, such as the *Bodhisattvabhumi* (3rd century CE), describe the female body as an impediment to achieving ultimate Buddhahood:

> Completely perfected Buddhas are not women. (…) All women are by nature full of defilement and of weak intelligence. And not by one who is by nature full of defilement and of weak intelligence is completely perfected Buddhahood attained.[27]

In contrast, Hindu and Buddhist Tantric texts and images re-envisioned women as agents of enlightenment and sources of enormous power. This, however, begs the question: did women play a primarily instrumental role in the service of male Tantrikas seeking to tap into their power, or were they agents in their own right? In Tantric texts, the majority of which were written from male perspectives, women are described in the following roles: as partners in sexual rites, whose sexual fluids were regarded as a distillation of Shakti; as semi-divine, witch-like beings worshipped for their bestowal of magical powers; and as independent, initiated practitioners and gurus.[28]

Most scholarship has focused on the first two roles but the (often overlooked) visual evidence demonstrates that women were also important autonomous practitioners and teachers of Tantra.

Both textual and visual sources can also challenge the perceived heteronormativity of Tantra. Hindu and Buddhist Tantric texts describe sexual rites carried out by men and women, and polarity symbolism rests on the balance of apparently 'feminine' and 'masculine' forces, often indicated by gendered names and nouns such as 'Shakti' and 'Shiva' or *prakriti* (creative force) and *purusha* (pure consciousness). However, in Tantra heteronormativity and gender are also deliberately disrupted through an emphasis on androgyny and the union of masculine and feminine forces within the body on ritual, symbolic and literal levels.

## TANTRIC VISUAL CULTURE

Despite an emphasis on initiation and secrecy, visual expressions of the Tantric experience were produced wherever the movement took hold in India and across Asia. Tantric paintings and sculptures supported meditation and visualization of the divine, functioning as images to inspire the practitioner rather than simply as devotional objects to be worshipped passively. This book presents a re-examination of Tantra through a series of visual case studies, almost all from the British Museum's collection, to illustrate a history of Tantra beyond the texts, which usually receive the most attention from scholars of the movement. The *Tantras* can be enormously enriched by an understanding of the material objects to which they gave rise. The range of objects in this book includes representations of Tantric deities and Tantrikas, objects used in Tantric practice, and objects that reflect reimaginings as well as misunderstandings of Tantra. Above all, the aims is to provide readers with the tools for recognizing certain signs and signifiers (from skull-cups and weapons to sexual acts) as specifically relating to the Tantric imaginary, in order to understand how its philosophy has been visualized throughout history. Each of these signs carries a range of different associations and meanings depending on the object's original intended audience (from rulers and lay devotees to monks and yogis), as well as its context, whether public and reflecting the 'right-hand' path or private and reflecting the 'left-hand' path. These multivalent tensions are key to understanding Tantra's often 'secret', enigmatic philosophies and rituals.

The power of the creative imagination has always been central to Tantra and is a running theme across this book. Advanced Tantrikas, with their god's-eye view of the world, could transform and re-create themselves and their surroundings using this power, by imagining and materializing the seemingly impossible. Visualization, which was fundamental to all aspects of Tantric practice, privileged material aids as practical tools of embodiment far more than any other South Asian religious tradition had done, resulting in the creation of complex ritual instruments, sculptures and paintings which served to fuel the Tantrika's imagination and practice. Imagination was also key when it came to reading the *Tantras* themselves, since they could be interpreted on both literal and symbolic levels. In symbolic readings the Tantrika had to imagine participating in transgressive acts, while literal readings would involve the practitioner apprehending the pure in the impure.

The power of the imagination also plays a role when the gaze is shifted and those outside the Tantric social milieu – from Mughal rulers to the hippies of the New Age movement – interpret and visualize the 'exotic' mystique of Tantra and its practitioners (fig. 8). In the modern era Tantra has become a blank canvas onto which people have projected certain ideals, shaping the movement to represent freedom from societal and cultural conventions and restrictions. To describe Tantra as an anti-establishment movement would not be incorrect, though it was many more things besides. Tantra was never a monolithic religion, but rather an adaptable sacred tradition that was incorporated into and appropriated by other belief systems, beginning with Hinduism and Buddhism. As this book will show, it constantly transformed in response to its social, political and cultural environments – for instance, in the association of Tantric goddesses such as Kali with Mother India by Bengali revolutionaries and artists during the British colonial period; and in the 20th-century appropriation and redefinition of Tantra by Western popular culture during the 1960s.

Tantra's one recurring thread (to take its literal meaning, 'to weave', as a central metaphor) has been its role as a fundamentally countercultural movement, from medieval India to 21st-century Britain. Granted, it has also been harnessed by ruling elites and members of the establishment for purposes of statecraft, particularly during times of political turbulence. Nevertheless, its radical potential for opening up new ways of seeing and changing the world has been enduring. Tantra transformed South Asia's major religions, challenged society's norms and inspired revolution. In the 21st century, its relevance continues, both in South Asia and around the world.

**Fig. 8**
**Detail of fig. 191, *TEJAS-BHUMI: Fire that is Earth, Shambala* series, Yokoo Tadanori**
Tokyo, Japan
1974
Silkscreen print, 97.8 × 67.9 cm
British Museum 2019,3005.7
Purchase made possible by the JTI Japanese Acquisition Fund

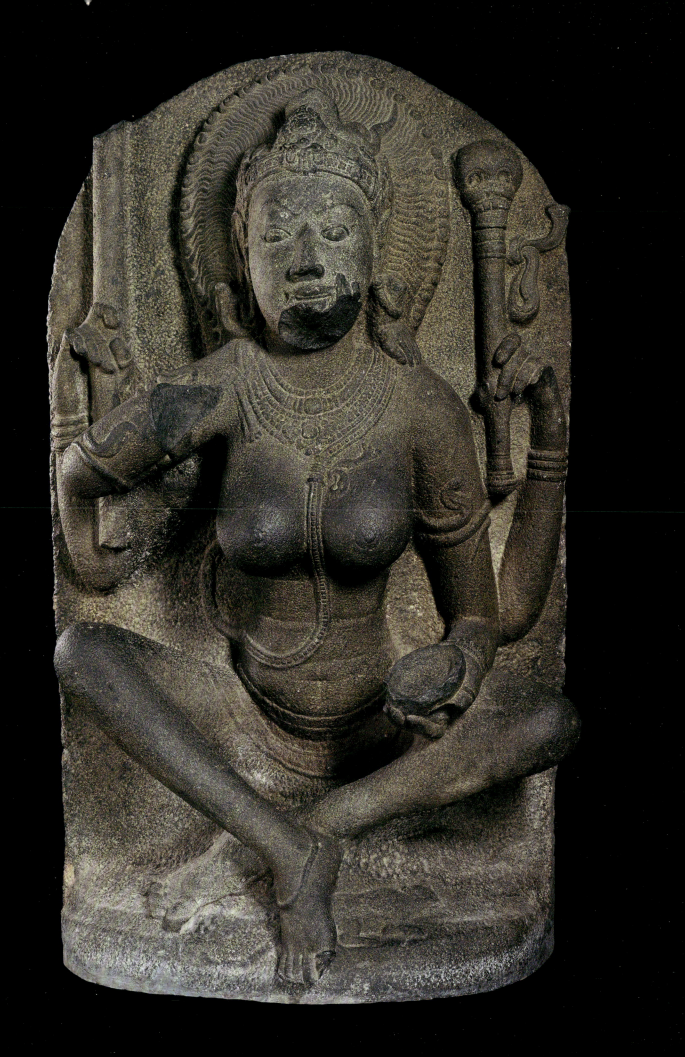

CHAPTER 1

# THE RISE
# OF TANTRA IN
# MEDIEVAL INDIA

Between the 4th and 6th centuries CE, two dynasties dominated the Indian subcontinent: the Guptas in the north and the Vakatakas in the southwest. Multiple attacks on the north from the Ephthalites of Central Asia (sometimes called the White Huns) accelerated the decline of the Gupta empire, which broke up *c.* 550 CE, around the same time that the Vakataka dynasty fell for reasons that are less clear. The subsequent destabilization of power led to the rise of feudal kingdoms with shifting boundaries, especially after the 7th century. New rival dynasties emerged with imperial ambitions for territorial expansion. Some had been vassals of the Guptas and Vakatakas, while others materialized as if from nowhere, eager to take advantage of opportunities to seize authority.[1] Although the medieval period in India, between the 7th and 12th centuries, was marked by precariousness and uncertainty, there was also a great flourishing of the arts, with the development of new regional styles of sculpture and the royal patronage of magnificent temples and monasteries.[2]

As this chapter will demonstrate, these monumental public spaces often incorporated or revolved around Tantric deities and teachings, since many of the new kingdoms' rulers were drawn to the movement's promise of power. This challenges the assumption that Tantra was an exclusively 'secret', marginal movement. While its origins may lie among ascetic, transgressive groups, from the 8th century onwards Tantric deities attracted popular worship and were integrated into mainstream spaces and the public religious domain as a result of royal patronage. This chapter goes on to examine how Tantric gods and practices of Hindu origin were creatively adapted and incorporated into Buddhist contexts. The central role of Shakti (divine feminine power) within the movement and the proliferation of martial goddesses that it inspired are also explored, along with the role of sex and erotic imagery, which were part of, but not confined to, Tantric traditions.

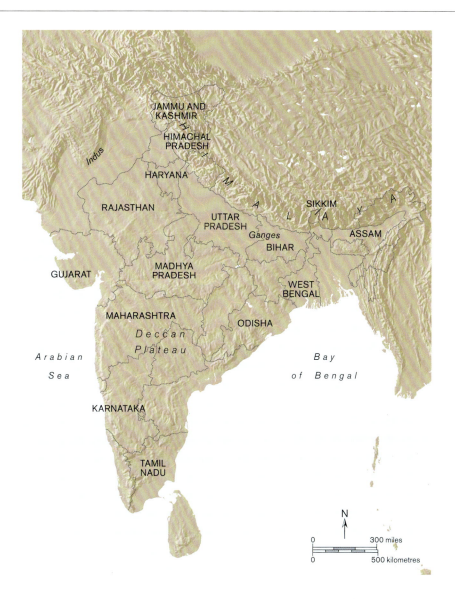

Fig. 9

Modern states of India
mentioned in the text


Fig. 10

Head of Bhairava

Uttar Pradesh, India

5th century

Terracotta, 10.2 × 7.6 × 10.5 cm

Los Angeles County Museum
of Art M.82.220

Gift of Mr John I. and Mrs
Maria C. Bicocchi

## BHAIRAVA THE SKULL-BEARER AND HIS FOLLOWERS

The story of Tantra begins with the Hindu god Shiva, an all-powerful
anarchic destroyer of worlds who delights in transcending social and
religious boundaries. Shiva perfectly embodies the Tantric spirit
and its tensions between eroticism and asceticism, auspiciousness and
inauspiciousness.[3] Like other Hindu deities, Shiva can be simultaneously
conceived as merging into one absolute god, as well as assuming numerous
other forms. His most explicitly Tantric persona is Bhairava ('Horrific'
or 'Fearsome'), protector of temples, kingdoms and devotees. His followers
regard him as a superior manifestation of Shiva.[4] A body of Hindu Tantric
texts dating from around the 6th century onwards revolved around Shiva
and Bhairava, including the *Siddhanta Tantras* and the *Bhairava Tantras*, and
by the 12th century their ideas and rituals were embedded in the religious
and cultural landscape of South Asia.[5]

The earliest known sculptures that have been identified as Bhairava (or
at least Bhairava-like) date to the 5th–6th centuries CE and were executed

in Uttar Pradesh during the rule of the Gupta dynasty (fig. 10).[6] They already depict some of his key characteristics, including wide, furious eyes. Bhairava became more present in temple iconography from the late 6th century onwards, at a time of increasing political instability. An imposing sculpture of the god was made shortly after the decline of the Guptas (fig. 11).[7] He holds a skull-cup in his right hand and a trident in his left. His eyebrows are arched to express his wrathful nature and a human skull and dismembered hands adorn his headdress. Bhairava's popularity extended to non-Tantric Hindu texts including the *Shiva Purana* and *Skanda Purana*, in which his origin myth is recounted. The god Brahma (regarded as the creator of the *Vedas*) insulted Shiva who, enraged, created Bhairava from his own anger and had him decapitate one of Brahma's heads. Bhairava obliged but, as punishment for his crime, the head remained stuck to his hand for twelve years, during which time he carried out the 'skull-bearer's vow' (*kapalikavrata*) in exile, wandering across impure cremation grounds, his body covered in ash, using the skull as his begging bowl.[8] The myth reveals the tensions between orthodox (Brahmanical) and Tantric Hindu traditions, the display of Bhairava's strength over Brahma articulating the superior powers of the Tantric path.

The role of the cremation ground as a site of impurity and Tantric power is key to Bhairava's identity, mythology and iconography. The *Netra Tantra*, an early 9th-century Kashmir text, identifies him as the 'Lord of the Demonic Dead' (Bhutanath) who protects his loyal devotees from demonic spirits: 'If a man has been marked by terrible *bhutas* and female demonic seizers, then a tribute should be offered to the lord of the demonic dead (…) one's [condition] immediately improves after making an offering to Bhairava [who is their leader.]'[9] Some of the earliest Tantrika ascetics emulated Bhairava's unusual appearance and behaviour in order to 'become' him. They included the itinerant Kapalikas ('skull-bearers') who seem to have had a presence in the north and south of India and as far as Nepal.[10] Kapalikas are mentioned in sources as early as the 5th century but most date between the 7th and the 12th centuries.[11] It is believed that the rites and mantras described in the *Bhairava Tantras* (which emphasize the worship of Bhairava) for the attainment of power, originated among Kapalikas and similar groups.[12] Like Bhairava, they dwelt in cremation grounds, covered their bodies in ashes and carried skull-cups to re-enact his penance. They worshipped the god with offerings of impure substances including blood and alcohol to achieve transcendence through transgression, inspiring both awe and revulsion.[13]

Surviving early images of Bhairava suggest what the Kapalikas might have looked like. A mid-10th-century bronze sculpture from Karnataka (south-west India) shows him holding a skull-cup and a trident (*trishula*) (fig. 12). He wears high sandals, typical in representations of wandering

**Fig. 11**
**Bhairava**
Uttar Pradesh, India
Late 6th century
Stone, 78 × 38 × 22 cm
Sarnath Archaeological
Museum 6618

**Fig. 12**
**Bhairava**
Karnataka, India
Mid-10th century
Bronze, 19.4 × 10.3 × 6.3 cm
British Museum 1967,1017.1
Funded by the Brooke Sewell
Permanent Fund

ascetics. Otherwise naked, save for ornaments that include a garland of
human heads draped across his body, he carries a severed head, which
oozes blood that is lapped up by a dog, Bhairava's inauspicious carrion-
feeding companion. In another of his four hands he wields a two-headed
drum (*damaru*), around which a cobra is coiled; Shiva periodically plays
the *damaru* to drum the universe into creation, dissolution and re-creation.
A cobra appears again below his genitals, emphasising his virile potency.
His large, exaggerated eyes suggest a crazed and intoxicated mood. This
bronze was probably enshrined or placed on an altar and may have been
used to stimulate visualizations and as an aid for meditation.

Sculptures of Bhairava were also made to adorn the exterior of temples
as guardians to protect the deity in the inner sanctum, who was often Shiva
himself. Many were built during the reign of the Hoysala dynasty (11th–12th
centuries), which ruled over most of present-day Karnataka in south-west
India (fig. 13).[14] A 13th-century Hoysala temple sculpture of Bhairava exhibits
an extraordinary attention to detail, morbid as well as beautiful, carved in
soft schist (fig. 14). He appears almost benign, with a gentle expression and
a head of tightly wound curls, until closer inspection reveals vampiric fangs
and Brahma's still-fresh head casually clutched in one hand. Apart from a
trident and drum he also carries a sword. To his left and right are his
ghoulish skeletal attendants, the *bhutas* or 'demonic dead'.

**Fig. 13**
**Sculpture of Bhairava**
**at Hoysaleshvara temple**
Halebidu, Karnataka, India
12th century
Stone

**Fig. 14**
**Bhairava**
Karnataka, India
c. 1200–50
Black schist, height 63.5 cm
British Museum 1966,1014.1
Funded by the Brooke Sewell
Permanent Fund

In Karnataka, Kalamukha ('black face') ascetics were particularly dominant between the 11th and 13th centuries, attracting royal patronage for the founding of monastic centres and temples.[15] Like the Kapalikas, the Kalamukhas emulated Bhairava.[16]

In Tamil Nadu (southern India), Bhairava temples appeared from around the 8th century and especially during the reign of the Chola dynasty (9th–13th centuries) that subsequently dominated the region.[17] An 11th-century granite temple sculpture from Tamil Nadu shows Bhairava as a naked ascetic, a wild shock of hair streaming out of his head like fire (fig. 15). His arched eyebrows and bulbous eyes reveal a controlled fury, while his fangs signal his violent side. His missing hand would have once held a skull-cup and his three others hold a trident, noose and drum. Statues of the god appear around the same time as the rise in popularity of songs dedicated to Shiva and Bhairava that were composed by a group of Tamil poet-saints called the Nayanars ('Hounds of Shiva') in the 6th–8th centuries.[18] Their visionary songs combined Tantric images and ideas with those of another Hindu tradition, Bhakti ('love' or 'devotion'), a major movement that developed around the same time as the rise of Tantra, and

Fig. 15
**Bhairava**
Tamil Nadu, India
11th century
Granite, 115.8 × 48 × 30 cm
British Museum 1967,1016.1
Funded by the Brooke Sewell
Permanent Fund

Fig. 16
**Karaikkal Ammaiyar**
Tamil Nadu, India
Late 13th century
Bronze, 23.2 × 16.5 cm
The Metropolitan Museum
of Art 1982.220.11

**Fig. 17**
**Karaikkal Ammaiyar,**
**Mohan Sthapati**
Chennai, Tamil Nadu, India
c. 1990–92
Bronze, 23.8 × 18 × 12.5 cm
British Museum 1992,0727.64

that focused on a direct and intimate relationship with a personal deity. The Nayanars came from a variety of social backgrounds but each road led to the same end: divine madness for Shiva, which often led them to transgress social parameters and to reject caste and gender rules.

A 13th-century Chola-period sculpture represents the 6th-century Nayanar Karaikkal Ammaiyar ('Mother from Karaikkal') (fig. 16). She is one of three women among the sixty-three Nayanars. Here she is seen singing the god's praises, accompanying herself with a pair of cymbals. A modern bronze depiction of her made in the 1990s by the sculptor Mohan Sthapati (fig. 17) reveals her enduring popularity and is based on an earlier image of her that was worshipped in the Kapaleshvara temple in Chennai, the capital of Tamil Nadu. When Karaikkal Ammaiyar abandoned her role as an obedient wife to become an ascetic follower of Shiva, she asked the god to take away her beauty and to replace it with the ghoulish appearance of his demonic retinue (evident in figs. 16, 17), which she described in her poetry:

> A female ghoul with withered breasts, bulging veins, hollow eyes,
> White teeth and two fangs,

Shrivelled stomach, red hair, bony ankles, and elongated shins,
Stays in this cemetery, howling angrily.
This place where my Lord dances in the fire with a cool body,
His streaming hair flying in the eight directions.[19]

This metamorphosis is decidedly Tantric in its radical disavowal of
Karaikkal Ammaiyar's expected social role in favour of a transgressive and
'polluted' one that affords her sacred power. Her behaviour echoes that of
the ascetic cremation-ground dwellers. In another of her poems she even
transcends her gender altogether by assuming the voice of a man wishing
to abandon his wife to pursue an ascetic path:

My heart!
Give up your bondage, your wife and children.
Saying that you take refuge here at His feet,
Think of Him and worship.[20]

She describes the cremation ground as a liberating, paradisiacal space in
which to overcome the fear of death and to burn away the ego:

In the cemetery where you hear crackling noises
and the white pearls fall out of the tall bamboo,
The ghouls with frizzy hair and drooping bodies,
Shouting with wide-open mouths,
Come together and feast on the corpses.
In the big, threatening cremation ground,
When The Lord dances,
The Daughter of the Mountain watches Him,
In astonishment.[21]

Another Nayanar named Chiruttontar ('Little Devotee'), depicted in a
modern sculpture by Mohan Sthapati (fig. 18), is the subject of a popular
story featuring Bhairava that is recounted in the *Periya Purana*, a 12th-
century hagiography of the Nayanars by Chekkilar (minister to the Chola
king, Kulottunga II). In this story, Bhairava pretended to be a mortal
ascetic, dressed in Kapalika garb, to test Chiruttontar's devotion to Shiva.
Chiruttontar offered him food but Bhairava insisted that he would only
accept the cooked flesh of Chiruttontar's own child. Out of respect and
devotion, Chiruttontar proceeded to cut off his son's head and prepared
the macabre feast, which Bhairava insisted they share. Before they
could take the first bite, however, Bhairava magically re-materialized
Chiruttontar's son. Chiruttontar had passed the test in his total surrender
to the god.[22]

**Fig. 18**
**Chiruttontar,**
**Mohan Sthapati**
Chennai, Tamil Nadu, India
c. 1990–1992
Bronze, height 35 cm
British Museum, 1992,0727.16

The stories and poetry of the Nayanars informed the foundation of Tamil Nadu's dominant Tantric tradition, known as Shaiva Siddhanta (together with its associated texts, the *Siddhanta Tantras*), which developed there from the 11th century and led to the rapid popularization of Tantra not only in southern India but across South Asia.[23] The Shaiva Siddhanta tradition was a 'right-hand' or *dakshina* form of Tantra centring on a more benevolent, five-faced form of Shiva known as Sadashiva.[24] It consisted of public rituals performed by Hindu priests following certain orthodox (Vedic) codes of conduct, including the adherence to pure/impure distinctions and the use of generally vegetarian offerings rather than the alcohol, blood and meat of the 'left-hand' or *vama* practices of the *Bhairava Tantras*.[25] Nevertheless, Shaiva Siddhanta also challenged Vedic rules by upholding the idea that a devotee's social background could be transcended through devotion to Shiva. Daily rituals involving the internalization of divinity through mantra recitation and visualization exercises were also Tantric in nature.[26]

Many Shaiva Siddhanta temples were built in Tamil Nadu by the Chola dynasty and became not only powerful sacred spaces but also displays of Chola political prowess. An inscription from the Tiruvalishvara temple, dedicated to Shiva, records that the Chola King Rajadhiraja II (r. *c.* 1163–1179) approached a Shaiva Siddhanta guru named Jnanashivadeva of Gauda and requested him to use his power to ward off an invading army from Sri Lanka. The guru worshipped Shiva for twenty-eight days continuously and, according to the inscription, the 'attackers of Shiva' were defeated.[27]

The Cholas were patrons of Shiva and the 11th-century Tamil sculpture of Bhairava (see fig. 15) was carved during their rule. Its quality and size strongly suggest that it was made for a temple commissioned by a member of the Chola court. Like the Hoysala temple sculpture (see fig. 14) it demonstrates the incorporation of fierce Tantric deities within the public and popular arena of temple worship during the medieval period, while also evoking the more extreme forms of left-hand Tantric practice. Bhairava and his skull-bearing followers would have been considered great sources of power.

Bhairava's presence in a public temple also reveals how fluid the boundaries were between left-hand and right-hand forms of Tantra itself.[28] Indeed, there is no single, monolithic Tantra; instead there are many shades of it, and its adaptability has always been the key to its success. The right-hand path made Tantric traditions accessible to a wider, more mainstream audience beyond the cremation-ground-dwelling ascetics. However, all acknowledged – whether with awe or horror – the power of the left-hand Tantrikas who, as mentioned, were often referred to as literal heroes in Tantric texts due to the dangers involved in their pursuit of a fast-track to enlightenment as well as supernatural abilities and worldly domination. Bhairava stood as a reminder of these complex ideas.

## BHAIRAVA'S BUDDHIST TRANSFORMATION

Bhairava assumed another guise – a Tantric Buddhist (Vajrayana) one – during the medieval period. While early Buddhist institutions and places of worship had attracted royal patronage since the 3rd century BCE, Tantric traditions revolving around Shiva posed significant competition across the subcontinent from the 6th century CE onwards, with the fall of the Gupta and Vakataka dynasties and the rise of multiple kingdoms all vying for power and territory.[29] The subsequent political instability informed not only the martial iconography of many Tantric deities but also the content of many of the *Tantras* themselves, which advised on how best to conquer enemies. For example, instructions on how to carry out a set of six magical actions (*satkarman*) using mantras recur across Tantric texts: pacification (*shanti*), subjugation (*vashikarana*), immobilization (*stambhana*), creation of hostility (*vidvesana*), driving away (*ucchatana*) and killing (*marana*). According to the 8th-/9th-century Tantric text *Mrigendra Agama*, *ucchatana* is performed by using 'destructive' mantras and making an offering into a fire. Such a rite could only be performed by an initiated Tantrika, either for themselves or for someone else, such as a ruler.[30] Warfare and worldly power could thus conceivably find justification and sacralization in the *Tantras*. The targeted 'victims' of these rites could be personal or political enemies, or other threats including diseases, natural disasters and emotional impediments.[31]

The rise of Tantra within Buddhism from around the 7th century CE occurred in response to its rise within Hinduism. Tantric deities and practices of Hindu origin were appropriated and then creatively adapted to suit Buddhist goals, particularly evident in eastern India (Bengal, Bihar and Odisha).[32] A growing body of Buddhist *Tantras* demonstrated an active engagement with the Hindu *Tantras*. These included the *Kriya Tantras* (*Tantras of Action*) and *Charya Tantras* (*Tantras of Observance*), which paralleled the *Siddhanta Tantras* in their lack of transgressive content. The *Mahayoga Tantras* (written by the end of the 8th century) and *Yogini Tantras* (written between the 9th and 10th centuries) most closely resembled the *Bhairava Tantras*.[33] These latter texts were believed to contain superior teachings for the most direct, rapid path to enlightenment and simultaneously offered instructions on the cultivation of worldly and supernatural powers. They described the ritual use of impure and forbidden substances, and sexual rites designed to access the latent power of the forbidden, while also challenging distinctions between the sacred and profane.

The *Yogini Tantras*, in particular, emphasized the role of cremation and charnel grounds, and also incorporated the language of military conquest, explaining how to vanquish enemies and armies. These texts and the practices they described are believed to have initially circulated among independent Buddhist Tantrika ascetics, often referred to as Siddhas or 'accomplished ones'. Siddhas resembled the skull-bearing Kapalika followers of Shiva in their appearance, behaviour and emulation of Tantric deities.[34] Buddhist Tantrikas, too, regarded cremation and charnel grounds as centres of immense power, as both sites of pollution and the homes of the most ferocious gods. It is clear that Hindu and Buddhist Tantrikas met and exchanged ideas; Buddhist *Tantras* not only borrowed from the Hindu *Tantras*, but also vice versa.[35] From the 8th through to the 12th centuries, the *Mahayoga Tantras* and *Yogini Tantras* were quickly absorbed into mainstream monastic Buddhist communities, where they were studied closely, especially in eastern India.[36] In these environments (governed by strict codes of conduct), the esoteric, layered and metaphorical passages of the texts focusing on transgressive practices could be interpreted symbolically, using substitutes for taboo substances or acts (such as milk and flowers, and through visualization techniques).[37]

Tantric Buddhism produced an outpouring of gods and goddesses in violent, dynamic guises, in marked contrast with the peaceful, benevolent characteristics of orthodox (Mahayana) Buddhist deities and Bodhisattvas. Most surviving early Tantric Buddhist images were produced in eastern India, especially during the reign of the Pala dynasty (8th–12th centuries), whose rulers funded major monastic establishments, including the monastery of Vikramashila in Bihar. Probably founded by Devapala (r. 812–850), Vikramashila occupied over a hundred acres of land with around a thousand monks, and more than fifty temples enshrining Tantric deities.[38] The Tantric guru Buddhajnana became its chief *vajracharya* (Vajrayana master), conducting rites such as the *homa* to guarantee the longevity and protection of the Pala dynasty. The *homa* was a votive ritual sacrifice involving the immolation of offerings into a fire (including milk, grains, incense and clarified butter or *ghee*). Originally an ancient Vedic ritual centring on the propitiation of invoked gods, it remained an important part of Tantric ritual in which a practitioner could visualize their own chosen deity at the heart of the fire.[39] The offerings now represented obstacles that were purified and transformed by the flames. Buddhajnana's *homa* was said to have been performed uninterrupted for many years in order to keep enemies of the dynasty at bay.[40] The Palas were struck by multiple succession conflicts as well as constant external threats, and from the 11th century the dynasty's stronghold in Bengal was challenged on all sides by competing forces. This included the Sena dynasty, who would ultimately defeat the Palas around 1170.[41] In such a climate, Tantric gurus, teachings and the material culture they inspired could thrive due to the multivalent nature of Tantric power and its rhetoric of martial conquest.

Mahakala ('Great Black One') is a Buddhist incarnation of Bhairava who is regarded as a Dharmapala or Protector of the Dharma (Buddhist teachings). The *c.* 12th-century *Mahakala Tantra*, which is named after him, devotes entire sections to methods for achieving political power.[42] An 11th/12th-century sculpture from Bihar of a seated Mahakala (fig. 19) shows many iconographic similarities to a sculpture of a seated Bhairava from Karnataka (see fig. 14). Mahakala wields a sword and trident, holds a skull-cup and wears a garland of heads. Cobras wind around his body and flame-like hair shoots out of his skull-decorated diadem. To his lower left and right are kneeling figures who present offerings, probably the donors who commissioned the sculpture and presented it to a Buddhist monastery or shrine.[43]

The Pala dynasty not only supported Buddhist institutions; they were also devotees of Shiva, and patrons of temples dedicated to him. Excavations at Vikramashila have revealed the presence of Tantric Hindu imagery at the site, including sculptures of Bhairava, which must have been incorporated and adapted for Buddhist worship, serving as visual sources of inspiration.[44]

A 12th-century Pala-period bronze from eastern India incorporates many of Bhairava's characteristics and symbols (fig. 20). The principal figure is Chakrasamvara, a Yidam or personal deity of Tantric Buddhist meditation, who functions as an aspirational role model and guide for devotees. During Vajrayana initiations, a guru will usually select a disciple's Yidam for them.[45] This example may have had a ritual function, to stimulate visualizations of the deity. The monasteries that studied the *Mahayoga Tantras* and *Yogini Tantras*, which flourished during the Pala period in eastern India, also housed workshops for producing Vajrayana (as well as more orthodox Mahayana) sacred objects like the Chakrasamvara bronze, which may have originated in one of them.[46] Chakrasamvara assumes the pose of a warrior here. His matted hair is piled up on top of his head, and he appears to snarl, revealing his sharp fangs and furious bloodshot eyes (highlighted by inlaid copper). His twelve arms carry an array of objects that align him explicitly with Bhairava, including a trident, decapitated head, skull-cup, noose and drum. Additionally he holds an axe and dagger, and stretches an elephant skin out behind him, alluding to Shiva's defeat of the elephant demon, Gajasura.[47] Clutched to his heart he holds a *vajra* (thunderbolt) and *ghanta* (bell), which are important Tantric Buddhist ritual implements (see Chapter 3).

Chakrasamvara assimilates the characteristics of Bhairava and transforms them into a powerful new Buddhist form. Both deities have been described as embodiments of the charnel ground itself, devouring its carrion and ornamented with blood and body parts.[48] However, the explicitly Hindu Bhairava himself also makes an appearance in the bronze,

**Fig. 19 (below)**
**Mahakala**
Bihar, India,
11th/12th century
Black stone, 61 × 29.8 × 12.7 cm
The Metropolitan Museum of
Art 1996.465

**Fig. 20 (opposite)**
**Chakrasamvara**
Eastern India
12th century
Bronze, copper, and silver,
14.6 × 11 × 3.5 cm
British Museum 1976,0927.1
Funded by the Brooke Sewell
Permanent Fund

trampled under Chakrasamvara's left foot. Under Chakrasamvara's right foot, with a skeletal frame, is the Tantric Hindu goddess Chamunda, also known as Kalaratri ('Night of Dread'). The eponymous *Chakrasamvara Tantra* recounts how the Yidam deliberately assumed the appearance of Bhairava in order to attract Shiva's Tantric followers in the hope of converting them to Buddhism.[49] Chakrasamvara believed that their path had been clouded by the obstacles of arrogance, pride and self-centredness. He succeeded in luring Bhairava himself, whom he proceeded to trample, along with Chamunda. This seemingly wrathful act is ultimately carried out for compassionate purposes in order to destroy Bhairava's and Chamunda's pride and convert them to Buddhahood. It also very clearly reveals the rivalry between Buddhist and Hindu Tantric traditions and institutions. It is significant that in this bronze Bhairava and Chamunda appear as corpses. The image of a deity trampling a corpse would assume many symbolic guises in different Tantric contexts in India and beyond. While here the Hindu gods become symbols of the ego that must be transformed, in other Tantric images (see fig. 26) the corpse may evoke actual Tantric practices involving engagement with the dead.

The emphasis on macabre symbolism inherent in images of Mahakala and Chakrasamvara might initially seem to contradict Buddhism's emphasis on non-violence to an outsider. They reflect the tension between the actual and symbolic role of violence in the *Tantras*, which evolved in the climate of instability that many kingdoms in India faced from the 6th century onwards. While these images of Tantric deities speak to a military imaginary, they were also often produced in monastic Buddhist contexts in which they could speak to a different, symbolic form of violence: the destruction of inner obstacles to enlightenment, such as jealousy and greed.[50] The sacralization of warfare and Tantric techniques for immobilizing enemies coexisted with the idea that these armed gods were effective forces of spiritual liberation. This visual vocabulary of violence is unique to Tantric iconography and recurs throughout its diverse traditions, from images of terror to the production of ceremonial weapons for subduing negative forces. In medieval India, it was also articulated especially vividly in images of Tantric goddesses as both bloodthirsty warriors and compassionate mothers.

Fig. 21
Folio from the *Devi Mahatmya,* Shrivirabhadra (scribe)
Nepal
1669
Black ink on paper, 8.3 × 21.7 cm
Cambridge University Library
MS Add.1588.3 (fol. 22v)

## DURGA, CHAMUNDA AND THE MATRIKAS: THE MANY SHADES OF FEMININE POWER

The Tantric worldview sees everything as animated by Shakti – unlimited, divine feminine power. The earliest known text to describe the idea of Shakti is the *Devi Mahatmya* (*Glory of the Goddess*), dated between *c.* 400 and 600 CE.[51] It identifies Shakti with Devi or Durga, the Supreme Goddess, from whom all other goddesses emerge. The *Devi Mahatmya* forms part of the *Markandeya Purana,* an orthodox Hindu text. Nevertheless, it presents its readers with an unmistakeably Tantric tour de force featuring a host of ferocious goddesses.[52] In the *Devi Mahatmya,* Durga is a weapon-wielding, lion-riding warrior who must fight a series of demons that threaten the stability of the universe. Famously, she slays the buffalo demon, Mahisha (an embodiment of ignorance), whom the gods had been unable to defeat. Durga appears, armed and clutching a skull-cup, in an illuminated 17th-century copy of the *Devi Mahatmya* from Nepal (fig. 21).

Durga's death-blow to Mahisha became one of the most popular subjects in medieval sculpture, especially in eastern India where she is still widely venerated.[53] In an 8th-century sandstone temple relief from Odisha (fig. 22) she uses one hand to snap back his neck and another to impale his throat with a trident. The relief was executed during the rule of the Bhaumakara dynasty (8th–10th centuries), who maintained their control over most of the region for two centuries. The Vaital Deul temple in Bhubaneswar, built during Bhaumakara rule, is a Shakti temple with an iconographic programme featuring Tantrika ascetics wielding skull-topped clubs (*khatvanga*) (fig. 23).[54] One of the Bhaumakara kings, Subhakaradeva I (r. *c.* 790–810), was described as having 'the protection of his subjects as his

**Fig. 22**
**Durga killing the buffalo**
**demon Mahisha**
Odisha, India
8th century
Sandstone, 44.5 × 33.5 × 11.8 cm
British Museum 1872,0701.89
Donated by John Bridge and
his nieces, Miss Fanny Bridge
and Mrs Edgar Baker

**Fig. 23**
**Vaital Deul temple**
Bhubaneshwar, Odisha, India
8th century
Stone

highest aim', and had 'pacified the affliction of the world caused by the doings of his kinsmen'.[55]

Durga's foot bears down on Mahisha triumphantly in the Odisha relief. She brandishes a bow and shield while her lower left hand clasps a snake that peers at Mahisha. Durga's face is damaged but it is possible to make out her benevolent expression amidst the turmoil of the scene. She looks down at the crumpled demon compassionately, ultimately having released him from suffering. Mahisha had been torn between wanting to marry and destroy Durga; sculptures of the goddess highlight her erotic appeal by portraying her voluptuous curves. Durga exhibits many Tantric characteristics that challenge traditional models of femininity.[56] Aside from her heroics on the battlefield, she also has a taste for wine, with which she intoxicates herself before annihilating her enemies. According to the *Devi Mahatmya*, her devotees must offer their own flesh and blood to satisfy and renew her; in return, she will grant wealth, power and liberation.[57] Durga was adopted by many rulers as their guardian and regarded as a source of their authority and strength. King Narasimhadeva I (r. 1238–1264) of the Eastern Ganga dynasty (11th–15th centuries), who retained a stronghold in Odisha, referred to himself as the 'son of Durga'.[58] Sculptures from

Konarak temple, which he built between 1241 and 1258, depict him worshipping her.

Durga does not always act alone; other wild, bloodthirsty goddesses often assist her. When confronted with the power-hungry demon brothers Shumbha and Nishumbha and their armies, the Hindu gods manifest their own Shaktis or female counterparts to support Durga; these goddesses are known collectively as the Matrikas ('Mothers').[59] A sandstone 10th-century temple panel from Madhya Pradesh (central India) depicts the Matrikas together (fig. 24). It was carved during the rule of the Gurjara-Pratihara dynasty (8th–11th centuries). Mahipala I (*c.* 910–?), along with his predecessors Nagabhata I (*c.* 725–760) and Mihira Bhoja (*c.* 836–885), are described in inscriptions as Shakti devotees (*bhagavatibhakta*).[60] Around 945 CE, the dynasty experienced succession conflicts involving numerous claimants to the throne, triggering its decline.[61] The Matrikas are joined by Shiva on the far left. Beside him are, from left to right: Brahmi, created from the god Brahma; Maheshvari, from Shiva; Kaumari, from Skanda; Vaishnavi, from Vishnu; the sow-headed Varahi, from the boar *avatar* or incarnation of Vishnu (Varaha); and Indrani, from Indra. They sit on their *vahanas* or vehicles (a swan, bull, peacock, mythical Garuda bird, buffalo and elephant respectively). On the far right is the seventh Matrika,

**Fig. 24**
**The Seven Mothers (Sapta-Matrikas) accompanied by Shiva**
Madhya Pradesh, India
10th century
Sandstone, 39.4 × 72 × 6.8 cm
British Museum 1880.230

Chamunda, the horrifyingly skeletal leader of the Matrikas, who is exceptionally created by Durga herself, bursting out of her as an embodiment of her battle rage.[62] She sits on her human corpse *vahana*. As the Seven Mothers (Sapta-Matrikas) the goddesses successfully defeat the demons in a whirlwind of carnage. Victorious, they celebrate by inebriating themselves on their victims' blood and dancing madly.[63] Finally, they enter Durga's body after fulfilling their duties. In the *Devi Mahatmya*, Durga proclaims: '"[Be]hold these manifestations of power entering back into me!" [T]hereupon, all the goddesses (…) went to their resting-place in the body of the Goddess'.[64]

Evidence suggests that the Matrikas were venerated in iconic form from the 5th century onwards by rulers, members of their courts and warriors.[65] An inscription from Gangadhar (Rajasthan, north-west India), dated to the 420s CE, notes that the Gupta king's minister built a shrine dedicated to the Matrikas there.[66] Their exceptional martial abilities seem to have been harnessed by the Gupta dynasty and later rulers to ensure victories on the battlefield. The Matrikas' mainstream popularity continued to grow, as demonstrated by the creation of shrines and niches dedicated to them across medieval India; meanwhile, they continued to play an important role in esoteric Tantric practice. By the 9th century, sculpted panels representing the Matrikas were often positioned as lintels above the entrances of temples, often dedicated to Shiva, which is almost certainly the case with the Madhya Pradesh relief.[67]

According to the *Vastushastras*, Sanskrit architectural manuals composed from the 5th century onwards, the Hindu temple was conceived as a symbol of the cosmos with the central deity residing in the inner sanctum (*garbhagriha*).[68] Hierarchies of other deities surrounded the heart of the temple, offering a protective function at the doorways and on the exterior walls. Many of the temple sculptures in this chapter, such as the Hoysala (fig. 14) and Chola Bhairava (fig. 15) examples, would have performed such a role, their intrinsic power harnessed in a public setting. Such images again reflect the dynamic fluidity between private and public expressions of Tantra as a source of power that could be tapped into. When these Tantric deities, originally associated with the marginal and the esoteric in early *Tantras*, were brought into the orthodox (Brahmanical) Hindu fold, they were not being tamed but conscripted, for their capacities as guardians, warriors and custodians of supreme knowledge.

The Madhya Pradesh relief reveals how the Matrikas were perceived by the 10th century, not only as bloodthirsty warriors but also loving mothers, as reflected in their name. Three of the Matrikas – Maheshvari, Vaishnavi and Indrani – hold children on their laps. This is not only to suggest their maternal qualities, but also to remind devotees to worship them because they were believed to inflict death and disease, of which children were frequent victims.[69] On the other hand, they were associated with fertility. Their seemingly contradictory qualities, intertwining morbidity and benevolence, beauty and horror, defined their Tantric identities.

This ambivalence is particularly evident in the figures of Varahi and Chamunda, who are depicted in sharp contrast to the other Matrikas. While Chamunda is emaciated and grotesque, Varahi is sow-headed, deliberately contrasting with the ideal feminine physiques of the other Matrikas. Both also hold *kapalas* or skull-cups containing wine or blood, a reminder of their roles as the most transgressive of the Mothers.

Varahi and Chamunda went on to lead independent roles, singled out for special worship, not only in dedicated niches within larger temple complexes dedicated to Durga or Shiva but also in numerous temples dedicated solely to them.[70] A 9th-century sandstone sculpture of Varahi, possibly from the Badoh-Pathari region of Malwa (central India), was carved during the rule of the Paramara dynasty (9th–11th centuries) and must have once been positioned inside a niche within a temple (fig. 25). The sculpture shows the four-armed goddess seated on a nestled buffalo (her vehicle), an animal appropriately associated with Yama, the god of death. Varahi's iconography intertwines the beautiful with the ferocious, mirroring her ability to both cause and prevent epidemics. The *Devi Mahatmya* describes her as having the strength to lift the Earth with her sow-snout and tusks, her most lethal weapons in battle.[71] She has a potbelly, which has been interpreted as a container of the universe but also hints at her insatiable appetite.[72] She holds a child and a bell (*ghanta*), though two other attributes in particular allude to her Tantric nature: the skull-cup containing wine or blood and the large fish that is held firmly between her teeth, fish (*matsya*) being one of the so-called polluting 'Five Ms' (*panchamakara*) of left-hand Tantric practice.[73]

Chamunda, the most Tantric of all the Matrikas, is named after two demon-generals, Chanda and Munda, whom she decapitated in battle, devouring their army, elephants and weapons in a riot of carnage.[74] Before this triumph she is referred to as Kali ('Black'), a form of the goddess who became particularly popular from the 18th century onwards (see Chapter 4). Chamunda's worship as an independent deity was well established in eastern India between the 9th and 14th centuries.[75] Surviving sculptures of the goddess consistently depict her as emaciated. An 11th-century inscription from Bangarh in Bengal, recording the building of a temple dedicated to Charchika (another name for Chamunda), begins with praise for the goddess, and provides insight into the connotations that her physique would have evoked for devotees at the time:

May the world be protected by the dust from the feet of Charchika, (…) fragrant powder for the heads of all the gods and demons. May

**Fig. 25 (overleaf, p. 48)**

**Varahi**

Malwa, India

9th century

Sandstone, 62 × 44 × 17.5 cm

British Museum 1872,0701.47

Donated by John Bridge and
his nieces, Miss Fanny Bridge
and Mrs Edgar Baker

**Fig. 26 (overleaf, p. 49)**

**Chamunda**

Odisha, India

9th century

Sandstone, 94 × 72.4 ×
29.2 cm

British Museum 1872,0701.83

Donated by John Bridge and
his nieces, Miss Fanny Bridge
and Mrs Edgar Baker

Charchika protect the world, who at the aeon's end, garlanded with human skulls, with her body becoming desiccated out of anxiety at the poverty of her fare, thinks: 'What shall I eat? If I devour this universe in a single bite, it will be no more than a fragment that will lodge between my teeth.'[76]

Here Charchika/Chamunda's gauntness signals not only her compassion for 'her fare' or devotees, but also her ravenous hunger, which even the consumption of the universe cannot sate. Her role as devourer of the world reflects the belief that at the close of each aeon the universe is destroyed and then re-created by the gods according to the Hindu concept of time as cyclical. The inscription notes that the temple was built by a Shaiva Siddhanta guru called Rajaguru Murtishiva during the reign of the Pala ruler Nayapala (r. *c.* 1042–1058).

A sandstone sculpture of Chamunda, carved in 9th-century Odisha, shows her dancing ecstatically after her rampage, shaking the very foundations of the universe (fig. 26). She is a horrifyingly macabre, skeletal vision to behold, with a skull-like face, unsettling grimace, glaring, protruding eyes, drooping breasts, protruding ribs and sunken belly. Her nakedness is ornamented with a garland of heads. Her eight bony arms, flying in all directions, clutch a skull-cup, severed head and weapons, including a sword and a trident with a corpse or *preta* (malevolent ghost) draped over its prongs. Her 'throne' is a trampled corpse with hands raised in supplication and surrender, his fingers brushing her toes. On the left a dog or jackal begins to chew his foot while two birds join in the carrion-feeding frenzy, including an owl perched on his head, suggesting the nocturnal setting of the cremation ground, Chamunda's favourite haunt.

While the corpse here can be interpreted as a mirror held up to the viewer to confront his or her own limited self-grasping, which Chamunda helps her devotees to destroy and transcend with her multiple weapons, it is also her vehicle (*vahana*), which serves and empowers her. Tantric texts also describe practices involving meditation while seated on a corpse (*shava sadhana*), carried out by only the most experienced practitioners in cremation- and charnel-ground settings. The *Vajramrita Tantra*, for example, describes how to invoke a spirit (*vetala*) residing within a corpse through the recitation of mantras invoking a wrathful deity (fig. 27). Aside from magical attainments, the practice is also said to 'confer happiness' and to grant 'the body, the speech and the mind [of the deities]'.[77] After the recitation of mantras, 'the *vetala* will emerge, emitting a deep sound and pronouncing a cry, filled with anger. (…) The *vetala*, once arisen, asks the practitioner to indicate his task: "Oh Great Hero, what is the action (to be performed)? Give me the command!"'[78] The *vetala* is described as having the power to grant whatever the Tantrika desires, be it a sword, invisibility ointment or

Fig. 27
**Folio from the**
*Vajramrita Tantra*
Nepal
1162
Palm leaf, 5 × 31 cm
Cambridge University Library
MS Or.158.1 (fol. 11v)

Fig. 28
**Chamunda**
Malwa, India
11th century
Sandstone, height 53.3 cm
British Museum 1872,0701.84
Donated by John Bridge and
his nieces, Miss Fanny Bridge
and Mrs Edgar Baker

flight. Thus, the corpse becomes a vehicle and agent for the Tantrika's own path of power and transformation.

An arresting 11th-century sandstone temple sculpture (fig. 28) shows the surviving upper portion of a large Chamunda image from Malwa, where the goddess was clearly popular, judging by the number of surviving sculptures dating between the 9th and 11th centuries, when the Paramara dynasty was in power.[79] Three of her hands hold a snake, dagger and skull-cup, while her matted hair is piled on top of her head in a bun, held up by a skull-encrusted headband. Although images of Durga and the other Matrikas challenge conventional models of femininity, their identities are still tied to an ambivalent tension between destructive and maternal qualities, even in the case of Varahi, who cradles a child in the Malwa sculpture (see fig. 25). Chamunda, however, possesses no such ambiguity. With her skeletal and gory appearance, she is a ruthless harbinger of chaos and carnage, and is thus the embodiment of Tantric power, tied to impurity and transgression. This aesthetic was not only confined to representations of goddesses but could extend to mortal women as well, as in the depictions of the Nayanar saint Karaikkal Ammaiyar (see figs. 16, 17), who disavowed her role as a dutiful wife and daughter to become 'a female ghoul with withered breasts, bulging veins, hollow eyes, white teeth and two fangs'.[80]

Another sandstone temple sculpture of an eighteen-armed Chamunda, possibly from Kalinjar (Madhya Pradesh, central India), dates to the 9th century, during the rule of the Gurjara-Pratihara dynasty (figs. 29, 30).[81] Numerous ghoulish denizens of the cremation ground join Chamunda, including her fellow Matrika Varahi in miniature form, hungrily drinking up the blood that drips from the severed head that Chamunda holds.

The corpse on which Chamunda acrobatically dances turns around to look up at her adoringly.[82] The Gurjara-Pratiharas' attraction to Chamunda is vividly illustrated in a play written by the 10th-century court poet Rajashekhara, entitled *Karpuramanjari*. The central character is a Tantrika called Bhairavananda who has supernatural powers and is described as 'drinking alcohol' and 'enjoying women' to obtain 'liberation'.[83] In the play he installs an image of Chamunda while women dressed as goddesses perform dances and 'others, bearing in their hands offerings of human flesh and terrible with their groans and shrieks and cries and wearing the masks of night-wandering ogresses, are enacting a cemetery scene'.[84] They are watched over by a king and queen, who are captivated by the

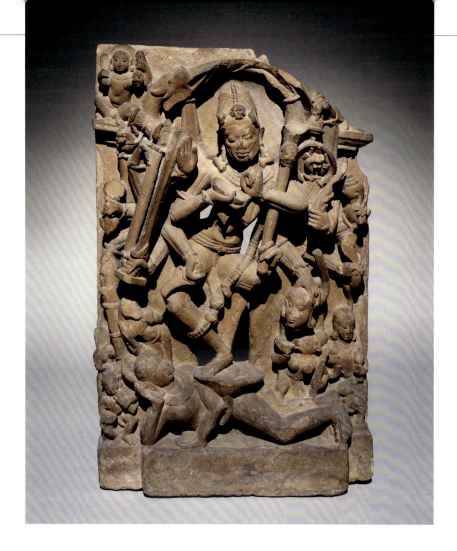

charismatic Tantrika. Bhairavananda promises to transform the king into a *chakravartin* or universal conqueror.

While the play was written to entertain and titillate, and literature of the medieval period is replete with caricatures of morally degenerate Tantric 'supermen' with expertise in black magic, it nevertheless demonstrates how strongly Tantrikas and their Tantric goddesses captured the imaginations of the courts during the medieval period. As agents of power, they appealed to rulers with worldly, military ambitions. The *Netra Tantra* describes the role that Tantric gurus played in protecting rulers from a range of adverse forces, both practical and supernatural, through apotropaic mantras.[85] Tantric masters also offered initiations to kings, not simply as a means for them to attain spiritual liberation, but to transform them into invulnerable leaders.[86] A 12th/13th-century inscription from Haryana (northern India) records King Surapala's relationship with his guru, Murtigan, 'by whose excellent initiation Surapaladeva became [a king] whose might was unequalled'. It states that anyone whom Murtigan initiated was transformed into a 'repository of [all] knowledge, lord of the whole Earth, and the foremost of men'.[87] At a time when there were many rival imperial centres, rulers sought initiation from Tantric masters to empower and legitimize their reigns, and to increase their authority as divine *chakravartins*. This practice would extend beyond India to the rest of Asia (see Chapter 3).

Fig. 29
**Chamunda**
Probably Kalinjar, Madhya
Pradesh, India
9th century
Sandstone, 89 × 61 × 21 cm
British Museum 1872,0701.82
Donated by John Bridge
and his nieces, Miss Fanny
Bridge and Mrs Edgar Baker

Fig. 30
**Detail of fig. 29, showing
Chamunda surrounded
by her retinue**

## YOGINIS: SHAPESHIFTERS OF THE SKY

By the 7th and 8th centuries the Matrikas had evolved into arguably
the most important Tantric deities in medieval India: the seductive yet
dangerous Yoginis, reigning witch-like goddesses of Tantric Hinduism.[88]
The Yoginis are prominent in the *Bhairava Tantras* classified as *Vidyapitha*
('Seat of the Wisdom Goddesses') texts, dating from around the 6th–7th
centuries CE.[89] These texts emphasized transgressive rites of a sexual
and sanguinary nature revolving around the Yoginis. The Yoginis were
shapeshifters who could metamorphose into women, birds, snakes, tigers
or jackals as the mood took them. Their most famous ability was the power
of flight.[90] Initiated Tantrikas sought to access their *siddhis* (supernatural
powers), from flight and immortality to control over others, by appeasing
the Yoginis in nocturnal cremation-ground settings with 'impure' sacrificial
offerings that were believed to nourish and energize them. These ritual
offerings ranged from blood and alcohol to the Tantrikas' own sexual fluids
released after ritual intercourse. If successful, the Yoginis would reveal
themselves to the Tantrika, offering the powers he or she desired and
granting exclusive admission to their 'clan'.[91] If not (due to lack of
initiation, experience or an offensive ritual mistake) the Tantrika could
become the Yoginis' breakfast. Not for nothing were Tantrikas often
described as heroes – the path of the Yoginis was a treacherous one that
required careful initiation from an experienced guru. The *Brahmayamala
Tantra*, a goddess-centred *Vidyapitha* text dating to the late 7th or early 8th
century, describes how to summon the Yoginis successfully in order to hear
their prophecies, but warns of the potential hazards:

> The [practitioner] of great spirit should recite the mantra, naked,
> facing south. After seven nights, the Yoginis come – highly dangerous,
> with terrifying forms, impure, angry, and lethal. But seeing this, the
> [practitioner] of heroic spirit should not fear; after prostrating, he
> should give them the guest-offering. [They become] pleased towards
> the practitioner endowed with [heroic] spirit, without a doubt.
> And touching him, they tell truly the [the future], good and bad.
> If by mistake a practitioner of weak spirit should tremble, the Yoginis
> (…) devour him that very moment.[92]

According to the *c.* 11th-century *Kaulajnananirnaya*, Yoginis might also offer
a Tantrika impure food (characterized by its inedibility) which, if eaten
without hesitation, could grant immediate power: '[if he consumes the
impure food] immediately when first given by the Yoginis, he becomes
equal to them'.[93] Even if there is initial hesitation, if the practitioner is able
to eat it without faltering 'he will undoubtedly attain *siddhi*, free from the

**Fig. 31**
**Yogini**
Kanchi, Tamil Nadu, India
10th century
Granite, 108 × 63.4 × 34.2 cm
British Museum 1955,1018.2
Donated by P. T. Brooke
Sewell Esq.

**Fig. 32**
**Yogini**
Kanchi, Tamil Nadu, India
10th century
Basalt, 116.8 × 73.7 × 50.8 cm
Detroit Institute of Arts 57.88

web of obstacles. Equal to the horde of Yoginis, he would obtain whatever he thinks about'.[94] Ritually ingesting, using or offering traditionally taboo substances could also result in a psychological breakthrough in accepting the Tantric worldview that all phenomena are infused with divine power or Shakti. According to this worldview, substances that might otherwise 'pollute' or corrupt one's being according to orthodox belief could be transmuted into divine ambrosia.

By the 10th century the Yoginis had prominently entered India's mainstream public religious landscape, with numerous temples dedicated to them, many constructed by royal patrons. The *Shilpa Prakasha* (9th–12th century), an architectural treatise from Odisha, notes that 'wherever temples are thus undergirded by Yoginis, the acquisition of *siddhis* is a certainty'.[95] A life-size 10th-century Yogini hewn in granite (fig. 31) once graced a temple in or near the city of Kanchi (Tamil Nadu).[96] From a distance her voluptuous nudity attracts the eye and invites the viewer to approach, but closer observation reveals the fearsome details of her fangs, angrily arched eyebrows, and earrings made from a dismembered hand and a cobra. She projects into the viewer's space, animatedly leaning out of the stone backdrop behind her, with unforgiving eyes and wild hair fanning out behind her in fiery waves. Her presence emanates power. With her four

Fig. 33
Map showing locations of
Yogini temples and sites

HIMALAYA

Indus

Yoginipur
(Delhi)

Ajmer ·   Naresar · · Mitauli
    Hinglajgadh ·   Lokhari · Rikhiyan   Kamakhya ·
   Jhalawar ·    Dudhai ·   Khajuraho   Ganges
    Ujjain ·     Badoh ·   · Shahdol
Broach ·       · Bheraghat

           Ranipur-Jharial ·
          Hirapur ·

Arabian
Sea

Bay
of Bengal

Kanchipuram ·

N

0            300 miles
0            500 kilometres

· Yogini temple sites
· Sites connected with Yoginis

arms, two of which are decorated with cobra armlets, she holds a skull-cup for alcohol or blood and a skull-topped staff. A now-broken arm probably once held sacrificial food up to her mouth. Along with at least eleven other Yogini sculptures, now dispersed across several collections worldwide, this figure would have been enshrined within a temple dedicated to them. This temple, which no longer exists, might have been commissioned by King Krishna III (939–967) of the Rashtrakuta dynasty (8th–10th centuries), who ruled over territories in the Deccan and had annexed the north of Tamil Nadu to his empire, defeating the Chola army in 949.[97]

The other surviving Kanchi Yogini sculptures display a range of visages, from benevolent to terrifying. One, now at the Detroit Institute of Art, arches her eyebrows angrily and holds up a club and shield as though readying herself to attack (fig. 32). A cobra has wound itself around her body and rears its head near her abdomen, while two others are coiled around her upper arms. Beneath her feet lies a headless corpse that has been carved onto the pedestal to suggest a charnel-ground setting; or perhaps this is one of her victims, satisfying her bloodthirsty desires.

Like the Matrikas before them, the Yoginis were believed to offer protection for kingdoms against epidemics or enemy forces, and to assist in the acquisition of new territories and the destruction of opponents.[98]

Between the 10th and 14th centuries numerous Yogini temples were built in cities across India (fig. 33). Eight of the surviving structures were patronized in parts of central India under Chandella dynasty rule (9th–13th centuries).[99] Most of the temples were circular and architecturally unique in their roofless design, perhaps in order to attract the Yoginis from the sky into the sacred courtyard.[100] It is possible that the Kanchi sculptures were once enshrined within a similarly open-air space, all set within interior niches, which is the case with the *c.* 900 CE Yogini temple in Hirapur (Odisha), possibly constructed after the fall of the Bhaumakaras by a chieftain of the Bhanja dynasty, a former feudatory whose leaders took advantage of the power vacuum to rule over the area temporarily. Surviving inscriptions describe the Bhanjas as 'favoured by the Goddess'.[101]

A total of sixty-four Yoginis encircle the interior walls, which measure around 7.5 m (25 ft) in diameter, all facing the courtyard as if expecting company (fig. 34). With semi-nude bodies, many stand and dance upon the animals that they can shapeshift into, including parrots (fig. 35), crows, jackals, antelopes, sows, tortoises and elephants. Others balance upon corpses (fig. 36) and dismembered heads, and some drink from skull-cups, associating them with the charnel ground.

The original function of this and of other Yogini temples remains mysterious. However, the iconography of their sculptures may reveal some clues. Images of dismembered body parts, corpses and skull-cups suggest that Tantric rituals may have been carried out within the space of the temple courtyard, involving the consumption and offering of wine, blood and flesh, which were believed to satiate the Yoginis, along with sexual fluids.[102] The *Vajrabhairava Tantra* provides a list of recommended liminal spaces for carrying out esoteric Tantric rites of a transgressive nature, including not only 'cemeteries', 'forests' and 'mountain peaks' but also 'temples of the divine mothers'.[103] It is also clear that Yogini temples were not secret, hidden places, but generally prominent and visible, so while their officiants were most likely Tantric adepts, they would have simultaneously invited more conventional forms of lay devotional worship from visitors, including offerings of flowers.[104]

Many rulers were Yogini devotees, such as the Western Chalukya dynasty that governed large parts of southern and central India between the 10th and 12th centuries. The *Manasollasa*, an encyclopaedic text written by or for the Chalukya king Someshvara III in 1131, includes a chapter entitled 'The Circle of Yoginis' which focuses on military strategy, including astrological diagrams to determine ideal times to attack enemies.[105] The 12th-century epic poem *Dvyashraya Kavya*, a history of the dynasty written by the scholar Hemachandra, presents a vivid picture of King Siddharaja's engagement with the Yoginis or 'filthy birds of night', whom he summons in order to receive prophecies:

[Even when the night comes] the duties of the king are by no means finished (…) he must rise from his couch to perform the [*vira* [hero] practice]. He goes forth, sword in hand, alone (…) extend[ing] his rambles beyond [the city] walls to some spot frequented only by the filthy birds of night, the Yoginis (…), female sprites, whom he compels to reply to his questions and to inform him of future events.[106]

While male Tantrikas, whether kings or ascetics, propitiated the Yoginis, female Tantrikas (as carriers of Shakti) could actually *become* them, inviting a more direct engagement through emulation and embodiment. Many *Tantras* insist that male Tantrikas should venerate women and never offend them, perhaps because they could be Yoginis in mortal disguise.[107] Indeed, as discussed in Chapter 2, the word 'yogini' often simply denotes a female Tantrika or practitioner of yoga. The Kanchi Yogini sculptures, with their sloped shoulders and animated life-size bodies, evoke living, breathing

**Fig. 34**
**Yogini temple**
Hirapur, Odisha, India
*c.* 900
Sandstone, laterite and grey chlorite

**Fig. 35**
**Yogini**
Hirapur, Odisha, India
*c.* 900
Grey chlorite

**Fig. 36**
**Yogini**
Hirapur, Odisha, India
*c.* 900
Grey chlorite

women, hinting at the blurred lines between female divinity and mortal womanhood. Although it is a fictional compilation of legends, the 11th-century *Kathasaritsagara* (*The Ocean of Rivers Story*) by Somadeva, believed to have been written for Queen Suryamati of Kashmir, features an insightful tale about a queen, Kuvalayavali, accessing the Yoginis' limitless power. In one chapter Kuvalayavali narrates how she succeeded in joining their sky-bound ranks, despite her initial hesitation at the gruesomeness involved:

At the conclusion of my worship, I suddenly saw that my friends [the Yoginis], having flown upward, were roaming about in the field of the sky, each by means of her own supernatural power. Beholding that [sight], I called in amazement, and made them descend from the sky; and, questioned by me regarding the nature of their supernatural power, they immediately said this: 'These supernatural powers of

witches' spells arise from the eating of human flesh…' Thus addressed by my friends, [and] most eager for the supernatural power of flight but anxious about eating human flesh, I hesitated for a moment. But then, out of my ardent desire for that supernatural power, I said to my friends, 'May this, my instruction, be conferred by you'.[108]

The propitiation of the Yoginis in the 16th century would take on new significance in an Islamic courtly context in the Deccan Sultanate of Bijapur (see Chapter 2), revealing the Yoginis' enduring reputations as granters of power and success as new political players appeared on India's stage.

The role of divine feminine power, or Shakti, remains central to any reading of Tantra both as a philosophy and as a set of practices across the different chronological and geographic contexts. Durga, the Matrikas and the Yoginis present visions of femininity that are dangerously transgressive, a pattern that is present in depictions of other Tantric goddesses, from Vajrayogini in Tibet (see Chapter 3) to Kali in colonial Bengal (see Chapter 4). Their power is often signalled by their appearance, with Tantric signifiers such as blood-filled *kapalas* and corpses serving as reminders of both their destructive powers and their *siddhi*-granting potential that could make or break a king. Whether or not the veneration of goddesses extended to a re-evaluation of mortal women's status is a separate question, requiring an examination of the role of women in Tantric practice according to textual sources, as well as visual depictions of female practitioners (see Chapters 2 and 3). While many Tantric texts instruct that women, as embodiments of Shakti, should be worshipped and have the capacity to be great masters, others suggest a more instrumental role as partners in sexual rites.

### *MAITHUNA* AND THE ROLE OF SEXUAL RITES

Sex and erotic imagery are not confined to Tantra. The exterior walls of hundreds of ancient and medieval temples across South Asia reveal the consistently important role of sexual symbolism across Tantric and orthodox sacred spaces alike. According to the *Vedas* and later Vedic texts, sexuality and religion were not mutually exclusive phenomena – creation itself was conceived as a product of divine coitus and the key goals of a fulfilling and righteous life were dictated by not only duty (*dharma*), prosperity (*artha*) and liberation (*moksha*) but also by *kama* (pleasure and desire).[109] Hindu and Buddhist monuments had long featured auspicious *mithuna* ('couple') figures embellishing exterior façades, both to generate prosperity and to protect the inner sanctum.[110] In a late 10th-century sandstone sculpture from Rajasthan that would have once been positioned on the vestibule of a temple (fig. 37), two lovers fondle each other, their lips about to touch, the man reaching for the woman's breast and she his phallus. There is nothing particularly 'Tantric' about this sculpture. The *Shilpa Prakasha* provides the following justification for the inclusion of erotic imagery in temple architecture:

> *Kama* is the root of the universe. All that is born originates from *kama*. (…) Without [the passionate engagement of] Shiva and Shakti, creation would be nothing but a figment. (…) Shiva is manifest as the great *linga* [phallus], Shakti's essential form is the *yoni* [vulva]. By their interaction, the entire world comes into being; this is called the activity of *kama*. (…) a place devoid of erotic imagery is a 'place to be shunned'. (…) erotic sculpture panels should be mounted in order to delight the general public.[111]

**Fig. 37**

**Erotic *mithuna* sculpture**

Rajasthan, India

Late 10th century

Red sandstone, 54 × 46 × 18.5 cm

British Museum 1964,0413.1

Funded by the Brooke Sewell Permanent Fund

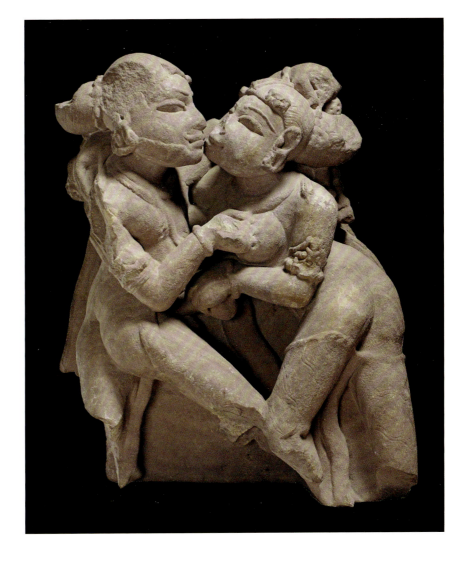

It is when transgressive sexual acts begin to appear, proliferating around the early 10th century in the form of *maithuna* ('sexual union', a more explicit form of *mithuna*) sculpture, that we begin to spot the depiction of what could be Tantric rites.[112] These depictions of transgressive acts included *rajapana* (the drinking of female discharge); in ancient texts dedicated to *kama*, such as the *c.* 3rd-century CE *Kama Sutra* by Vatsyayana, cunnilingus (as well as oral sex generally) was regarded as polluting, and a threat to societal and familial (reproductive) stability.[113]

An 11th-century sandstone sculpture (fig. 38), once part of a frieze and possibly from one of the Elephanta cave temples dedicated to Shiva in Mumbai (western India), depicts an orgiastic scene with Tantric ritual overtones. On the right, two bearded men stand either side of a woman who holds one of their phalluses between her breasts. On the left, another man appears to perform cunnilingus on a woman who, upside down, bends to reciprocate in an impossibly acrobatic manoeuvre. Like the figures in the *mithuna* sculpture, they all wear their hair tied in buns and are adorned with armlets and earrings. In this case we might describe them as Tantrikas. It is

**Fig. 38**
**Erotic *maithuna* sculpture**
Possibly from one of the
Elephanta cave temples,
Maharashtra, India
11th century
Sandstone, 45.5 × 75.5 cm
British Museum 1805,0703.264
Field collection of Sir Charles
Townley

THE RISE OF TANTRA IN MEDIEVAL INDIA

not unusual for temples to feature sculptures of ascetic followers of Shiva in erotic scenes, displaying their sexual potency.[114] More generally, they were revered and respected as figures who had mastered their minds as well as their bodies to affect dramatic spiritual transformations. Representations of ascetics on temple walls became particularly popular after the 5th century, coinciding with the rise of ascetic communities devoted to Shiva.[115]

Sculpted representations of *rajapana* appear on the exterior of Hindu temples oriented towards Shiva and Shakti between the 10th and 12th centuries, especially in Odisha.[116] According to Tantric texts including the *Yoni Tantra* (16th–17th century), *yoni-puja* ('veneration of the vulva') is carried out before *rajapana*.[117] It was believed that mortal women were carriers of Shakti, and that this power could be ritually accessed through their sexual fluids, whether discharge or menstrual blood. The same text notes that simply reciting '*yoni, yoni*' continuously will help a Tantrika in attaining *siddhis* and enlightenment because to venerate the vulva is equivalent to venerating the source of creation.[118] It describes the 'very secret' practice involving 'putting his mouth on the mouth of the female sex organ' and reciting the mantra 10,000 times, which 'wipes out numerous sins from 10,000 previous births in an instant'.[119] The *Brahmayamala Tantra* declares that a woman's sexual fluids or 'supreme nectar' (*paramrita*) has the power to grant all desires.[120] Aside from the possibility of viscerally tapping into this cosmic force in order to internalize it, *rajapana* also deliberately subverted traditional Vedic purity rules, which stressed the destructive dangers inherent in polluted substances. This subversion tapped into the suppressed energy of the forbidden, shattering dichotomies and triggering enlightenment.

The *Tantraloka*, written in early 11th-century Kashmir by the Tantric master and theologian Abhinavagupta (*c.* 975–1025), describes a secret 'sacrificial' ritual in which the Tantrika offers his own sexual fluids and his partner's to deities.[121] The pair must first enter the 'hall of sacrifice', a perfumed, consecrated space 'decorated with flowers'.[122] They mentally invoke a circle of deities and begin worshipping each other through kisses and caresses, until they reach a euphoric state in which their egos and attachments melt away. The *vira* ('hero') then worships the 'mouth of the Yogini' (*yoginivaktra*), the woman's vulva, and they proceed to intercourse. His semen and her vaginal discharge are 'reciprocally passed from mouth to mouth', creating a mixture that is then offered to the deities present before it is drunk by the pair with water and alcohol.[123]

The male and female Tantrikas must be fully in control of their sexuality and free of attachment, since the goal is to unite with divinity and attain *siddhis*, rather than pleasure for its own sake.[124] It has been argued that the literal performance of Tantric sexual rites was purely a way to offer and/or consume sexual fluids.[125] This 'de-eroticizing' of Tantra is misleading, however. Tantric sexual rites affirm the body and the sensual, sublimating and purifying ordinary sexuality, rather than repressing it, in order to generate power. A visualization (*dhyana*) of Shiva and the goddess Kamakaleshvari described in the *Shilpa Prakasha* describes the god performing the rite of *rajapana*:

> Lord of the Art of the Erotic, seated below, at the place of the jewel [the vulva], sustained in a posture of yoga, deeply absorbed in the dark limbs [of the Goddess], always engaged in sexual union together with the Goddess, who is the Lady of the Art of the Erotic, always drinking the [sexual] fluids of the Goddess at the level of the third eye [of wisdom].[126]

This description was written as a meditative visualization, but it also reflects the fact that Tantrikas imagined themselves as divine embodiments of Shiva and Shakti when they actively engaged in sexual rites. Similar practices are described in Tantric Buddhist texts (see Chapter 3), in which practitioners assumed the role of equivalent deities and harnessed desire in order to ultimately transcend it. The techniques of Hatha yoga (see Chapter 2) and Devata yoga (see Chapter 3) illuminate the symbolic dimension of sexual rites, involving the visualization of Tantric deities in union within the body of the practitioner.

Male Tantrikas or *viras* described in texts such as the *Tantraloka* may have been householders, ascetics or kings. Less clear, and still debated among scholars, is the social background of the women, who are often referred to as *dutis* ('female messengers') or as *shaktis*.[127] According to the *Tantralokaviveka*, a *c.* 13th-century commentary on the *Tantraloka* by the Kashmiri author Jayaratha, the female partner should be chosen 'without regard to caste', suggesting the desirability of transgressing Vedic caste but also suggesting that women in vulnerable positions, whether prostitutes or servants, could be taken advantage of.[128] The late 7th/early 8th-century *Brahmayamala Tantra*, however, gives the female Tantrika more agency as a practitioner in her own right:

> [She can be characterized as one who] has received the guru's instructions, is beautiful, is endowed with [all] auspicious features, has mastered the sitting postures, is of heroic spirit, steeped in the essence of the Tantras, is loyal to her guru, deity and husband, has conquered hunger, thirst and fatigue, dwelling always in non-duality, she has no qualms, is non-covetous, knows [how to reach] Samadhi [blissful awareness], knows Yoga, knows Knowledge [i.e. this doctrine], and has accomplished her ascetic observances.[129]

Women play different roles across Tantric texts, most of which were probably written by male authors, whether as autonomous gurus with innate powers or as partners in sexual rites, whose sexual fluids could be tapped into as a source of Shakti. Like the goddesses described earlier in this chapter, they could also be dangerously ambivalent and shapeshifting Yoginis in disguise, capable of destruction if displeased.

## TANTRIC SEX AND THE SECRET MUSEUM

The *maithuna* sculpture analysed above (fig. 38), which was acquired by the British Museum in 1805, received alternative Western interpretations between the 18th and 19th centuries, hinging on the fascination with, or disapproval of, the relationship between sexuality and religion. The sculpture once formed part of the collection of Charles Townley (1737–1805), a collector and connoisseur of mainly Greek and Roman antiquities.[130] We know that in 1784 Captain Alexander Allan, a cartographer for the East India Company and commander of the warship HMS *Cumberland*, brought this sculpture to London.[131] How exactly he acquired it in the first place is unclear, though we are told that it was 'detached from one of the ancient temples which are excavated in the solid rock upon the island of Elephanta near Bombay'.[132] The sculpture was first bought by a friend of Townley's, Thomas Astle, who displayed it at the Society of Antiquarians before it eventually became part of Townley's personal collection in Park Street.[133] His protégé, the French antiquarian Pierre d'Hancarville, described the sculpture in the supplement to his *Recherches sur l'origine, l'esprit et les progrès des arts de la Grèce* (1785), which mused on the erotic origins of ancient art, on the basis of Townley's collection: 'One can't imagine anything more luxurious, more unrestrained than the actions of the figures. (…) they resemble things of the same type that have been known to have been deposited in temples and generally in all the monuments devoted to Bacchus'.[134] A year later, another antiquarian and collector of Greek erotic sculpture, Richard Payne Knight, also saw the sculpture and included an enthused description of it in his *A Discourse on the Worship of Priapus and its Connection with the Mystic Theology of the Ancients* (1786):

> It contains several figures, in very high relief; the principal of which are a man and a woman, in an attitude which I shall not venture to describe, but only observe, that the action, which I have supposed to be a symbol of refreshment and invigoration, is mutually applied by both to their respective organs of generation, the emblems of the active and passive powers of procreation, which mutually cherish and invigorate each other.[135]

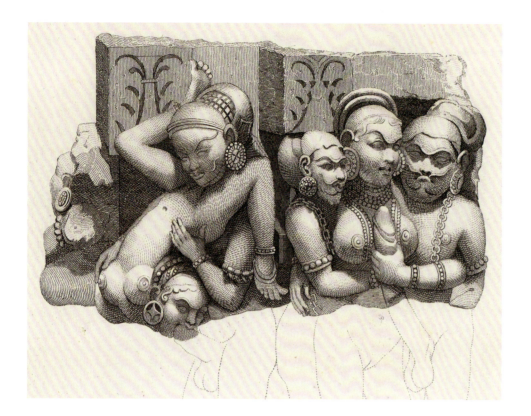

The sculpture was reproduced as an engraving and included as a frontispiece for the publication, with added outlines re-creating what the lower portion of the sculpture (now lost) might have looked like (fig. 39). The woman on the left is imagined giving fellatio to the male figure; interestingly, the engraver avoids making it appear as if the man is performing cunnilingus – perhaps this was deemed a step too far by Knight. On the right the central woman is imagined to be holding the phallus of the man to her left. Knight's study, which shocked readers at the time, sought to promote a better understanding of the theology behind ancient sexual symbols found across different cultures and religions, from Greek and Celtic to Egyptian and Indian artefacts.[136]

In 1865, more than sixty years after Townley's *maithuna* sculpture arrived at the British Museum, the Secretum or 'Secret Museum' was formally established to store all erotic objects deemed to be indecent, depraved or morally corrupting. Artefacts such as the *maithuna* sculpture were stored there and only select gentlemen were able to apply for special permits to view the material.[137] Women, children and the working classes were regarded as too impressionable and vulnerable to degeneracy.[138] This was in the wake of the Obscene Publication Act of 1857, which suppressed the sale of lewd material, including pornography. The *maithuna* sculpture remained in the Secretum until the 1960s.

Another sculpture in the Secretum was an 18th-century black sandstone *linga* and *yoni* from eastern India (fig. 40) that had been acquired by the East India Company officer Charles Stuart (1757/8–1828). It was probably

Fig. 39
Engraving depicting fig. 38 that illustrated Richard Payne Knight's *A Discourse on the Worship of Priapus* (London, 1786)
London
1786
Engraving, 25.7 × 23.9 cm
British Museum 2005,0805,0.1

originally set in the ground inside a temple or shrine, judging from the uncarved base. The *linga*, widely worshipped in temples across South Asia, is a symbolic cylindrical representation of Shiva's erect phallus, an abstract expression of his virility and creative power. It rises above an abstracted *yoni* or vulva, symbolising his divine sexual union with Shakti. A snake, often associated with the god, winds itself around the *linga*.

The creation of the Secretum and the placement of the *maithuna* sculpture (along with the *linga-yoni*) in such a space needs to be understood in the context of prevalent Victorian attitudes towards sexuality in late 19th-century Britain. Unlike the Romantic 18th-century antiquarians' brand of affirmative Orientalism, which exoticized and embraced the visual evidence they found in other cultures marrying sexuality with religion, the Victorian upper middle classes were generally much more hostile to what they perceived as the sinful, deviant sexual perversions described in the *Tantras* and the sculptures and paintings they inspired.[139] Anything that contravened reproductive, marital, heteronormative sex was regarded with suspicion. As discussed further in Chapter 4, by the 19th century the *Tantras* came to symbolize all that was 'wrong' with India, a land perceived as so corrupted by its misguided, irrational cocktail of sex and sacrality that it required British colonial rule to tame, regulate and redeem it.

**Fig. 40**
*Linga-yoni*
Eastern India
18th century
Sandstone, 59 × 35 cm
British Museum 1872,0701.119
Donated by John Bridge and
his nieces, Miss Fanny Bridge
and Mrs Edgar Baker

## CHAPTER 2

# TANTRIC YOGA
# AND THE COURT

This chapter introduces the Tantric techniques of Hatha yoga, which became the dominant form of yoga in India from around the 16th century onwards.[1] The term yoga stems from the Sanskrit root *yuj*, meaning 'to yoke' or 'to bind', suggesting the harnessing of the mind and body. The reception and representation of Hatha yoga practitioners (yogis and yoginis) in courtly paintings between the 16th and 19th centuries demonstrate how the allure of Tantra, with its promises of longevity and invulnerability, continued to retain a hold over those in positions of power.

Throughout this period, India's cultural and political landscape was dominated by several competing forces. In the north-west, kingdoms in Rajasthan and the Punjab Hills were governed by Rajput Hindu rulers, who were eventually conquered by a Turkic dynasty that arrived from Central Asia in 1526 and established the Mughal empire (1526–1857). Further south, the Deccan Plateau was ruled by independent Islamic sultanates between the 1490s and 1680s, until they were annexed by the Mughal empire. The complex interactions between these different forces resulted in the development of great traditions of courtly painting featuring not only scenes of life at court and tales of myth and legend but also documentary and poetic studies of Tantric practitioners.

## HATHA YOGA AND THE RISE OF KUNDALINI

Tantrikas are often referred to as yogis and yoginis. A yogini is a female human practitioner of yoga, though the same term is also used for a group of Tantric goddesses (Yoginis) as discussed in Chapter 1. Of the various types of yoga, Hatha yoga ('yoga of force'), which drew on earlier Tantric conceptions of the body and methods for internalizing divinity, remains the most well known.[2] Earlier, non-Tantric forms of yoga, such as Ashtanga ('Eightfold') yoga, described by Patanjali in his *Patanjalayogashastra* (*c.* 2nd–4th centuries), focused on cultivating concentration to attain a mindful state of blissful awareness (*samadhi*). In contrast, Hatha yoga harnessed the body as the ultimate instrument and site for self-deification.[3] It introduced a range of complex postures (*asanas*) accompanied by breath control (*pranayama*) and 'body locks' (*bandha*), which were muscular contractions used to direct the flow of *prana* (breath or life force) throughout the body. The earliest known text to codify the key practices of what we now understand as Hatha yoga is a Tantric Buddhist one: the 11th-century *Amritasiddhi* (*Attainment of the Nectar of Immortality*).[4] It describes the nectar of immortality (*amrita*) as residing in the skull, steadily dripping down through the body as a person ages. In order to preserve it and to ward off the shackles of mortality, the text recommends certain practices for using the breath to push the nectar upwards, back into the skull. It notes that Hatha yoga can be practised by both householders and ascetics. The 13th-century *Dattatreya Yoga Shastra* (*Yoga Treatise of Dattatreya*) takes this further, insisting that Hatha yoga can be practised by everyone, regardless of age, religion or caste:

> If diligent, everyone, even the young or the old or the diseased, gradually obtains success in yoga through practice. Whether Brahmin, Ascetic, Buddhist, Jain, Skull-Bearer or Materialist, the wise man endowed with faith who is constantly devoted to his practice obtains complete success. Success happens for he who performs the practices – how could it happen for one who does not?[5]

This emphasis on inclusivity is significant, as historically yogis were predominantly celibate male ascetics who had renounced the world. The *Tantras* and Tantra-related texts marked an important shift in detailing practices designed for all, including married householders and women. In later Hatha yoga texts oriented towards Shiva and Shakti, including the *c.* 1450 *Hathayoga-Pradipika* by Svatmarama, the techniques were elaborated to include visualizations of the Tantric goddess Kundalini. Awakening her inside the body subsequently became the key goal of Hatha yoga practice.[6]

Kundalini ('She Who Is Coiled', from the Sanskrit *kundala*, coil or rope) is understood as an individual's source of Shakti, located at the base of the spine and often imagined as a sleeping serpent. Around her is the intricate network of the yogic body, described in Tantric and Hatha yoga texts as made up of energy centres called *chakras* ('wheels' or 'circles'), seven of which are located in the perineum, the genitals, the solar plexus, the heart, the throat, between the eyes and at the crown of the head (or cranial vault).[7] A deity resides in each one. The *chakras* are linked to the three main channels of the yogic body called *nadis* ('tubes' or 'pipes'), which allow the body's life-force (*prana*) to flow. Each person possesses a yogic body that animates their material frame, which can be activated and instrumentalized. By mastering breath control and postures to direct the flow of *prana*, the practitioner awakens Kundalini from her slumber and she begins to rise like a current through the central *nadi* (*sushumna-nadi*) that runs parallel to the spine. As Kundalini rises through the yogic body, she comes into contact with the *chakras* and infuses them with power as the practitioner reaches higher spiritual planes. Shiva resides in the cranial vault (the seventh *chakra*) as pure consciousness (*purusha*) and when Kundalini climactically reaches this point they unite, thus enacting a Tantric sexual rite within the yogi's or yogini's own 'androgynous' body.[8]

This sublimation of sexual practice extends to the role of fluids, which are no longer literally produced, offered to deities and ingested as instructed in earlier Tantric texts. Instead, Hatha yoga texts advised the avoidance of ejaculation, though sexual fluids were still regarded as a potent source for ritual activity.[9] While Shiva is associated with seminal fluid or *bindu* (located in the cranial vault, visualized as white), Kundalini is associated with female menstrual or generative fluid or *rajas* (located in the perineum, visualized as red).[10] The advanced practitioner was able to direct and propel these gendered fluids using the breath, until their union at the crown of the head transformed and deified them, releasing *amrita*. This internalization of left-hand Tantric practice allowed for greater accessibility among those who did not engage explicitly with transgressive substances or acts.

The union of Kundalini (or Shakti) and Shiva in the body of the yogi or yogini could trigger an awakened, liberated state as well as access to *siddhis*, including bodily immortality, flight, levitation, control over nature, super-strength and the transcendence of pain.[11] According to the *Siddha Siddhanta Paddhati* (18th century or earlier), after eleven years of intensive practice a successful yogi or yogini is said to experience the microcosm of their body as equivalent to the macrocosm of the universe, while in the twelfth year their powers are said to exceed those of the gods.[12] The attainment of worldly and supernatural powers as consequences of, rather than obstacles to, the cultivation of spiritual enlightenment continued to define the Tantric goal. In a world permeated by limitless Shakti, ritual technologies to instrumentalize, master and transform this cosmic energy within the body of the practitioner continued to develop.

Some of the finest painted representations of Hatha yoga practitioners were commissioned by courtly Rajput patrons. In a late 18th-century painting from the Punjab Hills (possibly executed in the kingdom of Kangra in Himachal Pradesh) (fig. 41) an ash-smeared, mustachioed yogi is depicted

**Fig. 41**
**Yogi with seven *chakras***
Kangra, Himachal Pradesh,
India
Late 18th century
Gouache on paper, 48 ×
27 cm; 68 × 42 cm
(with frame)
National Museum of India
(Delhi), Ajit Mookerjee
Collection 82.485

with an inflated stomach, suggesting his retention of breath (*prana*).[13] Yogis often cover their bodies with ashes from a ritual fire (or sometimes from the cremation grounds) in imitation of Shiva. The figure here experiences a state of bliss as the Kundalini serpent goddess (represented as a coil within a pubic triangle near his perineum) prepares to move upwards. Each of the seven *chakras* is represented along the body's central column by a multi-petalled lotus inhabited by gods and their consorts: the elephant-headed Ganesha in the perineum; four-headed Brahma in the genital area; blue-skinned Vishnu in the solar plexus; Rudra Shiva as an ash-covered, leopard-skin-wearing yogi in the heart area; possibly an embodiment of the *jiva* (the soul or individual self) in the throat; Shiva again between the eyes, and Shiva for a final time above the crown of the head in the seventh *chakra*, accompanied by Shakti. This seventh *chakra* is referred to as *sahasrara* ('thousand-petalled'), here taken so literally that it has turned into a floral crown adorning the yogi's head, simultaneously evoking a snowy Mount Kailash, Shiva's Himalayan abode.

Three *nadis* are represented as vertical lines. Flanking the central one are the *pingala-nadi* on the right (associated with the sun and the feminine) and the *ida-nadi* on the left (associated with the moon and the masculine). These peripheral channels are the conduits of *prana*. Through the practice of breath control (*pranayama*), the yogi seeks to redirect *prana* into the otherwise neglected and 'empty' *sushumna-nadi* in the centre, the vital channel for awakening Kundalini and directing her power.[14] Two mirror-image tiny demons or *asuras*, holding a sword and shield, seem to fall helplessly through the yogi's 'yogic' and 'real' body, suggesting victory over his inner obstacles. The painting may have been commissioned to support a courtly patron's own Kundalini practice.

A seven-piece scroll from early 19th-century Rajasthan portrays an abstracted yogic body with no corporeal framework; only the *chakras* (which here number more than seven) and accompanying symbols are visible (fig. 42). The *sushumna-nadi* is visualized as a sinuous golden line linking each of the *chakras*. The scroll evokes the universe's three worlds of earth (*bhur*), atmosphere (*bhuvas*) and heaven (*svar*) in the body of the practitioner to draw even more explicit body–cosmos parallels.[15] It is designed to be read from the bottom to the top, re-creating an ascent from the subterranean world of the unconscious, through the terrestrial world represented by the yogic body, until reaching ultimate self-deification and identification with the universe in the heavenly world beyond the final *chakra*. The instructional Sanskrit inscriptions that appear along the length of the scroll reveal this to be a highly visual Tantric manual.[16] Details are provided on the *chakras* and symbols of the yogic body, including their significance, iconography, the powers they grant and the mantras that should accompany them as the yogi or yogini embarks on their practice.

**Fig. 42**

**Scroll depicting *chakras* and the rising Kundalini**
Rajasthan, India
Early 19th century
Painted scroll in seven parts, gouache on paper, length of complete scroll 406.4 cm; seven sections, each 62 × 45 cm
National Museum of India (Delhi), Ajit Mookerjee Collection 82.425; 82.542-1; 82.542-2; 82.542-3; 82.544-1; 82.544-2; 82.544-3

At the bottom are the inhabitants of the subterranean realm of the cosmic ocean (often identified with the unconscious): the tortoise Kurma (an incarnation of the god Vishnu) and the multi-headed king of the serpents, Sheshanaga (fig. 43). Both beings are associated with creation, supporting and stabilizing the foundations of the universe. Above Sheshanaga is the elephant-headed Ganesha in the *muladhara chakra* (perineum). His inclusion here is appropriate, since he is the Hindu god of beginnings and remover of obstacles.

Brahma, the god of creation, appears in a yellow lotus, above Ganesha, in the *svadhishthana chakra* (genital area) (fig. 44). He is followed by intersecting triangles representing the union of feminine and masculine principles and the red and coiled Kundalini herself.

Above Kundalini two gods are seated on lotuses (fig. 45). There are no identifying inscriptions but they may be Vishnu, situated in the *manipura chakra* (solar plexus), and Rudra Shiva, in the *anahata chakra* (heart). The *vishuddha chakra* (throat) does not appear to be included.[17]

The penetrating eyes staring at the viewer provide a corporeal landmark and indicate the location of the *ajna chakra* (between the eyebrows) (fig. 46). The Sanskrit inscription beside them explains: 'In the place of the eyebrows is the *ajna chakra* which has the form of two ruby-coloured lotus petals. In that lotus resides the deity who is the supreme self. The power of this ritual is knowledge (…) the state achieved is heightened awareness'. The inscription also explains that the mantra to be recited a thousand times in order to release this *chakra* is the so-called *ajapa* mantra, '*so ham*', which means 'I am That' ('That' being the universe). Golden swirls emanate from the pair of lotus petals, and an accompanying inscription explains that this spot above the eyebrows (the *triveni* or 'three-streams' *chakra*) marks the junction of the three *nadis* (*sushumna, pingala* and *ida*), which is paralleled with the confluence of three sacred Hindu rivers, the Ganges (*ida*), the Yamuna (*pingala*) and the mythical Sarasvati (*sushumna*). With the release of this *chakra*, the inscription notes, 'one should become the lord of yogis at whose mercy are the three times [past, present and future]'. The white lotus above the pair of eyes is identified by the accompanying inscription as the *chandra chakra*, located in 'the forehead', associated with the moon god, Chandra, and granting the 'power of immortality'. To meditate on this *chakra*, the inscription instructs that the *kamadhenu gayatri* mantra should be recited. The Kamadhenu is the wish-fulfilling cow-goddess whose image appears above the *chandra chakra*. As the inscription beside the mythical beast describes, 'The *amrita* flows from the Kamadhenu', from its udders onto the *chakra* below. This is the nectar originating from the union of Kundalini and Shiva at the crown of the head, dripping down and flooding the body. The Kamadhenu is described in the inscription as having 'the beak of a crow', the 'horns of a cow', the 'neck of a horse', the 'tail of a peacock' and the 'wings of a *hamsa* [sacred swan]'.

Above the Kamadhenu is the vibrant *brahmadvara chakra*, located above the forehead, in the form of a 'hundred-petalled lotus having the brilliance of Indra [king of the gods]' (fig. 47). The deity within the lotus is the sacred swan (*hamsa*), associated with the movements of the breath (*prana*). The power that the opening of this *chakra* grants is 'contemplation'. The golden *nadi* continues upwards towards a beautifully rendered fish whose presence is not explained by an inscription but which might refer to a yogic interpretation of one of the *panchamakaras* or 'Five Ms' (*matsya* or fish), according to the Tantric text *Agamasara* (15th/16th century). This text interprets *matsya* as two fish, representing the breath, which swim along the Ganges (*ida nadi*) and Yamuna (*pingala nadi*) until they are 'swallowed' by the Sarasvati, unblocking the *sushumna-nadi* and setting Kundalini free.[18] The *Agamasara* interprets the other 'Five Ms' thus: *mamsa* (flesh) is the practitioner's tongue from which mantras arise; *mudra* (parched grain) is the awakening of knowledge in the *sahasrara chakra*; *maithuna* (sexual union) is the union of Kundalini and Shiva in the cranial vault, and *madya* (wine) is the nectar generated from their union.[19]

**Fig. 43**
**Detail of fig. 42, showing**
**Section 1 from the scroll**
Rajasthan, India
Early 19th century
Painted scroll in seven parts,
gouache on paper, this section
62 × 45 cm
National Museum of India
(Delhi), Ajit Mookerjee
Collection 82.425

**Fig. 44**
**Detail of fig. 42, showing**
**Section 2 from the scroll**
Rajasthan, India
Early 19th century
Painted scroll in seven parts,
gouache on paper, this section
62 × 45 cm
National Museum of India
(Delhi), Ajit Mookerjee
Collection 82.544-3

**Fig. 45**
**Detail of fig. 42, showing**
**Section 3 from the scroll**

Rajasthan, India

Early 19th century

Painted scroll in seven parts,
gouache on paper, this section
62 × 45 cm

National Museum of India
(Delhi), Ajit Mookerjee
Collection 82.544-1

**Fig. 46**
**Detail of fig. 42, showing**
**Section 4 from the scroll**

Rajasthan, India

Early 19th century

Painted scroll in seven parts,
gouache on paper, this section
62 × 45 cm

National Museum of India
(Delhi), Ajit Mookerjee
Collection 82.542-3

Above the fish is the *akula kundalini chakra*, a 'hundred-petalled lotus', 'the colour of dawn', inhabited by Virat, the Cosmic Being (a manifestation of the divine principle in all physical bodies) (fig. 48). The inscription explains that meditation on this *chakra* grants creative power. To the upper left of this *chakra* is a square diagram or *yantra* divided into four triangles, each marked with an inscription, articulating the relationship between the individual and the cosmic. At the top is the god Shiva; on the right is *maya* (the creative force made up of the elements of the manifested world); at the bottom is the *jiva* (the individual self), and on the left is *avidya* (the individual's ignorance). Shiva playfully controls *maya*, which to the *jiva* tends to appear as a veil masking the divine oneness of reality, resulting in the individual's ignorance (*avidya*) of their own ultimate nature as Shiva. The *yantra* thus functions as a map for understanding the individual's path to and ultimate identification with Shiva, who is all-pervading. The inscription above the *yantra* describes the state achieved upon this realization, after meditating on the *chakras* below, as an all-encompassing awareness and at-oneness with the universe: 'the state of the Womb of the Universe (*Hiranyagarbha*) pervading the total (*vishva*) and individual (*deha*) [bodies]'.

The scroll ends with the thousand-petalled *sahasrara chakra* at the crown of the head, which is called the *brahmarandhra chakra* in the accompanying inscription, and is described as having 'the brilliance of all colours'. This is where 'Shri and Guru', identified as Shiva and Shakti in the image, reside in the lotus. The power granted by this *chakra* is 'consciousness'. According to the inscription, 'the universe is the deity' and 'the source of *maya* is Shakti (...) A thousand repetitions [of the *ajapa* mantra] will induce the feeling of being everything and the state of being all-pervasive'. Its repetition '21,600 times', with the in and out breath, will allow the practitioner to see the universe's nature as consisting of the interplay between *purusha* (consciousness) and *prakriti* (creative force), personified here as Shiva and Shakti, respectively.[20]

The final folio (fig. 49) is startling in its abstract formlessness and evocation of the supreme void (*paramashunya*). By reaching this state of ultimate liberation, the yogi or yogini is freed from the cycle of rebirth.

The quality and style of these paintings suggest that they were produced for a wealthy courtly patron. The coded nature of the iconography and its function as a visual manual for Kundalini practice make it probable that the scroll was intended for private use. It must have

**Fig. 47**
**Detail of fig. 42, showing**
**Section 5 from the scroll**
Rajasthan, India
Early 19th century
Painted scroll in seven parts,
gouache on paper, this section
62 × 45 cm
National Museum of India
(Delhi), Ajit Mookerjee
Collection 82.542-2

**Fig. 48**
**Detail of fig. 42, showing**
**Section 6 from the scroll**
Rajasthan, India
Early 19th century
Painted scroll in seven parts,
gouache on paper, this section
62 × 45 cm
National Museum of India
(Delhi), Ajit Mookerjee
Collection 82.544-2

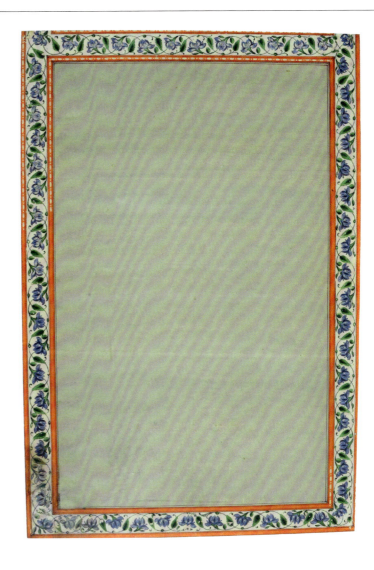

**Fig. 49**
**Detail of fig. 42, showing**
**Section 7 from the scroll**
Rajasthan, India
Early 19th century
Painted scroll in seven parts,
gouache on paper, this section
62 × 45 cm
National Museum of India
(Delhi), Ajit Mookerjee
Collection 82.542-1

been conceived for an informed and cultured elite, since only through a knowledge of Hatha yoga would the viewer be able to appreciate its many layers of esoteric meaning. As such, it is possible that the paintings might have been commissioned to show off the patron's knowledge to guests and other members of the court.

We know that Hatha yoga was practised by Rajput rulers; a vivid piece of visual evidence for this is a *c.* 1690–1700 portrait of Raja Mandhata, ruler of the kingdom of Nurpur (Himachal Pradesh) (fig. 50). He is shown in the posture of *siddhasana* ('pose of the perfected ones'), seated with one heel pressed against the perineum and another flat against the inner thigh, spine straight. The *Hathayoga-Pradipika* describes this posture as the chief of the *asanas* and a gateway to liberation, ideal for raising *prana* and Kundalini from the base of the spine upwards.[21] Here Mandhata is depicted employing this method to assist in the piercing and unblocking of three *granthis* or knots, which prevent the proper flow of *prana* and are located along the yogic body. These are named after Hindu gods who are used to represent the knots visually: Brahma-*granthi* at the base of the spine; Vishnu-*granthi* in the heart area, and Rudra-*granthi* (Shiva) between the eyebrows.[22]

**Fig. 50**
**Raja Mandhata in**
*siddhasana*
Nurpur, Himachal Pradesh,
India
*c.* 1690–1700
Gouache on paper, 20 × 14 cm
Cleveland Museum of
Art 1966.27

    This painting is a revealing example of royal self-representation.
By presenting himself as an initiated Hatha yoga practitioner, Mandhata
is also projecting himself as an ideal and accomplished ruler. Self-discipline
and control over the body can be understood here in the context of
self-mastery. Sacred lotus blossoms emerge from his crown, suggesting
his role as a divine *chakravartin* (universal conqueror). Many Rajput rulers
sought initiation from Tantric gurus to increase their clout as *chakravartins*,
just as medieval kings had done centuries before.

## THE NATH YOGIS AND ALCHEMICAL ELIXIRS

Various yogi sects in India practised Hatha yoga but the one most popularly associated with the practice was the Tantric Nath order, mainly based in northern India and founded by Gorakhnath around the 12th century. The Naths popularized the integration of Tantric methods for raising Kundalini with Hatha yoga practices, and many Sanskrit works outlining these techniques have been attributed to Gorakhnath.[23] In an 18th-century Rajput painting from Rajasthan, a haloed ruler and his entourage visit a group of Naths (fig. 51). There are certain visual clues identifying their affiliation as Naths – the most obvious is the wearing of small antelope horns around the neck.[24] Other clues are the presence of dogs (Bhairava's companions) and the wearing of cloaks and hats, though they are also shown naked, ash-smeared and with long, matted hair. The Naths held political sway with Rajput rulers of kingdoms in western India and the Punjab Hills and were often consulted as advisors in exchange for land grants and royal protection. In early 19th-century Jodhpur, Maharaja Man Singh even hired Naths as ministers to manage his kingdom of Marwar, convinced that his Nath guru and adviser, Ayas Dev Nath, had successfully used his powers to win him the throne in 1803.[25]

Aside from the alchemical transformations that Nath yogis enacted within their own bodies through Hatha yoga and the metamorphosis of sexual fluids into divine *amrita*, they also became famous for producing tangible alchemical concoctions. These consisted of sexually charged substances that could be ingested, promising a range of benefits, including longevity and invulnerability. The Tantric preparations included mercury (regarded as Shiva's semen), mica and sulphur (the vaginal and menstrual fluids of Shakti), along with other minerals and herbs, blended together to create a consumable, calcinated tablet.[26] Nath alchemists were particularly renowned for their skilful ability to transform and purify mercury, an otherwise hazardous and poisonous element, into divine ambrosia.[27] In an 11th-century text on Tantric alchemy, the *Rasarnava* (*Flood of Mercury*), framed as a dialogue between Bhairava and his consort, Bhairavi, the god explains its potency: 'through the use of mercury one rapidly obtains a body that is unaging and immortal, and concentration of the mind. He who eats calcinated mercury truly obtains both transcendent and mundane knowledge'.[28] Ancient Indian Ayurvedic medical texts such as the *Charaka Samhita* (*c.* 100 CE) and the *Sushruta Samhita* (*c.* 4th century CE) noted the therapeutic benefits of mercury but it is only later, after the 10th century, that it is described as a substance capable of granting immortality and even of transforming base metals into gold.[29] It is no surprise, then, that the Naths, as guardians of this esoteric knowledge, received royal support and patronage.

There are hundreds of documentary, poetic and satirical representations of yogis and yoginis produced in Indian courtly contexts. The first detailed depictions date from around 1560 and were commissioned under the court patronage of the Mughal dynasty.[30] Like the Rajputs, the Mughals were attracted to the spiritual and physical discipline of Hatha yoga, along with the otherworldly reputations of its practitioners and their alchemical elixirs. Many Mughal paintings depict rulers and other members of the court visiting these holy men and women, eager to consult them and to align themselves with their power. In textual sources of the period the Naths are often simply described as 'yogis', but it is often possible to identify their affiliation through descriptions of their attributes or references to alchemy and supernatural attainments. Abdul Qadir Badauni, who chronicled the Mughal Emperor Akbar's reign (r. 1556–1605), described Akbar's fascination with their rumoured abilities:

> His majesty also called on some of the Jogis [yogis], and gave them at night private interviews, enquiring into abstract truths; (…) the power of being absent from the body; or into alchemy, physiognomy, and the power of omnipresence of the soul. (…) The emperor ate and drank with the principal Jogis, who promised him that he should live three or four times as long as ordinary men.[31]

A *c.* 1600 Mughal painting from an album made for Akbar's son Prince Salim, the future Emperor Jahangir (r. 1605–1627), shows a Nath yogi dressed in a black robe and hat, accompanied by a white dog (fig. 52). The Persian verse above the image reads:

> I am the yogi of love who is infatuated with you.
> I desire you with every hair of my head.
> My shirt is made with the dust of his lane
> And that too is ripped to its hem and has blood from my eyes.[32]

Below the image the lines read:

> I am one with the seventy-two nations –
> I should have a rosary and an infidel's girdle.
> Your dog is better than the entire world of fidelity.
> If I am not your dog, the dog is better than me.[33]

The love described here is not of a worldly nature; the Nath is presented as the model of an ideal devotee, passionately longing for union with the divine and drawing a comparison between his faith and the dog's fidelity and devotion. The 'seventy-two nations', an oft-used reference in Persian

poetry, represent all of humanity.[34] Jahangir, like his Mughal predecessors, gave land revenue grants to the Naths of Jakhbar in the Punjab in exchange for alchemical medicine and blessings of longevity.[35] In 1661 or 1662 his grandfather, Emperor Aurangzeb (r. 1658–1707), wrote to Anand Nath, the abbot of a Nath monastic establishment in the Punjab, to request 20 g (1 oz) of treated mercury:

> It is desired that Your Reverence should carefully treat some more quicksilver [mercury] and have that sent, without unnecessary delay. A piece of cloth for a cloak and a sum of twenty-five rupees which have been sent as an offering will reach [Your Reverence].[36]

Nath yogis were believed to be capable of living for hundreds of years by regularly consuming a specially prepared combination of mercury and sulphur.[37] According to the French traveller François Bernier, who was in India during Aurangzeb's reign, they knew 'how to make gold and to prepare mercury so admirably that one or two grains taken every morning restore the body to perfect health'.[38]

The awe that mercury inspired is vividly portrayed in Mughal paintings of the period that depict a beautiful woman on horseback luring the silvery liquid out of a well (fig. 53). Mercury was conceived as the seminal fluid of Shiva, which had fallen to earth at various places. Such scenes illustrate a technique for extracting the liquid before capturing and treating it, as described in several alchemical texts including the 14th-century *Rasaratnasamucchaya* of Vagabhatta II:

> Upon seeing a well-adorned maiden who, having bathed after first coming into season, [rides by] mounted upon a horse, mercury, which is found in wells, [becomes] possessed of a desire to seize her, [and] rushes up out [of its well]. Upon seeing it, she gallops away. The mercury pursues her for the distance of one *yojana* [13–14 km, or 8–9 miles]. [When] that [mercury which is] born of Shiva then quickly returns to the well, it is caught in troughs dug in its path.[39]

The sexual connotations of the passage and image are clear. The mercury, 'born of Shiva', is attracted by the woman's beauty and fertility. Shiva is a virile god, a fact that is distilled in the abstract image of his *linga* or erect phallus. His seed is a major source of his power, which Nath yogis were believed to be able to harness and distil.

## SUFISM AND THE SEARCH FOR DIVINE UNION

In principle, Tantra challenged the hierarchical social order within orthodox or Brahmanical Hinduism by allowing people from different social backgrounds to be initiated, including those deemed 'impure' and excluded from the caste system. Since the Naths did not adhere to the purity constraints of upper-caste Hindus and claimed to be inclusive regardless of religion or caste, they readily engaged with others from different cultural and religious backgrounds, such as followers of Sufism or Islamic mysticism.[40] By the 9th–10th centuries Sufism had crystallized in Baghdad and Khorasan, before arriving around the 12th century in India, where it became informed by the subcontinent's various traditions, including Tantra.[41]

The Naths were known to frequent open kitchens run by Sufi ascetics.[42] An early 17th-century painting depicts a gathering of Naths receiving loaves of bread in a lodge (fig. 54). The figure dressed in black at the bottom left has been identified as a Sufi mystic.[43] The folio is an illustration from the *Mrigavati* (*Magic Doe-Woman*), a Sufi romance composed in Jaunpur (northern India) in 1503 by Qutban Suhravardi about a Hindu prince who disguises himself as a Nath and embarks on an adventure to find Princess Mrigavati.[44]

Fig. 53
**A woman luring quicksilver from a well**
Northern India
Mid-18th century
Opaque watercolour on paper,
40.6 × 55.9 cm
British Museum 1920,0917,0.197

A Mughal painting, executed *c.* 1570 during the reign of Emperor Akbar, shows a wandering dervish (Sufi ascetic) whose appearance echoes that of an itinerant yogi (fig. 55). He carries a snake-headed staff and wears talismanic ornaments. The bells and feather amulets are worn to ward off malevolent spirits. Akbar consulted Sufis as well as yogis and was known to host religious debates at his court in which Muslims, Hindus, Jains and Christians discussed their theological differences.[45] Sufis sought close, direct and personal experience of God (Allah), which could be achieved through methods designed to obliterate the inhibited self or ego (*fana*). This included one of the most important Sufi practices, the mantra-like performance of *dhikr*, a remembrance of God through the recitation of his many names in Arabic as found in the Qur'an.[46] Sufis were initiated and guided by a spiritual master (*shaykh* or *pir*) who taught the *dhikr* practice. Sufism quickly adapted to its surroundings in South Asia and began to assimilate compatible Tantric practices to facilitate its spiritual goals. In Bengal, Sufi texts exploring yogic techniques, including Saiyid Murtaza's *Yoga Kalandar* and Abdul Hakim's *Cari Mokamer Bheda* (both 17th century), adapted deities and mantras into Islamic angels and *dhikr*, and the *chakras* of an alternative yogic body into *maqams*, conceived as internal, ascending stages along the spiritual path to unity with God.[47] Hatha yoga appealed to Sufis in its affirmation of corporeality and the harnessing of the body as a sacred instrument and microcosmic mirror of the universe.

Around 1550 the Indian Sufi master Muhammad Ghawth Gwaliyari translated the Arabic version of *Amritakunda* (*Pool of Nectar*), a lost text on Hatha yoga drawing on Sanskrit sources, into Persian as the *Bahr al-Hayat* (*Ocean of Life*). The translation familiarized Sufis with Hatha yoga practices.[48] It was illustrated in 1600–4 in a manuscript made in Allahabad (Uttar Pradesh) for Jahangir (then Prince Salim). This was the first manuscript to illustrate the *asanas* (postures) in detail, accompanied by descriptions of practices including meditations on the *chakras*, divination by breath control through the right and left nostrils, and the summoning of Yogini goddesses (figs. 56, 57). The *Bahr al-Hayat* was the most widely disseminated literary source on yoga among Sufis.[49] In the text the author makes equivalences between yogic and Sufi terms and practices (such as chants and breath exercises). For example, the sounds emitted during the outbreath ('ham') and inbreath ('sa'), which together articulate the yogic terms *hamsa* (the sacred swan, associated with the breath) and *so ham* ('I am that'), are given an Islamic interpretation by the author. *Hamsa* becomes 'an expression for the spiritual lord (*rabb-i ruhi*)', while *so ham* becomes 'the lord of lords (*rabb al-arbab*)'.[50]

Eleven of the twenty-one yogis who appear in the folios are identifiable as Naths. One of the paintings illustrates the *khechari mudra* (flight pose), a practice to prevent the nectar of immortality dropping through the uvula

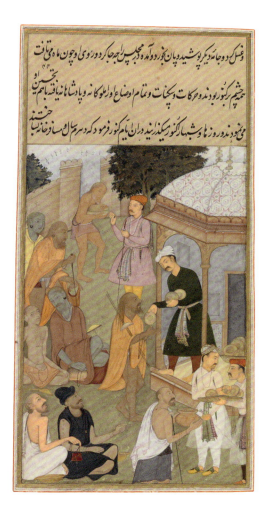

(above the throat) by forcing the tongue inside the palate and into the cavity leading to the skull (fig. 56). This is achieved by cutting the membrane connecting the tongue with the lower part of the mouth. Muhammad Ghawth Gwaliyari described the method, posture and its benefits thus:

> One places the tip of the sole of the left foot behind the right foot, and the end of the sole of the left foot beneath the genitals (…). One holds both hands backwards on both knees, and one also maintains the closure of the seal of the throat. (…) When this practice is perfected, one obtains a single station from the orbit of Earth to the Cupola [firmament], taking a single breath to go from the orbit of earth to the subterranean. Above, below, and centre are all three a single orbit; all three worlds are under the control of the wayfarer.[51]

Another folio depicts *garbhasana* (foetal posture) in which, according to the corresponding Persian text, 'One places the left foot on the right foot, holding the buttocks on both feet, holding the head evenly between the two knees, placing both elbows under the ribs, putting the hands over the ears, bringing the navel toward the spine' (fig. 57).[52] According to the author, this

**Fig. 54 (above left)**
**The feast of the yogis,**
**folio from the *Mrigavati***
Allahabad, Uttar Pradesh, India
1603–4
Opaque watercolour and gold
on paper, 28.3 × 17.5 cm (folio);
14.2 × 9.7 cm (painting)
The Trustees of the Chester
Beatty Library In 37 (fol. 44r)

**Fig. 55 (above right)**
**Dervish with a snake-
headed staff**
Northern India
*c.* 1570
Gouache and gold on paper,
19 × 12.8 cm
British Museum 1983,0727,0.1
Funded by the Brooke Sewell
Permanent Fund

posture is first accomplished 'when the child is in the womb of the mother'.[53] In this *asana*:

> One holds the breath; one brings it in the midst of the belly. One takes it above from below, and below from above, in this exercise to such a degree that the inner eye, winged imagination, wandering reflection, and incomparable thought – all four – emerge from their restrictions. They enter witnessing of the spiritual state and become one.[54]

The goals (Persian: *intiha*) of world-mastery and blissful awakening in both cases evoke a universe charged with limitless power that can be tapped into in order to unfetter and transform the body and mind. Just as Buddhism had adapted Hindu Tantric ideas and practices from around the 7th century, bringing them in line with the Buddha's core teachings, Sufism creatively borrowed from certain Hatha yoga techniques, aligning them with Islamic tenets.

Sufis and Naths, both renowned for their powers during the Mughal period, not only engaged with each other spiritually, but also competed as rivals for patronage on the political stage to prove who possessed the greatest miraculous abilities. The Sufi *shaykh* Nizam al-Din Awliya (d. 1325) recounts a story about a levitation contest between a Nath and a Sufi; the yogi succeeded in rising into the air but the Sufi triumphantly surpassed him by flying in the direction of Mecca (Islam's holiest city), then to the north and south, before returning, demonstrating his superior supernatural powers.[55] The Naths' pluralistic outlook is articulated in a collection of poetry entitled *Gorakhbani*, attributed to their *c.* 12th-century founder Gorakhnath (though the earliest surviving version of the text dates to around the 17th century). In one poem he describes himself as 'By birth a Hindu, in mature age a Yogi and by intellect a Muslim'.[56]

Many courtly paintings demonstrate a blurring of Sufi–yogi identities. A poetic late 17th-century painting, made in the Deccan (south-west India) during its rule by independent Islamic sultanates (1490s–1680s), shows a man with his legs bound with a *yoga-patta* (meditation band) and a crutch before him (fig. 58). He wears a *khirqa* or vibrant patchwork cloak (often associated with Sufis) slung over his right shoulder, and sits on a tiger skin (associated with Shiva). Other courtly paintings of both yogis and Sufis during this period show them with these attributes.[57] In a secluded forest the man is joined by a richly dressed and bejewelled woman, whom he reaches out to touch. They gaze at each other as she offers him a cup of wine, holding a wine flask in her other hand. In secular courtly scenes the wine cup often appeared as a symbol of pleasure in Mughal and Sultanate painting but here it takes on a mystical significance. The consumption of wine was usually prohibited within mainstream Islam; however, its intoxicating properties were transgressively employed as affirmative metaphors in Persian Sufi poetry, which was read widely by the Sultanate and Mughal courts, to describe surrender to divine union with God.[58] The 13th-century Persian poet Jalal al-Din Rumi, born in Afghanistan, wrote prolifically on love and inebriation, distinguishing between earthly wine that can lead one astray and divine wine that can dissolve the veils of illusion separating the devotee from God. He declared that 'God has created me from the wine of Love' and warned his readers: 'Don't be sober, because the sober one / Is very disgraced in the assembly of Love!'[59] Likewise, the 14th-century Sufi poet Mohammad Shams al-din Hafiz (*c.* 1320–90) from Iran, whose verses contain many references to wine, described God as a lover, passionately yearned for, in sensual and uninhibited terms. In one such verse the narrator turns to alcohol for comfort, symbolic of love or *'ishq* for God:

> Fill, fill the cup with sparkling wine,
> Deep let me drink the juice divine,
> To soothe my tortured heart;
> For love, who seemed at first so mild,
> So gently looked, so gaily smiled,
> Here deep has plunged his dart.[60]

**Fig. 58**
**A man and woman**
**sharing wine**
Deccan, India
Late 17th century
Gouache on paper, 18.2 × 12 cm
British Museum 1920,0917,0.123

To be 'drunk' was to lose control of reason and the self, and to embrace oneness with God. Intoxication (*sukr*) for Sufis represented an annihilation of the ego and union with the divine.[61] Interesting parallels with Tantric ideas arise in Sufi wine poetry, including the use of dissident language to transcend conventional norms, and the notion that polarities do not exist for the mystic who sees the world from God's perspective.

## INTOXICATION AND TRANSFORMATION: BECOMING SHIVA

Intoxication as a means of inducing expanded states of consciousness plays a role not only in Sufi poetry and Sufi-inspired paintings, but also among Nath yogis. A detail of the Rajasthani painting depicting a ruler visiting a community of Naths (see fig. 51) shows some of the yogis in the foreground making *bhang*, a hallucinogenic and edible preparation created from the leaves and flowers of the cannabis plant (fig. 59). They pound, knead and scoop the leaves, boil them in water or milk and strain them to produce the liquid, possibly adding spices including cardamom, turmeric, nutmeg, cloves, pepper and cinnamon. The consumption of *bhang* among yogis was a popular subject in Rajput and Mughal painting and was not only represented to allude poetically to its euphoric effects but also sometimes caricatured to suggest the yogis' stupor.[62]

Yoginis were also shown in states of intoxication. An 18th-century Mughal drawing of Nath yoginis shows one woman, on the left, smoking a *huqqa* (water-pipe) with which she may be inhaling *bhang*, opium or tobacco through scented water (fig. 60). The yogini next to her appears to lurch over, already inebriated.

Yogis and yoginis consumed *bhang* to achieve transcendent states and also to imitate Shiva, whose divine madness was understood as an intoxication from the drug to which he was notoriously addicted.[63] Shiva's deliberately disobedient behaviour, exceeding the boundaries of orthodox respectability, informed his identity as a Tantric god. A drawing of Shiva (probably from Kangra in the Punjab Hills, *c.* 1775–1800) shows his wife, Parvati, pouring him a cup of *bhang* as he woozily leans back, heavy-lidded and already pleasantly intoxicated (fig. 61). He is shown as a naked yogi with unruly, matted waist-long hair, a serpent winding itself around his chest. His appearance is deliberately androgynous, alluding to his composite form of Shiva and Parvati as Ardhanarishvara (the 'Lord who is half woman'), a literal expression of his synthesis of both masculine and feminine universal principles.[64] Shiva and Parvati are joined by their sons, Skanda and the elephant-headed Ganesha, in an idyllic family scene.

Artists in the Punjab Hills painted many uniquely evocative and visionary depictions of Shiva throughout this period for their courtly patrons.[65] An unusual series of paintings, *c.* 1790–1800 and also in the Kangra style, presents Shiva as Bhairava in various wild, Tantric guises.[66]

In one, he is joined by the goddess Varahi in a scene that might at first glance appear romantic until closer inspection reveals grisly details such as the corpse, skull-cup and thighbone that Bhairava casually holds in three of his multiple hands (fig. 62).

**Fig. 59**
**Detail of fig. 51, Nath yogis**
**preparing** *bhang*
Rajasthan, India
18th century
Gouache on paper, entire
painting 42.3 × 29.7 cm
British Museum 1933,0610,0.2
Donated by Laurence Binyon

In another of the paintings, Bhairava appears atop an elephant and is accompanied by an unidentified goddess (fig. 63). The white elephant, which has blunt tusks, may be the Vedic god Indra's *vahana* called Airavata, which according to myth was overpowered by Shiva's *vahana*, the bull Nandi. If the image articulates Bhairava's superiority over Indra, then the blue-faced goddess could be Indrani, the Shakti of a cuckolded Indra; Indrani is also one of the Sapta-Matrikas or Seven Mothers. In both this painting and the previous one (fig. 62), Bhairava is draped in a flayed elephant's skin, alluding to Shiva's defeat of the elephant demon, Gajasura.

Bhairava's flagrant display of supremacy over the other gods continues in another painting in the Kangra series, in which a red-skinned Bhairava rides a green parrot that may be Shuka, the *vahana* of the god of desire, Kama (fig. 64). According to myth, Shiva had been deep in meditation and Indra sent Kama to distract him by shooting him with his arrow of lust. He succeeded but Shiva was furious and incinerated him with his third eye. Kangra paintings typically depicted Kama with red skin, which may explain why Bhairava is that colour here – he has absorbed Kama's powerful eroticism, resulting in the perfect Tantric fusion of ascetic, macabre and erotic qualities. Indeed, despite Shiva's ascetic nature, Kama is in many respects his alter ego.[67] No doubt this unusual series was commissioned by a devout follower of Shiva and his manifestation as Bhairava. The lack of narrative content suggests that the images may have been intended to function as aids to meditation, perhaps commissioned by a patron wishing to identify with the god through

Fig. 60
**Three yoginis**
Northern India
18th century
Gouache on paper, 32.7 ×
19.6 cm
British Museum 1920,0917,0.11.30

visualizations and mantra recitations. The paintings are also courtly works of art designed to be seen up close and studied at leisure, either privately or by guests who would appreciate their jewel-like colours, intricate details and poetic mood.

Across the Kangra Bhairava series, the artist re-imagines what should be a macabre cremation ground as a paradisiacal scene, creating a paradoxical tension. Lush, blossoming trees and streams evoke perennial spring and tiny, colourful birds replace carrion-feeding ones.[68] In one painting Bhairava even holds a skull-cup in one hand (alluding to the head of Brahma) and a flower in another (fig. 65). Multiple snakes wriggle excitedly across his body and he is joined by his canine companions, who appear throughout the series. The setting is reminiscent of the cremation ground envisaged by the 6th-century poet and Nayanar saint Karaikkal Ammaiyar (see Chapter 1, fig. 16), who described it as an idyllic space in

**Fig. 61**

**Shiva and Parvati with
their family under a tree
on Mount Kailasha**

Kangra, Himachal Pradesh,
India

*c.* 1775–1800

Drawing on paper, 29.6 × 19.7

British Museum 1914,0217,0.11

which to burn away the ego, where 'white pearls fall out of the tall bamboo'.[69] In both her poem and the Kangra painting, a site associated with impurity and decay has been transformed into an idyllic space charged with auspicious power.

In another visionary depiction of a Tantric cremation-ground setting, painted by a Mughal artist in 1630–35, the difference in mood is striking (fig. 66). Here, Shiva (who could just as well be a mortal yogi emulating the god) appears before the chilling goddess Bhairavi (Bhairava's feminine counterpart), who sits cross-legged on a corpse, its head violently wrenched off. The image evokes a multiplicity of associations, including the ritual practice of meditating while seated on a corpse (*shava sadhana*) discussed in Chapter 1 in relation to sculptures of Chamunda (see fig. 26). Bhairavi is shown blood-red and cackling, with horns in the shape of spear-heads. Surrounding the pair are crematory fires, burning flesh, human bones and

**Fig. 62 (opposite, above)**
**Bhairava with Varahi**
Kangra, Himachal Pradesh,
India
*c.* 1790–1800
Gouache on paper,
17 × 23.5 cm
British Museum
1925,1016,0.17

**Fig. 63 (opposite, below)**
**Bhairava, possibly with Indrani, seated on an elephant**
Kangra, Himachal Pradesh,
India
*c.* 1790–1800
Gouache on paper,
17 × 22.8 cm
British Museum
1925,1016,0.15

**Fig. 64 (right, above)**
**Bhairava riding on a green parrot, possibly Shuka**
Kangra, Himachal Pradesh,
India
*c.* 1790–1800,
Gouache on paper,
17 × 22.8 cm
British Museum
1925,1016,0.19

**Fig. 65 (right, below)**
**Bhairava with two dogs**
Kangra, Himachal Pradesh,
India
*c.* 1790–1800,
Gouache on paper, 28.5 ×
34.2 cm
British Museum
1925,1016,0.16

॥श्रीभैरवीदेवी॥

dismembered body parts picked at by jackals. The painting may have been presented as a gift to the ruler of the kingdom of Mewar, Maharana Jagat Singh (r. 1628–1652), by the court of Shah Jahan.[70]

In contrast, the iconography in the Kangra Bhairava series (figs. 62–65) has an intimacy more reminiscent of the paintings inspired by the Bhakti tradition that were produced at the Kangra court around the same time. Bhakti, as explained previously in relation to the Nayanars (see Chapter 1), was the other major movement that developed around the same time as the rise of Tantra across India, focusing on cultivating a loving relationship with a personal deity. In Rajput painting from the 16th century onwards an emotional form of Bhakti was articulated through images of the romantic god and cow-herder Krishna and his lover, the *gopi* or cowgirl Radha (fig. 67).[71]

Krishna was perceived as the hero of love and passion, which had immediate appeal to Rajput rulers, reflecting escapist ideals of chivalry and sensuality. The couple's union came to signify the meeting of the individual (Radha) and the divine (Krishna).[72] For a courtly audience, such subject matter would have undoubtedly suggested that direct access to a deity could be achieved by realizing one's own inner divinity, a concept resonating with Tantric ideas.

Fig. 66
**The goddess Bhairavi with Shiva, Payag**
Northern India
1630–35
Gouache and gold on paper,
18.5 × 26.5 cm
The Metropolitan Museum
of Art 2011.409

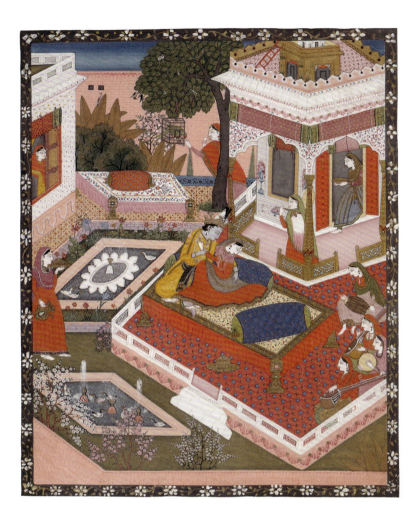

**Fig. 67**
**Krishna and Radha in**
**a terraced garden with**
**attendants and musicians**
Punjab Hills, India
*c.* 1830
Gouache on paper,
23.5 × 15.2 cm
British Museum 1948,1009,0.147
Bequeathed by Percival Chater
Manuk and Ms G. M. Coles,
funded by The Art Fund
(as NACF)

Near Kangra, in the kingdom of Mandi, Raja Sidh Sen (r. 1684–1727) was reported to possess Tantric powers and to own a book of magical spells. Rumours abounded about his supernatural abilities: he was said to levitate during yogic practice and to fly daily from Mandi to the source of the Ganges for ritual bathing.[73] His sword was even believed to bestow healing properties on water, which could then be used by women to cure infertility problems.[74] The most remarkable paintings executed during Sidh Sen's reign were portraits of himself as a self-deified Shiva incarnate, vividly illustrating the idea that only a god can worship a god, as stated in Tantric texts including the *Spandanirnaya* by Kshemaraja (a 10th-century Kashmiri Tantrika): 'having become Shiva one should worship Shiva'.[75]

In a painting from Mandi made 1725–27, Sidh Sen is ash-covered and four-armed, holding Shiva's attributes, including a trident, drum and leopard skin, as though engaged in role-play (fig. 68). He possesses Shiva's third eye of knowledge which provides enlightened insight beyond ordinary perception, and wears a large talismanic amulet and a necklace of *rudraksha* ('tears of Shiva') beads. The inscription above him reads: 'Shri Maharaja Sidh Sen Saheb Bahadur, Ruler of the State of Mandi'. Like the earlier image of Raja Mandhata depicted as a master of Hatha yoga (see fig. 50), this is another vivid instance of royal self-representation in a Tantric guise.

Both rulers are presented as deified monarchs, one by adopting the ritual technology of Kundalini practice and the other by assuming the attributes of a god. Since the ultimate aim of a Tantrika was to 'become' a deity, these paintings function as charismatic pieces of visual rhetoric, suggesting to viewers that these rulers have achieved their goal.

There was also evidently a certain fascination with the more extreme left-hand (*vama*) practices of Tantra among courtly circles. In a *c.* 1790 painting from the kingdom of Nurpur in the Punjab Hills, a yogini is shown engaged in a Tantric 'feast' with her consort, both clad in leopard skins (fig. 69). She serves him what is probably alcohol, poured from a thighbone into his skull-cup. They are in a cremation-ground setting, signalled by the human remains before them: a leg in a pyre, a burnt arm, skulls and other scattered bones. There is a strong suggestion that they are ritually consuming traditionally taboo substances, such as the *panchamakara* (Five Ms). Transgressing orthodox Brahmanical purity strictures suggests their engagement with the dangerous power inherent in impurity. The male consort's conical hat with strips of colourful cloth is a recurring attribute of Nath yogis in courtly Indian paintings.[76] He appears to wear a necklace of tiny human heads, which gives the image a fantastical quality. The sword he carries in his lap might suggest that he is a courtier or nobleman engaged in role-play, or may simply be a sign that he is embodying the martial quality of a god such as Bhairava.

The scene may evoke a *chakrapuja* or *ganachakra*, a sacramental Tantric ritual gathering common to both Hindu and Buddhist traditions, described in texts such as the *Hevajra Tantra* (8th–9th century) and the *Kularnava Tantra* (10th–13th century). It involved an assembly in which a group of initiated Tantrikas would ritually consume foods and substances that would then be offered to a Tantric deity.[77] These substances might be either literal or symbolic versions of the *panchamakara* or the *panchamrita* and *panchamamsa* (see Introduction). Sexual rites might also be carried out, again either literally or through visualization. These assemblies generally occurred in secluded spaces, such as caves and cremation grounds. According to the *Hevajra Tantra*:

> Feasting in the company-circle, (…) *siddhi* [power] is gained that fulfils the substance of all one's desires. One should set about this feasting in a cemetery or mountain-cave, in a deserted town or in some lonely place. One should arrange seats there, reckoned as nine, in the form of corpses, or tiger-skins, or rags from a cemetery. (…) one should place the yoginis in the eight directions. Then seated upon one's tiger-skin one should eat the food with eagerness, the sacramental herbs and the special flesh. Having eaten and eaten again, one should worship the mother-goddesses there. (…) The meritorious (pupil) should present to

**Fig. 68**

**Raja Sidh Sen of Mandi as
a manifestation of Shiva**

Mandi, Himachal Pradesh,
India

1725–27

Opaque watercolour and gold
on paper, 27.1 × 18.2 cm

Museum of Fine Arts, Boston,
Keith McLeod Fund 2001.137

**Fig. 69**

**Tantric feast**

Nurpur, Himachal Pradesh,
India

c. 1790

Opaque watercolour and gold
on paper, 22.54 × 15.88 cm

Los Angeles Museum of
Fine Art, Indian Art Special
Purpose Fund M.77.63.1

his master a sacred skull-cup in one piece which is filled with wine,
and then having made obeisance to him, he himself should drink.[78]

The *chakrapuja* was a rite practised in secret, and rumours of its scandalous
nature circulated to the extent that it continues to inform misunderstandings
of Tantra in India and the West. The Nurpur painting reflects the courtly
attraction to Tantric power, with a generous hint of caricature. It vividly
(and exaggeratedly) imagines what a *chakrapuja* might have involved,
appealing to courtly voyeuristic tastes and igniting dreams of bare-breasted
yogini seductresses.

## YOGINIS AS GURUS AND ROMANTIC HEROINES

Images of women as gurus and yoginis became increasingly common in
later 18th-century courtly paintings. In several Tantric texts women are
explicitly mentioned as practitioners who are equally capable, along with
male yogis, of obtaining great *siddhis*, ranging from flight and shapeshifting
to control over nature, the ability to predict the future and immortality.[79]
The *Brahmayamala Tantra* (7th–8th century) provides details about women

who are 'well versed in *samadhi*, yoga and the scriptural wisdom'.[80] *Samadhi* connotes the mastery of meditative visualization to the point of complete union with the deity. By the 13th century onwards women are also described as authoritative gurus.[81] The *Tripurarnava Tantra* (*c.* 16th–18th century) states that women, in their innate divinity, are natural-born masters:

> There are no rules for women; all are said to be gurus. Merely by receiving an authoritative mantra, she is the supreme guru. She can teach by means of the authoritative mantra and obtain books. A man does not have such authority, for woman is the supreme deity.[82]

The *Rudrayamala Tantra* (12th–13th century) details the qualifications necessary for a woman to progress from a practitioner to a powerful, commanding teacher:

> The woman practitioner (*sadhvi*) who has conquered her senses, has devotion for the teacher and engages in good conduct, who knows (…) the meaning of all mantras, who is skilful and always engaged in worship; (…) who has eyes as beautiful as the lotus flower; (…) She gives liberation and she explains the knowledge pertaining to Shiva – this woman indeed is fit to be a guru. (…) The initiation given by a woman is declared to be auspicious, and the mantras are known to be eight times more powerful [than those given by a man].[83]

As previously discussed, the Hatha yoga text *Dattatreya Yoga Shastra* (see p. 71) affirmed the egalitarian nature of the practice. In a description of the *vajrolimudra* technique, which was carried out as a means of preserving the yogi's and yogini's sexual fluids (*bindu* and *rajas*), the text also explicitly notes that it is open to both men and women: 'A man should strive to find a woman devoted to the practice of yoga. Either a man or a woman can obtain success if they have no regard for one another's gender and practise with only their own ends in mind'.[84] Tantric texts described mortal women as superior practitioners in their embodiment of Shakti, which increased their ritual status. While some texts focused on their role as partners in sexual rites, others stressed their autonomy as independent, initiated practitioners.

Rajput and Mughal paintings of yoginis articulate their authority and status while often idealizing their appearance, suggesting a correlation between beauty and divine power. Indeed, in the *Gupta-Sadhana Tantra* (*c.* 17th century), Parvati asks Shiva to describe the image of such a commanding woman and he provides her with the following visualization: 'Her eyes are like the blossoming petals of a lotus. She has firm, thick breasts, a thousand faces, a thin waist. She is eternal. Shining like a ruby (…) her face shines like the autumn moon adorned with bright shining earrings'.[85]

Such a visualization is aptly reflected in courtly paintings, such as an 18th-century Mughal example showing a Shaivite yogini sitting on a tiger skin and holding *rudraksha* beads, a *linga* installed outside her simple hut (fig. 70). Her dreadlocks (*jata*) are elegantly piled on top of her head and her blue skin suggests that she is covered in ashes. Her mystique and serenity radiate from the folio. Two women visit her to seek her counsel and make an offering of flowers. The subject of courtly women's nocturnal visits to yoginis became popular in Mughal painting from the 18th century.[86] The shimmering marginalia, with busy, clustered images of birds, deer, lions, palaces and courtiers, suggest the meeting of two worlds – the natural, spiritual world of the yogini and the courtly, secular world of her visitors.

Another mid-18th-century Mughal painting shows a woman who has travelled a great distance to visit two yoginis (fig. 71). Seated on the left, they are identifiable as Naths because of the small horns they wear around their necks. The visitor's hair is swept up and tucked into her turban, perhaps to disguise herself as a man because she is travelling alone. Indeed, at first glance she appears to be a young prince, but the artist highlights her breasts under her blouse. Holding *rudraksha* beads and carrying very few possessions, she may be seeking initiation from the elder Nath, whose age is expressively suggested with sensitive attention to detail. Tantra was initiatory, and its teachings were only accessible via a guru. In the *Gupta-Sadhana Tantra*, the goddess Parvati notes that prospective Tantrikas would be lucky to secure initiation from a female guru in particular: 'The initiation given by a woman is proclaimed to be auspicious and capable of giving the results of everything one wishes for, if, from the merit accumulated in many lives and by dint of much good luck, a person can acquire a woman as guru'.[87] The two yoginis appear to be discussing the woman's request. The abandonment of courtly life to pursue a self-disciplined path towards spiritual enlightenment was a popular subject in South Asian art and literature.

Hindu and Muslim rulers in India believed that the supernatural and occult powers possessed by both divine Yoginis and mortal yoginis could be harnessed to strengthen their kingdoms and realize their political ambitions. Temples dedicated to Yogini goddesses were built until the 14th century (see Chapter 1), and their propitiation continued in Islamic contexts. The 14th-century *Kamrupanchashika* (*Fifty Verses on Kamarupa*), the earliest known Persian text dedicated to yoga, includes practices for summoning sixty-four Yoginis, referred to as Islamic *ruhanis* (celestial beings).[88] In the text they are described as all-knowing, immortality-granting goddesses: 'We [the *ruhanis*] tell everything, for everything that goes on in all the world is all known and clear by the science of magical imagination. (…) We teach a science of who comes, and from where, and what he asks. Also know that this science lengthens life and makes one near-immortal'.[89] Their 'science' is also described as effective for curing illness and controlling people and events.[90]

**Fig. 70**
**A yogini with two disciples**
Northern India
Mid-18th century
Gouache on paper, 46 × 31.5 cm; 54.5 × 40 cm (with frame)
British Museum
1920,0917,0.20

**Fig. 71**
**A woman visiting two Nath yoginis**
Northern India
Mid-18th century
Gouache on paper, 29 × 21 cm
British Museum
1913,1218,0.10

In the 16th century, Islamic sultanates dominated the Deccan Plateau, covering parts of central and southern India. Paintings from the Sultanate of Bijapur are a compelling testament to the enduring appeal of the Yoginis as mediators of supernatural power. In 1570 Sultan 'Ali 'Adil Shah I (r. 1558–1580) authored and commissioned the *Nujum al-'Ulum* (*Stars of the Sciences*) manuscript, which demonstrated his erudite knowledge of astrology, magic, divination, talismans, mythical beings and politics in a work drawing on both Sanskrit and Persian sources.[91] One chapter describes the characteristics of 140 Yogini goddesses and again identifies them with *ruhanis*, presenting them as beings capable of granting a ruler victory in battle.[92] The *ruhanis* carry severed heads and skull-cups filled with blood, and some display animal features (figs. 72, 73). The author notes that the chapter has drawn on Hindu sources and that the *ruhanis* are associated with the myth of the goddess Sati.[93] According to this myth of cosmic dismemberment, Sati's body parts were scattered across South Asia and enshrined as Shakti Pithas, or Tantric Seats of Power.

One folio in the chapter depicts the *ruhani* Ariv with tiger paws and deadly-looking claws in place of feet, and carrying a bow and arrows (fig. 72). Most striking, however, is the fact she is busily biting down on a naked corpse. On the folio opposite is the monstrous Kalapasa, an embodiment of death, who holds an elephant goad and noose (fig. 73). In both cases their appearances contrast with their courtly attire. These *ruhanis* exude the same power as the sculpted Yoginis from Kanchi and Hirapur (see Chapter 1, figs. 31, 32, 34–36) with their macabre iconography and the inclusion of animals that suggests their ability to shapeshift at will. The weapons that Ariv and Kalapasa hold reflect a rhetoric of military conquest and warfare similar to that already encountered in medieval Indian representations of ferocious deities such as Bhairava and Chakrasamvara. As in these earlier Tantric Hindu and Buddhist representations, the *ruhanis'* weapons and ferocious characteristics in the *Nujum al-'Ulum* signal not only their ability to grant military victory on the battlefield, but also their role as spiritual guides who carry out the transformative destruction of ignorance. Shortly before the album was completed, in 1565, 'Adil Shah had led a confederacy of sultanates against the Vijayanagara kingdom to the south, winning the Battle of Talikota.[94]

Later paintings from the Deccan appear deliberately to blur the line between Yoginis as goddesses and yoginis as mortal women, romanticizing and even eroticizing the latter. This is seen in early 17th-century images commissioned during the reign of 'Ali 'Adil Shah I's successor, his nephew Ibrahim 'Adil Shah II (r. 1580–1627) (fig. 74).[95] In one example, an elegant, curvaceous ash-covered yogini, semi-nude apart from a coppery shawl and

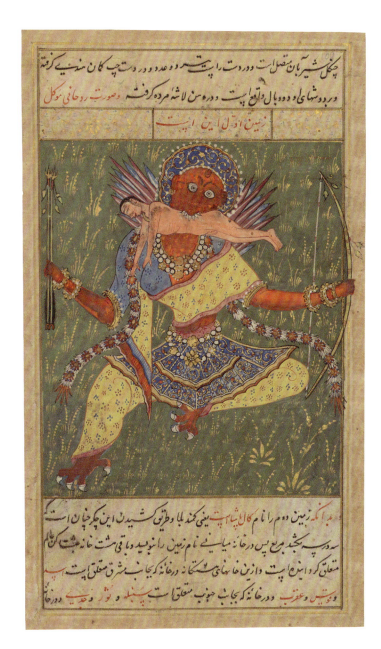

red loincloth, carries a *morchhal* (peacock-feather fan) and is accompanied by a parrot (associated with secrets and storytelling), which is perched on her shoulder and peers down at an excitable white dog, the companion of Bhairava (fig. 75).[96] The yogini's features are enhanced by golden earrings, a necklace, bangles and a hair ornament that keeps her topknot in place.

Similarly, in a painting executed around the same time in Bijapur, a yogini (mysteriously conversing with a mynah bird) is portrayed in elaborate, shimmering finery (fig. 76). She wears a red tunic (*chakdar jama*) in a masculine style, which distinguishes her as a female ascetic.[97] The romantic Persian inscriptions around the painting include couplets praising the unforgettable beauty of a woman who is black-haired, tall and fragrant. The ten couplets along the inner border describe a heart burning with love.[98] Such romantic longing could assume a sacred dimension in both artistic and literary contexts. For a Muslim audience, the figures of lover and beloved could symbolize the worshipper and God, according to the Sufi concept *'ishq*, or 'divine, fervent love'.[99] However, these yoginis are not necessarily mortal. There are visual parallels in both cases with the Yogini goddesses found in the *Nujum al-'Ulum* manuscript (which Ibrahim inherited from his uncle), suggesting their equally divine, powerful status.[100]

Rajput, Mughal and Sultanate courtly patrons were evidently attracted not only to the power of yoginis but also to their exotic and erotic mystery. The tension between the yogini as guru and romantic heroine is particularly visible in *ragamala* ('garland of melodies') illustrations, paintings inspired by classical Hindustani *raga* music, which originated in northern India. In these paintings, the moods of love, longing and devotion are conveyed via a rich

**Fig. 74 (above)**
**Ibrahim 'Adil Shah II**
Bijapur, India
*c.* 1615
Gouache and gold on paper,
17 × 10.2 cm
British Museum, funded by the
Research Fund 1937,0410,0.2

**Fig. 75 (left)**
**Yogini walking through
a landscape**
Bijapur, India
Early 17th century
Ink, gouache and gold on
paper, 27.7 × 17.8 cm
British Museum 1948,1009,0.73
Bequeathed by Percival Chater
Manuk and Ms G. M. Coles,
funded by The Art Fund
(as NACF)

**Fig. 76 (opposite)**
**Yogini with a mynah bird**
Bijapur, India
*c.* 1603–4
Opaque watercolour and gold
on paper, 39.2 × 27.6 cm (folio
with borders)
The Trustees of the Chester
Beatty Library In 11a.31

array of characters, including yoginis.[101] A *c.* 1740 painting from the Deccan (probably Hyderabad) depicts *Asavari Ragini*, a melancholy melody traditionally performed in the morning, which conjures a mood of wistfulness and contemplation (fig. 77). It is usually, as here, visualized as a solitary woman, clad in a peacock-feather skirt, mesmerizing snakes with her hypnotic presence. The figure in the painting is a Savara woman; the Savaras were a hill tribe often associated with the Malaya mountain range in the western Deccan. Legends circulated about their ascetic and yogic powers.[102] A Tantric Buddhist text takes the symbolism of the Savara's arrow to suggest the single-minded focus required to penetrate through delusion and induce enlightenment: 'Hey, Savara! With the conclusion of the teacher's direction, pierce your mind with your arrow! Nocking one arrow, pierce, pierce highest *nirvana*!'[103] The painting explicitly casts the Savara woman as a yogini, indicated by her topknot. The snakes may metaphorically suggest mastery of her own inner Kundalini. Their docility also indicates her power to control and tame predatory animals.

The Savara woman also wears bejewelled armlets, bracelets, anklets and head ornaments, indicating her royal status. Inscriptions accompanying other paintings of *Asavari Ragini* describe her as a romantic heroine driven to asceticism in the wilderness as a result of heartbreak, so it is possible that the painting suggests that she has abandoned a courtly life. This might relate her to a genre of Urdu literature, popular in 18th-century India, in which courtly women disguised themselves as yoginis and escaped the confines of their palaces to go in search of their beloved.[104] However, in this case the identity of her beloved is deliberately and titillatingly ambiguous – is it a man she had once known and lost, driving her to a life of asceticism, or is it the god Shiva with whom she now seeks divine union? The figure of the yogini across these paintings assumes different roles, from an occult agent of power and autonomous guru to a figurehead of divine and secular romantic longing. In the yogini's embodiment of these tensions, she is able to transcend conventional representations of womanhood (whether as wife, mother or lover) by inhabiting a role beyond the parameters of societal expectations.

Having outlined the Tantric methods of Hatha yoga, and the reception and representation of its practitioners between the 16th and 19th centuries in India, the following chapter will turn to the spread of Tantric Buddhist teachings across Asia. Despite the change of geographical location, there are clear continuities, testifying to the shared and fluid nature of Indian religious traditions among Hindu and Buddhist practitioners. The Tantric system of the yogic body and methods for raising Kundalini, for example, were adapted by Buddhist yogis beyond India. This was especially the case in Tibet where the manipulation of the yogic body through breathing techniques and visualizations remained fundamental techniques as part

**Fig. 77**
*Asavari Ragini*
c. 1740
Deccan (probably Hyderabad), India
Gouache on paper, 31.9 × 21.6 cm (including border)
British Museum 1964,0411,0.2
Funded by the Majorie Coldwell Fund

of the Tantric practice of Devata ('Deity') yoga. Devata yoga involves the embodiment of deities in union, reflecting a similar 'internalization' of sexual rites found in Hatha yoga. Similarly, just as [Y]oginis could be goddesses as well as mortal women, the equivalent Dakinis assumed an important role in Tantric Buddhism in Tibet and beyond as figures who frequently blurred the boundaries between the earthly and divine.

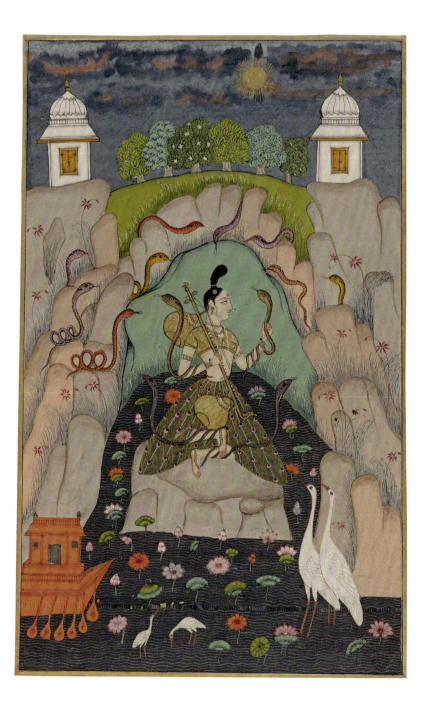

CHAPTER 3

# THE SPREAD
# OF TANTRA
# ACROSS ASIA

This chapter moves beyond India to explore how Tantric Buddhism (known as Vajrayana or 'Thunderbolt Vehicle') developed after it had spread across Asia by the 8th century CE. The Mahasiddhas ('Great Accomplished Ones'), whose lives were filled with miraculous episodes, were key transmitters of the teachings from India. A unique pantheon of Tantric deities evolved and thrived in Tibet, their iconography charged with sexuality and violence. Throughout the chapter the function and significance of ritual instruments will also be examined, from *yantras* and mandalas to ritual daggers (*kilas*) and flaying knives (*karttrikas*). Human remains were also (and continue to be) used as instruments in Tantric practice, including skull-cups (*kapalas*), two-headed skull-drums (*damarus*) and thigh-bone trumpets (*kanglings*).

N

0        1000 miles

0        1500 kilometres

→ Vajrayana Buddhism

→ Mahayana Buddhism before 700, and Theravada Buddhism

**Fig. 78**

Map showing the spread
of Tantric Buddhism
(Vajrayana) across Asia,
along with other Buddhist
traditions (Mahayana and
Theravada)

**Fig. 79**

**Padmasambhava**

Tibet

16th/17th century

Bronze and gold, height 18.8 cm

British Museum 1992,1214.49

Donated by Johannes
Nikolaus Schmitt and
Mareta Meade

## THE PATH OF THE THUNDERBOLT

As discussed in Chapter 1, Tantric Buddhism flourished in eastern India from around the 7th to the 12th centuries CE. This was where pilgrimage sites connected with the Buddha's life were located, including Bodhgaya where he is said to have attained enlightenment. Buddhist monasteries in India studied and taught the *Tantras*, attracting scholars, students and pilgrims from across Asia who returned home with portable bronzes, texts and ritual objects. This led to the rapid transmission of Vajrayana practices and material culture to other parts of Asia only shortly after the composition of the *Tantras* themselves. Vajrayana spread from eastern India (as well as from Kashmir, where there were also many Tantric masters) to Nepal and Tibet. There the movement thrived from the 8th century, even after the steady decline of Buddhism in India from around the 9th century, partly as a result of its loss of patronage due to the rise of Tantric Hinduism.[1]

Padmasambhava ('Lotus Born'), also known as Guru Rinpoche ('Precious Teacher'), is believed to have been one of the earliest Indian masters to bring Vajrayana teachings to Tibet. He was reputedly born a prince in Oddiyana (north-west India), but was sent into exile when it was discovered that he was carrying out Tantric rites. He wandered across cremation grounds to continue his practices. News travelled of Padmasambhava's ability to tame and conquer angry, malevolent spirits and he received invitations from King Tri Songdetsen (740–798) and the monk Shantarakshita to travel to Tibet in the 770s. He was asked to help construct Tibet's first Buddhist monastery, Samye, which was being disrupted by local spirits at night.[2] According to legend, Padmasambhava succeeded in subduing the spirits and even converted them to Buddhism so that they would become protectors of the faith. Buddhism (especially Vajrayana) was officially adopted by Tri Songdetsen as Tibet's state religion in 779, commemorated by a stone inscription at Samye which records that 'this practice of the Buddha's doctrine (…) shall never be caused to be abandoned or destroyed'.[3] A 16th-/17th-century gilt-bronze image of Padmasambhava shows him seated on a lotus throne, wearing regal attire as a reminder of his princely past (fig. 79). He holds a *vajra* and skull-cup. The front of his headdress is adorned with a sun and crescent moon, symbolizing his transcendence of dualities.

Some of the earliest examples of Tantric visual culture outside India have been preserved at Dunhuang (present-day Gansu province in north-west China), during a period when Tibetans ruled over the area (786–848). The fortress town of Dandan Oilik in the kingdom of Khotan (north-west China) has also yielded early artefacts with Tantric imagery. The town was located on the Silk Road, so-called because silk was exported along it from China to north-west India, and as far west as the Mediterranean.

A 7th-/8th-century wooden votive panel from Dandan Oilik represents an ithyphallic Shiva as Maheshvara (Great Lord) in his all-encompassing form (fig. 80). Each of his three heads suggests a different aspect of his

personality. On the god's left side is Shiva as incarnate terror, while on the right side is Shiva as feminine power. Between them is the central face of Shiva himself in whom all opposites are reconciled. A later medieval sculpture from Kashmir illustrates the Indian iconographic source of this imagery (fig. 81). The panel from Dandan Oilik shows Maheshvara holding the sun, moon, a *vajra*-like implement and a *damaru* in his four hands. He sits on his *vahana* (vehicle), the bull Nandi, who appears twice here. Maheshvara was adopted as a wrathful protector deity and exemplary Siddha ('Accomplished One') figure in Tantric Buddhism. This particular votive panel was found in a dwelling once inhabited by Buddhist monks.[4] Maheshvara was believed to protect inhabitants from external threats, including epidemics and attacks.[5]

In Tibet, Buddhism was suppressed during the 9th century by King Tri Udum-tsen (r. 836–842), probably as a result of the perceived decline of royal authority and the rise of powerful, well-funded Buddhist monastic establishments. He was ultimately murdered by a Buddhist monk, which

brought an end to the royal dynasty.[6] Between the 11th and 14th centuries Tibet saw the development of various Vajrayana schools of thought and practice. These schools were based largely on the *Mahayoga Tantras* and *Yogini Tantras*, including the Nyingma, Kagyu, Sakya and, later, Gelug (15th century) traditions, leading to the founding of major monasteries that became important political players in Tibet and often rivalled one another.[7] Although each of these traditions had its own lineage of Tibetan and Indian teachers, there was very little difference in the content of the teachings themselves. Many Buddhist Tantric practitioners, however, were non-monastic. Tantric gurus in Tibet were referred to as lamas, who might be either high-ranking monks and nuns or non-celibate, revered yogis and yoginis.[8]

A bronze of the lay lama Drakpa Gyaltsen (1147–1216), one of the heads of the Sakya order, shows him holding a *vajra* or thunderbolt (fig. 82).[9] The *vajra* is a Tantric symbol of the unbreakable force of the enlightened state, in which all inner obstacles have been obliterated to reveal the only unchanging, liberating truth: that all phenomena are temporary and therefore essentially empty (*shunya*).[10] Texts such as the *Hevajra Tantra* (8th–9th century) and *Vajramrita Tantra* (9th–10th century) also refer to the *vajra* repeatedly as a signifier for a Tantric god's phallus. It became the defining ritual implement and icon of Vajrayana which itself translates as 'Thunderbolt Vehicle'. The bronze Drakpa Gyaltsen holds not

Fig. 82

**Sakya master Drakpa Gyaltsen**

South-west Tibet or Mustang, Nepal

16th century

Bronze with copper and silver inlay, 19.5 × 13.2 cm

British Museum 1992,1214.20

Donated by Johannes Nikolaus Schmitt and Mareta Meade

Fig. 83

*Ghanta* and *vajra*

Tibet

19th century

Bronze, gold and bell metal, height 23 cm (*ghanta*); height 18 cm (*vajra*)

British Museum 1948,0716.11.a and 1948,0716.11.a-b

Bequeathed by Harry Geoffrey Beasley

only a *vajra* but also a *ghanta* (bell) in front of his chest, as a sign that he has embodied the god Vajradhara, who is traditionally shown wielding them in this way. Through this emulation, the lama seeks to identify his own body, speech and mind with those of the deity. When the *ghanta* is paired with the *vajra*, the symbolism becomes even richer and articulates the union of two gendered ideals that must be internalized: the *vajra* as 'masculine' compassion (*karuna*) and the *ghanta* as 'feminine' wisdom (*prajna*).[11]

Together, the *vajra* and *ghanta* became the most important Vajrayana ritual implements. Although there are no known surviving early Indian examples, others have been found in Indonesia, Cambodia, Nepal, Tibet and Japan.[12] The 19th-century Tibetan examples pictured here (fig. 83) were probably once used by a lama. The *vajra* has five prongs above and five below (in both cases arranged as four curved blades surrounding central ones); the prongs evoke the five Jina ('Conqueror') Buddhas: Akshobhya ('Unshakeable'), Vairochana ('Illuminator'), Amitabha ('Immeasurable Radiance'), Ratnasambhava ('The Jewel-Born One') and Amoghasiddhi ('Infallible Success').[13] The two ends also allude to perceived dichotomies, including permanence/impermanence, masculine/feminine and purity/impurity, which ultimately merge in the enlightened Tantric realization that dualities do not exist.[14] The bulbous centre in the middle of the *vajra* stands for *shunyata* (emptiness), out of which form emerges.[15] *Shunyata* refers to the concept outlined by the Buddha, and developed by the Buddhist philosopher Nagarjuna (*c.* 150–250 CE), that all phenomena are temporary, unfixed and therefore essentially empty. This does not imply that they do not exist, but rather that all living and inanimate things lack autonomy in isolation and are instead characterized by their divine interdependence and interconnectedness. According to the Tantric perspective, this implies a fluid world that can be sublimated and magically transformed through practice, just as Shakti was conceived as the divine power pervading all phenomena that could also be ritually channelled. The *ghanta's* ringing evokes the rise of form, while its dissipation into silence evokes *shunyata*.[16] The top of its handle is in the form of a *vajra* and the face in the middle represents the goddess Prajnaparamita ('Perfection of Wisdom').[17] In a ritual context the lama might have inserted the *vajra* into the opening of the *ghanta* to symbolize the union of feminine wisdom and masculine compassion.[18]

## THE DIVINE MADNESS OF THE MAHASIDDHAS

Instrumental in the transmission of Tantric Buddhist teachings from India to the Himalayas from around the 8th century were the Mahasiddhas, a diverse group of largely lay Indian practitioners, spanning several centuries, whose lives were later celebrated in literary hagiographies. Some Mahasiddhas were real historical figures while others were legendary. They came from eclectic social backgrounds, including former Hindu Brahmins (priests), royalty and servants.[19] Their vivid life stories were filled with accounts of supernatural and unorthodox, nonconforming behaviour resulting from their enlightened states. They became particularly popular in Tibet where many of them were claimed as founders of the various Vajrayana traditions that developed there.

By the 12th century a group of eighty-four Mahasiddhas, who lived between the 7th and 12th centuries, were recognized by the Indian author Abhayadatta Shri in *The History of the Eighty-Four Mahasiddhas* (Tibetan: *Grub thob brgyad bcu tsa bzhi'i lo rgyus*).[20] According to their hagiographies, many conducted their practices in charnel and cremation grounds, clearly influenced by followers of Bhairava such as the Kapalikas (see Chapter 1). Like the Kapalikas, many of the Mahasiddhas also famously engaged in sexual rites and practices involving impure substances. By ritually engaging with the transgressive, the Mahasiddhas subverted conditioned perceptions, confronting emotions such as fear, desire and disgust, and channelling suppressed forces. Several of the Mahasiddhas, including Gorakhnath, were also venerated as founding teachers by the Naths in India (see Chapter 2), again reflecting the many overlaps between Buddhist and Hindu traditions.

The stories of the Mahasiddhas often begin at a dissatisfied point in their lives when they meet a guru who awakens them and directs them on a rigorous Tantric path. Many are presented as embarking on radical, heroic quests for truth, defying social boundaries of caste and strategically employing seemingly mad behaviour to transcend established ethical, social and religious structures. Their main ambitions are the attainment of *siddhis* (powers or attainments), especially flight, which seems to have been one of the most popular powers across Tantric traditions during the medieval period. Flight could also be understood as the temporary departure of the mind from its physical body to travel to remote locations.[21] Other *siddhis* included invisibility, immortality, telekinesis and the ability to see into the netherworlds. As hagiographies of predominantly non-celibate and non-monastic individuals, the Mahasiddhas' stories highlighted the growing importance of the lay Tantric practitioner, attracted to the movement's intertwining of liberation- and power-seeking, and to the notion that it was not necessary to live a renunciant life in order to attain enlightenment.

The Mahasiddhas were also popularly depicted in painting and sculpture. The Tibetan teacher Katog Rigdzin Tsewang Norbu (1698–1755), for instance, noted that contemplating or visualizing images of the Mahasiddhas would bring one closer to attaining an enlightened state:

> Whoever thinks of a drawing or sees a drawing of the bodies of
> These supreme and great masters, the adepts, will be joyous
>      of mind.
> Just like these masters who have attained the supreme path towards
>      great enlightenment,
> It is certain that you will transform completely into Vajradhara.[22]

In other words, the Mahasiddhas were perceived as having embodied divinity and achieved a fast-track to enlightenment, making them aspirational role models to be visualized, contemplated and emulated.

An 18th-century *thangka* (painting on cloth) is part of a set of Mahasiddha paintings that may have once hung in a monastic assembly hall in Tibet (fig. 84). At the centre of this *thangka* is Saraha (known as the 'Arrow Shooter'), an 8th-century Mahasiddha who was born in eastern India. Though formally a Hindu Brahmin, he secretly followed the Buddhist path and eventually became a monk.[23] He holds an arrow, a reference to his guru (known as the 'Arrow-Making Yogini') who, according to versions of his hagiography, was a female arrow-smith. He first met her in a market where she was making and selling arrows. Attracted to her single-minded concentration as she aimed one, he approached to ask what she was doing. She replied: 'The Buddha's meaning can be known through symbols and actions, not through words and books', which led Saraha to interpret the arrow as a symbol of 'non-duality' that must be fired 'into the heart of dualistic grasping'.[24] Recognizing that she was a great Tantric yogini and stunned by her wisdom, he abandoned his monastic vows and became her disciple and consort. He composed many songs (*dohas*), including this one about his guru:

> This yogini's action is peerless. (…)
> Enlightened spontaneity shines forth.
> Beyond passion and absence of passion, (…)
> Here sun and moon lose their distinction,
> In her the triple world is formed.
> Perfecter of thought and unity of enlightened spontaneity
>      know this yogini.[25]

He affirmed the role of sexual rites in Tantric practice: 'Stay at home in the company of your mate. Perfect knowledge can only be attained [w]hile one

**Fig. 84**
**Saraha (centre) and other**
**Mahasiddhas**
Tibet
18th century
Painted textile, 83 × 59 cm;
185 × 107.5 cm (entire scroll)
British Museum 1956,0714,0.40

is enjoying the pleasure of the senses'.[26] And he stressed the importance of the body as a channel to enlightenment rather than an obstacle to it, in its microcosmic mirroring of the universe: 'Here [in my body] are the Ganga and the Yamuna (…) here are Prayaga and Varanasi, here the Sun and the Moon. Here are the sacred places, the [Shakti] Pithas [Seats of Power] (…) Never have I seen a place of pilgrimage and an abode of bliss like my body'.[27] In this quote Saraha refers to rivers and sites that are sacred to Hinduism, highlighting the fluidity of India's Hindu–Buddhist divine imaginary.

In the *thangka* Saraha is surrounded by other Mahasiddhas, including Virupa (top right), which literally translates as 'deformed' or 'ugly'. Indeed, many of the Mahasiddhas, including Virupa, are portrayed as unidealized, with exaggerated, mannerist features including straggly hair and beards, hunched bodies, bushy eyebrows and eccentric faces. Though undoubtedly humorous, this form of caricature is also designed to highlight their otherworldliness, power and transcendence of conventional beauty as a metaphor for their transcendence of convention generally.[28] Virupa had been a Buddhist abbot at the monastery of Nalanda (in present-day Bihar) but, like Saraha, abandoned his duties when he discovered the greater power promised by the 'left-hand' (*vama*) Tantric path. Here he is pointing at the sun, a reference to the most famous episode in his hagiography in which he demonstrates his control over the solar system itself. According to legend, he arrived at a bar but had no money to buy drinks, and promised the barmaid that he would pay her as soon as the shadow cast by the doorframe reached a certain point. He then proceeded to hold the sun in place by its beam, halting its movement and enabling him to guzzle up the bar's entire stock while outside chaos ensued as time appeared to have stopped. Finally, Virupa agreed to release the sun when the king intervened by paying for his drinks. The 13th-century Indian scholar Munidatta interpreted Virupa's intoxication in this episode in symbolic rather than literal terms, as a divine, enlightened state.[29] The deliberate suggestion of subversive behaviour and the role of divine intoxication speaks to the playful disobedience of the *bhang*-addicted god Shiva and the metaphors of drunkenness in Sufi wine poetry explored in Chapter 2.

On the reverse of the *thangka* is the outline of a stupa, a Buddhist shrine and a symbol of the enlightened mind of a Buddha (fig. 85). Three Tibetan syllables for Body, Speech and Mind are written along the centre, a mantra designed to consecrate the painting and to make it a suitable receptacle for the divine. The inscriptions along the base of the stupa include auspicious verses for the welfare of all beings. A pair of handprints is visible on either side; they must have belonged to a senior lama who blessed and sanctified the *thangka* after its completion.[30]

Fig. 85
Reverse of fig. 84, showing
stupa with inscriptions, and
handprints

The Mahasiddha Jalandhara, known as the 'Net Holder', is portrayed
in a dynamic 16th-century bronze sculpture from Tibet (fig. 86). Born into
the Brahmin (priestly) caste around the 9th century in the north-west of
the Indian subcontinent, Jalandhara became disillusioned with the idea of
cyclic existence (*samsara*) and retreated to charnel grounds to meditate until
he was visited by a Dakini (the Buddhist equivalent of a Yogini goddess),
who initiated him into yogic practices.[31] Jalandhara is also revered in India
by the Nath yogis as one of their first teachers.[32] In both Buddhist and
Hindu contexts he is regarded as a master of Tantric yoga. Devata ('Deity')
yoga is a Vajrayana practice that includes techniques and concepts very
similar to those involving the awakening of Kundalini in Hatha yoga,
including the notion of a yogic body with channels (*nadis*) and *chakras*,
viewed through a Buddhist lens and framework. According to one of his
hagiographies, the Dakini gave Jalandhara instructions to visualize his body
as a microcosm of the universe and to redirect his breath (*prana*) from the

**Fig. 86**
**Jalandhara**
Tibet
16th century
Bronze, 24.1 × 14.6 × 9.5 cm
The Rubin Museum of Art
C2003.13.4, HAR65218

left and right channels up through the central one (*avadhuti*, the equivalent of *sushumna*):

> All entities of experience, inner and outer,
> Gathered together in body, speech and mind,
> Right and left channels [*nadis*] emptied into the *avadhuti*,
> Eject everything through the gate of purity [at the crown
>     of the head]
> Arisen in the space of pure yoga
> That emptiness [*shunyata*] is the highest form of pleasure.
> Try to sustain the inseparable union of pleasure
>     and emptiness.[33]

After years of practice, he finally achieved realization of *shunyata* and was able to recognize that *samsara* is merely a projection of the mind.[34] Jalandhara makes the flame-*mudra* gesture by bringing his two thumbs and forefingers together to create a triangular shape. The empty space between his fingers symbolizes *shunyata*, while the triangle evokes the flame-like goddess Chandali (the Buddhist equivalent of Kundalini), who resides at the navel and blazes upwards towards the crown of the head when released. He is adorned with bone ornaments and tramples an ego-corpse embodying the limiting 'I am' conceit.

A 20th-century *thangka* from Solukhumbu in Nepal depicts all eighty-four of the Mahasiddhas, each with their distinctive attributes and identifying features, surrounding the blue Tantric Buddhist deity Vajradhara and his consort, the red Bhagavani (fig. 87). Vajradhara is regarded as the source of the enlightened teachings of the surrounding Mahasiddhas. Most of them are portrayed as semi-naked and shaggy-haired itinerant yogis in various postures, dancing, flying and engaged in sexual rites. Some carry *kapalas* and wear human bone ornaments in imitation of deities such as Chakrasamvara.

Only four out of the eighty-four Mahasiddhas are women. However, women generally played important roles in the lives of the male Mahasiddhas, reflecting the influence of Tantric ideas around Shakti, the centrality of goddess worship and the status of women as embodiments and transmitters of power in medieval India. One of the women, pictured in the *thangka* dancing on a tiger skin and carrying a *kapala*, is Lakshminkara, known as the Crazy Princess (fig. 88). She was already well-versed in the teachings of the *Tantras* when her brother, King Indrabhuti, arranged for her to marry a prince in Lankapuri. When she arrived, she was distressed to discover that her intended husband hunted animals and was not a practising Buddhist. She gave away all her dowry to the poor and escaped to a cave where she smeared herself with mud,

Fig. 87
The eighty-four
Mahasiddhas, with
Vajradhara and
Bhagavani
Solukhumbu, Nepal
1954
Painted cotton, 96 × 73 cm
British Museum 1989,1106,0.5
Donated by Prof. David L.
Snellgrove in honour of
Pasang Khambache Sherpa

Fig. 88 (above left)
Detail of fig. 87, showing
Lakshminkara

Fig. 89 (above right)
Detail of fig. 87, showing
Mekhala and Kanakhala

scavenged for food in cremation grounds and acted mad to evade capture
and pursue her spiritual practice, which reached such an advanced point
that soon Tantric deities were compelled to visit her.[35] She composed
a surreal and playful song the was addressed to her one of her disciples,
Mekhala, full of paradoxical and unbelievable images to remind the
disciple that the world is not fixed but contains unlimited possibility
and power:

> A frog swallows an elephant!
> It's amazing, Mekhala,
> Do not doubt.
> If it confounds you, adept,
> Drop concepts now! (…)
> Flowers blossomed in the sky! (…)
> A barren woman gives birth!
> A chair dances! (…)
> Amazing! An elephant sits on a throne
> Held up by two bees! (…)
> If you're stunned, adept,
> Drop your doubts![36]

Two more female Mahasiddhas are identifiable in the *thangka*: one of them
carries her own decapitated head while another holds a sword beside her
(fig. 89). They are the siblings, Mekhala ('The Elder Severed-Headed
Sister') and Kanakhala ('The Younger Severed-Headed Sister'). According
to their story, they were about to marry two brothers but unfounded gossip

was spread around the village about the pair so the engagements were humiliatingly called off. The sisters considered leaving the village but knew that their problems would pursue them. Finally, the Tantric master Kanha paid them a visit and when the two women told him their story he suggested they undertake the Chinnamasta *sadhana* (practice), which they mastered over the next twelve years. It involved visualizing and identifying with the goddess Chinnamasta ('She Whose Head is Severed'), who carries a sword and holds her own freshly decapitated head, signifying a radical beheading of the ego and the destruction of dualistic (mind vs body) thinking.[37] Once the sisters had mastered this visualization practice, they went in search of Kanha and, when they found him, asked him what he desired as an offering. To test their devotion and power, he asked them to cut off their own heads, and they did so, singing: 'through the grace of the Guru's instruction (…) we destroy the distinction between *samsara* and *nirvana*; (…) between acceptance and rejection; (…) between self and others. As tokens of the indeterminate, we offer these gifts'.[38] He quickly restored their heads to their bodies, declaring they were true masters: 'Behold these two great yoginis! They have reached their goal in joy! Now forgetting your own peace and happiness, live for the sake of others!'[39]

There were other great female Tantric masters beyond those cited by Abhayadatta Shri. One was the celebrated Tibetan princess Yeshe Tsogyal, who is depicted in sexual union with Padmasambhava in an 18th-/19th-century *thangka* (figs. 90, 91). Yeshe Tsogyal had been forced to marry against her will but then sought out Padmasambhava and became his consort and student, travelling with him and meditating in caves.[40] He told her that women have a greater chance of achieving Buddhahood because of their superior ability: 'Oh yogini who has accomplished the secret mantra, the human body is the basis for attaining enlightenment. Male or female, inferior body – it makes no difference. If possessed of the aspiration to enlightenment, a female body is actually superior.'[41] She mastered a variety of *siddhis*, such as the ability to restore life, and took on other male consorts. The manuscripts piled around the pair in the *thangka* represent Padmasambhava's *terma* or 'treasure teachings'. These were said to have been hidden during his lifetime by Yeshe Tsogyal for the benefit of future generations, and have been periodically discovered and revealed by his followers.[42]

## TANTRIC MIRACLES AT THE MING COURT

The story of King Tri Songdetsen's invitation to Padmasambhava in the 8th century reflects a recurring trend for rulers and political agents across Asia to summon charismatic Tantric masters to their courts to transform them into *chakravartins* or universal conquerors. Khubilai Khan (r. 1260–1294), who established the Mongolian Yuan dynasty in China in the 13th century, was drawn to the reputed powers of Tibetan lamas to strengthen his imperial authority and actively patronized them.[43] The Ming dynasty, which defeated the Yuan dynasty in 1368, went on to continue this imperial support, as evidenced by surviving diplomatic gifts to Tibetan lamas.

An early 15th-century Tantric ritual sceptre (*khatvanga*), made of iron, is skilfully inlaid with gold and silver in a style associated with the eastern Tibetan town of Derge (figs. 92, 93). However, it bears the reign mark of the Ming Yongle emperor (r. 1403–1424) on the upper part of the handle, indicating that it was made in a workshop in Beijing, possibly by specialist Tibetan craftsmen based there.[44] By the 15th century, the imperial centre of Beijing was home to many Tibetan monks and nuns, as well as Buddhist temples, including the royally patronized Da Longshan Huguo si ('Temple of Great and Mighty Benevolence that Protects the Dynasty').[45] The *khatvanga* was made at a time when contact between the Ming rulers and Tibetan monastic orders flourished for both spiritual and political reasons. The Yongle emperor, in particular, sought to cultivate strong relationships with Tibetan religious leaders and lavished them with invitations to his court, along with gifts bearing the imperial reign mark.[46]

The *khatvanga* appears as an attribute of Tantric deities in early medieval Indian sculptures (see, for example, Chapter 1, fig. 31) where it is rendered as a skull-topped staff. The Kapalikas and other early ascetic followers of

**Fig. 92**
*Khatvanga*
Beijing, China
1403–7
Iron with gold and silver inlay,
length 44 cm
British Museum 1981,0207.1
Funded by the Brooke Sewell
Permanent Fund

**Fig. 93**
Detail of fig. 92, showing
*khatvanga* terminal
depicting three human
heads in varying states
of decay

Bhairava were also said to carry *khatvangas*, as were the Buddhist Mahasiddhas.[47] Padmasambhava is described as wielding it to defeat the disruptive local spirits in Tibet.[48] In a Buddhist context, it was not only conceived as a weapon for defeating external enemies but also for conquering one's inner obstacles. As such, it was believed to embody *bodhichitta* or the 'will to enlightenment'.[49]

The Ming-period *khatvanga* may have been intended for a rite of identification with a Tantric Buddhist deity.[50] It is crowned with depictions of three human heads in varying states of decay: freshly severed, decomposing and skeletal (fig. 93). Not only do the heads vividly convey the realities of transience and mortality, they also symbolize, in ascending order, three hierarchical states or bodies of Buddhahood: the *nirmana-kaya* ('transformation body'), a Buddha's mortal, perishable body that manifests in the earthly realm; *sambhoga-kaya* ('bliss body'), a Buddha's heavenly body located in paradise; and *dharma-kaya* ('*dharma* body'), a Buddha's transcendent, boundless body which embodies the ultimate truth of Buddhist teachings.[51] Below the heads is a vase of plenty (*purnaghata*) that alchemically transforms all impurities into divine nectar (*amrita*), here inlaid with lotus, peony and chrysanthemum blossoms. There are crossed *vajras* below the vase as well as one above the skull.

Along with other imperial gifts, the *khatvanga* was presented by the Yongle emperor to the head of the Kagyu order in Tibet, the Fifth Karmapa Dezhin Shegpa (1384–1415), during his visit to the then-capital of Nanjing in 1407.[52] The emperor bestowed on him the title of Da Bao Fawang ('Great Precious Dharma King') and the Karmapa became the emperor's guru after initiating him and introducing him to Tantric teachings. During his time in Nanjing the Karmapa performed a fourteen-day funerary ceremony for Yongle's deceased parents at Linggu monastery, which triggered a series of miraculous displays. According to Chinese and Tibetan sources, Yongle's parents appeared as the Tantric meditational deity Manjushri and the goddess Tara. One Chinese writer recalled that 'golden deities (…) appeared in the clouds (…) golden coloured flowers grew on cypresses all over the city. One could also hear the sound of mantras and music coming down from the sky'.[53] A 1407 handscroll, entitled *Miracles of the Mass of Universal Salvation Conducted by the Fifth Karmapa for the Yongle Emperor*, depicts the miracles that took place around the monastery, including a rain of divine flowers and the appearance of heavenly lights (fig. 94) and beings manifesting in the clouds (fig. 95).[54]

However, many members of the Ming literati, along with Yongle's courtiers, often expressed disapproval at the emperor's patronage of Tibetan lamas, dismissing such spectacles as magical illusions. The scholar and imperial tutor-in-waiting, Li Jiding, commented wryly that the Karmapa's 'chanting [of the mantra] *O ma ni pad ma hum* [*Hail to the Jewel in the Lotus*],

in fact means "Let me trick you"'.[55] These critics were generally followers
of Confucianism, based on the teachings of Confucius (551–479 BCE),
a humanistic philosophy which centred on the institutions of society, family,
school and state, and which taught the importance of maintaining social
order and harmony.[56] Tantric Buddhism offered a new worldview that
challenged the emphasis on social hierarchy, and emphasized self-
transformation, power and ritual authority.

## DIVINE UNION AND EMBODIED TEXTS

The two principal qualities to be cultivated on the path towards
enlightenment, according to Tantric Buddhist teachings, are wisdom
(*prajna*) and compassion (*karuna*), which mutually depend on and inform
each other. Tantric texts and images use gendered symbolism to articulate
these polarities by visualizing a goddess (wisdom) and god (compassion) in
sexual union (*yab-yum*, literally 'father-mother' in Tibetan), conceived as
one mutually constituting force.[57] This divine union is articulated in
sculptures of meditational deities or Yidams such as the 16th-/17th-century
Tibetan gilded bronze of Raktayamari ('Red Enemy of Yama') and
Vajravetali ('Thunderbolt Zombie') (fig. 96), who transcend death itself in
their trampling of Yama (the Hindu god of death) and his buffalo *vahana*.
The trampling of Yama is understood as a conquering of the repetitive
cycle of rebirth and the suffering and fear it brings.

   The texts classified as *Mahayoga Tantras* and *Yogini Tantras* (written in
India between the 8th and 10th centuries), including the *Chakrasamvara
Tantra*, *Guhyasamaja Tantra* and *Hevajra Tantra*, present Vajrayana teachings
through a dialogue between a god and a goddess and employ sexually

**Figs. 94, 95**
**Details from *Miracles of the
Mass of Universal Salvation
Conducted by the Fifth
Karmapa for the Yongle
Emperor***
Probably Nanjing, China
Dated 1407
Handscroll, ink and colours on
silk, 66 cm × 4.97 m
The Tibet Museum, Lhasa

**Fig. 96**
**Raktayamari in union
with Vajravetali**
Tibet
16th/17th century
Bronze with turquoise, gold
and paint, 21.8 × 15.8 × 11.4 cm
British Museum 1880.125

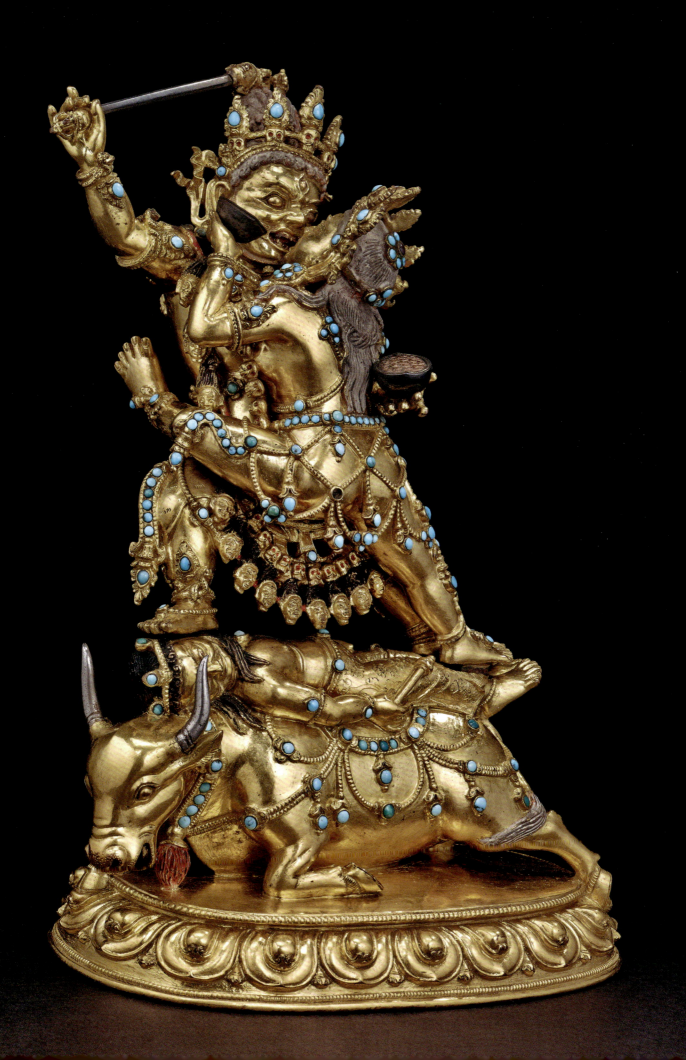

explicit language to describe rites for attaining liberation. Scholars have been split over whether to read these sexually charged descriptions (and the images they inspired) on literal or symbolic levels, partly because the texts employed what has been termed 'twilight' language.[58] This consisted of layered, ambiguous and metaphorical meanings and imagery, allowing for multiple interpretations and inspiring many commentaries. Only advanced Tantrikas, with the guidance of their guru, could navigate the true meanings of these texts. Although their content appears to be directed towards non-monastic, lay practitioners, we know that they were studied and appropriated by the celibate inhabitants of monasteries in eastern India from around the 8th century, where the symbolic, philosophical nature of the sexually explicit passages would have been emphasized.[59] *Yab-yum* iconography became one of the defining characteristics of Vajrayana from around the 11th century onwards and many *yab-yum* paintings and sculptures were produced for monastic establishments and temples, as well as for private use or for royal patrons.[60]

According to the Tantric Buddhist practice of Devata yoga, which could be carried out within a celibate monastic context, a practitioner must internalize the pair of deities and recognize in him- or herself both the female and male principles, merging the two within his or her own body. A similar 'internalization' of sexual rites is found in Hatha yoga and the methods for awakening Kundalini. The closely related practice of Devata yoga involves the manipulation of the yogic body through visualizations and breathing techniques.[61] There are two key stages, referred to as the 'generation' (*utpattikrama*) and 'completion' (*sampannakrama*) stages. During the 'generation' stage, practitioners visualize and identify with their chosen meditational deities. They must study their iconography and symbolism, for which sacred images, such as the paintings and sculptures presented in this chapter, are invaluable for constructing detailed visualizations.[62] The *Tantras* provided descriptions of the deities which the painters and sculptors meticulously drew on.

During the 'completion' stages, practitioners draw on advanced techniques for fully identifying the body, speech and mind with these deities.[63] These techniques involve working with the yogic body and its network of *chakras* and *nadis*. The *Hevajra Tantra* stresses that everyone has the transformative capacity to realize their own innate divinity, a source of tremendous, limitless power: 'all beings are Buddhas' and 'there is no being that is not enlightened, if it but knows its own true nature'.[64] As in Hatha yoga, there are three principal *nadis* that run from the head to the perineum. While the Hindu goddess Kundalini resides at the base of the spine, her Buddhist equivalent, the 'blazing goddess' Chandali (known as Tummo in Tibetan), is believed to dwell, fiery and snake-like, in the navel. By manipulating the breath (*prana*) that normally circulates along the left

Fig. 97
Milarepa
Tibet
18th century
Bronze, 12.7 × 8.4 × 6 cm
British Museum 1992,1214.21
Donated by Johannes
Nikolaus Schmitt and Mareta
Meade

and right *nadis* to flow through the central *nadi*, Chandali can be drawn up, piercing the *chakras* and untangling knots (*granthi*), understood as inner obstacles such as greed and ignorance, which can be converted to bliss, radiance and awareness.[65]

Visualized as a rising flame, the red, 'solar' Chandali as *prajna* (wisdom) and *shunyata* (emptiness) must be drawn up to the cranial vault to unite with the white, 'lunar' masculine principle (*karuna-upaya* or compassion and skilful means), the Buddhist equivalent of Shiva.[66] Chandali and the principle of *karuna-upaya* are associated with red and white sexual fluids, just as Kundalini and Shiva are in the Hindu Tantric context (see Chapter 2). They co-mingle to produce *amrita*, often referred to as *bodhichitta* (the 'will to enlightenment'), saturating the practitioner's being which, emptied of its ego-led limitations, is rendered androgynously divine and charged with *mahasukha ananda* (great bliss). The body is conceived as dissolved and empty apart from the radiant *bodhichitta*, an elixir of wisdom and compassion.[67] Through this process of self-divinization, all aspects of the body can be embraced, affirmed and instrumentalized on the path towards enlightenment. This also applies to usually disparaged human impulses – worldly desire or anger, for example, can be transmuted and directed towards destroying one's inner obstacles, mirroring the rich symbolism of sexually charged and wrathful Tantric deities.[68]

Milarepa ('Cotton-Clad Mila', 1040–1123), a Tibetan master of *siddhis*, is celebrated for his poetry describing his experiences of the Tantric path, including his mastery of waking Chandali through Devata yoga to generate inner heat, which enabled him to survive the freezing conditions in mountain caves during his solitary retreats, wearing only a cotton cloth (fig. 97):

> Continuance in Heat-Yoga without cold is indeed felicitous.
> With no cowardliness or dismay,
> Joyfully I follow the Tantric practice;
> With no effort I perfect the cultivation;
> With no distraction whatsoever,
> Remaining in solitude, I am truly happy.
> These are the pleasures of the body.
> Happy is the path of both Wisdom and [Compassionate] Means![69]

A Tibetan bronze shows Milarepa dressed in his simple cotton cloth with a meditation strap slung over his shoulder. He holds his right hand up to his ear as though reciting one of his poems.

The *Chakrasamvara Tantra*, which was probably composed by the late 8th century and transmitted to Nepal and Tibet from India around the 11th century, details visualization rituals and yogic techniques for achieving enlightenment.[70] The text inspired an 18th-century Tibetan *thangka* almost

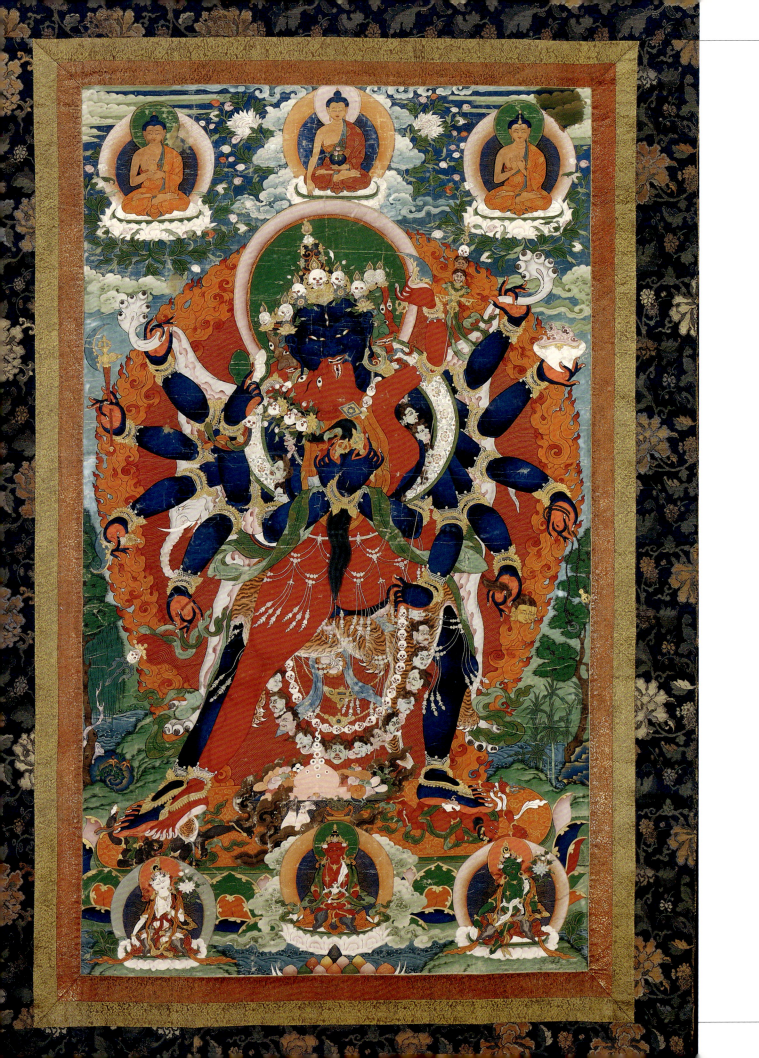

**Fig. 98**
**Chakrasamvara in union**
**with Vajrayogini**
Tibet
18th century
Painted silk, 129.5 × 77.6 cm
(image); 230.5 × 128 cm
(entire scroll)
British Museum 1957,0413,0.1

**Fig. 99**
**Detail of fig. 98, showing**
**Chakrasamvara's garland**
**of heads and tiger skin**

2 m (6 ft) in length, showing a four-headed, twelve-armed, velvet-blue Chakrasamvara embracing the goddess Vajrayogini, who swings one of her legs over his thigh (figs. 98, 99). Together, Chakrasamvara and Vajrayogini are two of the most popular Tantric Buddhist deities in Nepal and Tibet. Both trample the Hindu gods Bhairava and Chamunda, here portrayed as obstacles to enlightenment. The image is a perfectly composed yet explosive choreograph of sexual energy and dynamic ferocity.[71] The couple's red-rimmed, wild eyes and laughing, fanged mouths suggest their immense power. They each have a third eye, a reference to their omnipotence over all three worlds: the world of desire, which is our own world; the world of form, with its heavens; and the world of formlessness, with its liberating emptiness.[72] They are both deities to be adored and embodiments of the fusion of sexually charged fluids within the body of the Devata yoga practitioner. The blazing ring of flames around the pair corresponds to the fiery climax as Chandali reaches the crown of the practitioner's head.

Vajrayogini is an inflamed, blood-red colour, naked save for gold and bone ornaments. In her right hand she holds up a curved knife for hacking away at misplaced pride and the ego. Chakrasamvara holds up an array of symbolic objects including an axe, trident and noose with which he extinguishes attachment, anger, ignorance and worldly desire.[73] Again, he echoes Bhairava's attributes: stretching out an elephant skin behind him, representing his triumph over delusion; and wearing a tiger skin, painted with extraordinary attention to detail (fig. 99). Sex and death are inextricably entwined in this *danse macabre*. A garland of grisly decaying heads – each depicted with individual, almost humorous, character – hangs around Chakrasamvara's neck and he carries a skull-cup bubbling over with blood, along with a *khatvanga*. The interplay of sexual and violent symbolism in this and other *yab-yum* images speaks to the coming together of two uniquely Tantric forms of visual rhetoric. To represent the qualities of wisdom and compassion through images containing symbols of demonic wrath and military conquest not only evokes collapsing polarities but also

Fig. 100
**Hevajra in union with Nairatmya**
Tibet (Newari craftmanship)
17th century
Gilded bronze with gold,
21.5 × 14.8 × 8.9 cm
British Museum 1921,0219.2
From Louis Magrath King

highlights the belief that only the most ferocious deities can abolish the obstacles to enlightenment.

A 17th-century gilded bronze from Tibet depicts the Yidam Hevajra in union with the goddess Nairatmya ('Without Self'), whose name implies her supreme quality of *shunyata* (emptiness) (fig. 100). Both dance on the bodies of the Hindu gods Indra, Brahma, Shiva and Vishnu. Hevajra is the reigning deity of the *Hevajra Tantra* dating to the late 8th/early 9th century and probably composed in eastern India. Like other Tantric texts, the *Hevajra Tantra* describes the benefits of ritually engaging in sexual rites in order to transcend desire itself – 'healing' an internal obstacle by strategically embracing and affirming it. 'By passion the world is bound; by passion too it is released' is inscribed on a folio of a surviving 15th-/16th-century copy of the text (fig. 101).[74]

The *Hevajra Tantra* also clarifies that sexual rites should not be 'taught for the sake of enjoyment, but for the examination of one's own thought, whether the mind is steady or wavering'.[75] Even a celibate monk or nun could engage with this method through imaginative Devata yoga. The *Tantra* envisages Hevajra in anthropomorphic form as a sixteen-year-old boy, covered in cremation-ground ashes. In the text he proclaims the bliss that results from his union with Nairatmya:

> Fearful am I to fear itself,
> with my necklace made of a string of heads, and dancing furiously
>      on a solar disk. Black am I and terrible (...)
> But my inner nature is tranquil, and holding Nairatmya in loving
>      embrace, I am possessed of tranquil bliss.[76]

The survival of bronze sculptures of Hevajra commissioned during the reign of the Khmer kings of Cambodia (802–1431), dating between the 11th and 13th centuries, testifies to the arrival and popularity of *Hevajra Tantra* teachings beyond South Asia. King Jayavarman VII (r. 1181–1218) was a devout follower of Hevajra and was said to have commissioned a giant stone sculpture of him at the East Gate of the walled Khmer capital of Angkor Thom (north-west Cambodia), now at the Metropolitan Museum of Art, New York.[77] Many bronze figures of Hevajra were cast during Jayavarman's rule, including the example shown here (fig. 102), in which Hevajra dynamically balances on a corpse while eight Dakini goddesses dance ecstatically around him. This elaborately cast bronze, made *c.* 1200 in Cambodia, depicts Hevajra with sixteen arms. On the left his hands hold skull-cups containing the Hindu gods of earth (Prithvi), water (Varuna), fire (Agni), air (Vayu), the moon (Chandra), the sun (Surya), death (Yama) and wealth (Kubera). On the right his skull-cups contain animals symbolizing the eight Guardians of the Cardinal Directions or Dikpalas: an elephant, horse, ass, ox, camel, man, cat and *sharabha* (a mythical eight-legged beast, part-lion and part-bird). All reverentially look to Hevajra, who is presented as having mastery over each of them – a mastery that a Tantrika seeks to mirror.

An early 16th-century Tibetan *thangka* depicts four mandalas (sacred 'circles'), each featuring Hevajra and Nairatmya surrounded by goddesses manifesting from their union (fig. 103). Mandalas, commonly found on scrolls or as wall paintings, are circular diagrams depicting deities and their surrounding celestial environments and entourages. Their geometric forms capture the deities' cosmic, indefinable qualities. Originating in India, mandalas are also conceived as sacred ritual spaces, and may be traced on the ground to consecrate an area and to invoke deities before an important ritual, such as a Tantric initiation.[78] During the 'generation' stage of Devata yoga visualization, practitioners imagine themselves entering the mandala as though it were a palace, crossing over its encircling band (marking the point between the sacred realm of the deity inside and the profane world beyond it). They then visualize entering through one of the four doors representing the cardinal directions, protected by guardian deities, until they encounter the deity with whom they seek to identify, ultimately merging with them and taking their place at the centre of the mandala (fig. 103).[79] Charnel-ground scenes – suggested by the presence of corpses, skeletons, Siddha figures and scavenging animals – appear along the outer rings of each of the four mandalas depicted here. The charnel grounds that surround Hevajra mandalas (usually eight in number) are described in Tantric texts as inhabited not only by bodies and animals but also by zombies, ghosts, demons and fierce deities. They are 'gruesome', 'frightful with skulls', 'dark and terrible' and 'resounding with cries'.[80]

Although the *Mahayoga Tantras* and *Yogini Tantras* describe and endorse sexual rites in which desire is harnessed to transform desire, the language is often deliberately ambiguous, making the content open to both literal and symbolic readings. The question, then, is whether *yab-yum* images reflect actual physical practices of Tantric Buddhists, beyond purely philosophical metaphors. The *Hevajra Tantra*, for example, leaves little to the imagination, employing the symbols of the *vajra* and *padma* for the phallus and vulva throughout:

A knowledgeable yogi should continually worship
A superlative female consort who has disrobed (…)
Again and again unite by means of the thunderbolt [*vajra*] (…)

**Fig. 102**
**Hevajra**
Angkor, Cambodia
*c.* 1200
Bronze, 46 × 23.9 cm
Cleveland Museum of Art,
2011.143
Gift of Maxeen and
John Flower in honour
of Dr Stanislaw Czuma

Thus one attains extensive spiritual perfections and
Becomes the equal of all Buddhas.[81]

In the opening section of the *Chakrasamvara Tantra* sexual rites are
prescribed as essential:

The secret path without a consort
Will not grant perfection to beings.
Thus, attain enlightenment
By applying oneself most diligently
To the activities of erotic play.[82]

It is clear that sexual rites were also performed literally. Mahasiddhas,
for instance, are depicted performing sexual rites with their partners (see
fig. 87). In these cases, sexual yoga is performed with the partners visualized
as the *yab-yum* deities.

When an 18th-/19th-century gilded bronze from Nepal (fig. 104) was
acquired by the British Museum in 1893 it was originally registered as a
'bronze gilt god and goddess in princely human form; the former seated
nude, on his head a cap or turban; the latter with long hair, pendant
strings form waist-girdle'.[83] These figures appear to depict mortal
Tantrikas engaged in sexual rites in imitation of *yab-yum* deities. The act
of penetration is rendered explicitly, as it also often is in sculptures of
deities. Such rites were carried out by advanced practitioners in a state
of detached, meditative awareness in order to alchemically transform
emotions such as lust into enlightened states.[84] This is reflected in their
calm and controlled, smiling expressions. The goal of sexual yoga in a
Tantric Buddhist context was generally to retain and preserve sexual fluids
during intercourse and to visualize them rising to the cranial vault, where
the *amrita* (nectar of immortality) was believed to drip down as a person
aged, as described in the 11th-century *Amritasiddhi*.[85]

The qualifications for male and female Buddhist Tantrikas mirror those
of Hindu ones. For example, they are described as heroes and heroines (*viras*)
who must be initiated by gurus, become experienced practitioners of yoga
and acquire detailed knowledge of the Tantric teachings.[86] Just as many
Hindu Tantric texts proclaimed that Shakti flowed from and through human
women who must by extension be venerated, Tantric Buddhist texts creatively
adopted this idea. In the *Chandamaharoshana Tantra* (9th–10th century), the
goddess Vajrayogini reveals that all female beings are her embodiments and
must be worshipped, through offerings as well as sexual rites:

I am identical to the bodies of all women, and
There is no way that I can be worshipped

Fig. 104
**Tantrikas in coitus**
Nepal
18th/19th century
Gilded bronze with semi-
precious stones, 21 × 13 ×
15.5 cm
British Museum 1893,0410.4

Except by the worship of women. (…)
Visualizing that she is fully my embodiment,
He should make love to his woman.
Because of uniting the *vajra* and lotus,
I will grant enlightenment.[87]

Ultimately, both literal and symbolic interpretations of sexually explicit
Tantric passages and their accompanying creative visual expressions reflect
the overarching 'twilight' theme of collapsing polarities (male/female,
wisdom/compassion, sun/moon, etc), emphasizing the non-dualism
of phenomena and their essential emptiness or *shunyata*.

## DAKINIS: 'SHE WHO FLIES'

A pantheon of Tantric Buddhist deities thrived in Tibet, their iconography
not only charged with sexuality (in the case of *yab-yum* deities in union) but
also with violence, challenging us to question our assumptions about the
'face' of the divine.[88] Just as the Yogini goddesses were central to the Hindu
*Vidyapitha Tantras* from around the 8th century onwards (see Chapter 1),
the equivalent Tantric Buddhist Dakini goddesses (also often referred to
as Yoginis) were integral to the Buddhist *Yogini Tantras*.[89] The two bodies
of texts shared many ritual and theological concepts, particularly in their

**Fig. 105**
*Yantra*
Nepal
17th/18th century
Bronze, diameter 20 cm
British Museum 1992,1214.25
Donated by Johannes
Nikolaus Schmitt and
Mareta Meade

emphasis on the female principle of Shakti and descriptions of transgressive practices conducted in cremation and charnel grounds. Like the Yoginis, Dakinis ('She Who Flies') are conceived as both goddesses and witch-like, vampiric beings of the sky, to be feared but also venerated as powerful guides on the Tantric path who could assist the practitioner in acquiring supernatural *siddhis* in exchange for offerings, which included sexual fluids. They could assume mortal forms; women who became great Tantric masters were therefore often described as Dakinis.

Vajrayogini is both a Dakini and meditational deity whose popularity flourished in India between the 10th and 12th centuries, and whose role assumed particular importance in Tibet. She is sometimes portrayed with her consort, Chakrasamvara (see figs. 98–99), but also independently, as in a 17th-/18th-century bronze *yantra* from Nepal (fig. 105). The *yantra* geometrically frames and articulates Vajrayogini's power as she presides over her domain, which fans out around her. Situated at the top of the pyramidal diagram, she dances within an inverted triangle, a symbol of the vulva (*yoni*) and female creative power. *Yantras*, like mandalas, are ritual diagrams used as instruments to invoke deities during Tantric practice and as an aid to stimulate visualizations. They are also used for rites designed to fulfil certain worldly or supernatural ambitions; indeed, the Sanskrit root of the word *yantra*, *yam*, literally means 'to control', 'to restrain' or 'to bend'.[90]

*Yantras* were quintessentially Tantric in their function as ritual devices designed to harness a variety of powers.[91] Made of different materials, ranging from metal to ephemeral paper, *yantras* were understood as visual equivalents of mantras, capturing the essence of the chosen deity through variations of interplaying shapes including triangles, squares, circles and lotus petals. This particular *yantra* may have been used as a support for worship. Around Vajrayogini are the six points of a star made up of two interlocking triangles which together signify the union of feminine and masculine principles. Vajrayogini is positioned at the epicentre, the *bindu* (culminating point) that is understood as the emptiness (*shunyata*) from which all things cyclically arise and into which they dissolve.[92] The radiating rings include a variety of symbols that invoke Vajrayogini's cremation-ground realm, including skulls, pyres, Siddha figures, jackals and vultures. Other Buddhist recurring symbols include *vajras* and stupa shrines.

Vajrayogini is popularly shown in a lunging posture, trampling Bhairava and Chamunda, as seen in a Tibetan *thangka* (fig. 106). In this form, red and blazing, she is said to have appeared to the Mahasiddha Naropa in a vision, lending her the name Naro Dakini. She looks up towards her raised hand, her open mouth about to taste the blood pouring out of the skull-cup, transmuted into an elixir of *bodhichitta*. Her lowered right hand holds a flaying knife for severing attachment. The manuscript to her left contains the Prajnaparamita ('Perfection of Wisdom') teachings, while the sword of wisdom hovers in thin air to her right. Her retinue includes two dancing skeletal figures below her; they are the Smashana Adipati ('Lords of the Charnel Ground'), who provide protection for those engaged in Tantric practice and are a reminder of the impermanence of all things, including the human body, encouraging freedom from attachment. This emphasis on mortality, consistent across Tantric iconography, serves as a reminder not only to embrace all aspects of life but also that death itself is a state of transformative potential before the next rebirth.[93]

Vajrayogini is also known as Vajravarahi ('Thunderbolt Sow') when she is portrayed with a sow's head emerging from behind her right ear, as in an early 19th-century *thangka* (fig. 107), hinting at the creative Buddhist adaptation of Varahi, the earlier Tantric Hindu goddess (see Chapter 1, fig. 25). According to Buddhist teachings, three primary obstacles or poisons prevent beings from attaining enlightenment: ignorance, greed and aversion. They are symbolized by a pig, rooster and snake, respectively. The inclusion of an inauspicious female pig as part of Vajravarahi's iconography is therefore deliberate here, demonstrating her power to confront, harness, sublimate and transform ignorance. In this form she dances riotously upon a pitiful-looking anthropomorphic rendering of the human ego, her nakedness adorned with skulls in a flurry of overt eroticism and menacing violence. Her fangs and arched eyebrows are in threatening contrast to her idealized, feminine form,

**Fig. 106**
**Naro Dakini**
Tibet
18th/19th century
Painted cloth with silk brocade
borders, 26.3 × 23 cm
(image only)
British Museum 1992,1224,0.9
Donated by Johannes
Nikolaus Schmitt and Mareta
Meade

**Fig. 107**
**Vajravarahi**
Tibet
Early 19th century
Painted textile, 125 × 81 ×
4.5 cm
British Museum 1956,1208,0.17

described in Tantric texts as red like the 'China rose' and 'lovely with fresh youth'.[94] Like the Matrika Varahi, she defies traditional models of femininity with her long, unbound hair (as opposed to it being braided, tied or neatly presented) and she is often described as not only covered in blood but also menstruating.[95] As noted previously, menstrual blood was considered a polluting and therefore dangerous substance according to orthodox Indian traditions. Tantric practice deliberately engaged with it (either literally or symbolically) to harness its potent power and to destabilize and transcend limiting, traditional codes of purity, transmuting it from contaminated fluid to sacred energy.[96] The swirling, fiery ring around Vajravarahi evokes her role as a meditational deity for Chandali yogic practice and emphasizes her ability to burn through and to pulverize inner obstacles.

Many practices described in Tantric texts involved the internalization of Vajrayogini. The *Guhyasamayasadhanamala* (*c.* 11th–12th century), for example, describes the Devata yoga practice for transforming a Tantrika into the goddess by imitating her nature, attributes and appearance, from her nakedness and unbound hair to her lunging posture, or wearing red items of clothing to reflect her luminous colour.[97] The preparatory rite for this total assimilation is described in the text as a 'mantra bath' (*mantrasnanam*), during which the Tantrika mixes and applies a concoction of conventionally taboo and polluting substances in order to sacralize body, speech and mind:

In order to purify the body, speech, and mind, he should [take] the three kinds of divine liquid according to their availability, [namely, fermentations from] honey, molasses, [and] flour, and mix them with the five nectars [semen, blood, flesh, urine, and faeces] and place them in a chalice. [Then] having consecrated [the mixture] with the three-syllabled [purification] mantra [*om ah hum*], he should perform a 'mantra bath' using this liquid on all the major and minor limbs [of the body starting] from the left hand.[98]

Suggested areas for carrying out Vajrayogini practices included her favourite haunts, from cremation and charnel grounds to secluded, mountainous spaces such as caves. The ultimate goal was the dissolution of the Tantrika's limited self-perception, followed by a reconstruction or 'rebirth' of the practitioner as Vajrayogini herself.

Ritual objects associated with Vajrayogini allowed the practitioner to assume her character, thus internalizing divinity (fig. 108). She is consistently shown brandishing the curved flaying knife (*karttrika*), known as the 'knife of the Dakinis'. Its blade symbolizes the transformative wisdom of *shunyata*, with which she helps to cut through the entrails and flesh of demonic forces representing not only pride, jealousy, desire and aversion but also dualistic thinking, as expressed in the unenlightened mind's tendency to differentiate between the self and the other.[99] Grinding and blending these fetters in the blood-filled skull-cup, she transforms them into a nectar of enlightenment for her devotees. Just as three-dimensional *vajras* were made for practitioners to emulate and 'become' a deity such as Vajradhara, flaying knives were made as meditational tools so that the wielder might channel the Dakini and visualize flaying their own ego.[100]

In Japan, the Tantric figure of the Dakini acquired a new, culturally specific identity. While Buddhism first reached the island country in the 6th century from Korea, Tantric teachings were transmitted from China, famously via the Japanese monk Kukai (774–835), who established the Shingon ('true word', i.e. mantra) tradition.[101] Before the arrival of Buddhism, Shinto ('way of the gods') had informed the dominant belief system in Japan. Shinto is based on the worship of *kamis*, divinities associated with the natural world. In response to the rising popularity of Tantric Buddhist teachings, some *kamis* came to be associated or identified with Tantric deities. This was the case with Inari, a *kami* of the rice harvest, prosperity and fertility.[102] Inari became conflated with the Tantric figure of the Dakini, and renamed Dakini-ten (Dakini-deity) in Shingon contexts, including dedicated shrines and temples. This conflation may have occurred after Emperor Saga (r. 809–823) asked

**Fig. 108**
*Karttrika*
Tibet
c. 1900
Iron, bronze and silver, 15 × 19
× 4 cm
British Museum 1948,0716.12
Bequeathed by Harry Geoffrey
Beasley

Kukai to administer the Toji temple in Kyoto in 823, and the monk chose Inari to be its protector.[103]

Dakini-ten is usually depicted as a goddess riding a flying white fox, visualized in a 14th-century Japanese scroll painting as held aloft by billowing clouds and a pair of dragons (fig. 109). She holds a sword with a *vajra* handle in her right hand, and in her left she carries flaming wish-fulfilling jewels. The scroll was painted between 1336 and 1392, during the Nanbokucho period, when the northern and southern imperial courts were in conflict. Dakini-ten, who was not only associated with fecundity but also with worldly success and power, was invoked in imperial enthronement rituals to promote the legitimacy of emperors.[104] Like the wild, shapeshifting Dakinis and Yoginis of Tibet and India, Dakini-ten was also believed to be capable of causing ruin if dissatisfied, leading to her regular ritual appeasement by Japanese rulers and members of the elite.[105] In 1107 the statesman Fujiwara no Tadazane is said to have asked a Shingon monk to invoke Dakini-ten in order to ensure that he would be selected as regent to the emperor. He subsequently dreamt of a vixen-like woman with long, flowing hair. As he reached out to touch her, he suddenly awoke to find an auspicious fox tail in his hand. Shortly afterwards, he learned that he had received his promotion.[106]

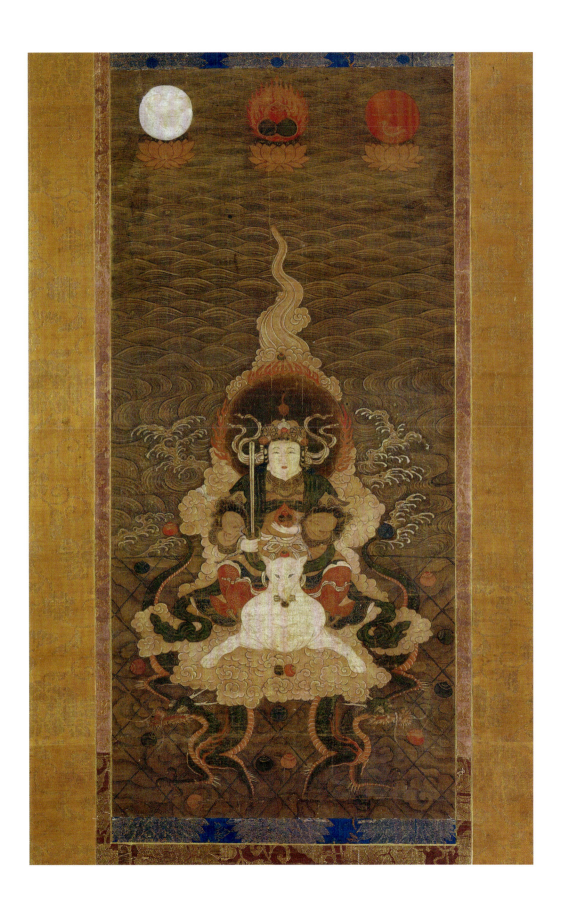

**Fig. 109**
**Dakini-ten**
Japan
1336–92
Ink, colour and gold on hemp,
74.9 × 33 cm; 162.9 × 49.5 cm
(with fabric mount)
The Metropolitan Museum
of Art 2000.274

**Fig. 110**
*Kila*
Tibet (Newari craftmanship)
18th/19th century
Rock crystal with eyes of inlaid
ruby, length 27 cm
British Museum 1992,1214.69
Donated by Johannes Nikolaus
Schmitt and Mareta Meade

## DHARMAPALAS AND THE ART OF VIOLENCE

Tantric iconography is unique in its inclusion, for sacred ends, of forms and content conventionally understood as hostile and demonic.[107] The significance of violence in representations of Dakinis and Yidams is also central to portrayals of Dharmapalas ('Protectors of the Dharma'), wrathful manifestations of the Buddhas in Tantric Buddhism. Their appearances are influenced by representations of Indian Rakshasas and Rakshasis, male and female demons with wild hair, fangs, bulging red-rimmed eyes and cavernous mouths. The purpose of their warlike imagery is encapsulated in a description of Vajrayogini as 'terrifying with anger, which is in fact displayed out of compassion'.[108] Indeed, their motivation is to emancipate all beings spiritually and to conquer destructive forces. This requires using the same weapons or tactics as the demonic 'enemies' (often symbols of inner obstacles), becoming 'fearful to fear itself' and 'dangerous to danger itself'.[109] Other obstacles might also include external ones, such as diseases and natural disasters. Many of the Dharmapalas were deities of non-Buddhist origin (i.e., Hindu or Bön, Tibet's indigenous religious tradition) who were understood to have converted to Buddhism. Some of the most popular Dharmapalas in Tibet are Mahakala (see Chapter 1), Yama Dharmaraja and Hayagriva.

The Dharmapala Hayagriva (the 'Horse-Necked One') is identifiable by the horse's head crowning the deity. He subdues the demonic roots of obstacles with the piercing sound of the horse's neigh. He is often represented as a *kila* ('stake', or *phurbu* in Tibetan), a ceremonial dagger, which is an important ritual instrument in Tantric Buddhism with a protective function. The *kila* is usually made of metal or wood, but the 18th-/19th-century example pictured here (fig. 110) is made of rock crystal which, along with iron, is regarded as a powerful medium for ritual daggers because of its translucency, symbolic of purity. Hayagriva's eyes are inlaid with ruby, which may indicate Nepalese craftmanship. The *kila's* origins lie in ancient India (it is used as a weapon by the god Indra in the *Rig Veda*) but no early examples from the region survive.[110] Padmasambhava is said to have used *kilas* to nail down and subdue the local spirits that were disrupting the building of Tibet's first Buddhist monastery in the 8th century.[111] The *kila* is wielded by the practitioner to destroy or neutralize obstacles, both internal and external. Groups of *kilas* are also planted around the practitioner to create a protective shield during a ritual.[112]

The *kila* is also an embodiment or symbol of Vajrakilaya ('Adamantine Stake'), a fierce Buddhist deity whose very pores are described as exuding miniature daggers that shoot out of him from every angle. He is vividly portrayed at the centre of an 18th-century *thangka*, six-armed, winged and covered in skulls and decapitated heads (fig. 111). The lower half of his

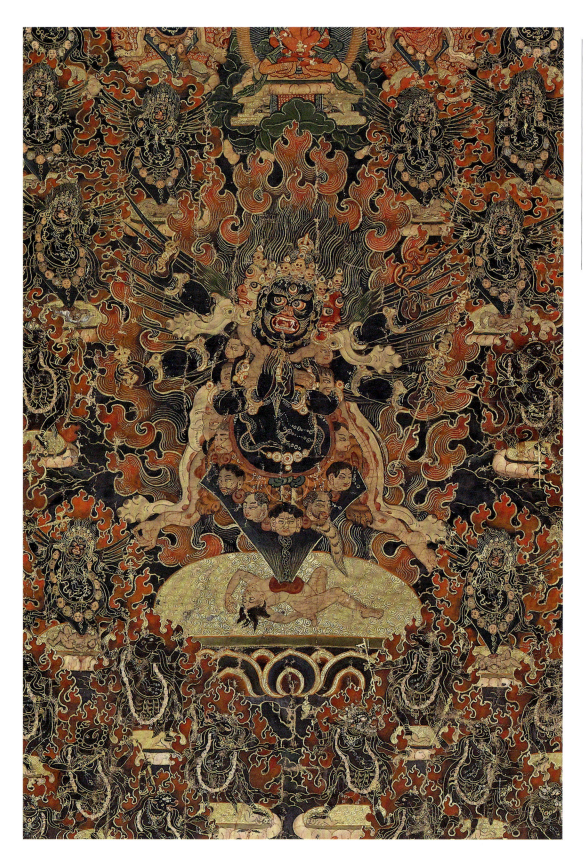

**Fig. 111**
**Detail of *thangka* depicting**
**Vajrakilaya**
Tibet
18th century
Painted fabric, 92.5 × 57.5 ×
4 cm
British Museum, 1956,1208,0.15

**Fig. 112**
*Kila*
Tibet
19th century
Bronze, 38 × 7 × 6.7 cm
British Museum 1893,0320.107

body terminates in a dagger blade, which pins down a writhing corpse symbolizing demonic obstruction.

The wielder of the *kila* identifies with this deity when performing protective rites. A 19th-century *kila* features the three faces of Vajrakilaya crowning the hilt, while his lower body is the triple-sided blade itself (fig. 112). Both the faces and the three sides of the blade symbolize the destruction of ignorance, hatred and desire (the three root poisons). Intertwining *nagas* (serpent spirits) decorate the blade, emerging from the mouth of a *makara* (sea-monster). In Tibet *nagas* are regarded as temperamental underworld spirits who control the rain and bodies of water, capable of inflicting misfortune and ill-health if displeased. *Kilas* are still often used to affect the weather and purify land, which sometimes involves subjugating the *nagas*.[113] Here their visual presence invokes their auspicious natures.

Yama Dharmaraja, the buffalo-headed Lord of Death and King of the Dharma, is invoked during practices associated with the *Vajrabhairava Tantra* (8th–10th century), ultimately with the aim of defeating the fear of mortality that results from attachment to the ego: 'If one hears this *Tantra* and, understanding it, holds to it and performs the recitation all the time, in this lifetime all his fears will be washed away'.[114] This is the same Yama who was shown being trampled (in his Hindu form) by Raktayamari and Vajravetali earlier in the chapter (fig. 96). Here he has been converted and his goal is to free all beings from the limitations of ignorance and to protect Buddhist teachings. The practices outlined in the *Vajrabhairava Tantra* also include the six magical actions (*satkarman*; see Chapter 1) for pacification, subjugation, immobilization, creation of hostility, driving away and killing. The victims of these rites could represent a multitude of threats, from opponents on the battlefield to diseases, natural disasters and emotional impediments.[115] The text also contains detailed instructions for how to paint and draw the image of Yama to facilitate effective visualizations.

In an 18th-century embroidered image of Yama (fig. 113), the enormous, bestial Dharmapala wields a skull-topped club and noose and balances balletically on a buffalo, which tramples and appears to rape an anthropomorphic representation of the ego (fig. 114). This recurring motif of a corpse being trampled can also be interpreted as the practitioner's own limited self-conception that is abandoned when they become the deity that subjugates it.[116] Embodying triumph over destructive forces, the scene occurs in the midst of a chaotic yet masterfully orchestrated blaze. Yama's erect phallus has a bright red tip, emphasizing his virility. The *thangka* may have originally hung in a monastic or private chapel to protect its inhabitants, as well as the surrounding community, from negative influences or events.

Ferocious Dharmapalas such as Achala ('Immovable One'), known as Fudo Myo-o ('Wisdom King Achala') in Japan, were harnessed by Japanese

Fig. 113
**Yama Dharmaraja**
Tibet
18th century
Embroidered textile, 117.5 ×
68.3 cm
British Museum 1961,1014,0.5
Donated by Louis Colville Gray
Clarke

Fig. 114
**Detail of fig. 113, showing**
**Yama Dharmaraja**

Fig. 115
**Actor Ichikawa Danjuro V**
**as the Dharmapala Fudo**
**Myo-o, Katsukawa Shunsho**
Japan
1780
Colour woodblock print,
32.8 × 15.1 cm
British Museum 1902,0212,0.202

emperors to protect the realm.[117] A colour woodblock print of Fudo, executed by the painter and printmaker Katsukawa Shunsho in 1780, is striking for its startlingly vivid, portrait-like quality (fig. 115). It represents one of the most famous Japanese actors of all time, Ichikawa Danjuro V, as Fudo, and captures a scene from a Kabuki play, a classical Japanese dance-drama. Danjuro was regarded as a living embodiment of Fudo, like his father, grandfather and great-grandfather, all of whom had been celebrated Kabuki actors. Danjuro I (his great-grandfather) had first promised to serve Fudo in 1688 at the Shingon Narita temple, and his descendants would all go on to play the fierce Dharmapala on stage. Not only was Fudo their guardian deity, he was also believed to manifest himself through them onstage, in a truly Tantric tour de force.[118] Danjuro V's distinctive facial features have been captured in the print, including his long nose and downturned mouth. He played the role of Fudo four times in his life, and this print may mark the final performance at the Nakamura theatre, capturing a popular scene known as 'The Stone Statue of Fudo' in a play entitled *Kite Kaeru Nishiki no Wakayaka* (*So Youthful! Brocades to Wear When Returning Home*).[119] Here he carries Fudo's sword, for cutting through illusion, and a rope that binds the enemies of the Dharma.

## HUMAN REMAINS IN TANTRIC BUDDHIST PRACTICE

In representations of Dakinis, Dharmapalas and Yidams, the *kapala* vessel overflowing with blood, flesh and organs is a recurring motif, just as it is in Hindu Tantric depictions of Bhairava, Chamunda and the Yogini goddesses (see Chapter 1).

A polychrome figure, which may have once formed part of an altar shrine, represents Ekajata Rakshasi ('Demoness with One Chignon'), one of the attendants of the Dharmapala Mahakala (fig. 116). Ekajata Rakshasi brandishes a *kapala* and prepares to chop up its contents with her flaying knife, her fury no match for any hindrances to spiritual awakening.

In Tantric practice *kapalas* made from human crania are important ritual objects associated with the Mahasiddhas as well as the Kapalikas (see Chapter 1). One 19th-century example is highly unusual because of the presence of mantras written in Tibetan on the inside of the cranium (fig. 117). The central mantras are related to the Yidam Yamantaka, including the line '*Om Yamantaka hum*', *om* and *hum* having no linguistic meaning but functioning as sacred syllables.[120] This line is described as the 'king of secret mantras' in the *Vajrabhairava Tantra*, capable of granting 'whatever accomplishment one wishes for', if harnessed correctly.[121] On the outside of the *kapala* three Tibetan syllables (*om ah hum*) have been chiselled into the bone, invoking the body, speech and mind of the deity,

designed to purify the contents and to make the skull-cup a suitable receptacle. The *kapala* may have been used in the context of a ritual dedicated to Yamantaka and his retinue that involved consecrating the vessel with the written mantras. It appears to have been sealed and stored away with unknown protective, volatile ingredients inside it; its damaged rim indicates that it was forcibly opened at a later date. It is possible that its original function was to subdue a wrathful, negative force (be it an external or internal one), which was literally locked away for safeguarding.[122]

*Kapalas* were often adorned with ornate metal bases and covers. A 19th-century example (fig. 118) may have been used as part of a ritual such as *sgrub chen* ('major practice session'), a communal Tantric practice performed by a group of lamas over several days.[123] It consists of a ritual of 'medicinal accomplishment' (*sman sgrub*), during which symbolic and consumable substances and medicinal pills are placed in containers (including *kapalas*) around a mandala and consecrated, alchemically transforming them into sanctified substances capable of granting *siddhis* such as longevity and enlightenment.[124] The substances in the containers might include the five elixirs (urine, excrement, semen, menstrual blood and brains) and the five meats (human, cow, horse, dog and elephant), or symbolic substitutes for them, together with medicinal ingredients such as sandalwood, saffron, juniper leaves, cloves, camphor and nutmeg. During the ritual, the deities of the mandala are visualized above the vessels containing the substances, dripping red and white *bodhichitta*-nectar that purifies and transforms their contents.[125]

Alternatively, this *kapala* may have been used during an 'inner offering' rite. During such a ritual, the practitioner (lay or monastic) visualizes the skull as his or her own severed head, into which internal poison-obstacles are poured.[126] These 'inner offerings' of substances might include substitutes for or visualizations of the five elixirs, symbolizing form, feelings, perceptions, karmic impulses, and consciousness, along with the five meats symbolizing confusion, miserliness, attachment, jealousy and self-grasping.[127] The practitioner, after internalizing his or her chosen Tantric deity, might imagine the contents (often in the form of alcohol or tea) brought to boiling point, transformed into a *bodhichitta*-nectar. This visualization is explicitly illustrated on the skull-cup's triangular altar-base with licking flames and severed heads that evoke a pyre. The practitioner then ritually imbibes the consecrated liquid from the skull-cup, purifying mind, body and speech. The brass cover features images of the god Guhyasamaja ('Secret Assembly'), with bow and arrow, and is crowned by a *vajra* to transform the contents of the skull-cup. Thus complete, the offering serves to jolt and unlock the practitioner from his or her attachments to a fixed sense of self and from the cravings that accompany this unstable conviction.[128]

Such use of human remains was a reminder of the impermanence of the body and the importance of non-attachment. Simultaneously, the vital force of the deceased individuals to whom these skulls had once belonged was believed to be inherent within them, making them effective power-objects. The quality and strength of this residual vital force in a particular skull depended on the status and spiritual advancement of its owner in life, or the context of his or her death, as well as on the nature of the practice.[129] The skulls of senior lamas who had attained enlightened states were especially desirable according to certain Tantric texts, but could be challenging to secure. Many were bequeathed or sourced from charnel grounds, but they could be ritually imagined as and transformed into the skulls of the desired individuals.[130]

Machig Labdron (1055–1149) was one of the most renowned Tantric masters and teachers in Tibet, and is regarded as a manifestation of the goddess of wisdom, Prajnaparamita. According to her hagiography, she was born in south-west Tibet. After training with lamas in a monastic context, she replaced her robes with rags and wandered among outcasts and lepers, receiving Tantric instructions from various different gurus.[131] She is most famous for developing, establishing and popularizing the Tantric meditation practice known as Chöd ('cutting off'), which involves visualizing the dissection of one's own body, and by extension the ego, presenting the remains as an offering to divine and demonic spirits.[132] In a 19th-century *thangka* from eastern Tibet she appears deified as a dancing Dakini (fig. 119). Surrounding her are enlightened beings and

Fig. 118
*Kapala* with brass stand and lid
Tibet
19th century
Human bone with brass, 28.2 × 18 × 20 cm (including base, *kapala*, and lid)
British Museum 1931,1124.1.a–c

**Fig. 119**
**Machig Labdron**
Kham province, Tibet
19th century
Pigments on cotton, 62.2 ×
40.3 cm
The Rubin Museum of Art
C2010.3, HAR57037

deities including Vajradhara (at top centre) and Prajnaparamita, who appears
as the orange goddess below him. Machig Labdron holds a two-headed
skull-drum (*damaru*, or Tibetan: *thod rnga*) and a *ghanta*, two ritual instruments
used in the practice of Chöd to invoke the spirits to feast on her body.[133]
There is another figure bearing Chöd instruments – the yogi figure (at top
left) who holds a trumpet made from a human thighbone (*kangling*) as well
as a *damaru*. He is Padampa Sangye, a celebrated Indian Tantric master
who travelled to Tibet and is regarded as the transmitter of the practice.
It is uncertain whether Machig Labdron actually met him and received his
teachings, but she became the main codifier of Chöd in Tibet.[134]

**Fig. 120**

*Kangling*

Tibet

19th century

Human bone, silver and white
metal alloy, copper alloy,
turquoise, and coral

British Museum 2016,3040.2

Donated by Carinne Bevan
and Gina Rober

**Fig. 121**

*Damaru*

Tibet

*c.* 19th century

Human bone and leather,
height 11.3 cm

British Museum 1919,-.473

The *damaru* and the *kangling* are played during Chöd rituals to invite the spirits to devour the Tantrika's body. The highly decorated 19th-century *kangling* shown here may have been used for this purpose (fig. 120). The ball-joint of the thighbone is partly removed to create the mouth for the trumpet, which in this example is encased in metal and embossed. The bone's marrow-canal is hollow and produces a howl-like sound.

A *damaru*, also dating to around the 19th century, consists of the tops of two severed crania, joined together and covered in hide (fig. 121). The practitioner would have played it in the right hand by turning the wrist back and forth, making the pair of leather clappers attached to it swing against the drum to create a rhythmic beat, the fading sound of which (like the *ghanta*) signifies *shunyata* or the empty, impermanent nature of all things.[135] In Hindu Tantric iconography in medieval India (see Chapter 1, figs. 12, 14 and 15) the *damaru* was an attribute of Shiva (and of his fierce manifestation as Bhairava), which he uses to drum the universe cyclically into creation, dissolution and re-creation.

Just as the skulls used to create ritual vessels are said to vary in their individual qualities, so too do those used for *damarus*. According to some

Tibetan sources, ideally the crania of a boy and girl (both around sixteen years of age) are combined, their potent vitality articulating male/female unity.[136] However, since skulls meeting these specific requirements could be difficult to acquire, abandoned ones found in the charnel ground were also used. Practitioners often directed that their skulls or other bones be donated to a lama or monastery after their death so that they might continue to accrue spiritual merit in the next life, ultimately bringing them closer to enlightenment.[137]

The Belgian-French explorer and writer Alexandra David-Néel, who visited Tibet incognito in 1924, witnessed the Chöd practice performed by a lama and described it as 'a macabre banquet' in which the practitioner:

> 'tramples down' all passions and crucifies his selfishness (…) The kangling in his left hand, the damaru lifted high in the right and bearing an aggressive staccato, the man stood in a challenging attitude, as if defying some invisible enemy (…) Then he began the ritualistic dance, turning successively towards the four quarters, reciting 'I trample down the demon of pride, the demon of anger, the demon of lust, the demon of stupidity.'[138]

Machig Labdron recommends carrying out the Chöd practice at night in a deserted and frightening place, such as a charnel ground, in order to directly confront the limitations of one's fear and to conquer it.[139] Fearlessness demanded the annihilation of self-grasping and the cultivation of compassion towards all things, including seemingly hostile conditions. In her *Great Collection of the Teachings on the Noble Practice of Severing the Demons* (Tibetan: *Gcod bka' tshoms chen mo'i sa bcad*) she advises:

> One cannot attain liberation
> by means of soothing and pleasing antidotes.
> Wander in grisly places and mountain retreats,
> do not let yourself get distracted
> by doctrines or books:
> no spiritual power can come from them.
> So, just get real experiences
> in horrid, desolate places.[140]

The goal of Chöd is to sever and dismember all ties to the idea of a fixed self that creates dichotomizing feelings – such as fear and desire, or attraction and aversion – which bolster internal obstacles of greed, anger and ignorance.[141] The demonic beings that are invoked to feast upon one's own corpse are symbolic projections of the Tantrika's restless mind. She continues:

The root of all demons is one's own mind.
If one feels attraction and desire
in the perception of any phenomenon,
one is captured by the demons. (…)
As form is empty in its nature,
do not feel attachment to it
but meditate on the emptiness. (…)
Eliminating one's own pride and ego-clinging
one pacifies the demons![142]

Machig Labdron remains an iconic cultural figure, not only among practitioners of Chöd but also in the popular Tibetan imagination. In 2019

**Fig. 122**
*Thangka* depicting Machig
Labdron, Arvind Tenzin Negi
Manali, Himachal Pradesh, India
2019
Pigment on cloth, 136 × 85 ×
95 cm
British Museum 2019,3028.1

**Fig. 123**
Arvind Tenzin Negi painting
*thangka* of Machig Labdron
commissioned by the
British Museum
2019

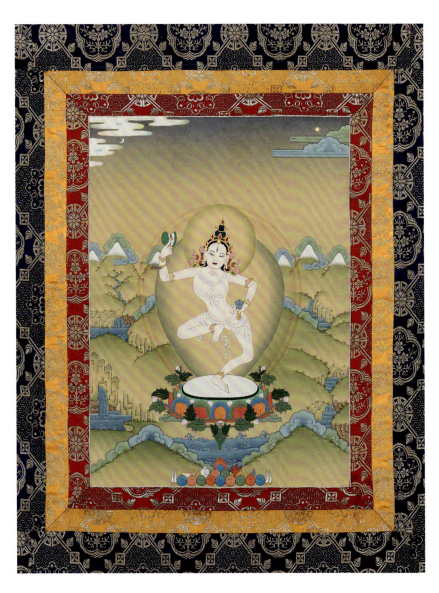

**Fig. 124**
*Rus gyan*
Tibet (acquired in Sikkim)
19th century
Human bone, 100.6 cm
(along waist)
British Museum 1911,0616.1

the British Museum commissioned a contemporary *thangka* of her by the Tibetan painter Arvind Tenzin Negi, who is based in the Himalayan town of Manali (Himachal Pradesh) (figs. 122, 123). Negi follows traditional techniques (including the use of pigments ground from minerals) and modes of representing divine figures that go back centuries in Tibet. This continuity of tradition is believed to make the image more powerful.[143] In Negi's *thangka* a crowned Machig Labdron dances on a lotus pedestal in a celestial landscape, holding the *damaru* and *ghanta*, the sun and moon rising above her. She is represented as a Dakini, in line with the Tantric blurring of mortal and divine identities, as seen in portrayals of Yoginis as goddesses (see Chapter 1) and yoginis as female practitioners of yoga (see Chapter 2).

Machig Labdron is shown wearing a delicate, net-like skirt or apron made of human bone (Tibetan: *rus gyan*). Versions of these garments, such as the 19th-century example shown here (fig. 124) were made from the bones of deceased lamas and bones found in charnel grounds, with the occasional addition of animal bones if human ones were unavailable. The only surviving early examples are Tibetan and Nepalese. They were accompanied by other ritual bone ornaments, including a crown, chest piece, bracelets,

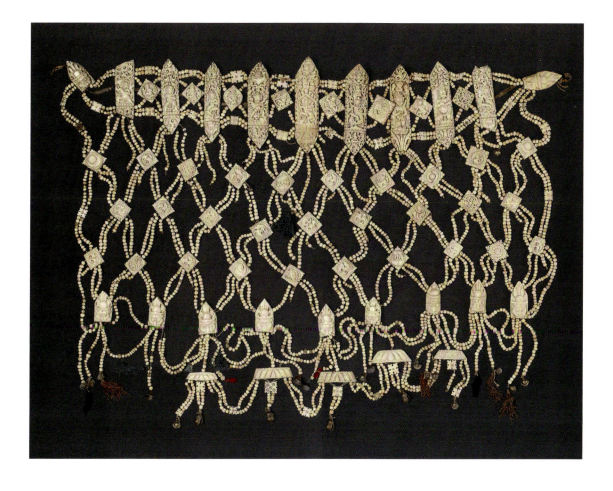

armlets and anklets. Together, the six ornaments symbolize the six Buddhist perfections (*paramitas*) necessary for attaining Buddhahood: patience, charity, meditation, mental discipline, perseverance and transcendent insight.[144]

Bone aprons such as these may have decorated life-size sculptures of deities, although they were generally worn by Tibetan monks and lamas during public festivals and ceremonies, including masked dances (Cham) in which the performers meditated on and transformed themselves into Dakinis, Yidams and Dharmapalas (fig. 125).[145] Cham dances, performed at monasteries in Tibet for lay audiences, re-enacted dramatic stories such as the arrival of Tantric Buddhism in Tibet from India and the defeat of demonic forces by Mahasiddhas. In the 17th century Ngagwang Lobzang Gyatso, the Fifth Dalai Lama and head of the Gelug order (1617–1682), who established a theocratic state centred around the Potala Palace in Lhasa, made Cham a regular public ritual.[146] In his manual on the ritual dance, he described its power to generate merit for all those watching and, above all, to expel negative hindrances: 'by making just one step of this dance, the hordes of devils are cut to pieces'.[147] By the 20th century Cham was being performed across all major Tibetan and Himalayan monasteries, including those in Sikkim and Bhutan.[148]

The 19th-century bone apron shown earlier (fig. 124) was acquired in Sikkim. A close-up view reveals the intricacy of the carving (fig. 126). The top belt section features alternating plaques depicting Dakinis, Dharmapalas and embracing *yab-yum* deities, supporting networks of smaller ones that hang like an apron in front of the wearer, with bells attached to the bottom. The images carved onto the plaques vary from Tantric deities and *apsaras* (celestial nymphs) to decorative floral patterns and auspicious symbols such as lion heads known as *kirtimukha* ('face of glory').[149]

This bone apron was collected by John Claude White, Political Officer for Sikkim between 1889 to 1908. He had also been part of the British military invasion of Tibet (1903–4) led by Francis Younghusband, which

**Fig. 125**
**Dance of the Sixteen Dakinis (*Rigma Chudrug Cham*) performed at the Kurjey Tshechu festival**
Bumthang, Bhutan
2016
This Cham dance is performed as an offering to Padmasambhava. The dancers' bone aprons are made from yak rather than human bone.

**Fig. 126**
Detail of fig. 124, showing plaques of carved human bone from a *rus gyan* with representations of embracing *yab-yum* deities (left) and a dancing Dakini (right)

aimed to challenge Russia's perceived ambitions in the region. In his memoir, White describes an inspection tour of Talung Monastery in Sikkim in 1891 where he was shown bone aprons:

> Here is preserved (…) some splendid specimens of 'Rugen' (apron, breastplate, circlet and armlets), exquisitely carved from human bones (…). All these treasures were produced for my inspection and examination (…) and were then most carefully put away and re-sealed, but before this was done some of the lamas put on the old dresses, to enable me to see them to greater advantage.[150]

Several photographs survive of the lamas who posed for White dressed in the bone aprons (fig. 127). These images were taken by Theodore Hoffman (of Johnston & Hoffman, an India-based photographic studio used regularly by the British government). White acquired the bone apron, which is now at the British Museum, in Sikkim but it is unclear how or from where. In the same memoir he describes Talung Monastery's collection of 'ritualistic paraphernalia' as being kept 'intact' with a 'carefully scrutinized' inventory, which would suggest that it remained

Fig. 127
**Lamas from Talung monastery pose wearing bone aprons and ceremonial dress for John Claude White, photograph by Theodore Hoffman**
Sikkim, India
1891

**Fig. 128**
**Detail of a *rus gyan***
**collected by Ignatius**
**Valentine Chirol**
Tibet
19th century
Human bone, glass and silk,
77 × 60.5 × 3.1 cm
British Museum 1930,0306.1
Donated by Sir Robert Greg

so after his visit and that this apron did not come from Talung, although we cannot be certain about this.[151]

A second 19th-century Tibetan *rus gyan* (fig. 128), acquired by the British diplomat Ignatius Valentine Chirol, was described as a 'Necromancer's bone apron' in *The British Museum Quarterly* (1930), associating it with black magic and the summoning of the dead: 'Aprons of this description (…) are worn as part of the equipment of sorcerers and priests of the unreformed sects of Lamaism when exorcizing the demons of death and disease; and in this connexion the figures and symbols represented on the carved plaquettes have magical significance'.[152] Tantric Buddhist belief in Tibet was often misunderstood by the British to be associated with black magic, fuelled by seeing bone aprons and Cham dances featuring monks dressed as the skeletal Smasahana Adipati ('Lords of the Charnel Ground'), which inspired morbid fascination.[153] Many 19th- and early 20th-century descriptions of the performance often referred to it as 'devil-dancing'.[154] Such stereotyping will be discussed in further detail in the following chapter, which will explore how Tantra was interpreted as India's 'darkest heart' by colonial officials and Christian missionaries stationed in 19th-century Bengal.

CHAPTER 4

# TANTRA AND REVOLUTION IN COLONIAL INDIA

Bengal in eastern India was an early centre of Tantra as well as the nucleus of British rule between the 18th and early 20th centuries. The Mughal Emperor Shah Alam had been forced to hand over Bengal, Bihar and Orissa to the East India Company officer Robert Clive after the Battle of Buxar in 1764, marking a critical moment in the British rise to power. The Company (a British trading organization founded in 1600) had by this time taken control of vast areas of India to expand its business interests as well as to extend colonial rule. Following an uprising in 1857, however, power was transferred from the Company to the British government. Throughout this period, Tantra informed the way many colonial officials, Orientalist scholars and Christian missionaries imagined India, as a subcontinent apparently corrupted by idolatry, black magic and sexual debauchery. This was embodied most vividly by the seemingly demonic and lascivious figure of the Tantric goddess Kali, whose widespread public worship in Bengal reached its height from the 18th century, during a period of disastrous economic and political crises. This chapter explores the ways in which Kali and other Tantric goddesses were harnessed by Indian revolutionaries as manifestations of Mother India precisely because they represented a threat in the colonial imagination, and ends by examining the impact that 19th-century Bengali mystics had on the popularization of Tantra.

Fig. 129
Map showing territory in
South Asia under direct
British rule in 1857

Territory under direct
British rule in 1857

## KALI: BENGAL'S 'CRAZY MOTHER'

Eastern India had been a central region for the development and rise
of Tantra. In Bengal, a heartland of Shaktism, one of the most popular
deities remains the Tantric Hindu goddess Kali ('Black' in Sanskrit),
associated with the creative and destructive nature of time. In the *Devi
Mahatmya* (*c.* 400–600 CE), Kali bursts forth from Durga's brow and devours
her enemies on the battlefield.[1] She is identified with Chamunda (see
Chapter 1) and is the form whom the goddess assumes before her defeat
of Chanda and Munda:

> Picking up the heads of Chanda and Munda, Kali approached
> Chandika [Durga] (…) 'Here, as a present from me to you, are
> Chanda and Munda, two beasts slain in the sacrifice of battle'.
> (…) The beautiful [Durga] spoke these playful words to Kali:
> 'Because you have seized Chanda and Munda and brought them
> here, you will henceforth be known in the world as the Goddess
> "Chamunda"'.[2]

Kali and Chamunda share similar iconographic traits, yet they are also
described and venerated as independent figures.[3] The image of the goddess

**Fig. 130**
**Kali** *yantra*
Bengal, India
Late 19th century
Painted cotton, 92 × 92 cm
British Museum 1994,0517,0.1

in her form as Kali assumed a new vitality in modern Bengal, stressing both her erotic potential and her battle-hungry characteristics.

A late 19th-century painted *yantra* dedicated to Kali (fig. 130) was probably once used to meditate on and invoke her. It is highly unusual because of its large size and its figurative details within the geometric composition. As in other Kali *yantras*, there are five downward triangles (representing the *yoni* or vulva) within an eight-petalled lotus, the central point evoking Kali herself. While other *yantras* typically present abstract shapes, here each side of the five triangles is imagined as an outstretched manifestation of the goddess; there are fifteen in total, each brandishing a bloodied sword and skull-cup, their faces full of individual character. Each of the eight petals is inhabited by a Matrika. Although there are usually seven Matrikas, an eighth is sometimes included, here the lion-headed Narasimhi. Four protective gods – Shiva, Ganesha, Vishnu and Skanda – are situated at the four corners of the *yantra*. The outer square includes four gaps or gateways indicating the cardinal directions, which invite devotees to visualize themselves entering the sacred space of the *yantra*, initially encountering the peripheral gods and goddesses before uniting with Kali at the centre.

At the centre of the *yantra* (fig. 131) Kali provocatively straddles and performs intercourse with Bhairava, who lies on top of Shiva (of whom he

Fig. 131
Detail of fig. 130, showing
Kali astride Bhairava, Shiva
and a corpse

is the ferocious manifestation). Shiva in turn lies on a corpse that is burning on a pyre. This layering of bodies suggests a cosmic hierarchy in which Kali functions as the supreme creative force (Shakti), while Bhairava and Shiva provide a foundational support. Bhairava is Shiva's most powerful Tantric form, and the corpse is a signifier of the cremation ground that Bhairava himself embodies (see Chapter 1). As discussed in Chapter 1, medieval Indian representations of Tantric sex could be distinguished from other erotic imagery in temple statuary by their depiction of transgressive acts (such as *rajapana*, the drinking of female discharge). This 19th-century *yantra* similarly depicts a subversive sexual rite, that of *viparita-rata* or 'reverse' sexual posture, with Kali on top, further elevating her authority and suggesting a deliberate inversion of hierarchical order. The significance of this position will be discussed again later in the chapter. The interplay of erotic and macabre imagery at the centre of this *yantra* also reflects the visual rhetoric seen in Tantric Buddhist *yab-yum* figures (see Chapter 3), suggesting not only the inseparability of sex and death at the heart of human experience but also a transcendence of dualistic categories.

Although Kali plays an important role in the *Devi Mahatmya*, and her manifestation as Chamunda received veneration in temples during the medieval period in eastern India, it was only in 18th-century Bengal that her popular worship gained momentum. Kali was heralded as a ruthless yet compassionate Mother and protectress by Ramprasad Sen (*c.* 1718–1775), a famous Bengali mystic and poet who popularized and transformed her into a benevolent and nurturing, simultaneously all-powerful, object of devotion.[4] His 'softening' of this Tantric goddess – to all appearances horrifying and bloodthirsty but in reality charged with compassion – made her accessible to a wider audience.

In a 20th-century print, Ramprasad is shown striding along a path, singing songs about Kali with his one-stringed *ektara*, followed closely by the goddess herself, as though he has attracted her with the power of his devotion (fig. 132). The Bengali text forming a halo around his head reads: 'Chanting the name of Kali Ma [Mother], I will keep beating my drum'. The sword of knowledge she carries symbolizes the death of the ego, represented by the garland of severed heads, through the transformative destruction of ignorance. She also carries a decapitated head and wears a girdle of dismembered hands. The trail of red footprints initially look bloodied, but could instead represent the red dye (*alta*) traditionally used to adorn married women's feet in Bengal, suggesting that she and Ramprasad are symbolically wedded. Indeed, Ramprasad's poetry describes his lover–beloved relationship with Kali in terms of euphoric union and the pangs of separation:

> She's playing in my heart.
> Whatever I think, I think Her name.
> I close my eyes and She's in there
> Garlanded with human heads.
> Common sense, know-how – gone.
> So they say I'm crazy. Let them.
> All I ask, my crazy Mother,
> Is that You stay put.
> Ramprasad cries out: Mother, don't
> Reject this lotus heart You live in,
> Don't despise this human offering
> At Your feet.[5]

By presenting himself as a 'human offering' at the feet of Kali in this verse, Ramprasad is surrendering himself entirely to the goddess. His admission of craziness also recalls the role of madness as a strategic means to commune with the divine and to reject social conventions, as practised by the Kapalikas and Nayanars (see Chapter 1), as well as the Mahasiddhas (see Chapter 3).

It is said that one evening in 1758 Ramprasad was overheard singing by the Maharaja of Nadia, Krishnachandra Ray (r. 1728–1782), who invited him to be his esteemed court poet.[6] Ramprasad's poetry resonated at a time

**Fig. 132**

**Ramprasad Sen and the goddess Kali, signed P. Chakraborty**

Bengal, India
20th century
Chromolithograph, 34.5 ×
28 cm
British Museum 2019,3030.1

**Fig. 133**

**The death of Ramprasad Sen, signed Kartik Das**

Bengal, India
20th century
Chromolithograph, 34.5 ×
28 cm
British Museum 2019,3030.2

when Bengal was experiencing political and economic crises, from Maratha invasions to the rise of the British East India Company. The latter raised land taxes when crops in the region failed (transferring the accumulated wealth back to Britain), resulting in the disastrous Bengal famine of 1770, which led to the deaths of over a million people and the disappearance of almost one-third of the region's population.[7] Amidst this turmoil, devotion to Kali as a mighty saviour and icon of strength increased, promoted through poetry, song and public festivals. The annual autumnal Kali Puja ('Kali Worship') festivals were spearheaded and promoted by Krishnachandra Ray, and are still celebrated in the region today.[8]

In 1775, at the end of the Kali Puja festival, Ramprasad is said to have waded into the river at Halisahar (the village where he was born), carrying an icon of Kali above his head, visible in the foreground of another modern print (fig. 133). He then immersed both the icon and himself in the water, at which point he experienced supreme bliss and divine union with Kali before dying.[9] In the print he is shown being cradled like a child by the goddess on a lotus. On the bottom right the accompanying text reads: 'Laying on Ma's [Mother's] lap, Ramprasad pleads, "I was born here, let me die here as well."'

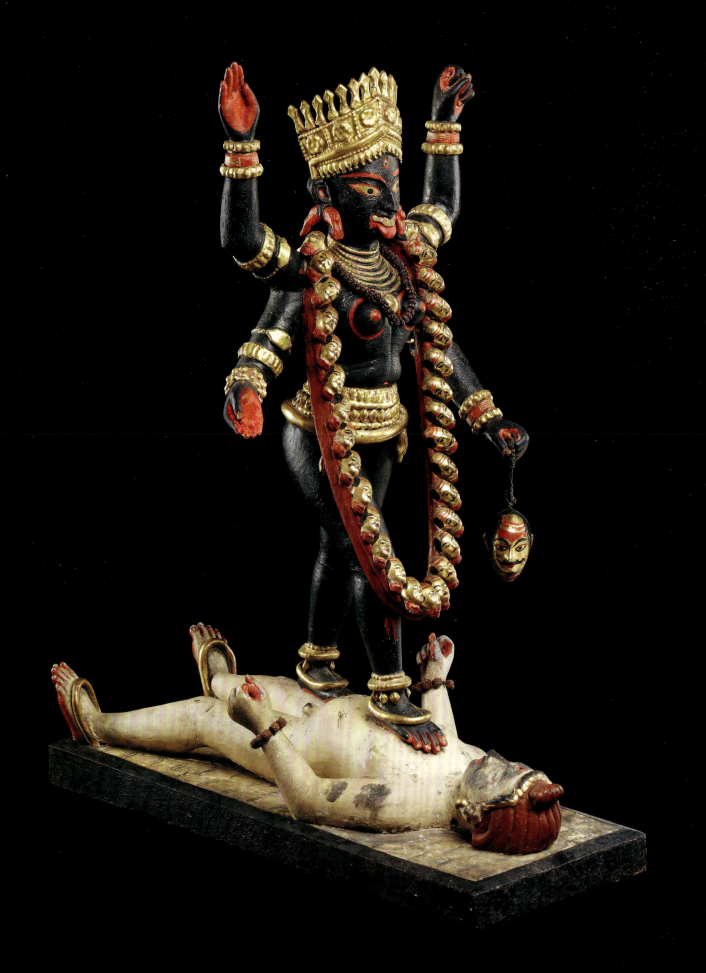

A late 19th-century figure of Kali made of painted and gilded clay (fig. 134) is similar to the one carried by Ramprasad and was probably produced in Krishnanagar where craftsmen made images like this to adorn the temporary shrines (*pandals*) for the festival.[10] The goddess is regally crowned and wears earrings made from corpses. Her mouth is smeared with blood and she sticks out her tongue as though thirsting for more. In the *Devi Mahatmya* she is described as having a 'widely gaping mouth, terrifying with its lolling tongue (…) that filled the directions with roars', and with which she 'devoured the forces of the enemies of the gods'.[11] Her erotic potential is highlighted by her full breasts. Her top left hand may have once held a sword while her top right hand displays the gesture of fearlessness, to reassure and protect devotees. The articulation of her creative and destructive aspects reflects her embodiment of the rhythm of the cosmos, which is created and then destroyed, only to be re-created according to the Hindu concept of time as cyclical. Her fierce appearance invites submissive surrender by her devotees.

Medieval Indian images of Chamunda depict her sitting or dancing on a corpse that is being gnawed on by jackals or pecked at by vultures, suggesting her use of the body as a *vahana* or vehicle (see Chapter 1, fig. 26). The corpse in these sculptures evoked the practice of *shava sadhana* for attaining a range of powers and benefits, as discussed in Chapter 1. The Buddhist Yidam Chakrasamvara was similarly depicted trampling a corpse-like Bhairava (see fig. 20), symbolizing both the destruction of the ego and the superiority of the Buddhist Vajrayana tradition, reflecting competition between Tantric Hindu and Buddhist institutions during the medieval period. In the later images of Kali, the cadaver has evolved into the supine, corpse-like god Shiva, who is also often described as her husband. According to Tantric belief, existence itself results from the erotic union between Shakti as creative force or *prakriti* (embodied here by Kali) and Shiva as pure consciousness (*purusha*).[12] The iconography of Kali striding over Shiva articulates her superiority, as without her he would remain inert and the universe would perish. Without Shakti, Shiva is literally a *shava* or corpse, emphasized by his deathly pallor. Indeed, in the *Brihannila Tantra* (*c.* 17th century) Shiva declares 'Without you, O great Goddess, I am the corpse'.[13] Despite this apparent transformation in the conception of the cadaver that Kali dominates, the echoes of the *shava sadhana* practice remain and some Tantric texts even make the association between the corpse and Shiva (or Bhairava) explicit. The *Brihat Tantrasara*, a 16th-century Tantric manual of ritual and iconography composed in Bengal by the Tantrika and Kali devotee Krishnananda Agamavagisha, includes a description of the rite involving a corpse and instructs the practitioner to 'offer the corpse flowers and make obeisance to it saying: "You are the lord of all heroic persons, (…)

you are the form of Ananda [Blissful] Bhairava, and you are the seat of the goddess'".[14] The text notes that appeasement of the corpse as an embodiment of the god will result in the attainment of all the practitioner desires, including magical powers.

## KALI AND COLONIAL ANXIETY

In 1698 the East India Company had bought three villages in Bengal (Kalikata, Sutanuti and Gobindapur) which were expanded and developed into the city of Calcutta (probably an anglicized spelling of Kalikata, named after Kali; it is now officially called Kolkata). The city was not only a nexus of British power but also a centre for her worship.[15]

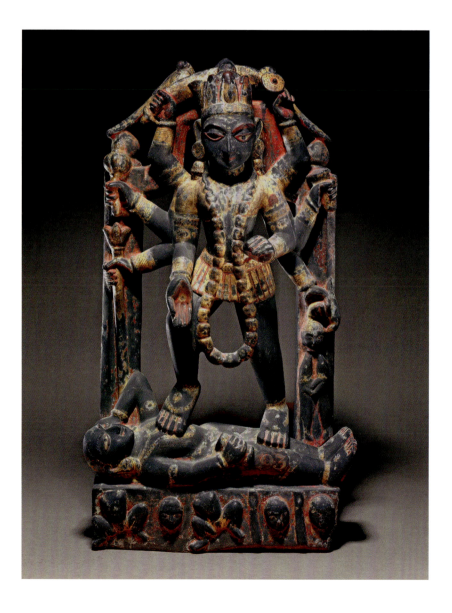

Fig. 135
Kali
Bengal, India
18th century
Black stone with red and gold paint, 71.0 × 41.5 cm
British Museum 1872,0701.69
Donated by John Bridge and his nieces Fanny Bridge and Edgar Baker

An 18th-century sculpture from Bengal of an eight-armed Kali, with remnants of red and gold paint (fig. 135), was acquired by Major-General Charles Stuart (1757/8–1828), a Company officer from Ireland who settled in Calcutta and lived there until his death. An unconventional military man, in his published writings he praised the country and its traditions, criticizing Christian missionaries and the notion that the West was morally superior.[16] In a pamphlet entitled *The Vindication of the Hindoos* (published anonymously in 1808), Stuart recounted an incident in 1806 when an Indian man who had converted to Christianity was sent by missionaries to Kalighat, Kali's principal temple in Calcutta. There he 'began to harangue the crowd, condemning their idolatry, their worship, and their sacrifices'.[17] Describing how the man was chased away, Stuart instructed his readers to 'leave the Hindoos in the undisturbed possession of their altars and their Gods'.[18]

Not only did Stuart collect sculptures of deities, which he displayed in his house-cum-museum, he was also said to worship them, though we do not know whether he did so with the Kali sculpture. Over a hundred of Stuart's Indian sculptures entered the British Museum's collection in 1872, including representations of Durga (fig. 22), Chamunda (figs. 26, 28, 29) and Varahi (fig. 25), as well as a *linga-yoni* (fig. 40).[19] One disapproving officer observed that 'Incredible as it may sound, there is at this moment a British general in the Company's service, who observes all the customs of the Hindoos, makes offerings at their temples, carries about their idols with him (…). He is not treated as a madman, but would not perhaps be misplaced if he had his idols (…) in some corner of Bedlam'.[20] His enthusiasm in adopting Indian customs led to him being called Charles 'Hindoo' Stuart.

A friend of Stuart's, the Company soldier Major Edward Moor, also collected images of deities, especially Hindu bronzes, of which over three hundred are now in the British Museum's collection. He went on to write *The Hindu Pantheon* (1810), which was one of the first encyclopaedic studies of Hindu mythology and imagery for a Western audience. It contained over a hundred plates, engraved mainly by John Dadley and William Raddon from line drawings made by Moses and/or Matthew Haughton. 'Plate 27' represented Kali (fig. 136).[21] Describing the image, Moor noted that

> Kali is said to assume this form to frighten sinners into repentance and virtue: her attitude seems a chasing one, put on to cause immediate terror (…) immense teeth and tusks are fixed in her lipless gums (…). The cast, however disgusting to the eye, is far from being devoid of merit: our engraving is taken from an exact portrait, and exhibits considerable expression.[22]

Moor invites the reader to imagine the feelings that such an image of Kali would have inspired:

**Fig. 136**
**Kali, Plate 27 from Edward
Moor's *The Hindu Pantheon*
(1810), Matthew Haughton
and/or Moses Haughton
the Younger (draughtsmen);
engraved by John Dadley**
London
Etching on wove paper; 31.5
× 25 cm
Publisher: Joseph Johnson;
printer: Thomas Bensley
British Museum 1940,0716.32

> Let the reader picture to himself (…) this 'goddess of horrid form' (…)
> of gigantic proportions, smeared with blood, among the ravings of
> bedlamites (…) and imagine what effect it must have on the timid minds
> of the trembling affrighted multitude, and what a hold such a religion
> must have on the sensibilities of its votaries.[23]

This projection of Kali as an all-powerful demonic goddess captured the
public's imagination back in London, inspiring a combination of curiosity
and aversion. The artist and poet William Blake (1757–1827) obtained a
copy of *The Hindu Pantheon* and used some of the illustrations as source
material for his own works, including Plate 27, which he revealingly drew
on in his vision of 'Lucifer' or Satan in an 1824 series of watercolours
illustrating Dante Alighieri's *Divine Comedy* (fig. 137).[24]

Indian artists who had previously worked for Mughal and Rajput
patrons now responded to British demand for illustrations of gods.

**Fig. 137**
**'Lucifer', Illustration for
Dante's *Divine Comedy*,
William Blake**
London
1824
Ink and watercolour over
pencil and black chalk,
52.7 × 37.2 cm (sheet)
National Gallery of Victoria,
Melbourne Butlin 812.69

They adopted Western pictorial conventions for their new clientele, such as linear perspective and realism, which were executed in a distinctively Indian mode that became known as the 'Company School' style of painting. In an early 19th-century Company painting that illustrates a Tantric goddess through a Western lens and aesthetic sensibility (fig. 138), the detached, almost forensic attention to gruesome detail transforms her into a virtual portrait rather than an icon, to the extent that it suggests a mortal woman in costume posing for the artist. The painting represents Kalaratri (identified with Kali). With her four arms she holds a sword, a cleaver, a skull-cup filled with blood and a severed head, the blood from its neck pooling on the ground. She is adorned with a long necklace of skulls and a cobra. Her teeth are pronounced and her unbound hair suggests dissolution and excess, in contrast with the hair of other goddesses, which is often braided, tied or neatly presented, symbolic of cosmic order.[25]

CalratriDevi.

**Fig. 138**
**Kalaratri**
Patna, Bihar, India
Early 19th century
Gouache on paper, 28.9 ×
23.9 cm
British Museum 1880,0.2024

Although there are Western commentaries on Tantric material
and practices dating back to the earliest European presence in India,
particularly from the 17th century onwards, the earliest Western reference
to the *Tantras* as a group of texts was a brief mention by the British
philologist William Jones, who worked as a judge in Bengal, in his *Asiatick
Researches* journal in 1790.[26] While the Company had generally avoided
interfering with local Indian traditions, this changed from around the early
19th century onwards under the influence of Christian evangelicals who
came to India to carry out missionary work.[27] As Kali's worship gained
momentum, many missionaries were scandalized by her, reductively
perceiving her as a symbol of India's depravity.

Western descriptions of Kali by the 19th century centred on her
bloodthirsty appearance as well as the threat of her sexual dominance.
Simultaneously, more detailed discussions of the *Tantras* began to be
published, particularly by missionaries who emphasized and misunderstood
their sexual and transgressive references. With few exceptions, Tantra
informed how they imagined India itself, as a subcontinent tainted by
irrationality, idolatry, sorcery and sexual degeneracy, in contrast with

Britain's apparent scientific and rational spirit of progress.[28] Accordingly, the Indian population was believed to require redemption and regulation through colonial rule.

In 1817 the Reverend William Ward, from the Baptist Missionary Society in Bengal, described 'many of the *tuntras* [sic]' as containing 'directions respecting a most (…) shocking mode of worship (…). Here things too abominable to enter the ears of man, and impossible to be revealed to a Christian public, are contained'.[29] By the late 19th century the Sanskritist Monier Monier-Williams had coined the term 'Tantrism' in the singular, which he believed had corrupted Hinduism from within: 'Tantrism is Hinduism arrived at its last and worst stage of medieval development', consisting of 'sanguinary sacrifices and orgies with wine and women'.[30]

A vivid early 20th-century lithograph portrays a brazen Kali clutching the head of a demon who lies decapitated beside her right foot (fig. 139). It became one of the most popular images produced by the Ravi Varma Press, originally founded by the artist of the same name, Raja Ravi Varma (1848–1906). This lithograph was reproduced in a missionary tract published by the Bible Churchmen's Missionary Society, *Glimpses of a Land of Sun and Sadness* (1928). Its author, Beatrice M. W. Grautoff, provided the following commentary:

> 'What an awful picture!' we exclaim as we look at the ferocious figure of Kali. Yet she is honoured and worshipped by intelligent Hindus, and little children are taught to pray to her. Look at her! (…) beside her lies the body of the murdered man. Her hands and face are stained with blood and her red tongue hangs out asking for blood, more blood! (…) Yet this savage female deity is called the gentle mother! (…). I am glad I was not born a Hindu and made to believe in Siva and Kali, aren't you?[31]

A year later the print was featured as the frontispiece of *Crime and Religious Belief in India* (1929) in which the author, Augustus Somerville, captioned the image as 'Kali, the Dreaded Goddess of Destruction'.[32] Somerville linked the worship of Kali to human sacrifices and began by noting that 'Crime in India may be said to originate from three main sources. Religious controversies and practices, women and land disputes. The first two are the most prolific factors (…). To it may be traced the majority of murders, dacoities and assaults that fill our police records'.[33]

Many ritual objects associated with Kali's worship survive from colonial Bengal. She has historically received offerings including wine, blood and animal sacrifices, such as goats and buffaloes, which were ritually beheaded to pacify and nourish her. This harks back to the descriptions in the *Devi*

**Fig. 139**
**Kali, Ravi Varma Press**
India
*c.* 1910–20
Lithograph with varnish,
35.6 × 48.3 cm
The Metropolitan Museum
of Art 2013.17

*Mahatmya* of ideal offerings to Durga and the Matrikas, including flesh and
blood in exchange for the granting of wealth, power and liberation (see
Chapter 1).[34] Kalighat temple, where regular goat sacrifices were and still
are carried out, attracted fascinated and disapproving Western visitors from
the 17th century onwards.[35] The sacred *ramdao* is a sword used for animal
sacrifice, with a curved blade to ensure decapitation in a single stroke
(fig. 140). Kali herself is often depicted wielding one to slay ignorance. The
eye of the goddess is engraved on the upper part of the blade, channelling
her presence so she can preside over the ritual sacrifice. At the moment
of death, the sacrificial animals are believed to be instantly liberated from
the cycle of *samsara*, just as Durga's beheading of Mahisha is regarded
as a compassionate act.[36] The buffalo evokes Mahisha, and is an animal
regarded as impure and therefore appropriate for Tantric sacrifice,
particularly during the annual Durga Puja festival, which is celebrated

**Fig. 140**

*Ramdao*

Bengal, India

18th century

Gold and steel, 4.5 × 52.5 ×

13.5 cm

British Museum 2006,0312.1

every October across Bengal to celebrate Durga's victory over the demon.[37] Goats are more frequently sacrificed and are often offered as extensions of the devotee's own pride and base instincts, such as lust, greed and envy, to be purged by the goddess, whether Kali or Durga.[38] As a repository of the ego, the head becomes an appropriate symbol with which to appease her.

During the 19th century, many British officials believed that goats and buffaloes were not the only sacrifices being made to Kali. Simplistic colonial interpretations of violence and transgression in Tantric texts perpetuated a stereotype that Tantrikas were little more than dangerous criminals. Kali was claimed to be the presiding goddess of the so-called Thugs (gangs of bandits) and their Thuggee 'cult'.[39] Colonial officials claimed that Thugs committed ritualistic murders involving the strangling of travellers with handkerchiefs as part of their Kali-worship, a stereotype that allowed the British to impose stricter controls over the local population. Although banditry occurred as a result of socio-economic instability, worsened by colonial taxation policies, the British sensationalized Thugs as an ancient cult of stranglers devoted to Kali, who presented a threat to British authority.[40] From 1830 onwards the British administrator William Henry Sleeman dedicated himself to suppressing Thuggee, claiming to have discovered details of their perverse practices and intentions via informants: 'it is the imperious duty of the Supreme Government of this country to put an end in some way or other to this dreadful system of murder, by which thousands of human beings are now annually sacrificed upon every great road throughout India'.[41] The Reverend Alexander Duff similarly described the sinister ways of the Thugs in 1839:

> [The] Thugs, find a ready and potent protectress in Kali. To the
> divinely revealed will and command of this goddess, they universally

ascribe their origin, their institutions, their social laws, and their ritual observances. Intense devotion to Kali is the mysterious link that unites them in a bond of brotherhood that is indissoluble; and with secrecy which for generations has eluded the efforts of successive governments to detect them.[42]

In Jabalpur (central India) a reformatory was established where supposed Thugs sentenced to life imprisonment were sent and where they were asked to theatrically re-enact the stages of their attacks on travellers for visiting photographers.[43] There was a demand for such vivid re-creations and three-dimensional models of the Thugs were even made by Indian craftsmen for sale to European collectors.

**Fig. 141**
**Model depicting 'Thugs'
attacking travellers**
Chennai, Tamil Nadu, India
Early 19th century
Painted wood and textile,
21 × 78 × 53 cm
British Museum As1847,0630.6
Donated by Mrs Catherine
Horne

Two such early 19th-century Thuggee models (figs. 141, 142) are part of a set of four commissioned by Benjamin Worthy Horne (1804–1870), a coach and railway proprietor who paid 14 guineas to have them made in Madras (present-day Chennai) by a local craftsman. The four models illustrate the different stages of attack, showing Thugs strangling and killing travellers with handkerchiefs, burying the bodies and holding tools including pick-axes. It is clear that they were subsequently displayed in the Museum because in 1857 the Chaplain of Newgate Prison made a complaint about them in *The Times*. He felt they were corrupting British audiences and inspiring young men to commit crimes around London:

> I have often thought, and still think, that the origin of garrotte robberies took place from the exhibition of the way the Thugs in India strangle and plunder passengers, as exhibited in the British Museum. However valuable as illustrations of Indian manners such representations may be, I could heartily wish that these models were placed in some more obscure position, and cease to be that which I fear they have been, the means of giving to men addicted to crime and violence an idea how their evil purposes may be accomplished.[44]

Reflecting on these models today, the colonial anxieties that fed into such representations are clear. This extends to a 19th-century handkerchief donated in 1878 by James M. Foster (a surgeon stationed in Assam) which was, according to the original register, 'used by Thugs' (fig. 143).

Fig. 144
'Procession of the Hindoo
Goddess Kali', in *Narrative
of the Indian Revolt from Its
Outbreak to the Capture of
Lucknow* by Colin Campbell
(1858)
Book illustration
British Museum Asia
Department Library DS478.N3

This handkerchief reflected not only an enduring British preoccupation with all things Thuggee-related, but also the desire to document and record with the aim of controlling their colonial subjects.[45] This had taken a more extreme turn decades earlier, in 1833, when seven skulls labelled as 'Thugs' were presented to Edinburgh's Phrenological Society.[46] They belonged to Indian men who had worked as professional bandits for the local elite but were executed as hereditary Thugs by the British. When the skulls were examined by phrenologist Robert Cox he noted that, unusually, they did not seem to show the 'base sentiments' he would have expected: 'Destructiveness is not a predominant organ in any of them; and yet they were murderers. (…) but the thugs murdered obviously for the sake of robbing, (…) and also because they had been trained to this mode of life from their infancy'.[47] Fictional renderings of the Thugs even made it onto the silver screen, a memorable example being Steven Spielberg's *Indiana Jones and the Temple of Doom* (1984), in which the bandits are immortalized as a cult that engage in black magic, child slavery and human sacrifices offered to Kali.

Fears around Tantra and the figure of Kali would escalate with the rise of revolutionary movements in Bengal. The Great Rebellion of 1857 was partly a military mutiny against the East India Company; it began among Indian soldiers from the Bengal Army and soon escalated with civilian uprisings.[48] Termed the 'Indian Mutiny' by the British, it was considered by some later Indian nationalists to be India's first war of independence. Colin Campbell's publication, *Narrative of the Indian Revolt from its Outbreak to the Capture of Lucknow* (1858), featured vivid, polemical, illustrations contextualizing the uprising, including one of a 'Procession of the Hindoo Goddess Kali' (fig. 144), which suggested that Kali, as a powerful Tantric goddess, was capable of inspiring organized political violence and subversive revolt.[49] Ruminating on the 'atrocities' committed by the rebels, Campbell compared them to the Thugs, in an attempt to de-politicize the uprising:

> It is hard, indeed, to account by any means for the atrocities which have been committed over so large a portion of India. Religious fanaticism has much to do with it, of course, as may be easily imagined so far as the Hindoos are concerned, when we remember that murder is the Alpha and Omega of a certain 'religious' sect of Hindoos – the Thugs (…) a sort of religious corporation; they worship the bloodthirsty goddess Kali, whom they seek to propitiate by sacrificing in cool blood as many unoffending individuals as they can.[50]

## KALI AND THE REVOLUTIONARY IMPULSE

The 1857 rebellion ultimately led to the British government taking over direct rule of India from the Company in 1858.

At the heart of the British colonial capital of Calcutta lay Kalighat temple (fig. 145), enshrining a divinely embodied icon (*murti*) of Kali. Kalighat was acknowledged as a Tantric Shakti Pitha ('Seat of Power') from at least the 15th century, and became a famous pilgrimage site around the middle of the 18th century.[51] The present building was constructed in 1809 and consists of one large room, the *garbhagriha* ('womb-chamber') or inner sanctum, surrounded by an elevated, circumambulatory balcony.

The Kali *murti* (fig. 146), adorned with garlands of flowers, is in full view as devotees circle around it. The icon of the goddess has four hands, and a large golden tongue that is held in place by an upper row of golden teeth. During the 19th century visitors to the temple could buy prints and paintings of the goddess to take home as devotional souvenirs.

A *c.* 1895 print published by the Bengal Art Studio (located on Sarkar Lane in Calcutta) depicts the *murti* of Kali (fig. 147). In the print the eyes and tongue are made prominent, immediately identifying the *murti's* chief characteristics. The eyes were particularly important for *darshan* (sacred vision), involving seeing and being seen by the deity in a reciprocal act of 'visual communion' that imparted power.[52]

Watercolour paintings sold around the temple were made quickly to cater to high demand, resulting in a uniquely bold and simple aesthetic,

**Fig. 145**
**Kalighat temple during the**
**British colonial period**
Calcutta (Kolkata), Bengal,
India
Early 20th century
Postcard

which became known as the 'Kalighat style' of painting.[53] In one example Kali is depicted haloed and four-armed, carrying a *ramdao* and a decapitated head (fig. 148). The peak in popularity of Kalighat paintings lasted from the 1850s to the 1880s, after which prints became affordable mass-produced alternatives. For pilgrims in the 19th century, souvenirs such as paintings and prints of the goddess sold at Kalighat were powerful devotional artefacts that extended the religious experience at Calcutta's most famous temple. This further popularization of devotion to Kali, which had begun a century before, heightened the possibility for revolutionary politics in and around Calcutta, the colonial capital and centre of Bengali anti-imperialism.

Since Kali was regarded by many British officials as demonic, dangerous and a threat to the stability of the colonial enterprise, Bengali

**Fig. 146**
**Garlanded Kali *murti* (icon)**
**at Kalighat**
1980s
Photographic print on paper,
73.5 × 48 cm
British Museum 1990,0707,0.85.2

**Fig. 147**
**Kali *murti* as worshipped at**
**Kalighat, Bengal Art Studio**
Calcutta (Kolkata), Bengal,
India
*c.* 1895
Chromolithograph, 42 × 31.5 cm
British Museum 2003,1022,0.26
Funded by the Brooke Sewell
Permanent Fund

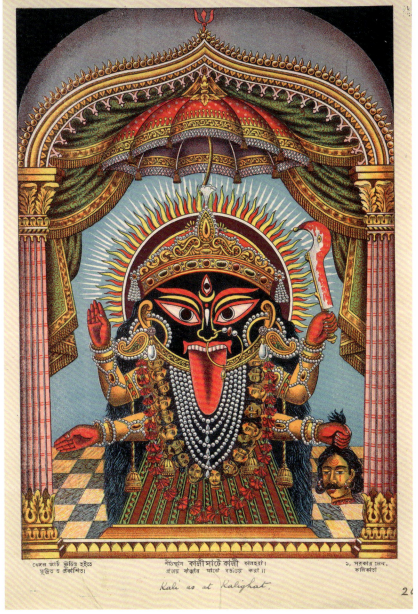

revolutionary writers and artists, for whom Kalighat became a central symbolic space, appropriated and harnessed her radical potential.[54] She was reimagined as a figurehead of resistance and a manifestation of an independent Mother India. This is evident in lithographs produced by printmakers such as the Calcutta Art Studio, established in 1878 on Bowbazar Street by Ananda Prasad Bagchi along with four art students who took over a year later. From the 1880s their most successful prints for the mass market became brightly coloured lithographs of Hindu deities and mythological scenes, which were often incorporated into domestic shrines for worship.[55]

A lithograph of Kali was produced by the Studio *c.* 1885–95 to advertise locally produced cigarettes made by the East India Cigarette

**Fig. 148**
**Kali**
Calcutta (Kolkata), Bengal,
India
Late 19th century
Gouache and silver paint on
paper, 46 × 27.5 cm
British Museum 2004,0408,0.7
Donated by Dr Achinto
Sen-Gupta

**Fig. 149**
**'Kali Cigarettes'**
**advertisement, published**
**by the Calcutta Art Studio**
Calcutta (Kolkata), Bengal,
India
*c.* 1885–95
Lithograph, 42 × 32.1 cm
British Museum 2016,3031.2

Manufacturing Company (fig. 149). Smoking these was seen as a patriotic duty, as the accompanying text suggests: 'If you care to improve the standard of goods manufactured in India, if you care about the poor, then dear Hindu brothers, please buy these (…) pure home-bred (…) Kali cigarettes'.[56] This advertisement anticipated the demands of the early 20th-century Swadeshi (self-sufficiency) movement, which called for the population to boycott British products. Different versions of the same popular image continued to circulate after 1905, the year in which Viceroy and Governor-General George Curzon ordered the partition of the province of Bengal into West Bengal (with Bihar and Orissa) and East

Printed at The Calcutta Art Studio. 185, Bowbazar Street, Calcutta.

### কালী সিগারেট।

যদি বিশুদ্ধ স্বদেশী সিগারেট ব্যবহার করিয়া খাস কাস প্রভৃতি পীড়ার আক্রমণ হইতে অব্যাহতি পাইতে চাহেন, তবে • ক • এই চিহ্ন অঙ্কিত কালী সিগারেট ব্যবহার করুন। কালী সিগারেটের তুল্য নির্দোষ সিগারেট এ পর্যন্ত আবিষ্কৃত হয় নাই।

### রূপসূ।

পুরুষবহ্নি, অমশিত, অশীর্ণ, পুরাতন সর্দি কাসি ও হাঁপানি প্রভৃতি জটিল রোগের অব্যর্থ মহৌষধ। ইউনানি শাস্ত্রানুমোদিত ব্যবহি মতিচ এই ঔষধ ব্যবহারে লক্ষ লক্ষ রোগী আরোগ্য লাভ করিয়াছেন। যিনি উপরিউক্ত রোগ সমূহে নানাবিধ ঔষধ ব্যবহার করিয়া হতাশ হইয়াছেন তিনি একবার রূপসূ ব্যবহার করিয়া দেখুন।

### কালী সিগারেট।

**বিশুদ্ধ স্বদেশী**

ইহা ইণ্ডিয়া সিগারেট ম্যানুফ্যাকচারিং কোম্পানি লিমিটেড দ্বারা প্রস্তুত।

**সোল এজেন্ট এ, এচ, জহর।**

১৭৯ নং হারিসন রোড।
কলিকাতা।

### কেশরাজ তৈল।

আসলযমে নকল লইবেন না, যদি আপনার শিরোঘূর্ণি, মস্তিষ্কের দুর্বলতা, চুলের অকাল পক্কতা, শিরঃ পীড়া প্রভৃতি পীড়া অন্য কোন কেশ তৈল ব্যবহারে আরোগ্য না হইয়া থাকে তবে ডাঃ এস, এম, ডোসেনের কেশরাজ তৈল এক লাস ব্যবহার করিয়া দেখুন! যদি সুগন্ধি মনোমুগ্ধ কর সুস্বাস্থ্যমুক্ত, মস্তিষ্ক শীতল কারক এবং সর্ববিধ শিরোরোগ নাশক কেশতৈল আপনি ব্যবহার করিতে চাহেন অথবা অতিরিক্ত মানসিক পরিশ্রমে কাতর হইয়া অন্য কোন কেশতৈলে আপনার উপকার না হয় তবে ডাঃ এস, এম, হোসেনের কেশরাজ তৈল ব্যবহার করুন।

**সোল এজেন্ট—এ, এচ, জহর।**
১৭৯ নং হারিসন রোড, কলিকাতা।

Bengal (with Assam). While the partition was purportedly carried out for administrative efficiency, weakening the growing nationalist movement in Calcutta was of equal importance. As the colonial administrator Herbert Hope Risley wrote in 1904, 'Bengal united is a power; Bengal divided will pull in different ways'.[57] The partition infuriated the Bengali intelligentsia, who recognized it as a deliberate ploy to weaken and sabotage the anti-colonial movement. Some of the initial steps to organize the revolutionaries were taken by Aurobindo Ghose (1872–1950).[58] In 1905 he published a widely read pamphlet, *Bhawani Mandir* (*The Temple of the Goddess*), in which he described his vision of India as Shakti which must be liberated by a group of politically active ascetics:

> For what is a nation? What is our mother-country? It is not a piece of earth, nor a figure of speech, nor a fiction of the mind. It is a mighty Shakti, composed of the Shaktis of all the millions of units that make up the nation.[59]

The circulation of printed media, both visual and written, was one way of fostering a collective vision and purpose. The writings of Bengali anti-colonial thinkers such as Aurobindo made extensive use of Tantric themes to promote their revolutionary activity. Kali, too, was identified as India personified, summoning her children to liberate and vindicate her. The land was also imagined as a vast cremation ground in the context of the partition, as articulated by the Bengali poet Mukunda Das (1878–1934):

> Mother, come with your fierce aspect
> Come with your awful spirits
> Come and dance on this vast cremation ground
> Which is Bharat [India].[60]

While the cremation ground is a favourite haunt of fierce Tantric deities such as Kali, here the poet gives the space politically charged resonance and suggests that its desolation mirrors India's state under colonial rule. In the Studio print for Kali Cigarettes (see fig. 149) Kali roams around a cremation ground, her foot on Shiva's chest, surrounded by body parts and wild ghoulish figures causing carnage in the background, while gods observe her from the heavens. In 1907 a version of the same print was collected for Risley, then the Director of Ethnography for India, by his assistant B. A. Gupte as part of an attempt to identify veiled, politically subversive content, which would eventually lead to the 1910 Press Act imposing censorship on a range of Indian publications deemed 'frankly seditious'.[61] In a letter to Risley, Gupte noted that 'Of those I could collect last evening, I feel that the one printed for a cigarette manufacturer is the most effective and significant'.[62]

He pointed out the 'artistically cunning "modulation" of the caste marks' on the heads adorning Kali; those without marks were understood as representing European heads.[63] He also believed that the bearded leonine figure in the top left corner of the image represented 'the symbolical British lion couchant', and that the 'decapitated red coated soldier' in the bottom right corner depicted the eventual fall of the British empire, leaving 'no doubt as to the intention of the designer'.[64] The use of decapitated heads to represent the British colonial oppressors as an obstacle destroyed by Kali would not be out of place in Tantric iconography; its language of military conquest had developed during another, earlier, period of political precariousness, as discussed in Chapter 1.

Two early 20th-century insurgent Calcutta-based groups inspired by the philosophy and symbolism of Tantra, and particularly by the violent potential of Kali, were the Anushilan Samiti and Jugantar, whose members vowed to overthrow British rule.[65] One of their textual sources of inspiration was a novel by the Bengali author Bankimchandra Chatterjee, *Anandamath* (*The Abbey of Bliss*) (1882). Set in the context of the so-called Sannyasi Rebellion in the 18th century, it was the story of a group of patriotic *sannyasis* (ascetics) fighting against the land taxes that the British raised after crops in Bengal failed.[66] The pivotal scene in the novel is set in a temple where one of the protagonists encounters icons of several goddesses who represent different 'states' of the motherland, including Kali (India's present condition as oppressed, shrouded in darkness and poverty-stricken) and Durga (symbolizing future hope in her brandishing of weapons, a demon trampled beneath her feet). In the novel, Kali and Durga are identified with the motherland, and the former is described as 'blackened and shrouded in darkness. She has been robbed of everything; that is why she is naked. And because the whole land is a burning ground, she is garlanded with skulls. And she's crushing her own [welfare] underfoot.'[67] Again, the cremation ground or 'graveyard' is equated with the ransacked subcontinent, while the trampled figure of Shiva is identified with the motherland's 'welfare'. It was up to the 'sons' of the motherland to restore her to her former glory. The novel became synonymous with the fight for Indian independence and the Calcutta Art Studio produced monochrome lithographic portraits of its author, reflecting the nationalist spirit of the time.

The Jugantar group promoted the anti-colonial cause via its polemical newspaper, *Jugantar Patrika*. In 1905 a writer for *Jugantar* called for citizens to:

> Rise up, O sons of India (…). Invoke the mother Kali. (…) The Mother is thirsting after the blood of the Feringhees [foreigners] who have bled her profusely. (…) With the close of a long era, the Feringhee Empire draws to an end, for behold! Kali rises in the East.[68]

These groups were feared by the British. Not only did this mounting anti-colonial activity lead to the 1905 partition of Bengal, it would also eventually result in the transfer of the British capital to Delhi in 1911.

In 1917 James Campbell Ker, the personal assistant to the Director of Criminal Intelligence in Delhi, published a confidential report (*Political Trouble in India, 1907–1917*) detailing the anti-colonial activities of Bengali revolutionaries and their allegiance to Kali. He was particularly disturbed by rumours surrounding their secret 'cult' rituals, believed to involve the consecration of bombs to the goddess, and quoted the *Sandhya*, a radical Bengali newspaper, which had proclaimed in May 1907:

> It is a matter of great rejoicing that an excellent kind of bomb is being manufactured. This bomb is called Kali Mai's *boma* [the bomb of Mother Kali]. (…) A son is wanted from every family who must practice the virtues of the Khatriya [Warrior]. Let them play with Kali Mai's *boma*.[69]

Ker pointedly chose an early 20th-century lithograph of the goddess printed by K. P. Hazra as the frontispiece (fig. 150). In the report he quotes Bipin Chandra Pal, an Indian independence movement activist who had described Kali's potential to readers of the *New India* newspaper in June 1907:

> The symbol of Kali may well be utilized now to arouse the dormant energies of the nation and to lead it on to realize its highest destiny through conflicts and struggles. (…) I would therefore recommend the organization of Kali Puja in every important village, every new-moon-day. (…) we have the tradition of Kali worship whenever there are epidemics and troubles in the country.[70]

Pal suggested sacrificing 108 white goats during these ceremonies to Kali in order to scare the British who were already familiar with 'one of the favourite euphemisms applied to the killing of an Englishman (…) "sacrificing a white goat to Kali"'.[71] Since the animal was perceived as representing a demonic or negative force, such a euphemism carried particular significance.[72]

In the same report Ker reproduced a print entitled *Rashtriya Jagruti (National Awakening)*, originally published in 1909 by Sridhar Waman Nagarkar in Nashik (western India) and, like the Calcutta Art Studio image, later censored (fig. 151).[73] The print depicts Durga killing the demon Mahisha, with portraits of nationalists surrounding them, including

Fig. 150
**Kali, frontispiece to James Campbell Ker,** *Political Trouble in India, 1907–1917,* **originally published by K. P. Hazra**
India
1917
Chromolithograph, 32.5 × 24 cm
The British Library T.21492

Fig. 151
*Rashtriya Jagruti (National Awakening),* **published in James Campbell Ker,** *Political Trouble in India, 1907–1917,* **originally published in 1909 by Sridhar Waman Nagarkar**
India
1917
Chromolithograph, 24.5 × 21.5 cm
The British Library T.21492

Aurobindo. The image is covered in captions revealing an anti-colonial reinterpretation of the mythological scene. Ker, citing a report made by the Inspector-General of the Central Provinces, translates the captions thus:

> Her lion or tiger is labeled 'Bahiskar' (Boycott) and is attacking the bovine monster labeled 'Pardeshi Vyapar' (Foreign Trade), (…). The demon near the severed head of the monster is labeled 'Vilayati Mal' (English Goods) (…) the same demon's head has been injured by the knife labeled 'Svavalamban' (Self-Independence). The demon being held by the hair [by the goddess] is labeled 'Desha Droha' (Disloyalty to Country).[74]

Here the warrior goddess, famous for saving the world when the gods could not, assumes the status of a Swadeshi heroine calling for the public to boycott British goods in favour of local products to punish Britain for its exploitation of India's economy. The import of machine-made thread and fabric from England, for example, had severely damaged India's textile industry.

## THE MAHAVIDYAS AND THE MOTHERLAND

Aside from Kali, one of the most powerful icons employed in Bengali revolutionary visual rhetoric was the Tantric goddess Chinnamasta ('She Whose Head is Severed'), who is revered in both the Hindu and Buddhist traditions.[75] Images of this goddess mainly date from around the 18th century onwards.[76] In a late 19th-century hand-coloured woodblock print of the goddess, made in Calcutta by an artist identified in the inscription as Lalashiu Gobin Lal (fig. 152), Chinnamasta clutches her own severed head, which animatedly drinks one of the three streams of blood spurting from her neck. The other two streams nourish her attendants, Varnini and Dakini, who offer Chinnamasta the heads of two sacrificial victims. In Chapter 3, the Mahasiddha sisters Mekhala and Kanakhala were singled out for their mastery of the Chinnamasta *sadhana* (practice), involving visualizing and identifying themselves with the goddess to enact a radical beheading of ego (see fig. 89).

The iconography of the woodblock print communicates the inseparability and interdependence of sex, life and death. Chinnamasta stands upon the copulating deities of love and desire, Kama and Rati. Rati is shown on top of Kama, which reflects the 16th-century *Brihat Tantrasara's* instruction to meditate on the deities in *viparita-rata* (the 'inverse' sexual position).[77] Rati's dominant stance not only signals the superiority of the female principle within Tantra, but also emphasizes the transgressive nature of this 'reversal' (the literal meaning of the word *viparita*) connoting an overturning of hierarchical norms.[78] The fact that Chinnamasta stands on the couple suggests that she both subjugates sexual desire and is fundamentally supported and energized by its power.[79] During the 19th century this aspect of the image would have resonated with Bengali terrorists who had taken a vow of celibacy and would have understood Chinnamasta's pose as expressing the transcendence of worldly lust. The belief that one should remain celibate until the motherland achieved independence from the British was popular during the colonial period, and was considered a form of sacrifice. The numerous secret revolutionary societies inspired by Aurobindo's vision of the *Bhawani Mandir* adhered to this practice; the retention of semen was regarded as a source of their strength.[80]

The British diplomat Ignatius Valentine Chirol (the collector of the Tibetan bone apron discussed in Chapter 3, fig. 128) commented on the circulation of Chinnamasta's printed image in his book, *Indian Unrest* (1910):

> She is represented holding in her hand her head, which has been severed from her body, whilst the blood gushing from her trunk flows into her mouth. A very popular picture of the goddess in this form

**Fig. 152**
**Chinnamasta, Lalashiu Gobin Lal**
Calcutta (Kolkata), Bengal, India
Late 19th century
Hand-coloured woodblock, 28 × 23 cm; 56 × 40.5 × 0.5 cm (with frame)
British Museum 1993,1008,0.2

চিন্নমস্তা ছিন্নমস্তীকা

লালা মিত্র গোবিন লাল কলিকাতা

কালী    তারা    ষোড়শী    ভুবনেশ্বরী    ভৈরবী

ছিন্নমস্তা    ধূমাবতী    বগলা    মাতঙ্গী    কমলা
দশমহাবিদ্যা।

*Dasa Mahavidya – The ten aspects of divine energy.*    37

has been published with a text to the effect that the great goddess as
seen therein symbolizes 'the Motherland' decapitated by the English,
but nevertheless preserving her vitality unimpaired by drinking her
own blood.[81]

Among Bengali revolutionaries the image of Chinnamasta decapitating
herself represented an ideal of heroic fearlessness and self-sacrifice.
Appropriately, the *Tantrasara* describes her invocation in rituals designed
to control, combat and conquer enemies.[82]

Chinnamasta, like Kali, is worshipped both independently and as one
of the ten Mahavidya ('Great Wisdom') goddesses. Depicted by the
Calcutta Art Studio in a *c.* 1895 lithograph (fig. 153), the Mahavidyas are,
from top left: Kali, Tara, Shodashi, Bhuvaneshvari, Bhairavi, Chinnamasta,
Dhumavati, Bagalamukhi, Matangi and Kamala. As indicated by their
iconography, evoking the cremation ground and their wild bloodthirsty
natures, they are often associated with violence and mortality in Tantric
literature.[83] The Mahavidyas are said to have emerged as manifestations

Fig. 153
**The Mahavidyas, published
by the Calcutta Art Studio,**
Calcutta (Kolkata), Bengal,
India
*c.* 1895
Chromolithograph, 41 × 30.5 cm
British Museum 2003,1022,0.37
Funded by the Brooke Sewell
Permanent Fund

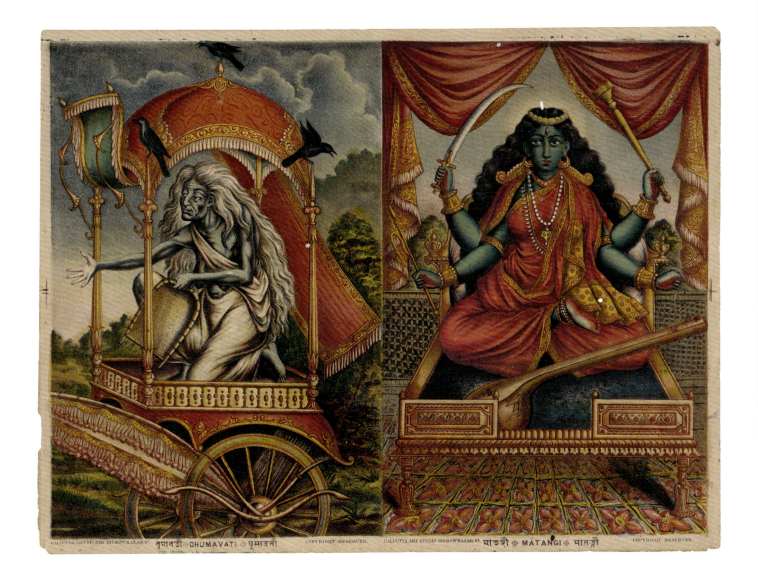

**Fig. 154**

**Dhumavati and Matangi, published by the Calcutta Art Studio**

Calcutta (Kolkata), Bengal, India

c. 1885–90

Lithograph, 29.8 × 40.3 cm

British Museum 2019,3015.1

of the goddess Sati's wrath. According to versions of the myth described in the *Brihaddharma Purana* and *Mahabhagavata Purana*, Sati's father, King Daksha, did not invite her husband, Shiva, to his *yajna*, a ceremonial sacrifice. Sati insisted on confronting Daksha but Shiva attempted to stop her. Enraged, her third eye became fiery and she metamorphosed into Kali. When a shaken Shiva attempted to escape, Sati generated all ten terrifying manifestations of herself, the Mahavidyas, who blocked his path.[84] Both *Puranas*, along with Tantric texts including the *Tantrasara*, note that the Mahavidyas grant not only enlightenment but also magical powers including the power of attraction and the ability to destroy enemies, drive them away, or immobilize them.[85]

Another Calcutta Art Studio print shows the Mahavidyas Dhumavati and Matangi (fig. 154). Matangi ('She Whose Limbs Are Intoxicated [with passion]') is an emerald-green goddess who is regarded as an embodiment of the impure. She is described as accepting inauspicious leftovers as offerings and is associated with the socially outcast, i.e. the *varna*-less class whose roles normally involve contact with pollutants.[86] She carries a noose,

Fig. 155
**Bharat Mata, D. Banerjee**
India
*c.* 1940–50
Chromolithograph, 24.7 ×
17.5 cm
Private collection

sword, goad and club and sits before a *veena* (a stringed instrument).
Dhumavati is the elderly Widow Goddess, who is accompanied by crow
companions, carrion-eating symbols of death. Unadorned, with dishevelled
hair, she is dressed in filthy white garments. Her widowhood signals her
inauspiciousness, since she does not fulfil the societal roles of wife and
mother.[87] Here she also resembles early descriptions of a deity that was
'invented' in the 19th century to personify the body of the Indian
subcontinent itself. Bharat Mata ('Mother India') first appeared as a
character in the form of a dispossessed mother in a play by Kiran Chandra
Bandyopadhyay (*Bharat Mata*, 1873) in which her condition under foreign
domination was described as bare, deprived and unkempt.[88] In an
allegorical Bengali narrative by Akshay Chandra Sarkar from the same
year, entitled *Dasamahavidya* (*The Ten Mahavidyas*), Bharat Mata is explicitly
compared to the Widow Goddess:

Bharat Mata is now Dhumabati [sic] – the widow. In her state of widowhood, she lacks food to nourish her body and clothes to cover herself. Her hair is rough from the lack of oil and unkempt. She has lost her teeth and suffering has made her gaze intense and piercing.[89]

It is clear, however, that Dhumavati is not as frail as she looks; Tantric texts such as the 19th-century *Shakta Pramoda* by Devanandanasimha of Muzaffarpur (Bihar, eastern India) describe her as ferocious and capable of destroying enemies and demons with fire radiating out of her furious eyes.[90]

The map of India began appearing in patriotic 'bodyscapes' of Bharat Mata from at least 1907, and especially after the 1930s when she was frequently superimposed upon it.[91] In these later images she is no longer imagined as a haggard figure in tattered garments but instead as an idealized young woman, usually portrayed in a *sari*, wielding a flag of India and/or superimposed on a cartographic outline of the country, as in an image signed by D. Banerjee dating to the 1940s (fig. 155). Here the land is no longer visualized as a cremation ground, but as the body of the goddess herself, giving visual expression to Aurobindo's description of the 'mother-country' as a 'mighty Shakti'.[92] Bharat Mata wields a flag supported by Shiva's trident and, in an interesting twist on Tantric iconography, she wears a garland of heads, not of her victims but of famous leaders of the Indian independence movement: Mohandas Karamchand Gandhi (1869–1948), Bal Gangadhar Tilak (1856–1920), Motilal Nehru (1861–1931), Chittaranjan Das (1869–1925) and Lala Lajpat Rai (1865–1928).[93] Their presence here both empowers the goddess and suggests their willingness to sacrifice their lives for the motherland.

## TANTRIC MASTERS AND THE TAMING OF A TRADITION

Almost a century after Ramprasad Sen's death, the charismatic Tantric master Bamakhepa (1837–1911) captured the Bengali popular imagination and consequently became a symbol of devotion. He resided near Tarapith temple, around 200 km (125 miles) from Calcutta in the district of Birbhum. Like Kalighat, Tarapith temple is regarded as a Shakti Pitha. Bamakhepa spent most of his time in its adjoining cremation ground, naked and intoxicated with *bhang* and liquor, which he drank from a skull.[94] His rejection of distinctions between pure and impure foods led him to consume flesh taken from the mouths of the dogs that followed him everywhere, while his meditations on corpses (*shava sadhana*) were said to grant him *siddhis*, including miraculous healing powers and the ability to raise the dead.[95]

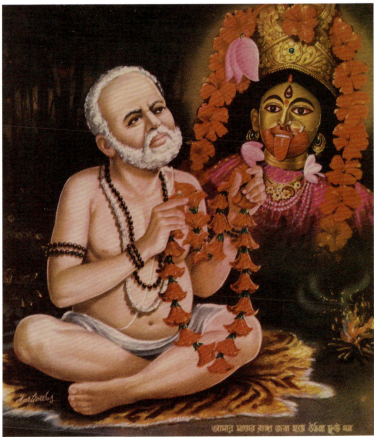

Bamakhepa's biographers stress his intimate relationship with Tarapith temple's resident deity: the inner sanctum enshrines a 1 m (3 ft) tall metal *murti* of Tara, a Mahavidya closely associated with death and destruction (fig. 156).[96] Today Tarapith has become a popular centre of devotional worship. Devotees approach the *murti* as a benign matriarch, offering her food, incense and, in keeping with her Tantric nature, alcohol.

In a modern print Bamakhepa is shown, sitting cross-legged on a tiger skin, offering a garland of flowers to the *murti* (fig. 157). In the accompanying Bengali caption he declares: 'My heart has opened up like my Mother's red hibiscus'. Tara wears a large, ornate crown and has a long, protruding tongue; her mouth is smeared with red pigment (*sindoor*), resembling blood. In the tenth-century *Mundamala Tantra* she is called 'She Who is Smeared with Blood' and 'She Who Enjoys Blood Sacrifice'.[97] Bamakhepa came to be regarded as a holy intercessor between devotees and Tara. His relationship with the goddess led to him consuming offerings left for the *murti*, before they had been dedicated to her, which prompted castigations from the temple's more orthodox Hindu priests.[98] Eating the *murti*'s offerings was an intentionally subversive gesture that articulated the intimacy of their relationship as Divine Mother and adoring son. It is said that in 1863 Bamakhepa was granted a vision of Tara in her capacity as ferocious destroyer and benign creator: he saw a 'demoness' with long teeth and fiery eyes, dancing on a burning corpse and wearing a tiger skin and

Fig. 156 (above left)
*Murti* (icon) of Tara in the inner sanctum of Tarapith temple
Birbhum, Bengal, India
2012
Author's photograph

Fig. 157 (above right)
Bamakhepa and Tara, signed Kartik Das
Bengal, India
20th century
Chromolithograph, 34.5 × 28 cm
British Museum 2019,3030.3

snake ornaments. Affectionately, she lifted him up and took him on her lap, and he lost consciousness as she took him to her breast.[99]

Though there is no evidence that Bamakhepa was directly involved in revolutionary politics, one of his disciples was. Tarapada Banerjee, who went on to become a Tantric guru known as Tarakhepa, was identified (along with Bamakhepa himself) as a threat to the colonial regime in a 1911 report by Francis Charles Daly, the Deputy Inspector-General of Police in India. Daly quotes his colleague, G. C. Denham (Superintendent of Police), who described Tarakhepa as a 'mysterious individual, who appears to be a political Sadhu [holy man] of a dangerous type'.[100] According to Daly, he was the 'spiritual guide' of an anti-colonial gang called the Sarathi Jubak Mandali, who published the seditious *Sarathi* magazine: 'He was looked upon by the members of the gang as a man of great wisdom and spiritual power, and he was believed to be an adviser of the gang in their actual work as well as in spiritual matters'.[101] His guru, Bamakhepa, 'was a person much venerated though (…) he was a disgusting creature, who drank intoxicating liquors from morning till night (…). He appears, however, to have been regarded by members of the revolutionary party as having possessed hypnotic power'.[102] Daly goes on to describe an incident in which a prominent member of the Anushilan Samiti group, Noni Gopal Sengupta, was arrested for terrorist activities against the British and 'while in jail, wrote a letter to his father asking him, as a last resort, to go to Bamakhepa and ask him to use his powers to get him acquitted'.[103]

Many members of the Western-educated Bengali middle classes (*bhadralok* or 'gentlemen') in Calcutta were frustrated by their career options under the colonial regime, often limited to menial clerical work.[104] Psychologically suspended between Western 'progressive' influence and a desire to reconnect with their own local cultural traditions, some were drawn to Tantric mystics outside the city. Perhaps the most famous was Ramakrishna Paramahansa (1836–1886), who was the priest of Dakshineswar temple dedicated to Kali and situated north of Calcutta. The goddess appeared to him in vivid visions and the *murti* enshrined in the temple was said to come to life in his presence.[105] Like Bamakhepa, he maintained an intimate and child-like rapport with the icon, embracing it, dancing with it and singing to it.

In a print captioned 'Lord Ramakrishna's ride to heaven' Ramakrishna appears alongside Kali, riding an airborne chariot above Dakshineswar (fig. 158). Her ambiguous identity as mother and ferocious deity is again apparent, reflecting a vision he once received of the goddess in her capacity as creator and destroyer of the universe. In the vision he saw a beautiful woman emerge from the Ganges, give birth and begin to cradle her child. Then, assuming a terrifying form, she devoured the child and re-entered the water.[106] Ramakrishna was initiated into Tantric rites by a female guru,

**Fig. 158**
**Ramakrishna's ride
to heaven with Kali**
Bengal, India
20th century
Chromolithograph,
34.5 × 28 cm
British Museum 2019,3030.4

Bhairavi Brahmani, during the early 1860s. She introduced him to practices involving engagement with the 'Five Ms' (*panchamakara*), ranging from eating fish out of a skull-cup to consuming scraps of flesh from the cremation ground. As he described it:

> I practised the discipline of the Tantra (…) I sometimes ate the leavings from a jackal's meal, food that had been exposed the whole night, part of which might have been eaten by snakes or other creatures. Yes, I ate that stuff. (…) I realized that the whole world was filled with God alone. One cannot have spiritual realization without destroying ignorance, so I would assume the attitude of a tiger and devour ignorance (…). I behaved like a child, like a madman, like a ghoul.[107]

He did not discriminate between the pure and impure since he perceived everything to be permeated by divine power. Since he believed that Kali manifested herself as a jackal and that dogs were the faithful companions of Bhairava, any food left over by them assumed a sacred quality. Rather than engage with the fifth *maithuna* (sexual union), he preferred to approach women as he did Kali, as mother-figures: 'my attitude towards all women,

**Fig. 159**
**Ramakrishna, Sarada Devi,**
**Vivekananda, Ramprasad**
**Sen and Bamakhepa**
**surrounding Kali, signed**
**P. Chakraborty**
Bengal, India
20th century
Chromolithograph, 34.5 ×
28 cm
British Museum 2019,3030.5

that of a child towards its mother, remained unshaken during the long period of practice according to the *Tantras*'.[108] At times he dressed as a woman in *saris* and jewellery in order to identify more fully with the goddess. He described this transcendence of gender as a conquering of the passions:

> How can a man conquer passion? He should assume the attitude of a woman. I spent many days as the handmaid of God. I dressed myself in women's clothes, put on ornaments, and covered the upper part of my body with a scarf, just like a woman. With the scarf on I used to perform the evening worship before the image.[109]

One of Ramakrishna's most famous disciples was the Calcutta-born Swami Vivekananda (1863–1902, born Narendranath Datta) who founded the Ramakrishna Mission and its monastic order. Vivekananda went on to introduce and popularize his guru, and modern Hindu teachings generally, most famously in a series of lectures at the Parliament of World Religions in Chicago in 1893. In a modern print (fig. 159) Vivekananda is shown at the centre of the composition, alongside (from left) Ramakrishna, Sarada Devi (Ramakrishna's wife), Ramprasad Sen and Bamakhepa, all united by a garland of flowers tied around Kali's neck. After Ramakrishna died in 1886 his disciples turned to Sarada Devi as their guru, worshipping her as the Divine Mother. In 1872 or 1873 Ramakrishna had announced that his wife was an incarnation of the Mahavidya Shodashi and he worshipped her during a *puja* dedicated to the goddess.[110]

Vivekananda, however, did his best to censor any potentially scandalous trace of Ramakrishna's Tantric proclivities, including the intense nature of his relationship with Kali, when presenting Ramakrishna as a global guru for a Western audience. Instead, he focused on interpreting his guru's message through the lens of Vedanta ('End of the Vedas'), an orthodox school of Hindu philosophy whose universalism had appealed to earlier Western thinkers from Ralph Waldo Emerson (1803–1882) to Arthur Schopenhauer (1788–1860). He also placed greater emphasis on Ramakrishna's interfaith belief that all world religions represented equally valid paths to the same goal. This interpretation of Ramakrishna, still dominant today, tends to obscure his complex Tantric background and was shaped by a desire to present an acceptable image of Hinduism to the West.[111]

On the other hand, despite the overwhelming claims by British writers (as well as Hindu reformers) that Tantra had corrupted orthodox Hinduism from within, there were some who came to appreciate Tantric texts for their deeper philosophical content. This is evident in the writings of John Woodroffe, a full-time Calcutta High Court judge and part-time (secret) Tantrika. In the 1910s and 20s Woodroffe co-authored books (under the pseudonym Arthur Avalon) with his Bengali collaborator and translator, Atul Behari Ghosh, that presented a somewhat sanitized re-evaluation of Tantric texts.[112]

A photograph of Woodroffe shows him dressed in a traditional Indian *dhoti* at the 13th-century Konarak temple in Odisha (fig. 160). Eager to disprove critics of Tantra who described it as a marginal movement, in his preface to *Principles of Tantra* (1914) he insightfully pointed out that Hinduism itself was in fact 'largely Tantric' and that 'Tantra was then, as it is now (…) the main, where not the sole, source of some of the most fundamental concepts still prevalent as regards worship, images, initiation, yoga, the supremacy of the guru and so forth'.[113] He argued that Tantra's notion of non-duality – that everything is pervasively infused with Shakti or power – reflected the latest discoveries of quantum physics, such as the concept that all matter is energy:

Fig. 160
John Woodroffe at the
Konarak temple in Odisha,
published in the 1973
edition of his *Introduction
to Tantra Sastra* (originally
published 1913)
Reprinted by Ganesh, Madras
1973

Where does [matter] go according to Shakta doctrine, but to that
Mother-Power from whose womb it came, who exists as all forms. (…)
There are no absolute partitions or gulfs. All is continuous (…). That
there should be such gulfs is unthinkable to any one who has even in
small degree grasped the notion of the unity of things. (…) The Shakta
doctrine is thus one which has not only grandeur but is greatly
pragmatic and of excelling worth.[114]

Like Vivekananda, however, Woodroffe was equally determined to skirt
over the more transgressive elements of Tantra in order to make it
palatable to Western tastes, opting for symbolic readings of passages
relating to the *panchamakaras* and sexual rites, for example, which he
described as 'of a purely mental and spiritual character'.[115] According to
this logic, he defines wine (*madya*) as the 'intoxicating knowledge acquired
by yoga; meat [*mamsa*] is not any fleshy thing but the act whereby the
*sadhaka* [practitioner] consigns all his acts to [God]; *matsya* [fish] is that
knowledge by which the worshipper sympathizes with the pleasure and
pain of all beings. *Mudra* [grain] is the act of relinquishing all association
with evil (…) and *maithuna* [sexual union] is the union of Shakti Kundalini
with Shiva in the body of the worshipper'.[116] Woodroffe did not entirely
succeed in eradicating the colonial associations of Tantra with sexual
hedonism and black magic. However, his publications on the subject
had a profound impact on scholarship and drew attention in the West to
the movement's philosophical dimensions. His promotion of a symbolic
interpretation of the *Tantras* earned him a reputation as the Western
'father' of Tantric studies, although his denial of their explicitly erotic and
taboo elements distorted their multivalent reality, ultimately demonstrating
his own Victorian bias.

## CHAPTER 5

# REIMAGINING TANTRA IN THE 20TH CENTURY

From its inception to the present day, Tantra has challenged religious, cultural and political conventions and opened up new ways of seeing and changing the world. This chapter will investigate modern reimaginings of Tantra in Asia and the West, beginning with an exploration of 20th-century artistic interpretations. In the 1970s South Asian artists associated with the Neo-Tantra movement from Kashmir, Bangladesh, Pakistan and India adopted Tantric symbols and adapted them to speak to the visual language of global modernism. Many were inspired by Tantra's engagement with social inclusivity and spiritual freedom. In Britain and the United States, Tantra had an impact on the period's radical politics, and was interpreted as a movement that could inspire anti-capitalist, ecological and free love ideals. Yoga and meditation were promoted in these milieux as transformative practices that could inspire minds to challenge the status quo, while Tantrikas captured the popular imagination in the West as countercultural role models.

Today, Tantra is as alive as ever. The chapter goes on to examine the philosophy's role among modern-day practitioners including the Naths, Aghoris and Bauls, revealing the enduring power of Tantric ideas and rituals. Tantra has also influenced modern feminist thought and artistic practice. In the contemporary art world, women have harnessed Tantric goddesses through the bodies of real women, seen through a feminist lens.

# THE ART OF TANTRA

From the 20th century to the present day, artists, writers, curators and filmmakers in Asia and the West have been inspired by Tantra, interpreting it as a movement that could contest and destabilize repressive attitudes towards gender, sex and politics. The British painter and writer Ithell Colquhoun (1906–1988), born in Shillong in north-east India, had a lifelong interest in Tantric philosophy and practices. Tantra seamlessly informed her engagement with Surrealism, an avant-garde movement that began in Paris during the 1920s. Surrealism aimed to shock the individual's conscious mind out of its conventional habits in order to awaken the revolutionary, creative potential of the unconscious. Colquhoun was drawn to spiritual movements and occult traditions that celebrated female power and challenged scientific rationalism, religious orthodoxy and social conformity.[1] She described 'Tantra in art, philosophy, feeling' as representative of 'the Magian Strain in Oriental culture' and argued that Tantra 'needs women because in its view their psycho-physical constitution contains elements absent from that of the male. This is the basic inspiration of all cults devoted to the Great Goddess and the reason for the suspicion with which they are commonly viewed in a male-oriented society'.[2]

Tantra influenced Colquhoun's artistic explorations of androgyny, feminism and alchemical metamorphosis.[3] This is particularly evident in her paintings dating to the 1940s, which explore the reconciliation of feminine and masculine principles, inspired by Tantra's potential to disrupt conventional ideas around gender by dissolving fixed polarities and binaries. As she put it, 'The division into male and female represents "a split in the psyche". The task is to replace this unresolved duality by a genuinely androgynous whole'.[4] Many of her paintings from the 1940s of this ideal androgynous being are inspired by the Tantric Hatha yoga idea of the yogic body with its *chakras* and latent Kundalini power (see Chapter 2). She described the *Shiva Samhita* (a treatise on Hatha yoga, *c.* 1300–1500) as an articulation of 'the androgynous nature of the developed human being, by sexual intercourses on all planes between the self and the very small and subtle flame whose form is intelligence'.[5] There are echoes of the Swiss psychoanalyst Carl Jung's interpretation of Kundalini (articulated in a 1932 seminar that shaped Western understandings of the practice) as an individual's *anima* or unconscious feminine side that could help to activate the psychological journey of individuation – the process of becoming a fully integrated being.[6]

*Mausoleum* (*c.* 1944), a watercolour by Colquhoun, depicts a central anthropomorphic skeletal figure cocooned within a phallic chrysalis, which appears to be in the act of formation or metamorphosis (fig. 161).[7] The red and blue channels encircling the figure and joining forces at its cranium allude to Colquhoun's interest in the *nadis* (channels) of the yogic body. According to Hatha yoga practice, the 'feminine' *pingala-nadi* and the 'masculine' *ida-nadi* are conduits of *prana* (breath or life force) that must be harmonized with the *sushumna-nadi* in the centre (suggested by the phallic

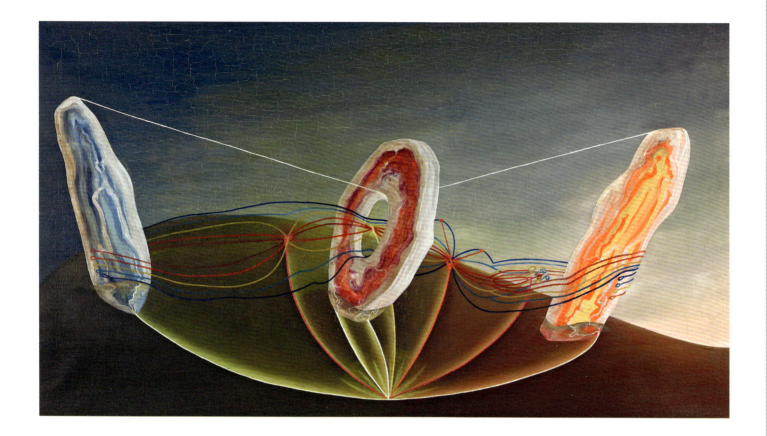

**Fig. 161 (opposite)**
*Mausoleum*, Ithell
Colquhoun
UK
*c.* 1944
Watercolour, pen, black ink
and gouache on paper, 31.1 ×
21.7 cm
British Museum 1990,1109.146

**Fig. 162 (above)**
*Sunset Birth*, Ithell
Colquhoun
UK
*c.* 1942
Oil on canvas, 39.3 × 71.2 cm,
Private collection

chrysalis in Colquhoun's watercolour) to propel the latent Kundalini upwards, resulting in divine union with Shiva in the cranial vault and the release of the seminal 'nectar of immortality' (*amrita*). The explicitly sexual white droplets bursting from the cranium of the figure in the watercolour suggest the transformative release of this nectar. The work's title, *Mausoleum*, suggests that the body is an impermanent tomb, which the Tantric practice of Kundalini seeks to make immortal. The composition and iconographic allusions of Colquhoun's painting also echo traditional South Asian representations of the Tantric goddess Chinnamasta with her two attendants (see Chapter 4, fig. 152). The streams of blood that gush out of the goddess's neck have been interpreted as a reference to the three *nadis*, Chinnamasta representing the central *nadi*, and the gushing blood suggesting the unblocking of all internal obstacles.[8] In both cases the images communicate the conjunction and inseparability of sex and death.

In an oil painting by Colquhoun entitled *Sunset Birth* (*c.* 1942) the body has disappeared almost entirely, leaving behind only the *nadis* (fig. 162). Made up of five channels, they weave through a large circular granite slab with a hole in the middle, stretching to touch two other flanking stones. These structures represent the megalithic monument of Men an Tol (located in West Penwith, Cornwall) to which Colquhoun had long been attracted and which, according to legend, possessed healing and fertility properties.[9] Their blue, red and yellow primary colours in the painting give them an organic quality and symbolize the elements according to alchemical tradition (red for fire, blue for air and yellow for earth).

Preliminary studies for the painting show that Colquhoun imagined the body of a naked woman for the composition.[10] Although the outline of a female body remains, the final result is more ambiguous. The channels of the yogic body meet at different points (the perineum, solar plexus, heart, throat, between the eyes and at the crown of the head) suggesting the location of the different *chakras*. The figure appears to absorb the power of the stones, conveyed by glowing, fiery lines that emerge from the earth, connecting and animating all four elements of the composition.

Painted by Colquhoun almost forty years later, *Torso* (1981) explores the yogic body according to Islamic Sufi tradition in a highly geometric style that abstracts the body entirely (though the title indicates the presence of a body) (fig. 163).[11] The Sufi system of six yogic centres (*lata'if*, singular *latifa*) varied according to different traditions and was visualized in different colours. Like the *chakras* according to Hatha yoga (see Chapter 2), the aim of Sufi practice was to awaken these centres through meditation, breathing techniques and recitations.[12] Two diagram studies for *Torso*, now in the Tate Archive, reveal that her choice of colours to represent each *latifa* was influenced by the system of the Naqshbandi order of Sufis, which developed in India from the 15th century. One of her studies features references to five *lata'if*, labelled clockwise: *khafi* (mystery, located above the eyebrows and blue), *qalb* (heart, below the left breast, red), *sirr* (conscience, middle of the breast, green), *ruh* (spirit, below the right breast, white) and, in the centre, *ikhfa* (arcanum or secret, at the top of the brain, black).[13] There is usually a sixth *latifa*, *nafs* (soul, beneath the navel, yellow), and the colours do not all correspond with Colquhoun's interpretation but she was probably more interested in an evocation of the Sufi yogic body rather than an exact rendering. The arrow in the painting may indicate the order in which to visualize each centre.[14] According to the Naqshbandi system, the heart is awakened first and the arcanum last.[15]

Before and after Indian independence from British rule in 1947 and the emergence of India and Pakistan as independent nation states, South Asian artists moved away from the Eurocentric style based on anatomical observation and naturalism that was taught at many colonial government art schools. Instead they sought to forge new, modern national styles influenced by the pre-colonial art of the past.[16] Some were inspired by the countercultural elements of Tantra relating to social inclusivity and personal freedom. They were particularly influenced by the Delhi-based art historian and curator Ajit Mookerjee (1915–1990), who owned a vast collection of sculptures, paintings and ritual objects which he published in his book *Tantra Art: Its Philosophy and Physics* (1966), emphasizing their philosophical content in order to reclaim Tantra from its popular associations with sexual orgies and sorcery.[17] His collection, which is now housed at the National Museum in Delhi, included two of the objects

**Fig. 163**
*Torso*, Ithell Colquhoun
UK
1981
Enamel on board, 26.7 ×
25.3 cm
National Trust

shown in Chapter 2: a Kangra painting of a yogi with seven *chakras* (fig. 41)
and a painted scroll from Rajasthan showing the rising Kundalini (fig. 42).
Mookerjee's book presented a range of popular and courtly Tantric
Buddhist and Hindu images, from *yab-yum* deities and Dakinis to *yantras*,
fierce goddesses such as Kali and erotic temple carvings, with a somewhat
de-historicized overview of their 'timeless' symbolic significance. The
publication went on to have a major impact on perceptions of Tantra not
only in India but also in the West. Like John Woodroffe, Mookerjee stressed
the symbolic significance of *maithuna* (sexual union), which for him centred
on the union of *purusha* (pure consciousness) and *prakriti* (creative force).
Mookerjee described Tantric practice as 'a scientific method' through
which one could 'become aware of one's own incredible potential, [and]
to realize and experience joy in being one with the cosmos (…) There is
no place for renunciation or denial in tantra. Instead, we must involve
ourselves in all the life processes which surround us. The spiritual is not
something that descends from above, rather it is an illumination that is to
be discovered within'.[18]

Many artists turned to Mookerjee's book for source material, adopting
the symbols associated with Tantric iconography and adapting them to
speak to the abstract visual language of global modernism, particularly the
Abstract Expressionist movement in the United States. At the same time,

following the occupation of Tibet by China in 1950, an influx of Tantric Buddhist *mandalas, thangkas* and bronzes found their way to India, carried by Tibetan refugees after the 1959 uprising in Lhasa and the exile of the Dalai Lama. Artists were particularly influenced by Mookerjee's interpretation of the universal qualities of certain Tantric objects: 'Continually pursuing fundamentals, Tantric art has always tried to integrate forms into geometrical and architectural patterns, the archetypes'.[19]

The Kashmiri artist Ghulam Rasool Santosh (1929–1997) became one of the leading proponents of this new visual language: 'Tantra (…) was not an intellectual exercise for me, but an internal urge, a call to understand the truth that is the source and underlying principle of everything; the truth that fashions the contours of our creative expression'.[20] Born in Srinagar (Kashmir) to a Shia Muslim family, he eventually settled in Delhi in 1960 after marrying a Hindu woman, much to their parents' disapproval, and assumed her surname (his family name was Dar).[21] Before encountering Mookerjee's publication Santosh had experienced a spiritual breakthrough during a pilgrimage in 1964 to a famous cave shrine in Amarnath in the Kashmir Himalayas, revered as a Shakti Pitha. Inside the cave is a large, ice-formed stalagmite that is regarded by devotees as a Shiva *linga*. 'Upon my return from the *yatra* [pilgrimage], a "new" poetry was born', he recalled.[22] 'It initiated me to study the Shiva-Shakti concept in Tantra. (…) I was in search of an image as an artist. An image that smacks of its soil, its tradition'.[23]

Santosh subsequently immersed himself in the philosophies of Kashmir Shaivism, as articulated by the Tantric master Abhinavagupta (*c.* 975–1025). Abhinavagupta described all phenomena as an expression of Shiva, including the self and the body, a realization that could lead to one becoming 'liberated while living', an experience he encapsulated as a 'luminous sea of subsiding waves'.[24] Abhinavagupta also privileged the power of the arts, citing the importance of *rasa* ('essence' or 'taste'), an emotional, transcendent state that could be inspired or evoked by an art form through *bhavas* (moods or emotions), and which he believed could inspire enlightenment. According to Abhinavagupta, the ultimate aesthetic experience was that of tranquillity (*shanta-rasa*) which he identified with the experience of ultimate union with Shiva.[25]

Santosh's work frequently evoked Tantric sexual rites as mirroring the union of Shiva and Shakti. An untitled painting from 1974 depicts two bodies merging in sexual union, indicated by two pairs of legs, suggesting one figure straddling the other (fig. 164). The bodies are made up of abstract shapes and glowing hues. Santosh described this iconography as constituting 'two bodies, *prakriti* and *purusha*, in union'.[26] The straddling figure (who may be female, although their gender is not emphasized) appears to hold their arms in the air, while a fiery circle is positioned at the base of their spine suggesting the presence of latent Kundalini energy being awakened through sexual contact. At the crown of this figure's head emerges what appears to be a third eye of enlightened awakening. As Santosh explained, 'Sex is elevated to the level of transcendental experience. I take the human form in all its dual male–female aspects in sexual union, in a state of unalloyed fulfilment, caught in a trance. I try to capture this intensity, order, and what is regarded as a yogic discipline'.[27] The painting is influenced by images of Kali straddling Shiva, suggesting her creative force and his static consciousness, their interaction sustaining the universe (See Chapter 4, fig. 131).

Santosh's works featuring gender-ambiguous bodies parallel Colquhoun's interests and echo Mookerjee's description of an image of Ardhanarishvara, a composite androgynous form of Shiva and Shakti as illustrated in a painting from Rajasthan, *c.* 1790–1810 (fig. 165): 'The male and female attributes are shown as part of the same body, hermaphroditically joined, thus anticipating a much later discovery; the idea that masculinity and femininity are two different factors is as illusory as the duality of body and soul'.[28]

Santosh was also inspired by the poetry of Lal Ded, a 14th-century female Kashmiri Tantrika, whose verses often reflected the syncretic religious traditions of his own birthplace in their references to Tantra and Sufism:

> The lord pervades everywhere,
> There is nothing like Hindu or Musalman [Muslim],
> All distinctions melt away;
> If thou art wise, know thyself
> See the Lord within.[29]

In one poem Lal Ded describes a vision of Shiva uniting with Shakti:

> I, Lalla, entered
> The gate of the mind's garden and saw
> Shiva united with Shakti.
> I was immersed in the lake of undying bliss.
> Here, in this lifetime,
> I've been unchained from the wheel
> Of birth and death.
> What can the world do to me?[30]

Her poems also allude to her practice of Hatha yoga and the awakening of the seven *chakras*:

> My mind boomed with the sound of *Om*,
> My body was a burning coal.

**Fig. 166**
*Untitled*, Ghulam
Rasool Santosh
Delhi, India
1970s
Paint on paper, 34.5 × 25.5 cm
British Museum 2003,1002,0.7
Donated by Dr Achinto
Sen-Gupta

Six roads brought me to a seventh,
That's how Lalla reached the Field of Light.[31]

Here the seventh 'road' alludes to the *sahasrara* or 'thousand-petalled' lotus
at the crown of the head; the 'Field of Light' describes the blissful release
of *amrita* and the state of enlightenment itself.

An untitled painting by Santosh in shades of red and pink includes
a central oval, egg-like shape out of which limbs protrude, suggesting
a figure seated in the yogic lotus position (*padmasana*) (fig. 166). Santosh
himself practised yoga, and he once said that he wanted his work to
communicate 'the practice of yoga-*sadhana*' and the mood present
'in temples, at shrines'.[32] Certainly his figures do assume the quality
of icons, enhanced by his use of sacred geometry, and at times become
almost entirely abstract. The egg-shape may suggest the creative,
reproductive fertility of the female form. However, again, the gender

**Fig. 167**
*Self-Portrait*, Ghulam
**Rasool Santosh**
India
1980
Watercolour painting, 36 ×
26 cm
British Museum 2003,1002,0.13
Donated by Dr Achinto
Sen-Gupta

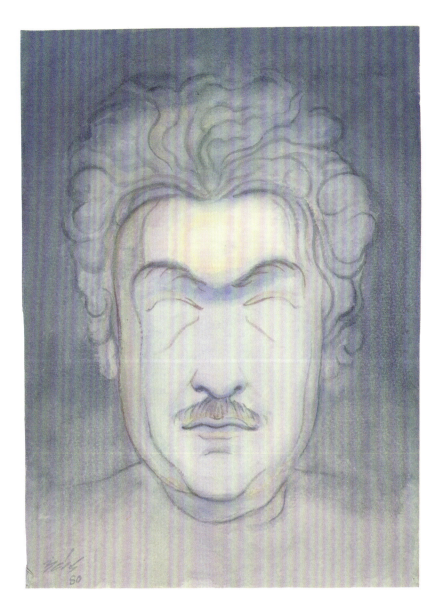

of this body is uncertain and even androgynous. This example lacks
even the suggestion of a head, which is deliberate in many of his
works: 'This was because heads mean individuation', he explained in an
interview.[33] In place of the head is an orange trident (*trishula*), the emblem
of Shiva. In his *Tantraloka* (early 11th century), Abhinavagupta describes
a ritual exercise in which the Tantrika should imagine his or her own
body being symbolically destroyed and then re-created through the
internalization of mantras and the visualization of Shiva's trident
permeating the body.[34]

A dramatic yet serene self-portrait from 1980 represents an eyeless
Santosh in shades of blue, his forehead glowing, his wavy hair snaking out
and his shoulders and chest dissolving (fig. 167). The mysterious emptiness
of his eye sockets suggests he is experiencing a deep, trance-like meditative
state (*samadhi*) and a dissolution of identity or ego as he becomes one with
his surroundings.

**Fig. 168**
*Untitled*, Biren De
India
1974
Acrylic on canvas, 65 × 65 cm
British Museum 1997,0121,0.2
Donated by Dr Achinto
Sen-Gupta

Another artist, Biren De (1926–2011), born in Faridpur (present-day Bangladesh), was equally struck by Mookerjee's collection of Tantric material. By the 1970s his paintings depicted the iconic concentric shapes of mandalas and *yantras*, framing luminous central deities (figs. 168, 169). This centre point is also referred to as the *bindu* and understood as a symbol of the cosmos and as an expression of cosmic creation (see Chapter 3); at the microcosmic level, in Hatha yoga practice, it is also understood as seminal fluid (see Chapter 2). De uses colour to suggest the light and energy emanating from the centre point of his own compositions. As Mookerjee described it, drawing parallels with contemporary physics, 'All creation, according to Tantra, is preceded by a focal tension, which is the centre of every creation (…). The microcosm of *bindu* illustrates the vital impetus in all things to multiply and reproduce. (…) physicists now generally believe that all creation of matter proceeds from one fundamental substance'.[35] De's paintings from the 1970s were also informed by his time in New York while on a Fulbright scholarship in 1958. New York was then the centre of the Abstract Expressionist movement, characterized by its nonrepresentational, often gestural approach to painting that sought to channel the unconscious. Mookerjee mentioned De in his publication (co-authored with Madhu Khanna), *The Tantric Way: Art, Science, Ritual* (1977), in a commentary on parallels between Tantric art and early 20th-century modernist abstract painting. This led to De being classified as a Tantric artist, though he was reluctant to accept this categorization: '[Mookerjee] thought I was his guinea

pig, but I am not a Tantric artist'.[36] Instead, he described himself as an agnostic. Despite this reluctance to be typecast, he did speak about his personal interpretation of Tantric philosophy and its impact on his work:

> For me, the essential meaning of tantra is expansion: expansion of consciousness. (…) By making us acknowledge the fragmented State of our existence, our inadequacies and limitations, it encourages us to strive to transcend these barriers (…) we also become aware of the vital Life-force, the vital energy (*kundalini*), that lies dormant in all beings. We are urged, therefore, to awaken, harness and direct the course of this energy towards an efflorescence of consciousness where polarity, or sense of duality, is finally resolved in Unity.[37]

**Fig. 170**
*Centrovision 299,*
**Mahirwan Mamtani**
India
1976
Oil on canvas, 80 × 80 cm
British Museum 2019,3040.1
Funded by the Brooke Sewell
Permanent Fund

Works by Santosh and De were included in a landmark exhibition in
Los Angeles at the Frederick S. Wight Art Gallery in 1985, 'Neo-Tantra:
Contemporary Indian Art Inspired by Tradition', curated by Laxmi P.
Sihare, Edith Tonelli and Lee Mullican. Tonelli noted in an interview,
'The thing that interested us about tantra was that we felt it was a universal
art. The concepts the artists deal with – nature, spirit, the universe – appeal
to a broad range of people. You can look at these paintings without
knowing anything about tantra and have a reaction to them'.[38] Soon the
term 'Neo-Tantra' became widely adopted by the art world to refer to the
works of Santosh and De, as well as those by other artists including
Mahirwan Mamtani (b. 1935) and Prafulla Mohanti (b. 1936), who also
featured in the Los Angeles exhibition and whose works explored the
concept and symbolism of the *bindu* in particular.[39]

   Mamtani (born in Bhiria, Pakistan), developed the concept of
'Centrovision' based on an 'impulse to transform my experience of the
world into a vision leading to the *bindu*'.[40] He explained that his use of
the 'mandala form with vibrational patterns migrates towards this *bindu*
in the centre', resulting in a 'vision of unity, wholeness or merging with the
universal consciousness or Self'.[41] This is vividly articulated in *Centrovision
299*, executed in 1976 (fig. 170). The geometric shapes of a mandala are
here rendered soft and fleshy, alluding to Tantra's affirmation of visceral
corporeality.

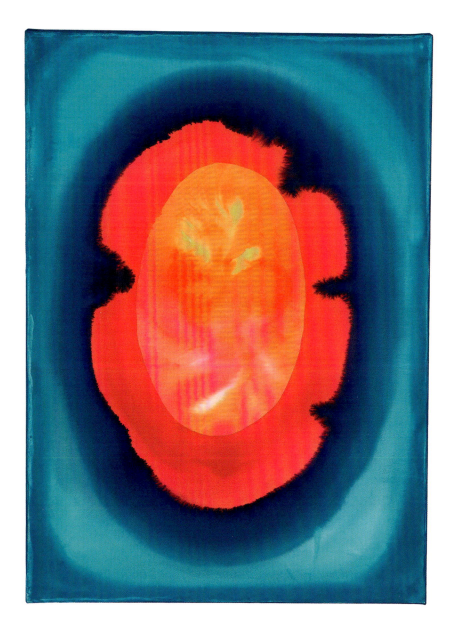

**Fig. 171**
*Kalika*, Prafulla Mohanti
India
1974
Watercolour, ink, gouache and
acrylic on paper and canvas,
75 × 55 cm
British Museum 2019,3039.1
Funded by the Brooke Sewell
Permanent Fund

A painting by Mohanti from 1974, also based on the *bindu* principle, invokes the goddess Kali (or Kalika) at its fiery centre (fig. 171). It is typical of the artist's oeuvre, made up of concentric oval shapes in different shades, the rims bleeding outwards. Born in Nanpur village in Odisha (eastern India), Mohanti described the origin of the recurring *bindu* symbol across his work: '[As a child], while drawing the circles (…) I was inviting the divine energies to come and live in them. As I looked around the village I saw the presence of the divine energy everywhere, in people and in the landscape. The circle became the Bindu (…) which glowed like the rising sun.'[42]

## COUNTERCULTURAL TANTRA IN BRITAIN AND THE UNITED STATES

From the late 1950s, Western interest in Indian culture and Tantra grew in tandem with a shared American-British countercultural revolution against conservative social, political and religious establishments. The next two decades saw the rise of sexual freedom, environmentalism, anti-capitalism and feminism, the Black Power movement, anti-imperialist sentiment and protests against the American military involvement in Vietnam. Against this backdrop, and as a result of an increasingly shrinking global village connected by travel and technology, enabling cross-cultural exchanges, Tantra offered an alternative, affirmative worldview for young Westerners that, to quote British philosopher Alan Watts (1915–1973), served as a 'marvellous and welcome corrective to certain excesses of Western civilization'.[43]

1968 was a particularly significant year of political upheaval. It was the year in which millions of students and industrial workers protested en masse across France against the capitalist nature of the government, resulting in its near-overthrow. Martin Luther King, Jr (1929–1968) was assassinated, resulting in a wave of riots across the United States, followed by intensified protests against the Vietnam War in Chicago. It was also the year that the Beatles travelled to Rishikesh in India to stay in the *ashram* of the guru Maharishi Mahesh Yogi (1918–2008), founder of the Transcendental Meditation movement (a form of silent mantra meditation). The Beatles' visit to India led to a rapid increase in young people's interest in the subcontinent and its spiritual traditions. Aurobindo Ghose, the leader of anti-colonial revolutionary groups in Bengal (see Chapter 4), became an internationally famous mystic who transmitted teachings on Tantra and yoga to the West. In 1968 he founded an experimental spiritual community called Auroville in Pondicherry (now Puducherry, southern India) with the aid of his French collaborator, Mirra Alfassa (1878–1973), also known as The Mother. This utopian community centred around his philosophy of Integral yoga, which taught that all existence stems from the same universal force, which can be accessed through yogic practice.[44]

Amidst the political uprisings and the promise of an alternative worldview, in 1968 Ajit Mookerjee collaborated with director Nik Douglas (1944–2012) and co-producers Mick Jagger (b. 1943) and Robert Fraser (1937–1986) to make an experimental 40-minute art film, *Tantra: Indian Rites of Ecstasy* (figs.172–175). The film was deliberately impressionistic and, according to its accompanying description, attempted to 'plung[e] the viewer without explanation into the sounds and visual splendour of Tantra art and ritual'.[45] It featured a collage of scenes and images, including details of Tantric sculptures and paintings, along with shots of worship and ritual.

Figs. 172–175
Stills from *Tantra: Indian Rites of Ecstasy*,
directed by Nik Douglas,
co-produced by Mick Jagger
and Robert Fraser (Ajit
Mookerjee: consultant)
USA
1968; released 1969
Film on videocassette, 40 mins

The film was divided into three parts: 'Invocation', 'Initiation' and 'Union', each a response to the question posed at the beginning of the film: 'Who am I?' Part 1 featured images of *yantras*, Kali, Durga, Chinnamasta, Vajrayogini and Chakrasamvara, alongside details of landscapes and flowers suggesting the sacrality of the natural world. According to the film's accompanying synopsis, the 'symbolism of Tantra is here used to awaken dormant forces within the human psyche, aided by the ancient chanting of primordial mantras recorded live in India'.[46]

Part 2 ('Initiation') included footage of male and female Tantrikas at the cremation ground of Tarapith in Bengal (fig 174), and a scene in which food offerings were presented to jackals at night.

Part 3 ('Union') centred on a yogi and yogini conducting a *homa* or *yajna*, involving the immolation of offerings into a fire (fig. 175), which functions as a liminal point between the worldly and sacred realms. The film's synopsis describes this scene as depicting 'the union of matter and spirit and the transcendence of all duality'.[47] The *homa* cuts between shots of erotic medieval temple sculptures from Khajuraho (central India), dancers playing the roles of the divine lovers Krishna and Radha, and a Tibetan *yab-yum* bronze. As the sounds of women and men chanting the seed of all mantras, *Om,* ring out, 'the alchemical marriage' of the yogi and yogini transforms into 'whirling ecstatic figures, indivisible, dancing the dance of life itself'.[48] Despite elements of artistic licence and a somewhat voyeuristic approach to recording practitioners, the film's portrayal of Tantra as a philosophy and set of practices through a rich vocabulary of visual signifiers, under Mookerjee's guidance, was uniquely nuanced at the time.

Mick Jagger, one of the film's producers, was the frontman of the Rolling Stones, a band which had formed in London in 1962. A few years after the film was made he approached the designer John Pasche (b. 1945) and asked him to create a logo for the band's record label inspired by the Tantric goddess Kali.[49] Pasche's design featured a protruding tongue, an attribute of the goddess originally suggesting her ravenous appetite on the battlefield. Pasche chose it to convey the band's rebellious, anti-establishment spirit and also to allude to Jagger's famously voluptuous mouth. This logo was first reproduced as a pair of lips with a lolling tongue on the inner sleeve of the Rolling Stones' *Sticky Fingers* album in 1971 and became their most iconic symbol (fig. 176).

The first major exhibition of Tantric material culture in the West ('Tantra') was held in the same year at the Hayward Gallery in London, which generated further international interest in the subject. Mookerjee's publication *Tantra Art: I* (1966) had been the initial inspiration for it, and his collection formed the backbone of the exhibition, which was curated by Philip S. Rawson (then curator of the Gulbenkian Museum of Oriental Art

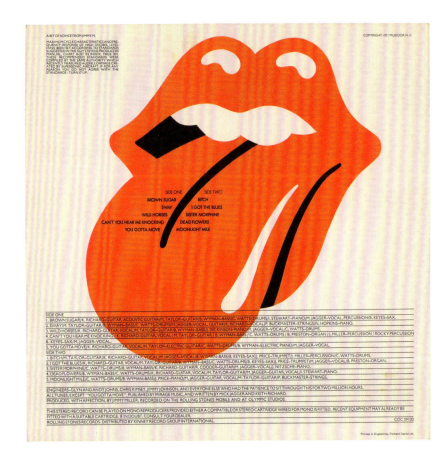

at the University of Durham). In the accompanying catalogue Rawson (1924–1995) interpreted Tantra as 'a vision of cosmic sexuality (…). It asserts that, instead of suppressing pleasure, vision and ecstasy, they should be cultivated and used.'[50] Each room gathered together objects from diverse periods and regions according to themes; these themes included the role of the erotic, the significance of violence and macabre symbolism, the yogic body and loosely related subjects such as representations of Krishna and Radha and cosmic diagrams. The poster for the exhibition featured a close-up of a 17th-century Nepalese scroll painting of the yogic body from Mookerjee's collection (fig. 177). To the left of the figure's heart *chakra* was the tantalizing description of 'an exhibition exploring the Indian cult of ecstasy', reflecting a particular reading of Tantra as a 'cult' that could challenge and overcome stifled attitudes to sexuality in the West.

This reading was not unlike that of the 18th-century British antiquarians (see Chapter 1) who had exoticized and idealized South Asian material that appeared to unite sexuality with religion. Indeed, it was noted in Chapter 1 that the reception of the erotic temple sculpture representing *rajapana* (fig. 38) underwent a transformation between the 18th and 19th centuries, from Orientalist praise to its categorization as licentious. By 1865 it had been hidden away in the British Museum's Secretum, where overtly erotic material was stored. Objects were still being deposited there until 1953 and, significantly, it would not be until the 1960s that its holdings began to be reallocated to other parts of the museum.[51]

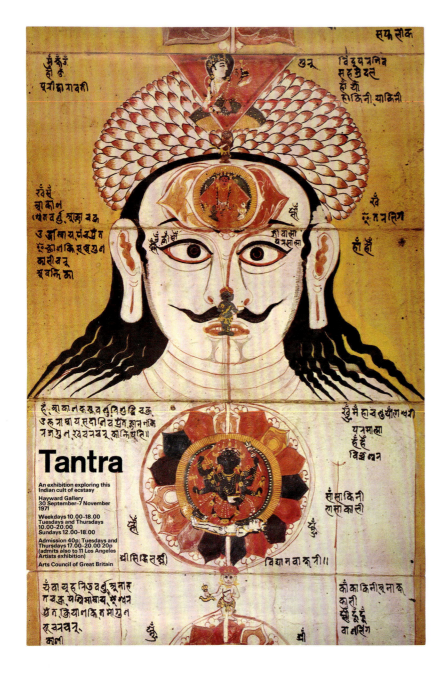

Fig. 177
'Tantra' exhibition poster
for the Hayward Gallery
London, UK
1971
Printed poster, 76 × 51 cm
Author's collection

Indian and Tibetan Tantric imagery – from deities embracing to fierce protector gods and portraits of yogis – exerted a strong stylistic influence on British and American designers. London-based design collaborative Hapshash and the Coloured Coat (Nigel Waymouth and Michael English) produced psychedelic posters communicating ecological and free-love ideals inspired by Tantric imagery. Waymouth (b. 1941) had been born in India and returned there many times from the 1960s onwards, also visiting Nepal and Tibet. He described the zeitgeist of the era as the 'young Western generation trying to break away from the values of our forefathers – war, empire, commercialism – [which] led to people's interest in Eastern religions'.[52] Indeed, by the 1970s Tantra was equated with social and political liberation, as well as spiritual freedom, an antidote to the

**Fig. 178**
*Tantric Lovers*, Hapshash
and the Coloured Coat
(Nigel Waymouth and
Michael English)
London, UK
1968
Pull-out poster from *Oz*
*Magazine*, 82.5 × 29.6 cm
British Museum 2019,3029.1

stranglehold of consumerist values over Western society. Waymouth's design vision was a utopian one: 'Our concept was to plaster the streets of London with this very brightly coloured and beautiful poster work (…) We felt like we were illustrating an ideal'.[53] His collaborator, English (1941–2009), later recalled: 'We believed and adopted anything that contradicted the rational world (…) Sexuality too was a strong force'.[54]

Their 'Tantric Lovers' gatefold pull-out poster was made in 1968 for a cover of *Oz*, an underground magazine published in London from 1967 to 1973, which covered contentious subjects from censorship and homosexuality to police brutality and the Vietnam War (fig. 178). The poster is based on Tibetan *yab-yum* imagery and features a gravity-defying nude couple, who may be divine or mortal, dancing on air as they kiss and embrace. Their legs wind around each other while the male figure's long hair billows softly. The serpent at their feet alludes to the goddess Kundalini. English described the representation of 'The Lovers locked together in eternal balance' as 'a symbol of the symmetry of space-time, as are the lovers each a reflection of the other. Independent yet interdependent'.[55] Waymouth adds that the image is 'all about male-female balance' and a call to 'make love, not war. (…) Tantric images of love were beginning to be understood at the time'.[56] He cites Jack Kerouac's semi-autobiographical novel *The Dharma Bums* (1958), as a source of inspiration. In one scene Japhy Ryder (modelled on Kerouac's friend, the Buddhist poet Gary Snyder) 'performs' *yab-yum* literally, interpreting it as a revolt against repressive attitudes to the body and sex:

> 'Here's what yabyum is, Smith,' said Japhy, and he sat cross-legged on the pillow on the floor and motioned to Princess, who came over and sat down on him facing him with her arms about his neck and they sat like that saying nothing for a while. (…) 'This is what they do in the temples of Tibet. It's a holy ceremony, it's done just like this in front of chanting priests. People pray and recite OMB Mani Pahdme Hum, which means Amen the Thunderbolt in the Dark Void. I'm the thunderbolt and Princess is the dark void, you see'.[57]

Ryder's quote captures the fact that many in the West were inspired by Tantra but did not necessarily have a comprehensive understanding of its original contexts and levels of interpretation (both literal and symbolic), often leading to a tendency to appropriate and adapt its most attractive or palatable elements. There was a general assumption that erotic Tantric images and the sexual rites described in Tantric texts reflected a liberal approach to sex based on pleasure rather than – or at least as well as – a means to attaining power and enlightenment.[58]

The Hapshash poster captured the sexual revolutionary spirit of the decade. Waymouth notes that 'the most powerful drug of the 60s wasn't

Fig. 179
*Save Earth Now*, Hapshash
and the Coloured Coat
(Nigel Waymouth and
Michael English), San
Francisco Art Lab
San Francisco, California, USA
Originally published in 1967;
reprinted in the 1990s, edition
of 250
Silkscreen print, 89 × 57.3 cm
British Museum 2019,3029.2

LSD – it was the birth control pill'.[59] The Pill, which became available in 1960 in the United States and 1961 in Britain, transformed attitudes to sex outside of marriage, allowing women greater freedom and independence. As Waymouth puts it, 'It led to a huge shift in culture and gave feminism a great engine to move forward'.[60]

A special edition silkscreen print was created and signed by the designers as a reprint of a 1967 original, emblazoned with the words 'Save Earth Now' (fig. 179). The image is an example of their use of design as

a 'spiritual and political statement', articulating their engagement with the burgeoning environmental movement and confronting the industrial damage inflicted on the planet's ecosystem by unregulated corporations.[61] Inspired by mandala imagery, a four-armed, weapon-wielding deity sits cross-legged at the centre. He resembles Manjushri, a Tantric Buddhist Yidam or meditational deity who wields a flaming wisdom-sword to annihilate ignorance. But this Hapshash ecological deity is an interfaith one – he carries a Wiccan pentacle and chalice, while the star and crescent around his neck is a symbol associated with Islam. Around the god are two rings, one made up of naked men and women dancing and embracing, and another evoking a paradise on Earth with flowering trees, sea and mountains in the distance. Beyond the rings the poster is harmoniously framed by fish at the bottom of the composition and birds flying at the top.

Waymouth describes the image as a 'Paradise Lost idea of the Earth'. It expresses the notion that an unpolluted world, free from the economical imperatives of greed and consumption, is impossible without 'contemplating the beauty of the Buddha's teaching, meditating and sitting still, and becoming aware (…) so sitting becomes political. Peace only comes with inner stillness. Mother Earth has to be respected completely'.[62] The Tantric conception of the world as a manifestation of divine feminine power was also a source of inspiration for this poster. The image was designed in 1967, a year before the iconic photograph of the Earth was taken from lunar orbit, later described as 'the most influential environmental photograph ever taken', capturing the fragility of the life-supporting planet.[63]

In the United States a parallel utopian optimism was taking hold of the younger generation. A poster from San Francisco advertises the momentous 'A Gathering of the Tribes for a Human Be-In' festival, which took place at Golden Gate Park on 14 January 1967 (fig. 180). It promoted communal living, ecological awareness, engagement with Asian religious traditions and the use of psychedelic drugs for the purpose of inducing altered states of consciousness.[64] Yoga and meditation were heralded as self-transformative practices that could inspire revolutionary minds to challenge and question capitalist structures. The bottom of the poster reads: 'Bring food to share, bring flowers, beads, costumes, feathers, bells, cymbals, flags', encapsulating the spirit of the bohemian Hippie movement. The poster is illustrated with one of the most iconic images of the 1960s, designed by Stanley Mouse (b. 1940) and Alton Kelley (1940–2008) – a photographic portrait (taken in Nepal by the artist Casey Sonnabend, b. 1933) of a yogi with long dreadlocks. A pyramidal shape is superimposed over his head and shoulders and a third eye surrounded by rays of light is visible above his brow. This third eye alludes not only to the Indian eye of awakening, which provides enlightened insight beyond ordinary perception, but also to the Eye of Providence or all-seeing eye of God, a Christian symbol, enclosed by

Fig. 180
*A Gathering of the Tribes for
a Human Be-In*, designed
by Stanley Mouse and
Alton Kelley, photograph by
Casey Sonnabend, signed
by Mouse and Kelley
San Francisco, California, USA
1967
Poster, 50.6 × 36.2 cm
British Museum 2019,3029.3

a triangle. This image encapsulates how yogis, with their reputations for ego-transcendence and supernormal abilities, captured the popular imagination in the West as countercultural role models. The poster lists the special guest speakers and performers at the festival, including Gary Snyder (Ryder in *The Dharma Bums*) and the Beat poet Allen Ginsberg (1926–1997), who had travelled around India in the early 1960s and recorded his experiences of meeting yogis and consuming *bhang* or cannabis with them to achieve euphoric, sublime states.[65] He chanted the mantra and sacred syllable *Om* onstage (fig. 181).[66]

Mantras had an impact on Ginsberg's own poetry. He described their recitation as 'a vehicle for the expression of nonconceptual sensations of the worshipper (…) the words become pure physical sounds (…) the names of the Gods used in the mantra are *identical* with the Gods (or powers invoked) themselves'.[67]

Similarly, the American jazz saxophonist John Coltrane (1926–1967) recorded an album in 1965 entitled *Om*, and described the syllable as: 'the first vibration (…) the first syllable, the primal word, the word of power' (fig. 182).[68] Avant-garde jazz music drew on global cultural sources and responded to the political climate of the period. The decolonization of territories across Africa and Asia in the second half of the 20th century along with the rise of the Black Power movement in the United States fostered new, non-Western and transnational forms of black spirituality. These included Islamic and Yoruban traditions, ancient Egyptian symbology, as well as the South Asian practices of yoga and meditation.[69] In 1966 Coltrane recorded 'Reverend King', inspired by Martin Luther King, Jr, which begins and ends with his chanting of the mantra, '*Om mani padme hum*' ('Hail to the Jewel in the Lotus'), along with fellow jazz musician Pharoah Sanders. The composition was released a year after Coltrane's death in 1968 in the album *Cosmic Music*, which included descriptions of the tracks inside the record jacket. This mantra was described as symbolizing 'the seven breaths of man and the truth that humanity is Divinity enshrouded in flesh

Fig. 181
Gary Snyder, Michael McClure, Allen Ginsberg, Maretta Greer and Lenore Kandel at the 'Human Be-In' festival, Golden Gate Park, San Francisco, 14 January 1967
1967; printed 1998
Lisa Law

**Fig. 182**
**John Coltrane and Alice**
**Coltrane, Van Gelder Studio,**
**Englewood Cliffs, New**
**Jersey, USA**
1966
Chuck Stewart Photography,
LLC

or earth-surroundings. In the heart of us is contained the One Identity'. Images accompanying the descriptions included photographs of an ancient Egyptian sphinx and a medieval statue of the Buddha.

Coltrane was interested in the Indian concept of *rasa* – an emotional state inspired by art through *bhavas* or moods – which he applied to his own musical practice, 'in which particular sounds and scales are intended to produce specific emotional meanings'.[70] His widow, jazz musician Alice Coltrane (1937–2007), noted that he 'always felt that sound was the first manifestation in creation before music', and that 'a cosmic principle' was 'the underlying reality' behind his music.[71] She later recorded a composition entitled 'Turiya and Ramakrishna' (*Ptah, the El Daoud*, 1970), dedicated to the 19th-century Bengali mystic and Kali devotee. She went on to adopt the Sanskrit name Turiya, a term connoting pure consciousness, and became the disciple of the Indian guru Swami Satchidananda (1914–2002).[72]

One of John Coltrane's collaborators, the American jazz trumpeter Don Cherry (1936–1995), was equally inspired by South Asian traditions and had studied under the Indian musician and mystic Pran Nath. Cherry

had a particular interest in Tibetan Tantric Buddhism and the writings of
the Sufi mystic Inayat Rehmat Khan Pathan (1882–1927), who emphasized
the sacred power of music.[73] In 1973 he released the free-jazz album,
*Relativity Suite*, which includes a composition entitled 'Tantra'. It begins with
a Buddhist mantra: *Om muni muni mahamuni shakyamuniye svaha* ('Om sage, sage,
great sage, sage of Shakya [Gautama Buddha], hail!'). Three years later, in
1976, Cherry recorded the album *Hear & Now*, which featured the opening
track 'Mahakali' ('Great Kali'). It begins with Tibetan bells, followed by
a trumpet–sitar dialogue, before erupting in a hailstorm of electric guitar
chords and drum beats, as if to signal the goddess Kali's dramatic arrival.

On the cover of the album Cherry is portrayed as an iconic modern-
day Siddha or yogi, seated in the 'lotus pose' (*padmasana*) (fig. 183). He
holds his trumpet in one hand and wears a necklace of *mala* beads, used
to keep count during the recitation of mantras. An unidentified Buddhist
deity floats above him, mirroring his posture to suggest their ultimate
inseparability. He is framed by streamers and auspicious conch shells,
with a stylized sky behind him reminiscent of traditional Tibetan
sacred paintings.

Along with Ginsberg, another Beat poet at the 'Human Be-In' festival
was Lenore Kandel (1932–2009), who had achieved notoriety the year
before, in 1966, when her small book of four poems, *The Love Book*, was

Fig. 185
**Cover of the Don Cherry
album *Hear & Now*,
designed by Lynn Breslin,
Atlantic Records**
USA
1976
Album, 31.5 × 31.5 cm

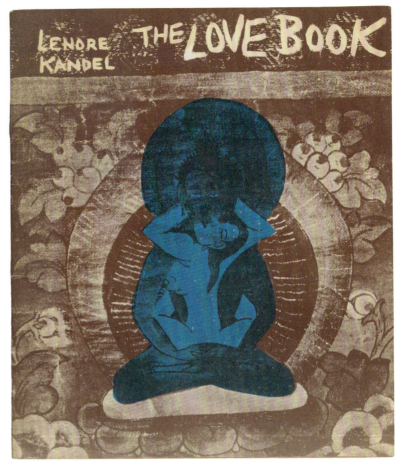

Fig. 184
Lenore Kandell holding
*The Love Book*
San Francisco, California, USA
1966

Fig. 185
Cover of *The Love Book* by
Lenore Kandell, published
by Stolen Paper Review/
Jeff Berner
San Francisco, California, USA
1966

published, extracts of which she read out to the festival's audience (fig. 184). Kandel described the poems, which contained Tantric references, as 'the invocation, recognition and acceptance of the divinity in man thru [sic] the medium of physical love'.[74] The original front and back covers of the book featured images of Vajrayana *yab-yum* deities in union, including Samantabhadra and Samantabhadri (fig. 185). The newly elected governor of California, Ronald Reagan, authorized a police raid on bookshops that sold the publication, impounding and banning it because it was deemed pornographic, violating state obscenity laws. In one poem, 'To Fuck with Love', she writes:

> pure love-lust of godhead   beauty unbearable
>          carnal incarnate
> I am the god-animal, the mindless cuntdeity    the hegod-animal
> is over me, through me    we are become one total angel
> united in fire    united in semen and sweat     united in lovescream
> sacred our acts and our actions
> sacred our parts and our persons.[75]

The attempt to ban the book led to the longest trial in San Francisco's history. During the hearing Kandel defended the poems as 'holy erotica'.[76]

REIMAGINING TANTRA IN THE 20TH CENTURY

**Fig. 186 (left)**
**Penny Slinger with her**
*Scrolls* (or *Chakra Man*
*and Woman*) series
UK
1977

**Fig. 187 (opposite, left)**
*Rose Devi*, Penny Slinger
UK
1976
Silkscreen from monoprint on
fine paper and collage, 25.4 ×
165.1 cm
Private collection

**Fig. 188 (opposite, right)**
*Chakra Woman*, Penny
**Slinger**
UK
1976
Body monoprint with collage
on paper, 25.4 × 167.6 cm
Private collection

The jury supported the obscenity charge, which would not be overturned until 1974. She said of the trial: 'Any form of censorship, whether mental, moral, emotional or physical, whether from the inside or the outside in, is a barrier against self-awareness.'[77] Her use of transgressive language plays on the often explicit sexual references found in Tantric texts. She was clearly familiar with the notion that Tantric practitioners who engaged in sexual rites visualized themselves as embodiments of deities representing, in the case of Tantric Buddhism, wisdom and compassion. The line 'I am the god-animal' in the extract quoted above speaks to Tantra's blurring of mortal and divine identities, particularly in relation to Yoginis and Dakinis who are described as manifesting themselves in mortal women. In the West

during the 1960s and 70s, which coincided with the rise of the Second-Wave feminist movement, many women were drawn to Tantric goddesses as powerful agents with the capacity to destroy, and who were often portrayed in sexually dominant positions (from Kali to Chinnamasta and Rati), appearing to confront patriarchal constructions of the ideal woman as passive and obedient.

Uninhibited, creative expressions of female sexuality and pleasure through a Tantric lens were also explored by the London-born artist Penny Slinger (b. 1947) (fig. 186). Her multi-media works of the 1970s fused Surrealist aesthetic practices with Tantric iconography, informed by her interest in the emancipatory potential of erotica and the radical feminist activism of the period. She had first encountered Tantric visual culture at the Hayward Gallery exhibition in 1971. Inspired by the scroll paintings of the yogic body that were on display, in 1976 she created her own highly personal equivalents, using her body to produce a series of provocative scrolls: 'I created the series laying sections of my naked body in turn on the [photocopying] machine. (…) I then put the body sections together to make the basis of my versions of the *Chakra Man* Tantric paintings that impressed me so much. (…) I saw them as imprints of slices of my being'.[78] Challenging notions of 'the body as shameful according to the Western canon, denying the sensual and sexual side of life', Slinger was drawn to Tantra as a 'non-sectarian, non-dogmatic (…) path of the goddess', uniting 'the physical with the spiritual'.[79] For her, the activating principle of Shakti 'represented permission to celebrate femininity'.[80]

In two scrolls from this series (*Rose Devi* and *Chakra Woman*) she placed her feet above her head to deliberately challenge orthodox Hindu conceptions of the body as hierarchically ordered (figs. 187, 188). While the head is conceived as the 'purest' part of the body, the feet are considered the most 'impure' because they come into contact with pollutants on the ground. Playing on the ambivalence of pure–impure distinctions in a deliberately Tantric form of subversion, Slinger also adds that 'coming into play was the line "put your head at the feet of the Goddess" and the idea that we as humans can only approach her by touching Her feet (a sign of reverence and respect in Hindu culture) and the sense that she is so vast and grand that only the hem of Her skirt or dust off Her feet may be accessible to us'.[81] Here Slinger both identifies with the goddess and submits to her. She was particularly influenced by Tantra's emphasis on Shakti as feminine power pervading all phenomena, which could be instrumentalized as an agent of corporeal and psychological transformation, and which was naturally present in the bodies of all women.

In both scrolls Slinger uses her fingers to pry open her vaginal labia, revealing her sex and emphasizing her pubic hair. She sticks out her tongue in imitation of the goddess Kali, who she harnesses for her disobedient unfettering of social and cultural conventions. With another pair of hands, Slinger brings her two thumbs and forefingers together to create a triangular shape, making the same gesture or *mudra* as the Mahasiddha Jalandhara in the Tibetan bronze sculpture in Chapter 3 (fig. 86), invoking the symbol for the source of Buddhahood, *dharmodaya*. As she explains, 'my *mudra* was a deliberate device to evoke the source of all, the triangle of infinite potential'.[82] Tantric symbols and images are collaged into the scrolls. In *Rose Devi* (fig. 187), the outline of Slinger's body dissolves into a red background. Roses, like lotuses seen in other yogic body images, mark her *chakras*, while dancing Vajrayogini figures are juxtaposed over her pubic area and feet. *Chakra Woman* (fig. 188) is replete with collaged images of Dakinis, *yab-yum* couples, the face of the wrathful manifestation of the goddess Tara, a *karttrika* (flaying knife) and Mahasiddha-inspired figures. As Slinger notes, 'the [Maha]siddhas represented for me the thought of enlightenment achieved within the living body, and often through very unconventional means'.[83]

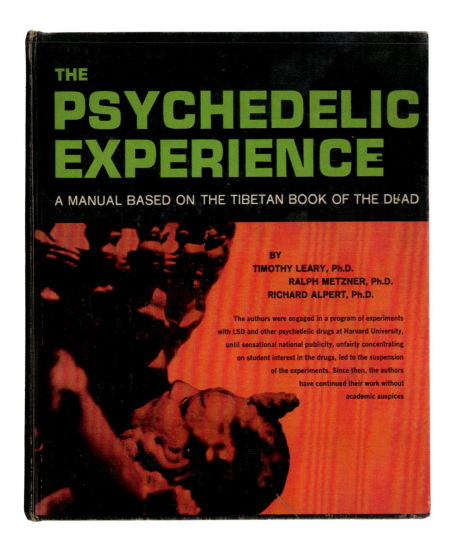

Fig. 189
*The Psychedelic Experience: A Manual Based on the Tibetan Book of the Dead*
by Timothy Leary, Ralph Metzner and Richard Alpert, published by University Books
New York, USA
1966 edition; original 1964
Printed book, 20.5 × 24 × 2 cm

Another method for emancipating the repressed West lay in the use of intoxicants as a means to induce expanded states of consciousness. Hallucinogenic substances such as cannabis and LSD were thought to have quasi-religious properties that could enable 'consciousness-expanding', 'instant nirvana', as described by the American psychologist Timothy Leary (another speaker at the 'Human Be-In' festival in 1967) who associated its effects with Tantric experience.[84] The properties of LSD, which was made illegal in the United Kingdom in 1966 and the United States in 1968, were known to heighten the senses and to induce vivid hallucinations, inspiring a wave of psychedelia-inspired art works, including those by Hapshash and the Coloured Coat. Leary (1920–1996) co-authored *The Psychedelic Experience* in 1964 (fig. 189), which took inspiration from the *Bardo Thodol* (known in the West as *The Tibetan Book of the Dead*) attributed to the 8th-century Tantric master Padmasambhava. The Tibetan text describes the hallucinatory stages experienced by the mind after death in the intermediary realm of the Bardo, during which visionary forms appear before the individual is reborn.[85] Leary interpreted the text as 'a key to the innermost recesses of the human mind' and regarded the stages it described as mirroring the experiences of taking LSD, from the 'psychological death' of the ego to 'rebirth'.[86] A line in *The Psychedelic Experience*, 'Turn off your mind, relax, float downstream' was made iconic by the Beatles in their song 'Tomorrow Never Knows' (*Revolver*, 1966).[87]

Aldous Huxley (1894–1963), who famously coined the term psychedelic (literally 'mind-manifesting') with the psychiatrist Humphrey Osmond, wrote the first 'psychedelic bible' of the era, *The Doors of Perception* (1954), which outlined his experience of taking mescalin. He had introduced Leary to Tantra in a letter dating to 1962:

> Tantra teaches a yoga of sex, a yoga of eating (even eating forbidden foods and drinking forbidden drinks). The sacramentalizing of common life, so that every event may become a means whereby enlightenment can be realized (…) LSD and the mushrooms should be used, it seems to me, in the context of this basic Tantrik idea of the yoga of total awareness, leading to enlightenment within the world of everyday experience – which of course becomes the world of miracle and beauty and divine mystery when experience is what it always ought to be.[88]

Huxley's perceptive interpretation of Tantra as the 'sacramentalizing of common life' and 'enlightenment within the world of everyday experience' recognized the role of transgression in rituals that engaged with taboo elements. He understood that these rituals were designed to challenge distinctions between purity and impurity, transforming 'forbidden foods and (…) drinks' into divine receptacles and instruments. Both Huxley and

Leary believed Tantra could teach Western society how to unlearn oppressive, puritanical and moralistic middle-class principles. Leary's well-known mantra-like phrase, 'turn on, tune in, drop out', encouraged revolt against conformity.[89]

Throughout the 1960s and 70s many European and American travellers embarked on the overland 'Hippie Trail' through Turkey, Iran, Afghanistan, Pakistan, India and Nepal. The trail was referred to as the Road to Kathmandu, Nepal's capital and often the final destination. The city was perceived as a utopian haven surrounded by sacred Hindu and Buddhist monuments, lush valleys and mountains. Before 1973 cannabis was sold legally in Kathmandu, and one of the most well-known businesses in Nepal was the Eden Hashish Centre run by D. D. Sharma.[90]

Posters advertising the Eden Hashish Centre to tourists featured images of Hindu deities, including a 1960s example depicting Shiva (fig. 190). The Centre's slogan, 'Let us take higher', appears below the image inviting people to 'come visit us any time for all your hashish needs'. Here Sharma shrewdly 'sells' the idea of *bhang's* transcendental properties and its associations with the unruly, intoxicated Tantric god (see Chapter 2, fig. 61) to the influx of hippies eager for a spiritual high. Customers could purchase 'temple balls' at the Centre and consume them in the Heavenly Pleasure Room at Sharma's nearby Eden Hotel.[91] All this would change in 1973 when the Nepalese government outlawed cannabis under pressure from the United Nations and especially President Nixon's administration (1969–1974), who were concerned that Kathmandu was becoming a centre for youth radicalism. The resulting negative media generated by the Western press threatened Nepal's growing tourist industry.[92]

One traveller who found his way to India in the early 1970s was the Japanese artist Yokoo Tadanori (b. 1936) who went on to create designs reimagining Tantric concepts and images fused with the aesthetics of psychedelia popularized in the West. His 1974 series of ten silkscreen prints, entitled *Shambala* (figs. 191, 192), evoke his fascination with the mythical and paradisiacal kingdom of Shambhala, which according to legend was in the shape of an eight-petalled lotus surrounded by mountain peaks, located north of India and the Himalayas.[93] Shambhala was believed to be inhabited by Tantric adepts and it was said that its king, Suchandra (or Chandrabhadra), met with the Buddha in India, who predicted that all beings who lived in Shambhala would achieve enlightenment. According to the 11th-century *Kalachakra Tantra*, an apocalyptic reign of chaos and conflict would descend on the world but Shambhala would preserve its ancient Tantric teachings and restore peace in the year 2424, marking a new enlightened era led by a spiritually advanced community.[94]

Before creating the prints, Yokoo dreamed that he saw a pure light and heard the voice of a monk he had once known uttering the words 'I bring

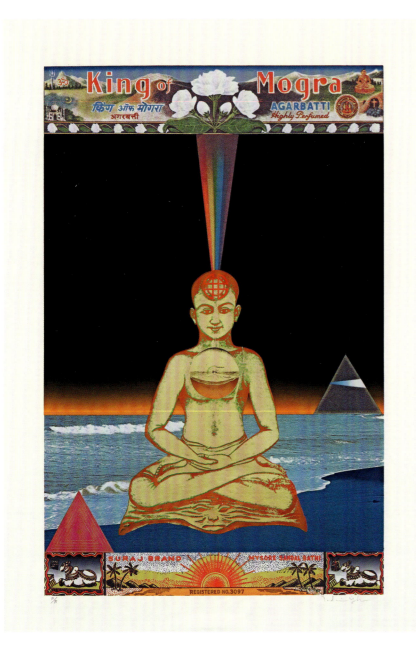

**Fig. 191**
*TEJAS-BHUMI: Fire that is Earth, Shambala* series, **Yokoo Tadanori**
Tokyo, Japan
1974
Silkscreen print, 97.8 × 67.9 cm
British Museum 2019,3005.7
Purchase made possible by the JTI Japanese Acquisition Fund

**Fig. 192**
*AP-DEVALOKA: Water that is Heaven, Shambala* series, **Yokoo Tadanori**
Tokyo, Japan
1974
Silkscreen print, 97.8 × 67.9 cm
British Museum 2019,3005.4
Purchase made possible by the JTI Japanese Acquisition Fund

the King of Shambhala', which convinced him to access the legendary kingdom within himself, through yoga and meditation.[95] Indeed, the prosperous, peaceful world of Shambhala was regarded by many as a state of mind. In 1973 a song called 'Shambala' was released in the United States, with lyrics by Daniel Moore, describing an idyllic realm that would 'wash away my troubles', and where 'everyone is kind'. The song alludes to the kingdom as a spiritual path within one's own being: 'How does your light shine, in the halls of Shambala?' In 1976 Chogyam Trungpa (1939–1987), a former Tibetan monk who introduced Tantric Buddhist teachings to the West, developed a training programme of meditation designed to re-create the kingdom of Shambhala on a global scale.[96] Yokoo's prints depict bodies seated in meditation, including one with a starscape around the heart *chakra* pinpointing the constellation Cassiopeia and the star Capella (fig. 191).

**Fig. 193**
**Couple having sex**
Possibly Bikaner, Rajasthan, India
*c.* 1690
Gouache on paper, 19.8 ×
13.3 cm
British Museum 1880,0.434

A rainbow streams from the crown of the figure's head, portraying both mind and body as a luminous source of light generating the immortal, enlightened 'rainbow body'.[97]

Another print by Yokoo includes a courtly couple performing sexual intercourse (fig. 192). This image is most likely adapted from a Rajput painting similar to a *c.* 1690 example from Rajasthan that forms part of a series illustrating a variety of sexual positions (fig. 193). The Rajput painting was influenced by ancient texts dedicated to *kama* (pleasure or desire) such as the *c.* 3rd-century CE *Kama Sutra* by Vatsyayana. According to this text, sexual pleasure for the people of the court was part of a wider, highly aestheticized lifestyle and therefore a carefully cultivated 'art'.[98] Contrary to popular belief, particularly in the West, Tantra had little to do with the science of pleasure it outlined. Instead, carnal craving was harnessed in Tantric rites to sublimate this very impulse, so that a sexual practice could become not an end in itself but primarily a means to achieving power and/or liberation. Here Yokoo's figures draw on the visual vocabulary that both the *Kama Sutra* and Tantra inspired, secular and sacred respectively, in order to suggest that Shambhala is a land free of sexual constraints.

The cosmic quality of Yokoo's images contrasts with the advertisements for incense that frame the compositions. In an accompanying preface to the prints the artist explains that the recurring shape of a triangle refers to 'a pyramid of dynamic energy' present at Shambhala 'which exchanges energy with our Sun'.[99] Yokoo had read *The Hollow Earth* (1964) by Raymond Bernard (real name Walter Siegmeister), which proposed the theory that there was a subterranean world inside the Earth inhabited by extra-terrestrials with superior spiritual and technological abilities. This subterranean world was sometimes identified with the mythical kingdom of Agartha, believed to be located under Tibet and often confused with Shambhala.[100] Yokoo imagined Shambhala as its capital:

> It is a legend about a land called Aghartha, which exists in a huge cavern in the centre of the Earth. (…) During various periods in history the supermen of Aghartha came to the surface of Earth to teach the human race how to live together in peace and save us from wars, catastrophes and destruction. The apparent sighting of several flying saucers soon after the [United States'] bombing of Hiroshima [in 1945] may represent one visitation.[101]

Here the residents of Agartha are presented as agents of healing in the wake of trauma. As he continues in the preface to his print series:

> I got more and more interested in flying saucers [appearing across some of the prints], which, in turn brought me back with an extraordinary swiftness to Shambala, the capital of an underground kingdom Aghartha. Shambala is a real place, as well as the center of cosmic consciousness. (…) Shambala is working upon us as the center of the universe which can lead us human beings spiritually. For me, to make 'SHAMBALA' [the series of prints] is a sort of meditation designed to join myself with the divine will of Shambala.[102]

Tantra lay at the heart of the shared countercultural movements of the 1960s and 70s. In Britain and the United States this resulted in the reinterpretation of many of its characteristics in the service of progressive thought, to resist capitalist culture and authoritarianism, to embolden collective action and to facilitate a consciousness-expanding worldview. Such readings of Tantra could also inevitably often lead to reductive interpretations of its teachings as well as forms of cultural appropriation. The galvanizing of Tantric and South Asian traditions to promote a utopian vision had by the 1980s lost much of its political bite with the rise of market-oriented neoliberal policies in the West. More recently, Tantra, yoga and 'mindfulness' have become big business at the service of the individual, even used by large corporations to encourage productivity in their workforce. Nevertheless, the rebellious spirit of Tantra, with its potential to disrupt prevailing social, cultural and political establishments, remains ripe for the reimagining.

## TANTRA TODAY

Tantra – as a worldview, philosophy and set of practices – is still as alive as ever, and assumes many forms. The British Museum has an archive of photographs of yogis and yoginis associated with different sects in India and Nepal, taken between the 1970s and 1990s by the Dutch photographer and writer Dolf Hartsuiker. Hartsuiker conducted interviews with the men and women he photographed as part of his fieldwork, culminating in a publication entitled *Sadhus: Holy Men of India* (1993).[103]

The archive includes portraits of Naths (fig. 194), whose historical roots were discussed in Chapter 2 and who still constitute one of the most important sects of yogis in South Asia. Today they are still credited with powers attained through their yogic and alchemical practices, including control over nature (from wild animals to the weather) and the ability to cure infertility problems.[104]

A photograph taken in 1992 in Girnar (Gujarat) during Shivaratri or 'Night of Shiva', an annual festival devoted to the god, depicts Ambai Nath (fig. 195). He sits in profile, adorned with the distinctive hoop earrings worn by Naths through slits in their ear cartilages (rather than the lobes) after they have been cut open with a knife during initiation. This practice, which is only documented in visual sources after *c.* 1800, has led to them being called Kanphata ('split-eared') yogis, a somewhat derogatory term.[105] According to some legends, Gorakhnath, regarded as the founder of the Naths, first prompted it in order to distinguish his followers from other sects.[106] The earrings can be made of a variety of materials, including wood, glass, crystal, silver, gold and ivory.

In a portrait of the Nath yogi Dishama Nath Bapujiat, taken in 1989 at Dwarka (Gujarat), he is shown smoking tobacco or cannabis from a *chilam* or conical pipe in front of memorial stones set around a cremation

Fig. 194
Manohar Nath Yogi in front of a wall painting of Shiva, photograph by Dolf Hartsuiker
Hardwar, Uttar Pradesh, India
1990
35 mm slide
British Museum 2014,3004.584
From the Hartsuiker Archive, donated by Mr Dolf Hartsuiker

ground (fig. 196). He wears the other distinctive accessory identifying him as a Nath, the horn-shaped pendant. While many Rajput and Mughal paintings of Naths showed them wearing pendants made of small antelope horns around the neck, today these have generally been replaced by whistles made from different materials, from bone (as here) to plastic. As Hartsuiker notes, the whistle is blown during morning and evening worship to 'invoke [the] Guru and tutelary deity'.[107]

While Nath yogis lost most of their political authority in the subcontinent between the mid-19th and early 20th centuries with the rise of British rule, this changed with Digvijay Nath (1894–1969), the spiritual leader or *mahant* of the Gorakhnath monastery in Gorakhpur (Uttar Pradesh), a Nath centre. In 1937 he joined the Hindu Mahasabha, a right-wing Hindu nationalist organization, and rapidly rose through the ranks. Exploiting Hindu–Muslim communal tensions following the 1947 Partition of India, in 1949 he played a leading role in a break-in of the Babri mosque in Ayodhya, placing statues of the Hindu gods Rama and Sita inside the mosque and alleging it was the birthplace of Rama.[108] His 'rebranding' of Nath identity as an exclusively Hindu one could not be further from the sect's early pluralistic and inclusive outlook that had led to dynamic exchanges between yogis and Sufis (see Chapter 2) and had

Fig. 195 (above left)
**Ambai Nath, photograph by Dolf Hartsuiker**
Girnar, Gujarat, India
1992
35 mm slide
British Museum 2014,3004.931
From the Hartsuiker Archive, donated by Mr Dolf Hartsuiker

Fig. 196 (above right)
**Dishama Nath Bapujiat, photograph by Dolf Hartsuiker**
Dwarka, Gujarat, India,
1989
35 mm slide
British Museum 2014,3004.153
From the Hartsuiker Archive, donated by Mr Dolf Hartsuiker

Fig. 197 (below)

Yogi Adityanath at

Gorakhnath temple

Gorakhpur, Uttar Pradesh,
India
2017

allowed the Naths to receive patronage from both Rajput and Mughal rulers. Digvijay Nath's successors have continued to play leading roles in right-wing politics in the state, including the current *mahant*, Yogi Adityanath, who was elected the Chief Minister of Uttar Pradesh for the Bharatiya Janata Party in 2017. Years earlier he had founded a youth militia organization, the Hindu Yuva Vahini, which aims to promote 'Hindutva [Hindu-ness] and nationalism' and has been involved in communal violence against Muslims.[109] A photo taken in 2017 shows Adityanath (dressed in saffron robes) at Gorakhnath temple with a framed picture of Digvijay Nath behind him, standing on the right (fig. 197).

The Aghoris ('Non-Terrible') are a sect of Tantrikas whose transgressive and deliberately provocative practices, centering around Bhairava, are often compared to those of the earlier, infamous Kapalika skull-bearers (see Chapter 1). Many Aghoris are based in the holy city of Varanasi in northern India, where thousands of Hindu pilgrims visit to bathe in the purifying waters of the river Ganges. According to myth, the city was also Bhairava's final destination after he wandered for twelve years carrying Brahma's head as penance. When he reached Varanasi it finally fell from his hand.

The Aghoris' practices include smearing their bodies with the ash of burnt corpses from funerary pyres, as seen in a photograph taken by Hartsuiker in Ujjain (Madhya Pradesh) in 1992 (fig. 198). Smearing oneself with crematory ash is a highly polluting act according to orthodox belief, and Hartsuiker explains that 'at the same time it is an intimidating display of power: transgressing taboos, having no fear of death and ghosts, clearly showing mastery over supernatural forces. And simultaneously, magically, it provides power: these ashes transmit the life-force of the cremated person'.[110] The cremation ground is regarded as a polluted and therefore inherently potent site for Aghoris in its association with decay and mortality, just as it was for the Kapalikas and Mahasiddhas.

For the Aghoris, the impure can be used as an instrument of power but their transgressive practices are above all an expression of the Tantric assertion that there is no distinction between what is conventionally perceived as pure and impure, or between the corporal self and the divine. By rejecting society's cultural conditioning, which tends to foster a discriminatory mentality (whether towards caste-less people or contact with the dead), the Aghoris transcend self-limiting ego-led emotions such as fear and aversion and instead nurture a non-discriminatory attitude.[111] The affirmation that all is sacred in the material world, including those forbidden things rejected by society, ultimately liberates the Aghoris from it. Hartsuiker notes that 'They aspire to a state of enlightenment in which there is no differentiation between opposites and no distinction between the soul and the Absolute. The Aghori way of dissolving this metaphysical

duality is to insist unconditionally on the identity of mundane opposites – bad is good, death is life, dirty is clean – and to act this out concretely'.[112]

A portrait of the Aghori Gauri Shankar Mishra (a former Brahmin *pandit* or scholar), taken in 1992 in Ayodhya (Uttar Pradesh), shows him drinking from a human skull-cup that has been painted red to resemble blood (fig. 199). Drinking out of a human skull is not only a tribute to Bhairava's penance and a mark of one's own fearless confrontation with mortality, it is also, as Hartsuiker points out, a 'magical act: a partaking of the dead person's life-force'.[113] This is comparable to the use of *kapalas* in Tibetan Tantric Buddhist practice (see Chapter 3), in which the unique vital force of the deceased individual is believed to be inherent within the skull, rendering it an effective power-object and an instrument capable of transforming negative forces into divine nectar.

Mishra told Hartsuiker that as part of his Aghori *sadhana* or practice he enacts a divinely inspired madness and deliberately subverts social niceties, recalling the behaviour of Bamakhepa and Ramakrishna (see Chapter 4). He 'drinks liquor (forbidden to caste Hindus and ascetics); eats the flesh of dead animals found in the street; talks, or rather raves incomprehensibly, quoting at length from the holy scriptures (which he is familiar with as a former *pandit*, a learned Brahmin scribe); and abuses people with foul obscenities'.[114]

**Fig. 198 (above)**
**Two Aghoris, photograph by Dolf Hartsuiker**
Ujjain, Madhya Pradesh, India
1992
35 mm slide
British Museum 2014,3004.1366
From the Hartsuiker Archive, donated by Mr Dolf Hartsuiker

**Fig. 199 (opposite)**
**Gauri Shankar Mishra, photograph by Dolf Hartsuiker**
Ayodhya, Uttar Pradesh, India
1992
35 mm slide
British Museum 2014,3004.1056
From the Hartsuiker Archive, donated by Mr Dolf Hartsuiker

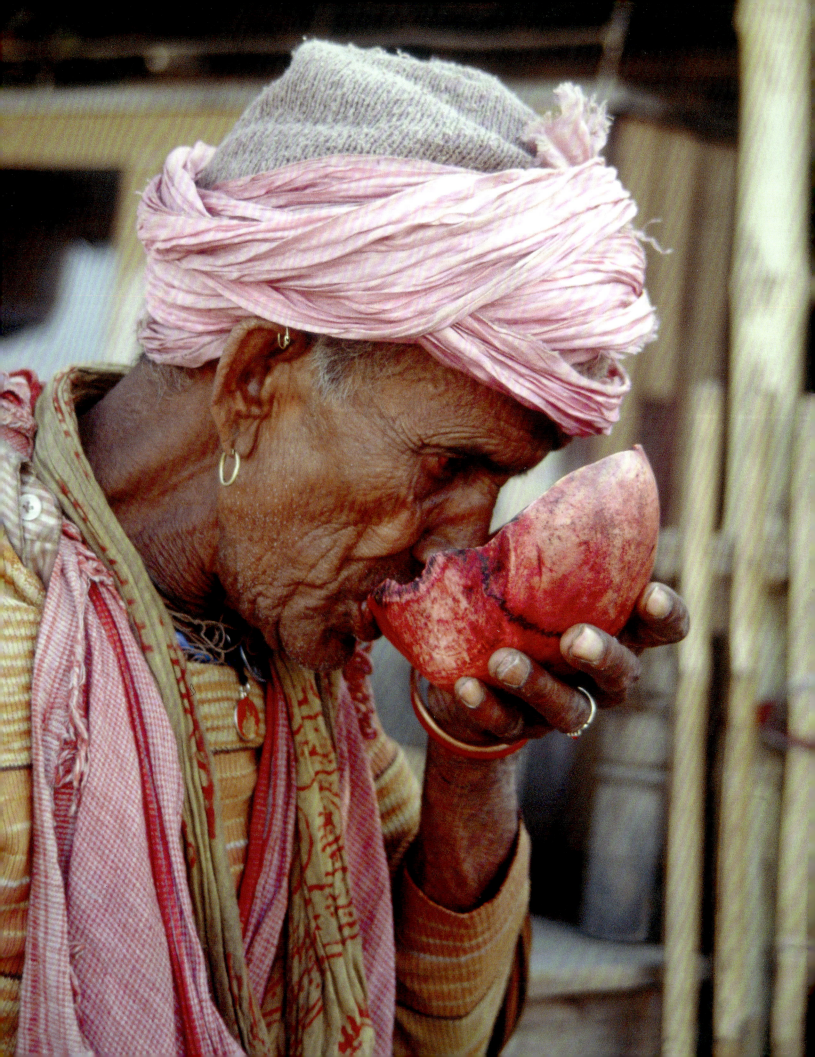

A photograph taken in 1992 shows Dashrath Ram, an Aghori from Varanasi, who belongs to the Kusht Seva ('Leprosy Service') Ashram founded by Awadhut Bhagwan Ram (1937–1992) (fig. 200). The latter became a major reformer of the sect by transforming the *ashram* into a social service centre dedicated to helping those stigmatized by society, including the *varna*-less 'untouchables', who from the 20th century have been referred to as Dalits ('oppressed').[115] A dedicated clinic was also built for those suffering from leprosy and other diseases deemed 'polluting'. This led to the founding of more *ashrams*, clinics and schools, which provided health and educational services for the socially marginalized. In the photograph Dashrath Ram drinks tea from a skull-cup. Hartsuiker notes that 'he did offend the onlookers

**Fig. 200**
**Dashrath Ram, photograph**
**by Dolf Hartsuiker**
Ujjain, Madhya Pradesh, India
1992
35 mm slide
British Museum 2014,3004 .1416
From the Hartsuiker Archive,
donated by Mr Dolf Hartsuiker

**Fig. 201**
*Shaitan Tantrik*, 2000
India
Printed pamphlet, 24.5 cm ×
18.5 cm
British Museum 2019,3029.5

on purpose by insisting on sharing the skull of tea with them. An offer they could not refuse, since it is *prasad*, divine food given by a holy man'.[116]

While Tantra is often equated with sexual hedonism in the West, today in India it is often dismissed or criticized as a marginal form of black magic, and practitioners associated with it, including the Aghoris, are often regarded as dangerous. This prevalent stereotype is partly a result of misunderstandings around some of the more transgressive left-hand practices, exacerbated by earlier colonial misinterpretations, and has been amplified by Hindi horror movies. *Shaitan Tantrik* (*Tantric Satan*, 2000) stars a villainous Tantrika who kidnaps women to conduct human sacrifices to the goddess Kali (fig. 201).[117] The accompanying poster features his

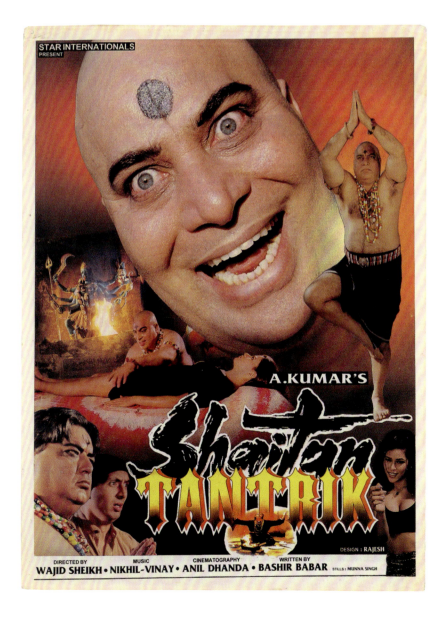

wide-eyed, maniacally grinning face with other shots of him standing in a yogic pose and groping at the body of one of his female victims, with a statue of Kali looming in the background. Indian newspaper reports continue to surface accusing Tantrikas of kidnapping and sacrificing children, among other criminal activities. These negative stereotypes are made worse by charismatic charlatans who claim to be Tantric masters and take advantage of Tantra's reputation by reductively promoting it as a form of black magic, offering their services for large sums of money.[118] Less well understood in many parts of India is the reality that Tantra is not independent of Hinduism and Buddhism but has pervaded and transformed both faiths since the early medieval period.

## TANTRA AND THE FEMALE GAZE

The Bauls (connoting 'madman' or religious ecstatic) are wandering bards with close ties to Tantra, mainly based around Bengal and Bangladesh. They are famous for their mystical songs, which they perform with simple stringed instruments, and for their syncretic beliefs that fuse Tantric, Bhakti and Sufi ideas, centring on the idea that divinity (whether in the form of Shiva, Shakti, Krishna, Radha or Allah) is present and accessible within the human body, which is itself a microcosm of the universe.[119] The Baul movement was at its peak during the 19th and early 20th centuries in Bengal, while many of its most celebrated songs (transmitted orally from guru to disciple) are attributed to Lalan Fakir (c. 1774–1890) and his disciple Duddu (1841–1911).[120] Those initiated into the Baul tradition come from all social backgrounds, including the rural poor, and can live as either married householders or ascetics.

The Bauls hold women in high esteem as bearers of Shakti. Parvathy Baul (b. 1976), a practitioner and teacher, was initiated and taught songs by her guru, Sanatan Das Baul (fig. 202). When she performs, she plays the one-stringed *ektara* along with a *duggi* (drum). She was drawn towards the Baul way of life at the age of sixteen:

> Baul freedom is limitless. It gives one such sense of peace, such freedom from one's bond even with oneself. (…) Baul philosophy goes beyond the natural link between biological man-woman and masculinity-femininity. Baul goes beyond religion, caste, creed and any limited identities.[121]

She has spent many years learning the songs of previous generations of Baul singers. The following is her translation of 'The Ananda Bazaar', by the Baul guru Haure Goshai, which describes the experience of awakening Kundalini through Hatha yoga, articulating the sect's Tantric worldview that all material reality is sacred, including the body itself:

**Fig. 202**
**Parvathy Baul performing**
**with *ektara* and *duggi***
India
2017

O the mad one, O my heart
Let us go to the bazaar of Ananda [bliss]
If you want have the true Darshan [sacred vision].
(…)
Go to the four-petalled lotus,
Awaken *kula kundalini*.
Find the stillness inside;
Find the silence in the heart and mind.
At the sacred space between your eyes
The jewel is hidden in the form of Shiva.[122]

As a practising artist, she also creates woodcut prints with her husband, Ravi Gopalan Nair, including one representing a group of female Baul musicians (fig. 203). Her inspiration comes from 'the metaphors, stories and history of the Baul oral tradition' which 'was not written down, as it is a process of "transmission" from Master to disciple, so there hasn't been any efforts to create images. But as a practitioner, I felt the need to create the images (…) which could create (…) visualization[s] of the Baul poetry'.[123]

Parvathy Baul is inspired by Bengali Tantric masters, including Bamakhepa (see Chapter 4) who persists in the popular imagination as an icon of power and devotion. In another of her woodcuts he stands, haloed and almost naked, standing in the cremation ground at Tarapith, with smoke from pyres billowing behind him, surrounded by dogs and human remains (fig. 204). Bamakhepa is remembered today for his dramatic visions of the goddess Tara, which often occurred in the cremation ground at night, not only because it was her residence, but also because the primal fear and close proximity to death encouraged her maternal instincts to protect her devotee.

A Tantrika who took initiation from Bamakhepa in 1902, Nigamananda Paramahansa (born Nalinikanta Chattopadhyay, 1880–1935), described his own visionary experience of Tara vividly. Bamakhepa had brought him to the cremation ground at midnight with three burnt bodies, and instructed him to meditate on Tara. Demonic apparitions haunted and distracted him. Bamakhepa would cry 'Tara! Tara!' every time Nigamananda's focus wavered. Eventually he felt his ego dissolve in a kind of 'ecstasy of death', achieving divine union with the goddess through a vision of her as a beautiful woman. He requested a vision of her cosmic form, and she became vast, with thousands of heads, tongues, bodies, weapons, grinding teeth, and eyes emitting fire.[124]

Contemporary female artists such as Parvathy Baul have been inspired by Tantric iconography, while others have playfully subverted it. Although many – if not most – Tantric traditions emphasize the role of women and goddesses, their traditional representations have sometimes been described as male constructions of 'femaleness'.[125] Certainly their often ambivalent characteristics, veering between overt eroticism and destructive violence, can be read as reflecting a male fear of feminine power. Nevertheless, this same ambivalence, which challenged traditional models of womanhood, has been a source of empowerment for modern women who continue to reclaim their spiritual authority in creative and emancipatory ways.[126] A monumental 1985 mixed-media painting by the Bengal-born British artist Sutapa Biswas (b. 1962) evokes Kali in a feminist guise. Its title, *Housewives with Steak-Knives*, challenges the stereotype of the submissive wife confined to the kitchen (fig. 205). Here the 'Housewife' as Kali (who may be Biswas herself) is four-armed and muscular, swinging an enormous, threatening blade (more machete than steak-knife), her hairy armpits defying traditional expectations of femininity. Her upper right hand displays the gesture (*mudra*) of peace and protection while her lower right hand holds a red flower (symbolizing her creative aspect) and a flag depicting two photocopied early 17th-century paintings by the Italian

**Fig. 203**
Female Baul performers at
a village festival, Parvathy
Baul (concept, drawing,
printing) and Ravi Gopalan
Nair (wood engraving)
India
2017
Woodcut, 78 × 56.5 cm.
British Museum 2019,3031.1

**Fig. 204**
Bamakhepa at Tarapith
cremation ground, Parvathy
Baul (concept, drawing,
printing) and Ravi Gopalan
Nair (wood engraving)
India
2017
Woodcut, 48.5 × 63.5 cm
British Museum 2019,3031.2

**Fig. 205**
*Housewives with Steak-Knives*, **Sutapa Biswas**
Leeds, UK
1985
Acrylic, pastel and xerox
collage on canvas-mounted
paper, 275 × 244 cm
Bradford Museum and
Galleries 1994-011

Baroque artist Artemisia Gentileschi. These paintings illustrate the apocryphal Old Testament story of the murder of the Assyrian general Holofernes by Judith, who seduced and beheaded him after he laid siege to Bethulia. The graphic violence of these paintings, and the fact Gentileschi returned to the subject multiple times, led to the theory that she was enacting a form of catharsis after she was raped by fellow painter Agostino Tassi, resulting in a lengthy, traumatic legal trial.[127] This visual expression of justice carried out by two women (Judith was assisted by her maid), and its autobiographical significance for Gentileschi, served as an inspiration to Biswas in her uniting of cross-cultural, defiant feminine forces.[128]

Even more striking is the garland of grotesque heads that Kali wears in Biswas's painting. Biswas describes them as figureheads of the white authoritarian patriarchy.[129] Adolf Hitler is clearly identifiable, while the larger, grinning fair-haired head has been likened to former British Conservative Prime Minister Edward Heath.[130] Biswas herself has noted that the latter head also represents the generic acquisitive colonial collector with a penchant for looting.[131] Across from Hitler's head is a monocle-wearing archetype of the 'upper echelons of [colonial] society'.[132] Below him is the bearded head of Leon Trotsky, whose presence Biswas notes 'was intended to be an uncomfortable or complicating presence to the whole dynamic. Not least because Karl Marx and Rosa Luxemburg are of course two of my heroes'.[133] Kali's politically charged, topical garland of heads in this painting makes an interesting parallel to the one worn by Kali in the late 19th-century Calcutta Art Studio print (see Chapter 4, fig. 149) in which the heads were deemed suspiciously European-looking, as well as the garland of heads of the loyal 'sons of India' worn by Bharat Mata (Mother India) in a print made in the 1940s (see Chapter 4, fig. 155). Just as Kali was reimagined by anti-colonial revolutionaries as an icon of Mother India rising to fight against her oppressors, here Biswas channels the goddess's power to challenge patriarchal structures.[134]

Like Biswas, Bharti Kher (born in London in 1969 to Indian parents), now based in Delhi, draws on the bodies of real women in her creation of dramatic and resonant 'urban goddesses'.[135] Her life-size sculptures are made from casts of the bodies of friends and acquaintances, whose naked muscular, fleshy, strong and dimpled features are infused with a powerful gravity, blurring the boundaries between mortal and divine. Her sculpture *And all the while the benevolent slept* (2008) is an evocation of the Tantric goddess Chinnamasta (fig. 206). Headless and squatting on a log, Chinnamasta holds up what is presumably her own skull while copper wires shoot out at all angles from its open neck, like jets of blood. The skull is a cast of the reconstructed skull of Lucy, the female *Australopithecus* found in Ethiopia in 1974, who is the oldest known human ancestor (3.2 million years old). This nod to human origins alludes to Chinnamasta's

embodiment of the foundation and cycle of life itself. In another hand
the figure balances a jarringly quaint teacup on a saucer, a witty signifier
of bourgeois domesticity, which was transplanted from Britain to India
during the colonial period. One wonders at the fate of the original owner
of this teacup at the hands of the confrontational goddess. Here the
teacup has become a substitute for a Tantric skull-cup used to catch the
gushing fluid. The menacing, violently graphic but simultaneously playful
nature of the figure is made all the more unsettling by the sculpture's
uncanny realism and immediacy. Kher describes the goddesses she is
attracted to, including popular images of Kali, as ones that are 'strangely
masculine'.[136] This interest in gender fluidity extends to her own sculptures
– here Chinnamasta has breasts but a phallic shape emerges from her
groin, binding her to the log. In some images of Chinnamasta, she is
shown squatting over the passive body of the god Shiva while being
penetrated by his erect phallus in the *viparita-rata* position (as Kali is shown
in Chapter 4, fig. 131), which is equally suggested here, the log (as inert as
the corpse-Shiva) evoking his presence. The deliberate gender ambiguity of

**Fig. 206**
*And all the while the
benevolent slept*, **Bharti
Kher**
Delhi, India
2008
Fibreglass, porcelain, plastic,
pedestal in mahogany wood,
and copper wires, 178.5 ×
220 × 121 cm

**Fig. 207**
*The Messenger*, Bharti Kher
Delhi, India
2011
Fibreglass, wooden rake, sari,
resin and granite, 188 × 136 ×
84 cm

Kher's figure recalls the *c.* 3rd-century description of the woman-on-top sexual position by Vatsyayana in the *Kama Sutra* in which it is not called the 'reverse' posture but *purushayitva*, 'to play the man's role'.[137]

Kher's *The Messenger* (2011) is another of her 'urban goddesses', this time conjuring a yogini follower of Shiva complete with pitchfork, alluding to his trident or *trishula* (fig. 207). She raises one of her legs, supported by a muscular arm, in a yogic pose that is emphasized by her meditative expression. The *sari*, barely concealing her nudity, wraps itself around her neck and is pierced by the pitchfork as if to suggest a disavowal of dress and, by extension, the containment of female sexuality. She at once embodies the autonomy of a wandering, flesh-and-blood yogini from a Sultanate painting (fig. 76), the gravity of a Yogini temple goddess hewn in stone (fig. 31), and the uncontainable energy of a Tibetan Dakini (fig. 106).

# CONCLUSION

As a body of beliefs and practices, Tantra has historically appealed to a broad spectrum of people from different social, political, religious and cultural backgrounds in South Asia and beyond. Those who engaged with the material described across the chapters of this book have included the following kinds of audiences: rulers and members of the court seeking worldly benefits, who commissioned Tantric objects and architecture; Tantric specialists (from gurus and yogis to lamas and monks) cultivating *siddhis* via esoteric means, who wielded ritual instruments as well as objects used for meditational purposes; members of the general public seeking prosperity, health, protection and spiritual gains, who would have encountered public devotional sculptures and acquired pilgrimage souvenirs after visits to sacred sites; and, in the final two chapters, anti-colonial revolutionaries and avant-garde artists who reimagined Tantra as an insurgent source of inspiration. The book has also highlighted the role of women, and the uniquely powerful roles they were able to play as autonomous practitioners and gurus due to Tantra's emphasis on the divine feminine.

Tantra is, above all, a form of corporeal spirituality: an affirmation of the visceral qualities of existence, and a vision of the world as sacred power or Shakti, which can be accessed through the body itself. This validation of the body as a channel for spiritual transformation was articulated succinctly by the 8th-century Tantric master Padmasambhava, who is said to have declared that 'the human body is the basis for attaining enlightenment'.[1] A Tantrika breaks down perceived distinctions between the body and the universe, and the self and the divine, in order to ultimately 'become' a Tantric god or goddess. The previous chapters have explored the range of different mental and bodily practices for achieving this, from visualizations and mantras to yoga and the adoption of a deity's attributes, all of which inspired masterpieces of sculpture, painting and ritual objects. Tantra is also a means of harnessing and releasing myriad forms of power, both supernatural and worldly. According to the Tantric worldview, the fabric of the phenomenal world, characterized by its fluidity and malleability, can be transformed rather than transcended.

Western misunderstandings of Tantra date back to the 19th century, as discussed in Chapter 4. Indeed, the most contentious characteristic of Tantra, and the key reason for its misinterpretation by Christian missionaries, Orientalist scholars and, more recently, New Age enthusiasts, is the role of sexual rites in Tantric practice. Once attacked by colonial officials as perverse, since the 1960s Tantra as a tradition has been celebrated as the 'art of sexual ecstasy'. Tantric visual culture features a proliferation of erotic images and many Tantric texts include descriptions of sexual rites, but these make up only a small proportion of the content. While *kama* ('desire') was a principle goal of life according to orthodox Hinduism, one of the central aims of Tantric sex was to unite with divinity and attain *siddhis*, rather than pleasure for its own sake. Here again we see a validation of the body and the sensual as a means of achieving liberation and generating power. As discussed in Chapters 1, 2 and 3, sexual rites could be imagined as an internal union of deities using visualization exercises, or carried out literally by a couple assuming the roles of Shiva and Shakti, or Buddhist deities embodying wisdom and compassion such as Chakrasamvara and Vajrayogini.

One of the main reasons Tantra has been misunderstood for so long is because of its apparent contradictions. Early British translators of the *Tantras* focused on the most titillating passages and uninitiated readers interpreted them literally, without recognizing their philosophical underpinnings or the complex tensions between Tantra's left-hand (*vama*) and right-hand (*dakshina*) paths, which allowed for multiple readings. On the other hand, early 20th-century writers such as John Woodroffe attempted to skirt over the more transgressive passages by interpreting them purely symbolically. This book has sought to provide the interpretive tools for understanding that such tensions between literal and symbolic registers can co-exist and are part of what make Tantra unique. The tension between public and private is also a recurring one. Most objects in the book were created for public spaces, but the Tantric texts that inspired them often describe secret rites that can only be grasped by the initiated.

This tension between the literal and the symbolic, and the private and the public, also informs the role of transgression in Tantra, particularly in its intentional violation of Brahmanical laws of purity, which is far more key to Tantra than sex alone. Tantric engagement with the taboo (again, both literally and/or symbolically), from alcohol and blood to human remains, challenged orthodox Hindu and Buddhist codes of conduct in order to channel the repressed powers of the forbidden and to confront emotional obstacles to enlightenment. Whether or not the transgressive elements of Tantric texts are taken literally, both left-hand and right-hand approaches harness the same reservoir of subversive and convention-defying symbols to transcend polarities. Distinctions between purity and impurity are broken down in order to create the conditions for the practitioner's self-deification. This gave rise to a range of visual symbols drawing on the potency of the taboo in depictions of Tantric deities, including skull-cups (*kapalas*) overflowing with entrails. The *kapala* has been a frequent Tantric signifier and in representations of gods and goddesses it is filled with sacrificial offerings as well as symbolic negative forces, to be transmuted into ambrosia. It is hoped that the case studies in this book will enable the reader to recognize certain symbols and iconographic patterns as central to the Tantric imaginary, allowing them to 'read' the philosophy through its imagery. Indeed, it is easier to understand Tantra through its visual vocabulary than through its texts and rituals alone, which are often highly esoteric and intentionally cryptic to the uninitiated. As the Japanese monk Kukai (774–835) noted:

> In truth, the esoteric [Tantric] doctrines are so profound as to defy their enunciation in writing. With the help of painting, however, their obscurities may be understood. The various attitudes and *mudras* [ritual gestures] of the holy images all have their source in the Buddha's love, and one may attain Buddhahood at the sight of them (…). Art is what reveals to us the state of perfection.[2]

The visual rhetoric of military conquest and warfare adopted by Tantric gods and goddesses likewise elucidates Tantric ideals, as explored in Chapters 1 and 3. These fierce and heavily armed deities were protectors of the realm, with the potential to drive away, immobilize, confuse and annihilate its enemies. Simultaneously, these enemies could be understood as internal obstacles, such as misplaced pride and ego, which only the most ferocious deities have the power to obliterate. Such co-existing tensions in meaning altered depending on who was approaching the deity – whether a ruler, a lay householder or a monk. A *vajra*, for example, is not only a sacred ceremonial weapon but also a symbol of the unbreakable force of the enlightened state, while the *ramdao* is wielded by temple priests to make animal sacrifices to Kali, whose own sword of knowledge cuts through attachments to the ego. As described in Chapter 4, sacrificing a 'white goat' to Kali became a famous euphemism during the colonial period in India, when the goddess's violent nature was heralded by anti-colonial rebels in Bengal as a form of resistance. This was partly an instrumentalization of earlier British anxieties around Tantric deities such as Kali, who was viewed as demonic and capable of inspiring ritualistic murders, leading to the sensational Thuggee stereotype that still persists to this day.[3]

This book has set out to dispel myths around Tantra as either a sexual or Satanic cult by tracing the history and influence of the movement in India, from its origins, major beliefs and artistic expressions to its global reach. Tantra grew to become one of the most successful philosophical movements in India, transforming South Asia's major religions, especially Hinduism and Buddhism. Tantra is often disavowed as an intrinsic part of South Asian culture due to its associations with black magic, despite the fact that many of the *Tantras* themselves were originally composed in Sanskrit by *pandits* based in Hindu and Buddhist monastic centres. Wherever it took hold across Asia, Tantra was able to adapt to its political and cultural contexts and to respond to different belief systems (including Bön in Tibet and Shinto in Japan). From the 20th century onwards, Tantra has come to mean much more than the original intentions outlined in the texts, as discussed in Chapter 5. It is hoped that readers will have acquired a deeper understanding of Tantra that will allow them to appreciate the diversity and vitality of its philosophies and practices, and the richness of its artistic traditions, through the contexts to which the objects described belonged. Above all, it is hoped that readers have also been stimulated and challenged to question their own ideas about the nature of the divine.

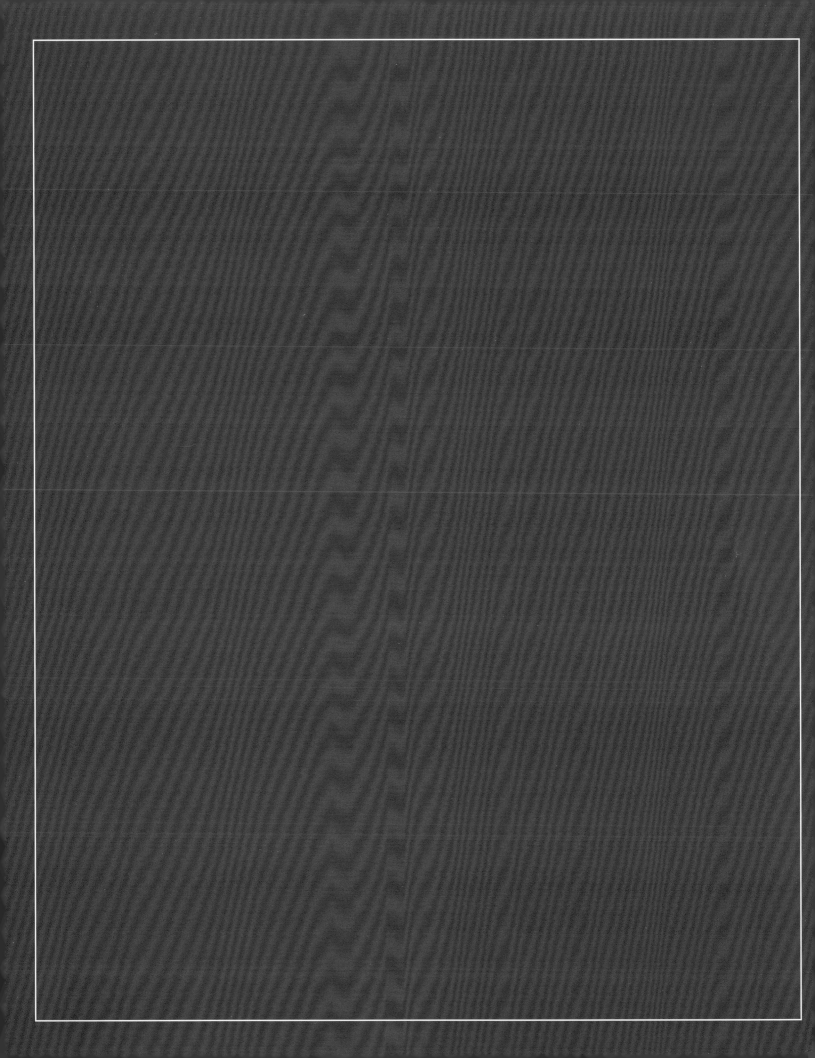

# RESOURCES

# NOTES

**PRELUDE**
**(pp. 8–11)**

1    For a detailed study of Kamakhya and Assamese Tantra, see: Urban, *The Power of Tantra*.

2    The festival dates back to at least the 11th century and is first described in the *Devibhagavata Purana*. *Devibhagavata Purana of Ksemaraja Sri Krsnadasa* (Delhi, 1986), 9.9.35–37. See: Urban, *The Power of Tantra*, 53–54.

3    It has been suggested that the temple's priests pour vermilion powder into the water. Urban, *The Power of Tantra*, 84.

4    The *Dharma Sutras*, Hindu texts outlining socio-religious duties dating between the 3rd century BCE and 1st century CE, state that even touching a menstruating woman is contaminating. See: Olivelle, *Dharmasutras*, 102–103, 108–109, 151–52, 263.

5    Ramos, 'The Visual Politics of Menstruation', 52–68. The sculpture's iconography conforms to early images of the goddess Lajja Gauri, who was not originally conceived of as menstruating but was instead meant to suggest birth and divine creation. While at Kamakhya devotees apply *sindoor* to the figure's vulva, at other temples the worship of Lajja Gauri is performed by ablutions of *ghee* or clarified butter applied to the pudendum, a substance equated with semen according to early Vedic texts. Crucially, though, pregnancy and menstruation were not mutually exclusive according to the *c.* 10th-century *Kalika Purana*, composed in Assam. In this text, the god Vishnu unites with the goddess Earth during her menstrual period, resulting in the birth of Naraka, who becomes the king of Kamarupa (present-day Assam) and a devotee of Kamakhya.

**INTRODUCTION**
**(pp. 12–23)**

1    Brown and Harper (eds.), *The Roots of Tantra*, 121–22; White, 'Bhairava', 488.

2    Apart from the *Tantras* themselves, there are also other Sanskrit instructional texts containing Tantric material, such as the *Agamas* and *Samhitas*.

3    See: Flood, *An Introduction to Hinduism*; Lipner, *Hindus: Their Religious Beliefs and Practices*.

4    Fowler, 'Brahmanical Hinduism', 156–57.

5    Flood, *An Introduction to Hinduism*, 158; Padoux, *The Hindu Tantric World*, 8; White (ed.), *Tantra in Practice*, 3–40.

6    Harvey, *An Introduction to Buddhism*, 133.

7    Lipner, 'Samsara'.

8    Padoux, *The Heart of the Yogini*, 104.

9    Padoux, *The Heart of the Yogini*, 19.

10   Padoux, *The Hindu Tantric World*, 107.

11   Sanderson, 'Saivism and the Tantric Traditions', 667; Brown and Harper (eds.), *The Roots of Tantra*, 3; Padoux, *The Hindu Tantric World*, 30.

12   Bhattacharyya, *Guhyasamajatantra*, Vol. 53, 20–21. Quoted in Snellgrove, *Indo-Tibetan Buddhism*, 171.

13   Sferra, 'A Fragment of the *Vajramritamahatantra*', 425.

14   Ibid.

15   Mimaki and Tomabechi (eds.), *Pancakrama*, verses 30–24a. Quoted in Wedemeyer, *Making Sense of Tantric Buddhism*, 122.

16   Wedemeyer, *Making Sense of Tantric Buddhism*, 105–206; White, 'Tantra', in Jacobsen et al. (eds.), *Brill's Encyclopedia of Hinduism*, 169; Gray, 'Tantra and the Tantric Traditions of Hinduism and Buddhism', 11; Flood, *An Introduction to Hinduism*, 190.

17   Urban, *The Power of Tantra*, 102.

18   English, E., *Vajrayogini: A Study*, 41.

19   Sferra, 'A Fragment of the *Vajramritamahatantra*', 418.

20   Ibid., 426.

21   Sanderson, 'The Saiva Age: The Rise and Dominance of Saivism', 288.

22   Sastri (ed.), *Svacchandatantra with the Commentary (Svacchandoddyota) of Rajanaka Ksemaraja*, verses 4.539c–545. Quoted in Sanderson, 'The Saiva Age: The Rise and Dominance of Saivism', 293–94.

23   See: Lorenzen, *The Kapalikas and Kalamukhas*; Törzsök, 'Kapalikas', 355–61.

24   Goodall and Isaacson, 'Tantric Traditions', 122; White, 'Tantra', in Jacobsen et al. (eds.), *Brill's Encyclopedia of Hinduism*, 173.

25   Törzsök, 'Women in Early Sakta Tantras', 363; White (ed.), *Tantra in Practice*, 17; Flood, *An Introduction to Hinduism*, 191.

26   Buhler, *The Laws of Manu*, 195–97. See also: Wadley, 'Women and the Hindu Tradition', 117–18, Hiltebeitel and Erndl (eds.), *Is the Goddess a Feminist?*, 95.

27   Dutt, Nalinaksha, *Bodhisattvabhumi* (Patna: Jayaswal Research Institute, 1978), 66. Translated by Jan Willis in: Willis, J. 'Nuns and Benefactresses', 69. See also: Shaw, *Passionate Enlightenment*, 27; Kajiyama, 'Women in Buddhism', 53–70; Sponberg, 'Attitudes toward Women and the Feminine in Early Buddhism', 3–36; Paul, *Women in Buddhism: Images of the Feminine*.

28   Törzsök, 'Women in Early Sakta Tantras', 342; Biernacki, *Renowned Goddess of Desire*, 33; Shaw, *Passionate Enlightenment*, 4.

**CHAPTER 1:**
**THE RISE OF TANTRA**
**IN MEDIEVAL INDIA**
**(pp. 24–67)**

1    Davidson, *Indian Esoteric Buddhism*, 26, 33.

2    Mitter, *Indian Art*, 48.

3    See: Doniger, *Siva: The Erotic Ascetic*.

4    Sanderson, 'The Saiva Age: The Rise and Dominance of Saivism', 45.

5    The *Siddhanta Tantras* and *Bhairava Tantras* are classified as *Mantramarga* ('Path of *Mantras*') texts, *Mantramarga* being a branch of Tantric Hinduism also sometimes referred to as Tantric Shaivism. Hatley, 'Tantric Saivism in Early Medieval India', 615; Sanderson, 'Saiva Texts', 10–42; Flood (ed.), *The Blackwell Companion to Hinduism*, 205; White, 'Bhairava', 485; Goodall and Isaacson, 'Tantric Traditions', 122.

6    Pal, *Indian Sculpture*, 244.

7    Many thanks to Laxshmi Rose Greaves for drawing my attention to this sculpture and to other examples of Bhairava-like images from Ahichhatra. Greaves, 'Brick Foundations: North Indian Brick Temple Architecture and Terracotta Art'.

8    White, 'Bhairava', 488; Visuvalingam, Elizabeth-Chalier, 'Bhairava's Royal Brahmanicide: The Problem of the Mahabrahmana, A Post-Structuralist Hermeneutic of Hindu Mythico-Ritual Discourse Based on the Phenomenology of Transgressive Sacrality', in Hiltebeitel (ed.), *Criminal Gods and Demon Devotees*, 167.

9    *Netratantram [Mrtyunjaya Bhattaraka] with the Commentary Udyota of Ksemarajacarya*; edited by Vajravallabh Dwivedi (Delhi: Parimal Publications, 1985), 19.207–211. Quoted in White, 'Bhairava', 489.

10   Lorenzen, *The Kapalikas and Kalamukhas*, 97–140; Flood (ed.), *The Blackwell Companion to Hinduism*, 208.

11   Törzsök, 'Kapalikas', 355.

12   Flood (ed.), *The Blackwell Companion to Hinduism*, 212.

13   Törzsök, 'Kapalikas', 358.

14   Settar, *Hoysala Sculptures in the National Museum, Copenhagen*, 80.

15 Their name may refer to the black streaks that marked their foreheads, differentiating them from other sects. Lorenzen, *The Kapalikas and Kalamukhas*, 97; Flood (ed.), *The Blackwell Companion to Hinduism*, 208.

16 Most references to the Kalamukhas come from South Indian inscriptions dating between the 9th and 13th centuries. Törzsök, 'Kapalikas', 356.

17 Diamond, et al., *Yoga: The Art of Transformation*, 106.

18 Flood (ed.), *The Blackwell Companion to Hinduism*, 220. See also: Dehejia (ed.), *The Sensuous and the Sacred*, 118.

19 *Tiruvalankattu Mutta Tirupatikam*, 1.1. Quoted in Craddock, 'The Anatomy of Devotion', 134.

20 *Tiruvirattai Manimalai*, 13. Quoted in Craddock, 'The Anatomy of Devotion', 142.

21 *Tiruvalankattu Mutta Tirupatikam*, 2.8. Quoted in Craddock, 'The Anatomy of Devotion', 136.

22 Hudson, D. Dennis, 'Violent and Fanatical Devotion Among the Nayanars: A Study in the *Periya Puranam* of Cekkilar', in Hiltebeitel (ed.), *Criminal Gods and Demon Devotees*, 397.

23 Flood (ed.), *The Blackwell Companion to Hinduism*, 209–11, 217; Gray, 'Tantra and the Tantric Traditions of Hinduism and Buddhism'.

24 Sanderson, 'Saivism and the Tantric Traditions', 668.

25 Sanderson, 'The Saiva Age: The Rise and Dominance of Saivism', 250.

26 Flood (ed.), *The Blackwell Companion to Hinduism*, 211, 217.

27 Sanderson, 'The Saiva Age: The Rise and Dominance of Saivism', 260.

28 Ibid., 254.

29 Davidson, *Indian Esoteric Buddhism*, 177; Hatley, 'Tantric Saivism in Early Medieval India', 622.

30 The *Vajrabhairava Tantra* (8th–10th century) stresses the need for the *satkarmans* to be 'performed in full meditative equipoise, or otherwise the devotee will bring down the rites on himself'. Siklos, 'Vajrabhairava Tantras: Tibetan and Mongolian Texts', 115.

31 Davidson, *Indian Esoteric Buddhism*, 177; Davidson, *Tibetan Renaissance*, 35.

32 Harvey, *An Introduction to Buddhism*, 181; Davidson, *Indian Esoteric Buddhism*, 74, 86, 112; Linrothe, *Ruthless Compassion*, 5; Hatley, 'Converting the Dakini', 37–38.

33 Isaacson and Sferra, 'Tantric Literature: Overview', 307–20; Sanderson, 'Saivism and the Tantric Traditions', 678.

34 Linrothe (ed.), *Holy Madness*, 39.

35 Davidson, *Indian Esoteric Buddhism*, 202, 217–18; Linrothe, *Ruthless Compassion*, 237.

36 Huntington and Bangdel, *The Circle of Bliss*, 25.

37 Ibid., 243; Linrothe, *Ruthless Compassion*, 253.

38 Sanderson, 'The Saiva Age: The Rise and Dominance of Saivism', 98–99.

39 Payne, 'Homa: Tantric Fire Ritual'.

40 Sanderson, 'The Saiva Age: The Rise and Dominance of Saivism', 91, 93.

41 Davidson, *Indian Esoteric Buddhism*, 61.

42 Davidson, *Tibetan Renaissance*, 31.

43 The inscription reveals that 'this is the pious gift of Dahapati'. Translation by S. P. Tewari.

44 Sanderson, 'The Saiva Age: The Rise and Dominance of Saivism', 116, 124.

45 Pal (ed.), *The Art of Tibet*, 44; Rhie and Thurman, *Wisdom and Compassion*, 215; Huntington and Bangdel, *The Circle of Bliss*, 252.

46 Linrothe, *Ruthless Compassion*, 9.

47 Zwalf (ed.), *Buddhism: Art and Faith*, 115.

48 Davidson, *Indian Esoteric Buddhism*, 213.

49 Linrothe, *Ruthless Compassion*, 187, 277.

50 Ibid., 217.

51 See: Coburn, *Encountering the Goddess*.

52 Many of the early medieval *Puranas* devoted to Shiva and Shakti, though ostensibly orthodox Vedic texts, reveal a blurring of Brahmanical-Tantric boundaries. Sanderson, 'The Saiva Age: The Rise and Dominance of Saivism', 250; Flood, *An Introduction to Hinduism*, 110, 113, 181.

53 Blurton, *Hindu Art*, 170.

54 Hatley, 'From Matr to Yogini: Continuity and Transformation', 113.

55 Banerji, 'Neulpur Grant of Subhakara: The 8th Year', 1–8.

56 Flood, *An Introduction to Hinduism*, 176–77; Hatley, 'From Matr to Yogini: Continuity and Transformation', 113.

57 Coburn, *Encountering the Goddess*, 83.

58 Kulke, 'Jagannatha as the State Deity under the Gajapatis of Orissa', 201.

59 Coburn, *Encountering the Goddess*, 63–64.

60 Sanderson, 'The Saiva Age: The Rise and Dominance of Saivism', 52.

61 Davidson, *Indian Esoteric Buddhism*, 58.

62 Coburn, *Encountering the Goddess*, 61.

63 Ibid., 66–67.

64 Ibid., 71.

65 Harper, Katherine Anne, 'The Warring Saktis: A Paradigm for Gupta Conquests', in Harper and Brown (eds.), *The Roots of Tantra*, 121–22, 128; Hatley, 'From Matr to Yogini: Continuity and Transformation', 6.

66 Sullivan, 'Tantroid Phenomena in Early Indic Literature', 12; Willis, *The Archaeology of Hindu Ritual*, 179.

67 Hatley, 'From Matr to Yogini: Continuity and Transformation', 1, 7; Blurton, *Hindu Art*, 166.

68 Mitter, *Indian Art*, 34–35; Blurton, *Hindu Art*, 47.

69 Kinsley, *Hindu Goddesses: Visions of the Divine Feminine*, 155.

70 Donaldson, *Tantra and Sakta Art of Orissa*, 373, 381.

71 Donaldson, 'Orissan Images of Varahi, Oddiyana Marici, and Related Sow-Faced Goddesses', 158–59.

72 Donaldson, *Tantra and Sakta Art of Orissa*, 176.

73 Agrawala, 'A Rare Image of Varahi', 167.

74 Coburn, *Encountering the Goddess*, 62.

75 Sanderson, 'The Saiva Age: The Rise and Dominance of Saivism', 231.

76 Sircar, 'Murti Siva's Bangarh Prasasti', 34–56, quoted on 49–50.

77 Sferra, 'A Fragment of the Vajramritamahatantra', 425.

78 Ibid.

79 Atherton, 'Chamunda and Early Hindu Tantrism in Western India', 61.

80 *Tiruvalankattu Talavaralarum Tiruppatikankalum*, 1.1. Quoted in Craddock, 'The Anatomy of Devotion', 134.

81 Guy and Willis, *L'Escultura en els Temples Indis*, 107; Krishna, *Art Under the Gurjara-Pratiharas*, 164.

82 See: Donaldson, 'The Sava-Vahana as Purusa in Orissan Images', 107–41.

83 Suru (ed.), *Karpura-Manjari by Kaviraja Rajasekhara*, 1.22. Quoted in White, *Kiss of the Yogini*, 142.

84 Suru (ed.), *Karpura-Manjari by Kaviraja Rajasekhara*, 4.15. Quoted in White, *Kiss of the Yogini*, 143.

85 Sastri, M. K. (ed.), *Netratantra with the Commentary (Netroddyota) of Rajanaka Ksemaraja*. Quoted in Sanderson, 'The Saiva Age: The Rise and Dominance of Saivism', 273.

86 Sanderson, 'The Saiva Age: The Rise and Dominance of Saivism', 258.

87 *Epigraphia Indica*, Vol. 1 (Calcutta & Delhi: Archaeological Survey of India, 1892), 61–66, verses 11.13–14.

88 Hatley, 'From Matr to Yogini: Continuity and Transformation', 2, 10; Hatley, 'Goddesses in Text and Stone', 195; White, 'Yogini', 823.

89 Sanderson, 'Saiva Texts', 21.

90 White, *Kiss of the Yogini*, 27.

91 Ibid., 11, 19; White, 'Yogini', 823.

92 *Brahmayamala / Picumata*, National Archives of Kathmandu MS. No. 3-370, Nepal-German

Manuscript Reservation Project Reel No. A42/6, 14.213–218. Quoted in Hatley, Shaman, 'What is a Yogini? Towards a Polythetic Definition', in Keul (ed.), *'Yogini' in South Asia*, 28.

93 Bagchi (ed.), *Kaulajnananirnaya and Some Minor Texts*, 11.7cd–10.

94 Ibid.

95 Boner and Sarma, *Silpa Prakasa*, verse 98.

96 Kaimal, *Scattered Goddesses*, 27.

97 Ibid., 110; Dehejia, *Yogini Cult and Temples*, 182.

98 Hatley, 'Goddesses in Text and Stone', 216. See also: White, *Kiss of the Yogini*.

99 Dehejia, *Yogini Cult and Temples*, 90.

100 White, *Kiss of the Yogini*, 12.

101 Dehejia, *Yogini Cult and Temples*, 89.

102 Ibid., 13.

103 Siklos, *Vajrabhairava Tantras: Tibetan and Mongolian Texts*, 95.

104 Dehejia, *Yogini Cult and Temples*, 59, 186.

105 White, *Kiss of the Yogini*, 13.

106 Retold in: Forbes, *Ras-mala: Hindu Annals of Western India*, 238.

107 Hatley, 'Goddesses in Text and Stone', 208; Hatley and Kiss, *The Brahmayamalatantra or Picumata*, Vol. 2, 126; Hatley, 'From Matr to Yogini: Continuity and Transformation', 9.

108 Sastri, J. L. (ed.), *Kathasaritsagarah*, 3.5.102a–4a, 105a–6b. Quoted in White, *Kiss of the Yogini*, 212.

109 Flood, *An Introduction to Hinduism*, 190–91.

110 Rabe, Michael D. 'Secret Yantras and Erotic Display for Hindu Temples', in White (ed.), *Tantra in Practice*, 434; Donaldson, 'Propitious-Apotropaic Eroticism in the Art of Orissa', 76.

111 Boner and Sarma, *Silpa Prakasa*, 1.90b–106, 499, 500, 501, 502, 539.

112 White, *Kiss of the Yogini*, 140.

113 Nevertheless, the *Kama Sutra* does contain passages dedicated to oral sex. See: Doniger, *Kamasutra: A New Complete English Translation*, 67.

114 Donaldson, *Hindu Temple Art of Orissa*, 1166.

115 Sears, 'Encountering Ascetics', 189.

116 White, *Kiss of the Yogini*, 99.

117 Schoterman (ed.), *The Yoni Tantra*, 2.22–24.

118 Ibid., 3.16–17.

119 Ibid., 3.1, 12.

120 *Brahmayamala/Picumata*, National Archives of Kathmandu MS. No. 3-370; Nepal-German Manuscript Reservation Project Reel No. A42/6, 24.53c–54b. Quoted in Törzsök, 'Women in Early Sakta Tantras', 344.

121 See: Dupuche, *Abhinavagupta*.

122 Padoux, *The Hindu Tantric World*, 92.

123 Ibid., 93. See: Dupuche, *Abhinavagupta*, stanza 127.

124 Padoux, *The Hindu Tantric World*, 87, 92, 95.

125 White (ed.), *Tantra in Practice*, 16; White, *Kiss of the Yogini*, 76.

126 Boner and Sarma, *Silpa Prakasa*, verses 2.533–34.

127 Custodi, 'Review of "The Kiss of the Yogini"', 539–44. See: Törzsök, 'Women in Early Sakta Tantras'; Shaw, *Passionate Enlightenment*; Biernacki, *Renowned Goddess of Desire*; Kragh, 'Appropriation and Assertion of the Female Self', 85–108; Padoux, *The Hindu Tantric World*, 48; White (ed.), *Tantra in Practice*, 18.

128 Padoux, *The Hindu Tantric World*, 92. See: Dupuche, *Abhinavagupta*, stanza 101.

129 Kiss, *The Brahmayamala Tantra or Picumata*, 45.185c–188.

130 Bryant, *The Museum by the Park*, 73.

131 De Almeida and Gilpin, *Indian Renaissance: British Romantic Art and the Prospect of India*, 52.

132 Caption on engraving depicting the erotic sculpture that illustrated Richard Payne Knight's *A Discourse on the Worship of Priapus* (London, 1786); British Museum, 2005,0805.0.1.

133 Bryant, *The Museum by the Park*, 73; Mitter, *Much Maligned Monsters*, 91.

134 Translation from French to English by Qamar Maclean. Thanks are due also to Pauline Dorio. D'Hancarville, *Recherches sur l'origine, l'esprit et les progrés des arts de la Grèce*, 104–105.

135 Payne Knight, *A Discourse on the Worship of Priapus*, 47.

136 De Almeida and Gilpin, *Indian Renaissance: British Romantic Art and the Prospect of India*, 52.

137 Objects stored in the Museum Secretum were provided with unique identification numbers. The number 'M. 633' was painted onto the erotic sculpture from India.

138 Gaimster, 'Sex and Sensibility at the British Museum', 14; Shah, 'Sexuality on Display: A Case Study'.

139 Urban, 'The Extreme Orient', 130.

## CHAPTER 2:
## TANTRIC YOGA AND THE COURT
## (PP. 68–111)

1 Mallinson and Singleton, *Roots of Yoga*, 374.

2 Early Tantric texts often use the term 'yoga' to refer to a broad range of practices designed to achieve self-deification. Hatha yoga drew on these (sometimes transgressive) techniques through complex visualizations, sublimating them within the body of the yogi or yogini, while also introducing new bodily practices. Tantric texts pre-dating (as well as post-dating) Hatha yoga ones teach systems of yoga, such as Somadeva Vasudeva's *Yoga of the Malinivijayottaratantra* (personal correspondence with James Mallinson, October 2019). See also: White, David Gordon, 'Yoga in Transformation', in Diamond, et al., *Yoga: The Art of Transformation*, 38.

3 Padoux, *The Hindu Tantric World*, 39, 74–75; Diamond, Debra, 'Yoga: The Art of Transformation', in Diamond, et al., *Yoga: The Art of Transformation*, 28.

4 Mallinson, 'The *Amrtasiddhi*: Hathayoga's Tantric Buddhist Source Text'.

5 Mallinson, 'Translation of the *Dattatreyayogasastra*', 3.

6 Hatley, 'Kundalini'; Flood, *An Introduction to Hinduism*, 98; Diamond, Debra, 'Nath Siddhas', in Diamond, et al., *Yoga: The Art of Transformation*, 128.

7 The term 'subtle body' (*sukshma-sharira*) has also been used. However, as James Mallinson notes, this is a Vedantic term that is not present in Hatha yoga texts (personal correspondence, October 2019). The *chakras* of the yogic body are not always seven in number; the number varies according to traditions and texts. Padoux, *The Hindu Tantric World*, 76; Flood, *The Tantric Body*, 160; Hatley, 'Kundalini', forthcoming.

8 Flood, *The Tantric Body*, 157–58; Padoux, *The Hindu Tantric World*, 75–76; Menzies (ed.), *Goddess: Divine Energy*, 173–74.

9 Padoux, *The Hindu Tantric World*, 94; Flood, *An Introduction to Hinduism*, 190–91; White, *The Alchemical Body*, 199–201.

10 Mallinson and Singleton, *Roots of Yoga*, 220, 245; White (ed.), *Tantra in Practice*, 15.

11 Mallinson, 'Siddhi and Mahasiddhi in Early *Hathayoga*', 327–44.

12 Diamond, Debra, 'The Subtle Body', in Diamond, et al., *Yoga: The Art of Transformation*, 166.

13 Sears, Tamara, 'Portraying the Guru', in Diamond, et al., *Yoga: The Art of Transformation*, 117; Ahuja, *Rupa-pratirupa: The Body in Indian Art*, 169.

14 Menzies (ed.), *Goddess: Divine Energy*, 175; White, *The Alchemical Body*, 226.

15 Khanna, Madhu, 'Devi Kundalini: The Narrative of the Subtle Body', in Menzies (ed.), *Goddess: Divine Energy*, 176, 178–79, 185.

16 Many thanks to Varun Khanna for helping me translate the Sanskrit inscriptions across the scroll.

17  Usually the number of petals identifies the specific *chakra*, but here the artist has not strictly adhered to this formula.

18  White, *Kiss of the Yogini*, 254; Benard, *Chinnamasta*, 32; Satpathy, *Dasa Mahavidya and Tantra Sastra*, 106; Bose and Haldar, *Tantras: Their Philosophy and Occult Secrets*, 113.

19  White, *Kiss of the Yogini*, 254; Benard, *Chinnamasta*, 32; Satpathy, *Dasa Mahavidya and Tantra Sastra*, 106; Bose and Haldar, *Tantras: Their Philosophy and Occult Secrets*, 113.

20  James Mallinson notes that the *ajapa mantra* is repeated naturally with the in and out breath, and the textual sources state that we breathe in and out 21,600 times per day (personal correspondence, October 2019).

21  Mallinson and Singleton, *Roots of Yoga*, 109.

22  Diamond, Debra, 'The Subtle Body', in Diamond, et al., *Yoga: The Art of Transformation*, 166.

23  Gorakhnath is said to have been a disciple of Matsyendranath, regarded as the original guru of the Naths. Mallinson, 'Nath Sampradaya', 426; White, *Sinister Yogis* 198–99; Flood, *An Introduction to Hinduism*, 98.

24  Mallinson, 'Yogic Identities: Tradition and Transformation'.

25  Mallinson, 'Nath Sampradaya', 421; White, *Sinister Yogis*, 26, 197.

26  White, *The Alchemical Body*, 5.

27  Ibid., 222.

28  Ray and Kaviratna (eds.), *Rasarnava Rasaitiava*, 1.20–22. Quoted in White, *The Alchemical Body*, 174.

29  White, *The Alchemical Body*, 52.

30  Mallinson, 'Yogic Identities: Tradition and Transformation'; Sharma, 'Representation of Social Groups in Mughal Art', 20, 23, 30; Ernst, Carl W., 'Muslim Interpreters of Yoga', in Diamond, et al., *Yoga: The Art of Transformation*, 59, 69; Losty and Roy, *Mughal India: Art, Culture and Empire*, 117.

31  Quoted in White, *Sinister Yogis*, 220.

32  Translated in Sharma, 'Representation of Social Groups in Mughal Art', 28.

33  Translated in Ibid., 28.

34  Ibid., 28.

35  Ernst, 'Accounts of Yogis in Arabic and Persian Historical and Travel Texts', 414; Shah, trans. Shea and Troyer, *The Dabistan*, 234, 247, 255; Goswamy and Grewal, *The Mughals and the Jogis of Jakhbar*. The 13th-century Venetian merchant and explorer Marco Polo noted that the yogis he met in India lived for 200 years as a result of the alchemical elixirs of mercury and sulphur they consumed (White, *The Alchemical Body*, 9).

36  Reproduced with translation and notes in: Goswamy and Grewal, *The Mughals and the Jogis of Akhbar*, 120–24.

37  White, *Sinister Yogis*, 217.

38  Bernier, trans. Bhattacharya, *Voyage dans les Etats du Grand Mogol*, 245. Quoted in White, *The Alchemical Body*, 9.

39  Kulkarni (ed.), *Rasaratnasamucchaya of Vagbhatta*, 1.85–88. This method is also described in Misra (ed.), *Rasendracudamani of Somadeva*, 15.13–15; Sastri, R. (ed.), *Anandakanda*, 1.53b–62a; *Rasakautuka*, Bikaner ASL MSS no.4203, fol. 4a.6–9; *Sivakalpadruma of Sivanatha*, Bikaner ASL MSS no. 4349, fol. 2b.1–6. Quoted in White, *The Alchemical Body*, 203.

40  Ernst, 'Situating Sufism and Yoga', 23; Mallinson, 'Nath Sampradaya', 426.

41  Ernst, 'Situating Sufism and Yoga', 21, 23.

42  Ibid., 23.

43  Diamond, Debra, 'Yogis in the Literary Imagination', in Diamond, et al., *Yoga: The Art of Transformation*, 209.

44  Ibid.; Leach, *Mughal and Other Indian Paintings from the Chester Beatty Library*, 189.

45  Akbarnia, Ladan, 'Wandering Dervish with a Snake-Headed Staff', in Calza (ed.), *Akbar: The Great Emperor of India*, 197.

46  Ernst, *Sufism: An Introduction to the Mystical Tradition of Islam*, 92.

47  Hatley, 'Mapping the Esoteric Body', 351–68.

48  Ernst, 'Being Careful with the Goddess', 191.

49  Ernst, 'Situating Sufism and Yoga', 21, 41; Ernst, 'Being Careful with the Goddess', 191; Leach, *Mughal and Other Indian Paintings from the Chester Beatty Library*, 556–57.

50  Ernst, 'Sufism and Yoga According to Muhammad Ghawth', 11.

51  Ernst, 'Translation of Chapter 4 of the *Bahr al-Hayat*'.

52  Ibid.

53  Ibid.

54  Ibid.

55  Malik (ed.), comp. Hasan 'Ala Sijzi, *Fawa'id al-fu'ad by Nizam al-Din Awliya' Bada'oni*, 84. Quoted in Ernst, 'Situating Sufism and Yoga', 34. See also Hatley, 'Mapping the Esoteric Body', 363; Digby, *Wonder-Tales of South Asia*.

56  Quoted in Lorenzen, 'Religious Identity in Gorakhnath and Kabir', 21. See also: Bouillier, 'Nath Yogis' Encounters with Islam', 3.

57  Linrothe (ed.), *Holy Madness*, 402. Thank you to Peyvand Firouzeh, James Mallinson and Debra Diamond for sharing their thoughts on the iconography of this painting with me.

58  Ernst, *The Shambhala Guide to Sufism*, 115; Schimmel, *As Through a Veil*, 78; Khare, 'The Wine-Cup in Mughal Court Culture', 168; Morrow (ed.), *Islamic Images and Ideas*, 93; Saeidi and Unwin, 'Persian Wine Tradition and Symbolism', 97–114.

59  Quoted in Schimmel, *As Through a Veil*, 125. See also: Chittick, *The Sufi Path of Love*.

60  Quoted in Arberry, *The Rubaiyat of Omar Khayyam and Other Persian Poems*, 60; Saeidi and Unwin, 'Persian Wine Tradition and Symbolism', 97.

61  Mojaddedi, 'Getting Drunk with Abu Yazid or Staying Sober with Junayd', 1–13; Schimmel, *As Through a Veil*, 9, 49, 60–61.

62  Leach, *Mughal and Other Indian Paintings from the Chester Beatty Library*, 514.

63  Kramrisch, *Manifestations of Shiva*, 198.

64  Blurton, *Hindu Art*, 77; Ahluwalia, *Rajput Painting*, 21.

65  See: Panthey, *Iconography of Siva in Pahari Paintings*.

66  Ahluwalia, *Rajput Painting*, 158.

67  See: Doniger, *Siva: The Erotic Ascetic*.

68  Blurton, *Hindu Art*, 194.

69  *Tiruvalankattu Mutta Tirupatikam*, 2.8. Quoted in Craddock, 'The Anatomy of Devotion', 136.

70  Haidar, Navina, 'The Cremation Ground', in Diamond, et al., *Yoga: The Art of Transformation*, 196.

71  See: Goswamy and Fischer, *Pahari Masters*; Archer, *The Loves of Krishna*, 42; Archer, *Kangra Painting*.

72  See: Miller, *Love Song of the Dark Lord*.

73  Desai, et al., *Life at Court: Art for India's Rulers*, 35; Archer, *Indian Painting in the Punjab Hills*, Vol. 1, 346, 367; Kramrisch, *Manifestations of Shiva*, 159.

74  Seyller and Mittal, *Pahari Paintings in the Jagdish and Kamla Mittal Museum*, 91.

75  Vasugupta, *Spanda-Karikas: The Divine Creative Pulsation; the Karikas and the Spanda-Nirnaya of Ksemaraja Translated into English by Jaideva Singh* (Delhi: Motilal Banarsidass, 1980), 50. Quoted in Flood, *An Introduction to Hinduism*, 164.

76  Mallinson, 'Yogic Identities: Tradition and Transformation'.

77  Linrothe (ed.), *Holy Madness*, 335; Davidson, *Indian Esoteric Buddhism*, 328.

78  Snellgrove, *The Hevajra Tantra*, 115–16.

79  Törzsök, 'Women in Early Sakta Tantras', 357–58, 360; Dehejia and Coburn, *Devi: the Great Goddess*, 386.

80  Hatley and Kiss, *The Brahmayamalatantra or Picumata*, Vol. 2, 7.

81 Biernacki, *Renowned Goddess of Desire*, 46–47, 51–52.

82 Upadhyaya, Sitala P. (ed.), *Tripurarnava Tantra* (Varanasi: Sampurnanand Sanskrit University, 1992), 1.196–97. Quoted in Urban, *The Power of Tantra*, 138.

83 Tripathi, Ramaprasada (ed.), *Rudrayamala (Uttara Tantra): Prathama and Dvitiya Vibhaga*, 2 vols (Varanasi: Sampurnananda Sanskrit University, 1991), 2.108–11. Quoted in Biernacki, *Renowned Goddess of Desire*, 49.

84 Mallinson, 'Translation of the *Dattatreyayogasastra*'. Hatha yoga was not without its explicitly sexual rites; *vajrolimudra* was carried out as a means of preserving the yogi's and yogini's sexual fluids (*bindu* and *rajas*) during intercourse and also of drawing up a mixture of these fluids via the urethra from one another (essentially combining Shiva and Shakti), as described in the *Dattatreya Yoga Shastra*. The ability to retain semen during intercourse served as the ultimate demonstration of power and sublimated desire. See: Mallinson, 'Yoga and Sex', 183; White, *The Alchemical Body*, 199.

85 Dvivedi (ed.), *Guptasadhana Tantra*. Quoted in Biernacki, *Renowned Goddess of Desire*, 47.

86 Desai, et al., *Life at Court: Art for India's Rulers*, 81.

87 Dvivedi (ed.), *Guptasadhana Tantra*, 2.18b–20. Quoted in Biernacki, *Renowned Goddess of Desire*, 7.

88 This has previously been mistaken for the *Kamrubijaksa (Kamarupa Seed Syllables)*. Thank you to James Mallinson for clarifying (personal correspondence, October 2019).

89 Quoted in Ernst, 'Being Careful with the Goddess', 196.

90 Ibid.

91 Diamond, Debra, 'Yoginis', in Diamond, et al., *Yoga: The Art of Transformation*, 124; Haidar, et al., *Sultans of Deccan India*, 98; Leach, *Mughal and Other Indian Paintings from the Chester Beatty Library*, 865.

92 Leach, *Mughal and Other Indian Paintings from the Chester Beatty Library*, 865.

93 Ibid.

94 Haidar, et al., *Sultans of Deccan India*, 88.

95 Hutton, *Art of the Court of Bijapur*, 87.

96 The image is framed by incomplete inscriptions in Arabic which have been re-pieced from different manuscripts, and are not directly related to the subject of the painting, but which contribute towards the poetic mood. Thank you to Zeina Klink-Hoppe and Nadia Jamil for translating these inscriptions and sharing their thoughts on their relationship with the image. The top and bottom read as one verse by the 8th-century poet Abu al-Atahiya (born in Al-Kufah in Iraq): 'Abu al-Atahiya said: "What are people but with the world and its friend, whichever way it turns, they turn."'

97 Haidar, et al., *Sultans of Deccan India*, 98.

98 Ibid.

99 Hutton, *Art of the Court of Bijapur*, 84, 94; Dehejia and Coburn, *Devi: the Great Goddess*, 386; Aitken, Molly Emma, 'Transcendence and Desire in Ragamala Painting', in Diamond, et al., *Yoga: The Art of Transformation*, 220.

100 Diamond, Debra, 'Yoginis', in Diamond, et al., *Yoga: The Art of Transformation*, 125.

101 Aitken, Molly Emma, 'Transcendence and Desire in Ragamala Painting', in Diamond, et al., *Yoga: The Art of Transformation*, 219–22; Ramos, 'A Garland of Melodies', 61.

102 Linrothe, *Holy Madness*, 398.

103 Sen, *Caryagitikosa Facsimile Edition*, 138. Quoted in Davidson, *Indian Esoteric Buddhism*, 227.

104 Hutton, *Art of the Court of Bijapur*, 93.

## CHAPTER 3:
## THE SPREAD OF TANTRA ACROSS ASIA
## (pp. 112–71)

1 Davidson, *Tibetan Renaissance*, 28–29; Linrothe, *Ruthless Compassion*, 239; Huntington and Huntington (eds.), *Leaves from the Bodhi Tree*, 69. A later additional factor for the decline of Buddhism in eastern India was the conquest of Gaur by the Turkic military general Bakhtiyar Khalji in the 13th century, along with the rise of the Delhi Sultanate. This chapter highlights material from across Asia, but certain Tantric centres, such as Bhutan, Mongolia and Indonesia, have been omitted owing to the nature of the British Museum's collection.

2 These are often described as Bön spirits. Bön, the indigenous religious tradition of Tibet, intermingled with Indian Buddhism and has remained a powerful and popular force. Its many local and nature gods are still venerated. Dalton, 'Padmasambhava'; Linrothe (ed.), *Holy Madness*, 45; Huntington and Bangdel, *The Circle of Bliss*, 38.

3 Li and Coblin, *A Study of Old Tibetan Inscriptions*, 190.

4 Whitfield, *Silk, Slaves and Stupas*, 151.

5 Iyanaga, 'Daijizaiten (Siva/Mahesvara)'; Sorensen, Henrik H., 'Central Divinities in the Esoteric Buddhist Pantheon in China', in Orzech, Sorensen, and Payne (eds.), *Esoteric Buddhism and the Tantras*, 116; Gallo, 'The Image of Maheshvara'; Williams, 'The Iconography of Khotanese Painting'. On the reverse of the panel is an image of either the Silk God of Khotan or the Persian prince Rustam.

6 Davidson, *Tibetan Renaissance*, 15, 65, 72; Huntington and Bangdel, *The Circle of Bliss*, 39.

7 Davidson, *Tibetan Renaissance*, 3; Linrothe (ed.), *Holy Madness*, 45.

8 Linrothe (ed.), *Holy Madness*, 46.

9 I am grateful to Yannick Laurent for identifying the figure as Drakpa Gyaltsen through a translation of its accompanying inscription.

10 Beer, *The Encyclopedia of Tibetan Symbols and Motifs*, 233; Huntington and Bangdel, *The Circle of Bliss*, 21.

11 Huntington and Bangdel, *The Circle of Bliss*, 21.

12 Chandrasekhar, 'Vajrayana', 226.

13 Ibid.

14 Ibid.

15 Harvey, *An Introduction to Buddhism*, 184.

16 Beer, *The Encyclopedia of Tibetan Symbols*, 243.

17 Zwalf (ed.), *Buddhism: Art and Faith*, 202.

18 Huntington and Bangdel, *The Circle of Bliss*, 220.

19 See: Abhayadatta, trans. Robinson, *Buddha's Lions*; Pal, 'Arhats and Mahasiddhas', 72; Linrothe (ed.), *Holy Madness*, 38.

20 See: Abhayadatta, trans. Robinson, *Buddha's Lions*; Linrothe (ed.), *Holy Madness*.

21 Baker, *Tibetan Yoga*, 108. See also: Davidson, *Indian Esoteric Buddhism*, 233.

22 Quoted in Schaeffer, *Dreaming the Great Brahmin*, 40.

23 Willis, *Tibet: Life, Myth and Art*, 109; Zwalf, *Heritage of Tibet*, 96.

24 Quoted in Schaeffer, *Dreaming the Great Brahmin*, 29. See also: Luczanits, Christian, 'The Eight Great Siddhas in Early Tibetan Painting', in Linrothe (ed.), *Holy Madness*, 79; Shaw, *Passionate Enlightenment*, 132.

25 Snellgrove, 'The Tantras', 235–36.

26 Quoted in Shaw, *Passionate Enlightenment*, 22.

27 Quoted in Padoux, *The Hindu Tantric World*, 73.

28 Davidson, *Indian Esoteric Buddhism*, 288.

29 Ibid., 258.

30 Thank you to Christian Luczanits for examining the series of Mahasiddha *thangkas* and transliterating the accompanying inscriptions.

31 Dowman, *Masters of Mahamudra*, 103.

32 Linrothe (ed.), *Holy Madness*, 409, 411; White, *The Alchemical Body*, 99–100.

33 Dowman, *Masters of Mahamudra*, 245–46.

34 Abhayadatta, trans. Robinson, *Buddha's Lions*, 162.

35 Shaw, *Passionate Enlightenment*, 111. See also: Kragh,

'Appropriation and Assertion of the Female Self', 85–108.

36  sDe-dge, *Sems nyid kyi rtog pa 'joms pa'i lta ba zhes bya ba*, 2433 fol.47, b.5-48a.3. Quoted in Shaw, *Passionate Enlightenment*, 96.

37  Shaw, *Passionate Enlightenment*, 111, 113; Benard, *Chinnamasta*, 10.

38  Dowman, *Masters of the Mahamudra*, 318.

39  Ibid.

40  Gardner, 'Yeshe Tsogyel'; Linrothe (ed.), *Holy Madness*, 71. See also: Kunga, Drime and Yeshe Tsogyel, *The Life and Visions of Yeshe Tsogyal: The Autobiography of the Great Wisdom Queen* (Boulder: Snow Lion, 2017).

41  Quoted in Gardner, 'Yeshe Tsogyel'.

42  Harvey, *An Introduction to Buddhism*, 205.

43  Huntington and Bangdel, *The Circle of Bliss*, 45; Watt and Leidy, *Defining Yongle*, 61.

44  LaRocca, *Warriors of the Himalayas*, 25; Watt and Leidy, *Defining Yongle*, 76; Thurman and Weldon, *Sacred Symbols*, 136.

45  Harrison-Hall, *China*, 182, 186.

46  Weirong, Shen, 'Tantric Buddhism in Ming China', in Orzech, Sorensen, and Payne (eds.), *Esoteric Buddhism*, 551; Harrison-Hall, *China*, 182, 186; Thurman and Weldon, *Sacred Symbols*, 136; Huntington and Bangdel, *The Circle of Bliss*, 47; Clark, Bartholomew, and Berger, *Tibet: Treasures*, 152.

47  Huntington and Bangdel, *The Circle of Bliss*, 358; Beer, *The Encyclopedia of Tibetan Symbols*, 253.

48  Beer, *The Encyclopedia of Tibetan Symbols*, 253.

49  Huntington and Bangdel, *The Circle of Bliss*, 358; Zwalf (ed.), *Buddhism: Art and Faith*, 211.

50  Zwalf (ed.), *Buddhism: Art and Faith*, 211.

51  Huntington and Bangdel, *The Circle of Bliss*, 358.

52  Harrison-Hall, *China*, 186; LaRocca, *Warriors of the Himalayas*, 27; Huntington and Bangdel, *The Circle of Bliss*, 47; Clark, Bartholomew, and Berger, *Tibet: Treasures*, 134.

53  Fu Weilin, *Mingshu (Book of Ming), Edition of Jifu congshu of Qing)* (Taipei: 1964–66), *juan* 160 3154. Quoted in Weirong, Shen, 'Tantric Buddhism in Ming China', in Orzech, Sorensen, and Payne (eds.), *Esoteric Buddhism*, 555.

54  Lin, Lina, trans. Silin Chen, 'Gifts of Good Fortune and Praise-Songs for Peace', 125.

55  Fu Weilin, *Mingshu (Book of Ming), Edition of Jifu congshu of Qing)* (Taipei: 1964–66), *juan* 160 3154. Quoted in Weirong, Shen, 'Tantric Buddhism in Ming China', in Orzech, Sorensen, and Payne (eds.), *Esoteric Buddhism*, 557.

56  Confucianism co-existed with the Daoist religion, developed from the ideas attributed to the sage Laozi who is believed to have lived in the 6th century BCE, which conceived Dao as the underlying force behind all things in nature. By meditating on this force and withdrawing from society, Daoism taught that it was possible to achieve union with this force, and with nature. Daoism shared much in common with certain Tantric goals, including the pursuit of immortality through bodily and alchemical practices. See: Teiser, 'The Spirits of Chinese Religion', 3–37.

57  In nondual symbolism, the female is also *shunyata* (emptiness) as well as wisdom, and the male is also skilful means (*upaya*) as well as compassion.

58  Linrothe, *Ruthless Compassion*, 6.

59  Ibid., 243; Davidson, *Indian Esoteric Buddhism*, 338; Heller, *Tibetan Art*, 88; Shaw, *Passionate Enlightenment*, 177.

60  Linrothe, *Ruthless Compassion*, 6, 231.

61  See: Baker, *Tibetan Yoga*; Huntington and Bangdel, *The Circle of Bliss*, 230; White (ed.), *Tantra in Practice*, 15, 17.

62  Huntington and Bangdel, *The Circle of Bliss*, 240, 264.

63  Ibid., 230; Harvey, *An Introduction to Buddhism*, 353–54.

64  Snellgrove, *The Hevajra Tantra*, 75.

65  White (ed.), *Tantra in Practice*, 15; Huntington and Bangdel, *The Circle of Bliss*, 231, 292.

66  Kilty, 'Brief Presentation of Channels, Winds, and Drops', 145–50.

67  Harvey, *An Introduction to Buddhism*, 354–55.

68  White (ed.), *Tantra in Practice*, 15.

69  Chang (trans.), *The Hundred Thousand Songs of Milarepa*, 70–71.

70  See: Gray, *The Cakrasamvara Tantra*; Huntington and Bangdel, *The Circle of Bliss*, 51.

71  Rhie and Thurman, *Wisdom and Compassion*, 215; Zwalf (ed.), *Buddhism: Art and Faith*, 122.

72  Rhie and Thurman, *Wisdom and Compassion*, 279; Huntington and Bangdel, *The Circle of Bliss*, 264.

73  Zwalf (ed.), *Buddhism: Art and Faith*, 138; Zwalf, *Heritage of Tibet*, 96; Willis, *Tibet: Life, Myth and Art*, 104; Menzies, *Goddess: Divine Energy*, 24.

74  Snellgrove, *The Hevajra Tantra*, 93.

75  Ibid., 91.

76  Ibid., 110.

77  Woodward, 'Esoteric Buddhism in Southeast Asia', 329–54; Woodward, 'Tantric Buddhism at Angkor Thom', 57–67; Boeles, 'Two Yoginis of Hevajra',

14–29; McGovern, 'Esoteric Buddhism'. Also see: Acri, *Esoteric Buddhism in Mediaeval Maritime Asia*.

78  See: Brauen, *The Mandala*; Bühnemann (ed.), *Mandalas and Yantras*; Tucci, *The Theory and Practice of the Mandala*.

79  Willis, *Tibet: Life, Myth and Art*, 38–39; Harvey, *An Introduction to Buddhism*, 352.

80  Konchog Lhundrub's (1497–1557) commentary on the *Hevajra Tantra*, written in 1551. Quoted in Watt, 'Mandala of Hevajra', no. 1360.

81  Snellgrove, *The Hevajra Tantra*, 99.

82  *Cakrasamvara-tantra*, Mal translation, printed in Tibet as *rGyud gyi rgyal po dpal bde mchog nyung ngu*, fol. 17b.6–7. Quoted in Shaw, *Passionate Enlightenment*, 142.

83  It is possible that this bronze was made with a 19th-century Western audience in mind, as it was acquired in Nepal by Maximilian August Scipio von Brandt (1835–1920), a German diplomat. For similar examples see: Pal (ed.), *Himalayas*, 102; Postel, Neven, and Mankodi, *Antiquities of Himachal*, fig. 156.

84  Shaw, *Passionate Enlightenment*, 169; Harvey, *An Introduction to Buddhism*, 356.

85  Mallinson, 'The *Amrtasiddhi*: Hathayoga's Tantric Buddhist Source Text'.

86  Shaw, *Passionate Enlightenment*, 174.

87  George (trans.), *The Candamaharosana-tantra*, 123.

88  Linrothe, *Ruthless Compassion*, 6.

89  Hatley, 'Converting the Dakini', 37–86.

90  Bühnemann, Gudrun, 'Yantras', in Bühnemann (ed.), *Mandalas and Yantras*, 570; Zeiler, 'Yantras as Objects of Worship', 68, 71, 74; Khanna, Madhu, 'Tantric Goddess Yantras', in Menzies (ed.), *Goddess: Divine Energy*, 166.

91  Bühnemann (ed.), *Mandalas and Yantras*, 32–34.

92  The term *bindu* has both macrocosmic and microcosmic associations; at the level of the individual it also refers to sexual fluids, as discussed in Chapter 2.

93  Heller, *Tibetan Art*, 196; Linrothe and Watt, *Demonic Divine*, 126.

94  *Guhyasamayasadhanamala* (GSSi K280r2 and GSS34 Kii2v6), Ms. K Oxford, Bodleian Library. Ms. Sansk c. 16 (R). No. 1455. Quoted in English, E., *Vajrayogini*, 51.

95  English, E., *Vajrayogini*, 159.

96  Ibid., 42, 159.

97  Ibid., 119.

98  *Guhyasamayasadhanamala* (GSSi, GSS2; K279V4/K4V2), Ms. K Oxford, Bodleian Library. Ms. Sansk c. 16 (R). No. 1455. Quoted in English, E., *Vajrayogini*, 117.

99 Huntington and Bangdel, *The Circle of Bliss*, 356; Thurman and Weldon, *Sacred Symbols*, 132, fig. 60; Beer, *The Encyclopedia of Tibetan Symbols*, 261.

100 Zwalf, *Heritage of Tibet*, 86; Huntington and Huntington (eds.), *Leaves from the Bodhi Tree*, 152.

101 Early Buddhist teachings first reached Japan in the 6th century from Korea. Shingon was based on the revelations of the *Mahavairocana Sutra* and *Tattvasamgraha Sutra* that Kukai had studied in China. Early Tantric masters were supported by the Japanese emperor and aristocratic families, who were drawn to their rumoured powers. See: Gardiner, 'Tantric Buddhism in Japan'; Linrothe, *Ruthless Compassion*, 12; Harvey, *An Introduction to Buddhism*, 226.

102 Smyers, *The Fox and the Jewel*, 1, 8.

103 Ibid., 17.

104 Ibid., 18; Grapard, 'Of Emperors and Foxy Ladies', 127–49.

105 Smyers, *The Fox and the Jewel*, 21.

106 Ibid., 84. An early 20th-century hand-coloured woodblock print, mounted as a hanging scroll, represents Dakini-ten as worshipped at Toyokawa Inari, a temple in the city of Toyokawa in Japan (British Museum 1987,0728.0.1). Despite the 1873 Meiji government decree to formally separate Shinto from Buddhism, involving differentiating between *kamis* and Buddhist deities which had previously shared the same sacred spaces, such temples as Toyokawa retained their Shingon identities. In this image, Dakini-ten carries sheaves of corn. Today it is still common to find Shingon priests serving at Inari shrines.

107 Linrothe, *Ruthless Compassion*, 8.

108 Kalff, 'Selected Chapters from the Abhidhanottaratantra', fol. 221r1–5.

109 Snellgrove, *The Hevajra Tantra*, 110.

110 Pal, *Tibet: Tradition and Change*, 165; Beer, *The Encyclopedia of Tibetan Symbols*, 245.

111 Pal, *Tibet: Tradition and Change*, 165; Huntington and Bangdel, *The Circle of Bliss*, 503.

112 Beer, *The Encyclopedia of Tibetan Symbols*, 245; Pal (ed.), *The Art of Tibet*, 244.

113 Beer, *The Encyclopedia of Tibetan Symbols*, 247; Huntington and Bangdel, *The Circle of Bliss*, 506.

114 Siklos, 'Vajrabhairava Tantras: Tibetan and Mongolian Texts', 167. See also Huntington and Bangdel, *The Circle of Bliss*, 468; Linrothe and Watt, *Demonic Divine*, 177; Linrothe, *Ruthless Compassion*, 68.

115 Davidson, *Tibetan Renaissance*, 35.

116 Rhie and Thurman, *Wisdom and Compassion*, 290.

117 Linrothe (ed.), *Holy Madness*, 42.

118 Clark, et al. (eds.), *The Actor's Image*, 162.

119 Ibid. I am grateful to Alfred Haft for translating the title of the play.

120 Thank you to Christian Luczanits for providing a transliteration of the *kapala's* visible mantras.

121 Siklos, 'Vajrabhairava Tantras: Tibetan and Mongolian Texts', 159.

122 I am grateful to Ayesha Fuentes for sharing with me her research on this *kapala*, which will be published in her forthcoming 'On the Use of Human Remains in Tibetan Ritual Objects'. I am also grateful to Joanne Dyer for her use of DStretch in order to increase the legibility of the inscriptions and for her analytical testing which confirmed that the red pigment is cinnabar/vermilion.

123 Fuentes, 'On the Use of Human Remains in Tibetan Ritual Objects'.

124 Garrett, 'The Alchemy of Accomplishing Medicine', 207–30.

125 Cantwell, 'The Medicinal Accomplishment (Sman Sgrub) Practice', 49–95; Garrett, 'The Alchemy of Accomplishing Medicine', 207–30; Cantwell, 'Reflections on Pema Lingpa's Key', 163–75.

126 Huntington and Bangdel, *The Circle of Bliss*, 346; Clark, Bartholomew, and Berger, *Tibet: Treasures*, 116; Zwalf, *Heritage of Tibet*, 84–85.

127 Huntington and Bangdel, *The Circle of Bliss*, 346.

128 Ibid.

129 Christian Luczanits notes that the power ascribed to *kapalas* is not uniform but depends on the source (personal correspondence, July 2018). For more information see: Fuentes, 'On the Use of Human Remains in Tibetan Ritual Objects'.

130 Huntington and Bangdel, *The Circle of Bliss*, 347. Ayesha Fuentes notes, regarding the sourcing of human remains in Tibetan Tantric practice, that they are often bequeathed by deceased practitioners, and then prepared as ritual objects by specialist religious authorities. Although the bones can be sourced from disposed corpses, this is now illegal (personal correspondence, November 2019).

131 Linrothe (ed.), *Holy Madness*, 369; Huntington and Bangdel, *The Circle of Bliss*, 155; Orofino, Giacomella, 'The Great Wisdom Mother and the Good Tradition', in White (ed.), *Tantra in Practice*, 407.

132 Sheehy, 'Severing the Source of Fear', 47; Orofino, Giacomella, 'The Great Wisdom Mother and the Good Tradition', in White (ed.), *Tantra in Practice*, 396.

133 A *damaru* is any two-headed drum, while a *thod rnga* ('skull-drum') is a *damaru* made specifically of skulls (personal correspondence with Ayesha Fuentes, November 2019).

134 Huntington and Bangdel, *The Circle of Bliss*, 155; Sheehy, 'Severing the Source of Fear', 40.

135 Beer, *The Encyclopedia of Tibetan Symbols*, 259; Zwalf, *Heritage of Tibet*, 91–92.

136 Linrothe (ed.), *Holy Madness*, 325.

137 I am grateful to colleagues who helped coordinate two workshops at the British Museum on the role, history and care of Tibetan ritual objects made with human remains. The discussions that took place during these workshops have informed this section of the chapter. The first was facilitated by Ayesha Fuentes (July 2019) and involved the following scholars: Christian Luczanits, Emma Martin, Nicholas Crowe, Crispin Paine and Thupten Kelsang. The second workshop was facilitated by Thupten Kelsang (October 2019), centring around a conversation on the display and interpretation of Tibetan human remains with members of the UK-based Tibetan diaspora. This involved the following participants: Tenzin Kunga, Tenzin Choephel, Dhondhup Samten, Lobsang Choedon Samten, Tsering Passang and Drukthar Gyal.

138 David-Néel, *Magic and Mystery in Tibet*, 150, 158.

139 Sheehy, 'Severing the Source of Fear', 41, 46.

140 'Jam mgon Kong sprul Blo gros mtha' yas (ed.), *Gdams ngag mdzod*, 456–66. Quoted in Orofino, Giacomella, 'The Great Wisdom Mother and the Good Tradition', in White (ed.), *Tantra in Practice*, 406.

141 Sheehy, 'Severing the Source of Fear', 46; White (ed.), *Tantra in Practice*, 406.

142 Jam mgon Kong sprul Blo gros mtha' yas (ed.), *Gdams ngag mdzod*, 456–66. Quoted in Orofino, Giacomella, 'The Great Wisdom Mother and the Good Tradition', in White (ed.), *Tantra in Practice*, 413, 416.

143 I am grateful to Bryan Mulvihill for facilitating this commission.

144 Huntington and Bangdel, *The Circle of Bliss*, 361.

145 Schrempf, 'Tibetan Ritual Dances', 103.

146 Samuel and David, 'The Multiple Meanings and Uses of Tibetan Ritual Dance', 10.

147 De Nebesky-Wojkowitz, *Tibetan Religious Dances*, 111; Schrempf, 'Tibetan Ritual Dances', 98.

148 Samuel and David, 'The Multiple Meanings and Uses of Tibetan Ritual Dance', 10.

149 The varying styles of the plaques and beads suggest that the *rus gyan* is a patchwork of recycled pieces made by different hands over the course of several centuries (as late as around the 19th century and possibly as far back as the 15th century judging by the iconography and style of one of the Dakini plaques) (personal correspondence with Christian Luczanits, August 2018).

150 White, J. C., *Sikhim & Bhutan*, 66–67.

151 I am grateful to Emma Martin for alerting me to the bone apron's provenance details and for directing me to the photograph and publication by John Claude White.

152 Braunholtz, 'A Necromancer's Bone Apron from Tibet', 29.

153 In 1923 Berthold Laufer published a piece in the *Field Museum of Natural History* on the 'Use of Human Skulls and Bones in Tibet', describing such phenomena as a corruption of the Buddha's original teachings: 'At the outset, these relics of an age of savagery and a barbarous cult leave no small surprise in a land whose faith is avowedly Buddhistic, and whose people have made such signal advances in literature, poetry, painting, sculpture, and art industries. Buddha was an apostle of peace and universal love, averse to blood-shed, and forbidding the taking of human and animal life. He repudiated all outward ceremonies and offerings.' Laufer, 'Use of Human Skulls and Bones in Tibet', 2.

154 Samuel and David, 'The Multiple Meanings and Uses of Tibetan Ritual Dance', 9.

## CHAPTER 4:
## TANTRA AND REVOLUTION
## IN COLONIAL INDIA
## (pp. 172–213)

1 Coburn, *Encountering the Goddess*, 61–63.

2 Ibid., 62.

3 Kinsley, *Tantric Visions of the Divine Feminine*, 16.

4 McDermott, *Mother of My Heart*, 7.

5 Sen, *Grace and Mercy in Her Wild Hair*, 55.

6 McDaniel, *The Madness of the Saints*, 138.

7 Hunter, *Annals of Rural Bengal*, 32; McDermott, *Mother of My Heart*, 15, 24–25, 31.

8 Urban, Hugh B., 'India's Darkest Heart: Kali in the Colonial Imagination', in McDermott and Kripal (eds.), *Encountering Kali*, 172.

9 His death is described in the late 19th-century *Tantratattva* by Shivachandra Vidyarnava. McDaniel, *The Madness of the Saints*, 139; McDermott, *Mother of My Heart*, 56.

10 This sculpture, which might have otherwise had an ephemeral existence, was probably collected by a colonial official who then gave it to the British Museum in 1894. Blurton, *Hindu Art*, 158; Dallapiccola, *Hindu Visions of the Sacred*, 70–71.

11 Coburn, *Encountering the Goddess*, 61.

12 Gupta, Hoens, and Goudriaan, *Hindu Tantrism*, 55.

13 Kaul (ed.), *Brhannilatantra*, 7.86. Quoted in Biernacki, Loriliai, 'The Yogini and the Tantric Sex Rite, or How to Keep a Secret', in Keul (ed.), *'Yogini' in South Asia*, 221. See also: Donaldson, 'The Sava-Vahana as Purusa in Orissan Images', 107–41.

14 Agamavagisa, *Brhat Tantrasara*, 438–39. Quoted in Kinsley, *Tantric Visions of the Divine Feminine*, 204.

15 McDermott and Kripal (eds.), *Encountering Kali*, 60.

16 See: Fisch, 'A Solitary Vindicator', 35–57; Davis, *Lives of Indian Images*, 163.

17 Stuart, *Vindication of the Hindoos*, 55.

18 Ibid., 58.

19 His collection was sold at auction in London in 1829 and 1830, mostly bought by John Bridge. The Bridge collection was acquired by the British Museum from Bridge's heirs in 1872.

20 Sherer, *Sketches of India*, 187.

21 Moor, *The Hindu Pantheon*, pl. 27. The plate is captioned as: 'Kali, Bhawani, Parvati or Durga'. As Moor explains in the accompanying text, these are 'names of the same goddess (or Sacti [Shakti], or personization of an energy) in different characters' so he 'sometimes use[s] the names indiscriminately'.

22 Ibid., 159.

23 Ibid., 147.

24 Clark and Suzuki (eds.), *The Reception of Blake in the Orient*, 49; Burke, 'The Eidetic and the Borrowed Image', 290.

25 Kinsley, *Tantric Visions of the Divine Feminine*, 84.

26 Jones, *Works*, Vol. 4, 93.

27 Urban, *Tantra: Sex, Secrecy, Politics*, 47.

28 Urban, 'The Extreme Orient', 127; Urban, Hugh B., 'India's Darkest Heart: Kali in the Colonial Imagination', in McDermott and Kripal (eds.), *Encountering Kali*, 174.

29 Ward, *A View of the History*, p. 247.

30 Monier-Williams, *Brahmanism and Hinduism*, 116, 122–23, 130.

31 Grautoff, *Glimpses of a Land*, 59–61.

32 Somerville, *Crime and Religious Beliefs*, frontispiece.

33 Ibid., i–ii (introduction).

34 Coburn, *Encountering the Goddess*, 83.

35 McDermott and Kripal (eds.), *Encountering Kali*, 5.

36 The *Brihat Tantrasara* (16th century) stressed decapitation, and the subsequent offering of the head and blood to the goddess, as the superior form of sacrifice. This was a deliberate subversion of the orthodox method of animal sacrifices to specifically male deities which, according to Vedic texts, should be carried out through the more sanitized method of strangulation or suffocation. See: Urban, 'The Power of the Impure', 281; Doniger, *The Origins of Evil in Hindu Mythology*, 155.

37 Urban, 'The Power of the Impure', 280.

38 Samanta, 'The "Self-Animal" and Divine Digestion'.

39 Bayly, et al., *The Raj*, 341; Wagner, *Thuggee*, 25.

40 Urban, *Tantra: Sex, Secrecy, Politics*, 82; Wagner, 'The Deconstructed Stranglers', 932; Wagner, *Thuggee*, 138.

41 Sleeman, W. H., 'Anonymous Letter', in *The Calcutta Literary Gazette* (1830). Quoted in Bruce, *The Stranglers*, 82–83.

42 Duff, *India and India Missions*, 267.

43 Bayly, et al. *The Raj*, 227.

44 Quoted in Godfrey, *Masculinity, Crime and Self-Defence*, 27.

45 Bayly, et al. *The Raj*, 227–28.

46 Wagner, 'Confessions of a Skull', 27–51.

47 Cox, 'Remarks on the Skulls', 525.

48 For further information about the uprising of 1857, see: Chakravarty, *The Indian Mutiny*.

49 Campbell speculated on the origins of the rebellion, citing a popular conspiracy theory at the time concerning the mass distribution of *chapatis* (unleavened flatbreads) across the country, along with lotus flowers among the Bengal army, shortly before its outbreak. It was widely believed that these functioned as a form of code to rally Indian citizens to rebel against the Company, and they were even symbolically associated with the goddess: 'These symbols of the cake [*chapati*] and the lotus have excited great curiosity (…) A writer in "Household Words," (…) says that cakes and lotus flowers are the symbols of the Queen of Heaven, the Hindoo goddess of mercy, and mother of God. (…) "The flower was circulated to rally the votaries of the goddess of the lotus. And the cakes have precisely the same significance as the lotus flowers"' (Campbell, *Narrative of the Indian Revolt*, 4). Sergeant William Forbes-Mitchell, who fought alongside Campbell, described their capture of a mausoleum during the siege of Lucknow: 'There were scores of

men armed with great burning torches (…) these men were (…) shouting "Jai Kali ma ki [Victory to Mother Kali]!'" (Forbes-Mitchell, *Reminiscences of the Great Mutiny*, 80).

50  Campbell, *Narrative of the Indian Revolt*, 208.

51  Ramos, *Pilgrimage and Politics in Colonial Bengal*, 21.

52  Eck, *Darsan*.

53  Jain, *Kalighat Painting*.

54  By 1905 Swadeshi leaders were symbolically pledging allegiance and devotion to Kali at Kalighat (Sarkar, *The Swadeshi Movement in Bengal*, 312–13). In 1910 Valentine Chirol confirmed: 'The [anti-British Swadeshi] movement was placed under the special patronage of Kali and vows were administered to large crowds in the forecourts of her great temple at Calcutta and in her various shrines all over Bengal' (Valentine, *Indian Unrest*, 83).

55  See: Pinney, *Photos of the Gods*; Mitter, 'Mechanical Reproduction', 1–32; Guha-Thakurta, *The Making of a New 'Indian' Art*, 82; Ramos, *Pilgrimage and Politics in Colonial Bengal*, 77.

56  I am grateful to Koel Chakraborty for translating the print's inscriptions.

57  Quoted in Sarkar, *Modern India*, 107.

58  Wolfers, 'Born like Krishna in the Prison-House'; Wolfers, 'The Making of an Avatar'; Wolfers, 'Empire of Spirit' (forthcoming).

59  Ghose, *Bande Mataram*, 920.

60  Goswami, *Charankavi Mukunda Das*, 218.

61  Letter dated 11 December 1908, from Gupte to Risley in the Royal Anthropological Institute Photographic Collection, London. Quoted in Kaur and Mazzarella (eds.), *Censorship in South Asia*, 38.

62  Ibid.

63  Ibid.

64  Ibid.

65  Urban, Hugh B., 'India's Darkest Heart: Kali in the Colonial Imagination', in McDermott and Kripal (eds.), *Encountering Kali*, 184; Sarkar, *The Swadeshi Movement in Bengal*, 312–13.

66  The rebellion flared up in Bengal following the disastrous famine in 1770 and continued in sporadic bursts of intensity until the turn of the century.

67  Chatterji, trans. Lipner, *Anandamath*, 150.

68  *Jugantar*, 1905. Quoted in Valentine, *Indian Unrest*, 346.

69  *The Sandhya*, 6 May 1907. Quoted in Ker, *Political Trouble in India*, 82.

70  Pal, B. C., *New India*, June 1907. Quoted in Ker, *Political Trouble in India*, 46–47.

71  Valentine, *Indian Unrest*, 86.

72  The Tantric *Kalika Purana* (10th century), composed in the neighbouring region of Assam during the reign of the Pala dynasty, devotes its final chapters to military tactics and governance, and suggests visualizing an animal as the adversary one wishes to conquer: 'First the sword is consecrated, and the buffalo or goat is consecrated with the name of the enemy. (…) Having severed its head, he should offer it to the Goddess with great effort. (…) With this slaughter, the life of the enemy, having fallen into danger, is also slain.' Sastri, V. (ed.), *Kalikapuranam*, 67.145–52. Quoted in Urban, 'The Path of Power', 806.

73  Ramaswamy, *The Goddess and the Nation*, 111.

74  Ker, *Political Trouble in India*, 384.

75  See: Benard, *Chinnamasta*.

76  Van Kooij, 'Iconography of the Battlefield', 261.

77  Pal (ed.), *Hindu Religion and Iconology*, 79–80.

78  While many Sanskrit texts describing erotic play use this term, Vatsyayana's *c.* 3rd-century *Kama Sutra* refers to it as *purushayitva*, 'to play the man's role' (Doniger, *Redeeming the Kamasutra*, 111). The 16th-century *Yoni Tantra* (composed in Assam) describes the goal of the *viparita-rata* position as the collecting together of seminal and menstrual fluids, regarded as a source of power and enlightenment and later offered and consumed as part of the Tantric rite: 'He should make a sacrificial offering [*bali*] with his own semen and menstrual blood (…) The goddess herself is in the form of the *shakti* [female partner], if the intercourse is performed in the inverse position [*viparita-rata*]. (…) with the nectar of the vulva and penis, the best of adepts should make a food offering' (Schoterman [ed.], *The Yoni Tantra*, 2.16–26). See also: Urban, 'Desire, Blood, and Power', 75; Biernacki, Loriliai, 'The Yogini and the Tantric Sex Rite, or How to Keep a Secret', in Keul (ed.), *'Yogini' in South Asia*, 219.

79  Kinsley, *Tantric Visions of the Divine Feminine*, 154–55.

80  On the importance of ascetic self-fashioning and the 'revolutionary *sannyasi*' icon for the emergence of radical politics during the Swadeshi movement (1905–08), see: Wolfers, 'Born like Krishna in the Prison-House'.

81  Valentine, *Indian Unrest*, 102.

82  Pal (ed.), *Hindu Religion and Iconology*, 81.

83  Kinsley, *Tantric Visions of the Divine Feminine*, 63.

84  For short summaries of the myth see: Eck, *India: A Sacred Geography*; Kinsley, *Hindu Goddesses: Visions of the Divine Feminine*; McDaniel, 'Sacred Space', 73–88.

85  Kinsley, *Tantric Visions of the Divine Feminine*, 37, 219; Pal (ed.), *Hindu Religion and Iconology*, 446, 448.

86  Kinsley, *Tantric Visions of the Divine Feminine*, 216–19.

87  Ibid., 182; Narayanan, 'Auspiciousness and Inauspiciousness', 698.

88  The play's particular innovation lay in representing Mother India as an embodied female form who suffered at the hands of foreigners determined to abuse her and rob her of her bounty. Sarkar, T., *Rebels, Wives, Saints*, 180.

89  Nag (ed.), *Akshay Sahitya-Sambhar*, Vol. 1, 257.

90  Devanandanasimha, *Sakta-pramoda* (Bombay: Khemraja Srikrsnadasa Prakasan, 1992), 283–85. See also: Kinsley, *Tantric Visions of the Divine Feminine*, 180; Chowdhury Sengupta, 'Colonialism and Cultural Identity', 175.

91  Ramaswamy, *The Goddess and the Nation*, 164. The first temple to her, which opened in Varanasi in 1936, featured a giant marble relief map of India. Inaugurated by Mohandas Karamchand Gandhi, the temple does not contain an image of a deity, only a map of India set in marble relief.

92  Ghose, *Bande Mataram*, 920.

93  Another head belongs to the historic ruler of the Maratha kingdom, Shivaji Bhonsle (r. 1674–1680), remembered for his alliances with and battles against the Mughal empire, Deccan Sultanates and European forces. His inclusion here reflects the fact that he was later adopted as a national hero by some Indian Hindu nationalists, including Bal Gangadhar Tilak. This modern appropriation was (and still is) problematic, since his defeat of Mughal rule was often paralleled with the fight against British oppression, a misleading comparison that could carry latent Islamophobic connotations.

94  McLean, 'Eating Corpses and Raising the Dead', 16.

95  Banerjee, *Logic in a Popular Form*; Gangopadhyay, *Mahapith Tarapith*, 170.

96  The following authors discuss some of the more important events of his life: Morinis, *Pilgrimage in the Hindu Tradition*; Banerjee, *Logic in a Popular Form*; Gangopadhyay, *Mahapith Tarapith*; McLean, 'Eating Corpses and Raising the Dead' (forthcoming); McDaniel, *The Madness of the Saints*. These are gathered from oral sources compiled by Bengali biographies including: Bandopadhyaya, S. K., *Tarapith Bhairava* (Calcutta: 1376 B.S. [Bengal era]); Cakravarti, G., *Banglar Sadhaka* (Calcutta: 1387 B.S.); and Banerjee, *Sri Sri Bama Ksepa*.

97  Diksit, *Tara Tantra Shastra*, 117.

98  Banerjee, *Sri Sri Bama Ksepa*, 53.

99 Ibid., 36.

100 Daly, *First Rebels*, 75.

101 Ibid., 34.

102 Ibid., 35.

103 Ibid.

104 Sarkar, '"Kaliyuga", "Chakri" and "Bhakti"'. See also: Chatterjee, *The Nation and its Fragments*.

105 McDaniel, *The Madness of the Saints*, 95; Urban, *Tantra: Sex, Secrecy, Politics*, 148.

106 Nikhilananda, *The Gospel of Sri Ramakrishna*, 21.

107 Gupta, trans. Nikhilananda, *Ramakrsna Kathamrta*, 2:544.

108 Saradananda, *Sri Ramakrishna the Great Master*, 227. See also: Kripal, *Kali's Child*, 117–30.

109 Gupta, trans. Nikhilananda, *Ramakrsna Kathamrta*, 2:603.

110 McDaniel, *The Madness of the Saints*, 203–204.

111 Urban, *Tantra: Sex, Secrecy, Politics*, 155.

112 Urban, 'The Extreme Orient', 124. See: Taylor, *Sir John Woodroffe, Tantra and Bengal*.

113 Woodroffe, *Principles of Tantra*, 1.

114 Woodroffe, *Shakti and Shakta*, 305, 315, 335.

115 Woodroffe, *Tantra of the Great Liberation*, cxix.

116 Ibid.


## CHAPTER 5:
## REIMAGINING TANTRA IN THE
## 20TH CENTURY
## (PP. 214–71)

1 Shillitoe, *Ithell Colquhoun*, 38; Ferentinou, 'Ithell Colquhoun: Surrealism and the Occult'; Ferentinou, 'The Iconography of Coniunctio Oppositorum', 38.

2 Colquhoun, *Sword of Wisdom*, 287, 289.

3 Shillitoe, *Ithell Colquhoun*, 30, 116–17.

4 Colquhoun, 'The Night Side of Nature', 170–71.

5 Ithell Colquhoun's notebook (TGA: 929/5/35/3), Tate Archive Collections, Tate Britain, London. Quoted in Ferentinou, 'The Iconography of Coniunctio Oppositorum', 385.

6 Jung, *The Psychology of Kundalini Yoga*, 21–22.

7 I am grateful to Isabel Seligman for alerting me to this painting and to Colquhoun's interest in Tantra. Seligman, 'A Wordless, Thoughtless Vacuum' (forthcoming); Shillitoe, *Ithell Colquhoun*, 282.

8 Benard, *Chinnamasta*, 103.

9 Shillitoe, *Ithell Colquhoun*, 272.

10 Ibid., 273.

11 Ibid., 130.

12 Ernst, 'Situating Sufism and Yoga', 25.

13 The studies are at Tate Archive Collections, Tate Britain, London: TGA 929/5/2/2. I am grateful to Richard Shillitoe for alerting me to these studies and providing me with these details.

14 Shillitoe, *Ithell Colquhoun*, 402.

15 Ernst, 'Situating Sufism and Yoga', 25.

16 See: Mitter, *Indian Art*; Mitter, *The Triumph of Modernism*.

17 Mookerjee, *Tantra Art: Its Philosophy and Physics*. See also: Brown, *Art for a Modern India*, 51; Sen-Gupta, 'Neo-Tantric 20th Century Indian Painting', 105.

18 Mookerjee, *Tantra Asana*, 15–16.

19 Mookerjee, *Tantra Art: Its Philosophy and Physics*, 13.

20 Santosh, G. R., 'Understanding Tantra', in Singh (ed.), *Awakening: A Retrospective of G. R. Santosh*, 39.

21 Brown, Rebecca M., 'Seeking Oneness: G. R. Santosh's Political, Historical and Philosophical Syncretism', in Singh (ed.), *Awakening: A Retrospective of G. R. Santosh*, 29.

22 Santosh, G. R., 'Understanding Tantra', in Singh (ed.), *Awakening: A Retrospective of G. R. Santosh*, 39.

23 Quoted in Khanna, Madhu, 'The Twilight Language of Tantric Symbols', in Singh (ed.), *Awakening: A Retrospective of G. R. Santosh*, 48.

24 Quoted in Padoux, *The Hindu Tantric World*, 94.

25 See: Masson, J. L., and M. V. Patwardhan, *Santarasa and Abhinavagupta's Philosophy of Aesthetics* (Poona: Bhandarkar Oriental Research Institute, 1970); Higgins, 'An Alchemy of Emotion', 43.

26 Santosh, G. R., 'Understanding Tantra', in Singh (ed.), *Awakening: A Retrospective of G. R. Santosh*, 40.

27 Quoted in Sen-Gupta, 'Neo-Tantric 20th Century Indian Painting', 112.

28 Mookerjee, *Tantra Art: Its Philosophy and Physics*, 110.

29 Kaul, *Kashmir's Mystic*, 13.

30 Quoted in Schelling, Andrew, *Love and the Turning Seasons: India's Poetry of Spiritual and Erotic Longing*, (Berkeley: Counterpoint Press, 2014), 88.

31 Ded, *I, Lalla*, 53.

32 Quoted in Kaul, Shantiveer, 'The Journey: The Artist and His World', in Singh (ed.), *Awakening: A Retrospective of G. R. Santosh*, 24.

33 Interview with Mohan Kishen Tiku for *The Times Weekly*, quoted in: Singh, Kishore, 'A Biography: The Artist as Yogi', in Singh (ed.), *Awakening: A Retrospective of G. R. Santosh*, 204.

34 Abhinavagupta, trans. Raniero Gnoli, *Tantraloka* (Milan: Adelphi, 1999), verses 295–328. Quoted in Padoux, *The Hindu Tantric World*, 77.

35 Mookerjee, *Tantra Art: Its Philosophy and Physics*, 27–28.

36 Quoted in Sareen, 'Biren De (1926–2011)'.

37 Tonelli (ed.), *Neo-Tantra*, 24.

38 Greenstein, 'A View of India's Modern Tantric Art'.

39 Brown, *Art for a Modern India*, 50.

40 Tonelli (ed.), *Neo-Tantra*, 28.

41 Ibid.

42 Mohanti, *Shunya*, 2.

43 Watts, 'Tantra', 57.

44 Wolfers, 'The Making of an Avatar', 278.

45 Douglas, Nik, *Tantra: Indian Rites of Ecstasy*, Mystic Fire Video, 1998 VHS re-release, accompanying description on reverse of tape.

46 Ibid.

47 Ibid.

48 Ibid.

49 Egan, *The Rough Guide to The Rolling Stones*, 96.

50 Rawson, *Tantra: Catalogue of an Exhibition*, 5.

51 Frost, 'The Warren Cup', 65.

52 Personal correspondence with Nigel Waymouth (October 2018).

53 Quoted in Henke and Puterbaugh (eds.), *I Want to Take You Higher*, 103. See also: Grunenberg (ed.), *Summer of Love*, 107.

54 English, M., *3D Eye*, 12. See also: Owen and Dickson, *High Art*, 122.

55 Golding, Peter, *Inspirational Times: The Art of Rock from Beat to Punk via Psychedelia* (London: Sotheby's, 2003), 8.

56 Personal correspondence with Nigel Waymouth (October 2018).

57 Kerouac, *The Dharma Bums*, 17.

58 Oliver, *Hinduism and the 1960s*, 93.

59 Personal correspondence with Nigel Waymouth (October 2018).

60 Ibid.

61 Ibid.

62 Ibid.

63 Nature photographer Galen Rowell declared in 1995 that William Anders's 'Earthrise' photograph was 'the most influential environmental photograph ever taken'. Quoted in *Life* Magazine, *100 Photographs that Changed the World* (Life Books: New York, 2003), 172.

64 Henke and Puterbaugh (eds.), *I Want to Take You Higher*, 69.

65 See: Ginsberg, *Indian Journals*.

66 Rorabaugh, *American Hippies*, 63.

67 Ginsberg, 'Reflections on the Mantra', 148–49. See also: Trigilio, '"Will You Please Stop Playing with the Mantra?"', 189. In his anti-war poem, 'Witchita Vortex Sutra' (1966), Ginsberg invoked 'Sri Ramakrishna master of ecstasy eyes / half closed who only cries for his mother' and 'Durga-ma

covered with blood / destroyer of battlefield illusions'
to assist in ending the Vietnam war: 'I lift my voice
aloud, / make Mantra of American language now, /
I here declare the end of the War!' (Ginsberg, *Collected
Poems 1947–1980*, 407).

68  Quoted in Porter, *John Coltrane*, 265.

69  See: Berkman, 'Appropriating Universality', 47–48.

70  Hentoff, Nat, liner notes to *Live at the Village Vanguard*
by John Coltrane (Impulse!, 1961). Quoted in
Porter, *John Coltrane*, 211.

71  Coltrane and Rivelli, 'Alice Coltrane Interviewed',
22. See also: Clements, 'John Coltrane and the
Integration of Indian Concepts', 155–75.

72  Oliver, *Hinduism and the 1960s*, 132–33.

73  Lavezzoli, *The Dawn of Indian Music in the West*,
318–21.

74  Kandel, Lenore, 'With Love', in *The San Francisco
Oracle*, 1/4 (16 December 1966), 3.

75  Kandel, *The Love Book*, 4.

76  Knight, Brenda, *Women of the Beat Generation: the
Writers, Artists and Muses at the Heart of a Revolution*,
(Berkeley: Conari Press, 1996), 281. See also: Lawlor
(ed.), *Beat Culture*, 169.

77  Kandel, Lenore, 'With Love', in *The San Francisco
Oracle*, 1/4 (16 December 1966), 3.

78  Penny Slinger's personal website:
https://pennyslinger.com/Works/scrolls/

79  Personal correspondence with Penny Slinger
(July 2019).

80  Ibid.

81  Ibid.

82  Ibid.

83  Ibid.

84  Leary, Metzner and Alpert, *The Psychedelic Experience*;
Oliver, *Hinduism and the 1960s*, 69; Grunenberg (ed.),
*Summer of Love*, 15.

85  See: Trungpa and Fremantle (trans.), *The Tibetan
Book of the Dead*.

86  See: Leary, Metzner and Alpert, *The Psychedelic
Experience*.

87  Ibid., 14.

88  Huxley letter to Leary, 2 February 1962. Quoted in
Forte (ed.), *Timothy Leary*, 108.

89  Leary, *Flashbacks*, 260.

90  Liechty, 'Building the Road to Kathmandu', 24.
See also: Liechty, *Far Out*.

91  Liechty, 'Building the Road to Kathmandu', 24.

92  Liechty, *Far Out*, 278.

93  Huntington and Bangdel, *The Circle of Bliss*, 475.

94  See: Sopa, et al. (eds.), *The Wheel of Time*.

95  Quoted in Smee, Sebastian, 'In MFA Exhibit

"Seeking Shambhala", Everything is Illuminated',
*Boston Globe* (30 March 2012).

96  See: Midal, Fabrice, *Chögyam Trungpa: His Life and
Vision* (Boston, London: Shambhala, 2004).

97  The 'rainbow body' (Tibetan: *ja lü*) is one that has
transcended the cycle of death and rebirth (*samsara*).
Baker, *Tibetan Yoga*, 209.

98  Doniger, *Kamasutra: A New Complete English Translation*,
292; Ramos, '"Private Pleasures" of the Mughal
Empire', 12.

99  Tadanori, Yokoo, 'Preface', *Shambala* [print series]
(Tokyo: Nantenshi Gallery, March 1974), British
Museum: 2019.3005.1-10.

100  See: Whitsel, 'Walter Siegmeister's Inner-Earth
Utopia', 82–102.

101  Quoted in Berressem, et al. (eds.), *Between Science and
Fiction*, 110.

102  Tadanori, Yokoo, 'Preface', *Shambala* [print series]
(Tokyo: Nantenshi Gallery, March 1974), British
Museum: 2019.3005.1-10.

103  See: Hartsuiker, *Sadhus*.

104  White, *Sinister Yogis*, 232.

105  Mallinson, 'Yogic Identities: Tradition and
Transformation'.

106  Mallinson, 'Nath Sampradaya', 419.

107  Hartsuiker, *Sadhus*, 45.

108  After India achieved independence in 1947, the
British partitioned India, and a new, predominantly
Muslim, nation was formed – Pakistan (East
and West). The hastily drawn boundaries along
predominantly religious lines forced many millions
to abandon their homes and move between Pakistan
and India, resulting in chaos and at least one million
deaths due to sectarian violence and riots. See also:
Bouillier, 'Nath Yogis' Encounters with Islam', 1.

109  See: Jaffrelot, 'The Other Saffron'.

110  Hartsuiker, Dolf, Hartsuiker Archive, British
Museum, serial no. 1064 (slide no. 3105), 'Aghori
babas'.

111  Barrett, 'Aghoris', 281.

112  Hartsuiker, *Sadhus*, 37.

113  Ibid.

114  Hartsuiker, Dolf, Hartsuiker Archive, British
Museum, serial no. 753 (slide no. 2385), 'Gauri
Shankar Mishra'.

115  Barrett, 'Aghoris', 283.

116  Hartsuiker, Dolf, Hartsuiker Archive, British
Museum, serial no. 1115 (slide no. 3209), 'Dashrath
Ram'.

117  Urban, *Tantra: Sex, Secrecy, Politics*, 39. See also: Iyer,
'Nevla as Dracula'.

118  Tantra is also still vividly present in the world
of modern politics. Indian politicians have been
known to visit Tantric masters to ensure successful
campaigns by engaging in rituals designed to
increase their political potency, and this has even
extended to past Prime Ministers including Indira
Gandhi. See: Jaffrelot, 'The Story of Indian
Politicians and Tantrics'.

119  Openshaw, 'Bauls', 285.

120  The earliest evidence of a unified 'Baul sect' dates
to the 19th century. See: Urban, 'The Politics of
Madness', 15, 23–24.

121  Quoted in Halder, 'Singing Is Like My Personal
Prayer'.

122  Quoted in Sahai, 'Poetess and Minstrel'.

123  Parvathy Baul's personal website:
http://parvathybaul.com/#Artworks

124  Saraswati, Nigamananda, *Mayer Kripa*, (Halisahar:
Swami Atmananda, Saraswati Math, 1382 B.S.),
3–13. Quoted in McDaniel, *The Madness of the Saints*,
151–52.

125  Padoux, *The Hindu Tantric World*, 48.

126  See also: Hiltebeitel and Erndl (eds.), *Is the Goddess a
Feminist?*

127  Garrard, Mary D., *Artemisia Gentileschi: The Image of
the Female Hero in Italian Baroque Art* (Princeton, NJ,
USA: Princeton University Press, 1989), 208.

128  Pollock, 'Tracing Figures of Presence, Naming
Ciphers of Absence', 217; Kokoli, *The Feminist
Uncanny*, 143.

129  Personal correspondence with Sutapa Biswas,
May 2019.

130  Kokoli, *The Feminist Uncanny*, 142.

131  Personal correspondence with Sutapa Biswas,
May 2019.

132  Ibid.

133  Ibid.

134  A year before the painting was executed, in 1984,
Kali was also symbolically cast as the inspiration
for India's first feminist publishing house (based in
New Delhi and founded by Urvashi Butalia and
Ritu Menon), Kali for Women, which specialized
in promoting female empowerment through
publications by women activists and scholars
(covering previously taboo subjects including sex,
menstruation and the body) in multiple South Asian
languages and in English.

135  Sinha, 'Bharti Kher', 123; Petersen, *Migration into Art*,
161; Brown, 'Quite Strangely Masculine', 32–47.

136  Quoted in Brown, 'Quite Strangely Masculine', 33.

137  Doniger, *Redeeming the Kamasutra*, 111.

## CONCLUSION
## (PP. 272–75)

1   Quoted in Gardner, 'Yeshe Tsogyel'.

2   Kukai, *Memorial on the Presentation of the List of Newly Imposed Sutras, AD 806*. Quoted in Shoshin, Moriyama, (ed.), *Bunkashijo yori mitaru Kōbo Daishi den* (Tokyo: Buzanha shu musho, 1931), 249. Translated in de Bary, *Sources of Japanese Tradition*, 155.

3   The Thugee stereotype was recently perpetuated by the British Conservative MP Jacob Rees-Mogg: 'Thuggee is a religious cult around the goddess Kali that murders travellers', TalkRADIO, 3 June 2019; Rees-Mogg, Jacob, *The Victorians: Twelve Titans Who Forged Britain* (London: Virgin Digital, 2019), 142.

# BIBLIOGRAPHY

Abhayadatta, trans. James B. Robinson, *Buddha's Lions: The Lives of the Eighty-Four Siddhas* (Berkeley: Dharma Publishing, 1979).

Acri, Andrea, *Esoteric Buddhism in Mediaeval Maritime Asia: Networks of Masters, Texts, Icons* (Singapore: ISEAS Yusof Ishak Institute, 2016).

Agamavagisa, Krsnananda, *Brhat Tantrasara* (Kolkata: Navabharat Publishers, 1984).

Agrawala, R. C., 'A Rare Image of Varahi in the British Museum', in *Oriental Art*, 9/3 (1963), 167.

Ahluwalia, Roda, *Rajput Painting: Romantic, Divine and Courtly Art from India* (London: British Museum Press, 2008).

Ahuja, Naman P., *Rupa-pratirupa: The Body in Indian Art* (Delhi: National Museum, 2014).

Almeida, Hermione de, and George H. Gilpin, *Indian Renaissance: British Romantic Art and the Prospect of India* (Aldershot, Burlington: Ashgate, 2005).

Arberry, A. J., *The Rubaiyat of Omar Khayyam and Other Persian Poems: An Anthology of Verse Translations* (London: Everyman, 1954).

Archer, W. G., *Indian Painting in the Punjab Hills* (Delhi: Oxford University Press, 1973).

Archer, W. G., *Kangra Painting* (London: Faber, 1952).

Archer, W. G., *The Loves of Krishna* (London: George Allen and Unwin, 1957).

Ardalan, Ziba (ed.), *Bharti Kher* (London: Parasol Unit, 2012).

Atherton, Cynthia Packert, 'Chamunda and Early Hindu Tantrism in Western India', *Orientations*, 26/2 (1995).

Bagchi, Prabodh Candra (ed.), *Kaulajnananirnaya and Some Minor Texts of the School of Matsyendranatha* (Kolkata: Metropolitan Printing and Publishing House, 1934).

Baker, Ian A., *Tibetan Yoga: Principles and Practices* (London: Thames & Hudson, 2019).

Banerjee, S. K., *Sri Sri Bama Ksepa* (Kolkata: Sri Byomkesh Bysack, 1971).

Banerjee, Sumanta, *Logic in a Popular Form: Essays on Popular Religion in Bengal* (Chicago: University of Chicago Press, 2010).

Banerji, R. D., 'Neulpur Grant of Subhakara: The 8th Year', in *Epigraphia Indica*, 14 (1919–20), 1–8.

Barrett, Ronald L., *Aghor Medicine: Pollution, Death, and Healing in Northern India* (Berkeley: University of California Press, 2008).

Barrett, Ronald L., 'Aghoris', in Knut A. Jacobsen, Helene Basu, Angelika Malinar, and Vasudha Narayanan (eds.), *Brill's Encyclopedia of Hinduism*, Vol. 3 (Leiden, Boston: Brill, 2011), 281–84.

Bartholomew, Terese Tse, et al., *Tibet: Treasures from the Roof of the World* (Santa Ana: The Bowers Museum of Cultural Art, 2003).

Bary, Theodore de, *Sources of Japanese Tradition*, Vol. 1 (New York: Columbia University Press, 2001).

Bayly, Christopher Alan, et al., *The Raj: India and the British, 1600–1947* (London: National Portrait Gallery Publications, 1990).

Beach, Milo C., Eberhard Fischer, and B. N. Goswamy, *Masters of Indian Painting* (Zurich: Artibus Asiae Publishers, 2011).

Beer, Robert, *The Encyclopedia of Tibetan Symbols and Motifs* (London: Serindia Pub, 2000).

Benard, Elisabeth Anne, *Chinnamasta: The Aweful Buddhist and Hindu Tantric Goddess* (Delhi: Motilal Banarsidass, 1994).

Bentor, Yael, *Consecration of Images and Stupas in Indo-Tibetan Tantric Buddhism* (Leiden, New York: Brill, 1996).

Berger, Patricia Ann, *Empire of Emptiness: Buddhist Art and Political Authority in Qing China* (Honolulu: University of Hawaii Press, 2003).

Berkman, Franya J., 'Appropriating Universality: The Coltranes and 1960s Spirituality', in *American Studies*, 48/1 (2007), 41–62.

Bernier, François, trans. France Bhattacharya, *Voyage dans les Etats du Grand Mogol* (Paris: Fayard, 1981).

Berressem, Hanjo, et al. (eds.), *Between Science and Fiction: The Hollow Earth as Concept and Conceit*, trans. Bernd Herzogenrath (Berlin: LIT Verlag, 2012).

Bhattacharyya, Benoytosh, *Guhyasamajatantra*, Vol. 53 (Baroda: Gaekwad Oriental Series, 1931).

Biernacki, Loriliai, *Renowned Goddess of Desire: Women, Sex, and Speech in Tantra* (Oxford: Oxford University Press, 2007).

Bloom, Lisa E., *With Other Eyes: Looking at Race and Gender in Visual Culture* (Minneapolis: University of Minnesota Press, 1999).

Blurton, T. R., *Hindu Art* (London: British Museum Press, 1992).

Boeles, J. J., 'Two Yoginis of Hevajra from Thailand', *Artibus Asiae*, 23 (1966), 14–29.

Boner, Alice, and Sadasiva Rath Sarma (trans.), *Silpa Prakasa: Medieval Orissan Sanskrit Text on Temple Architecture* (Leiden: Brill, 1966).

Bose, D. N., and Hiralal Haldar, *Tantras: Their Philosophy and Occult Secrets* (Kolkata: Firma KLM, 1981).

Bouillier, Veronique, 'Kanphatas', in Knut A. Jacobsen, Helene Basu, Angelika Malinar, and Vasudha Narayanan (eds.), *Brill's Encyclopedia of Hinduism*, Vol. 3 (Leiden, Boston: Brill, 2011), 347–54.

Bouillier, Veronique, 'Nath Yogis' Encounters with Islam', *South Asia Multidisciplinary Academic Journal*, online (2015), 1–18. Online resource: https://journals.openedition.org/samaj/3878

Brauen, Martin, *The Mandala: Sacred Circle in Tibetan Buddhism*, trans. Martin Wilson (London: Serindia Publications, 1997).

Braunholtz, H. J., 'A Necromancer's Bone Apron from Tibet', in *The British Museum Quarterly*, 5/1 (1930), 29–30.

Brown, Rebecca M., 'A Distant Contemporary: Indian Twentieth-Century Art in the Festival of India', *The Art Bulletin*, 96/3 (2014), 338–56.

Brown, Rebecca M., *Art for a Modern India, 1947–1980* (Durham, London: Duke University Press, 2009).

Brown, Rebecca M., 'P. T. Reddy, Neo-Tantrism, and Modern Indian Art', *Art Journal*, 64/4 (2005), 26–49.

Brown, Rebecca M., 'Quite Strangely Masculine: Bharti Kher's Androgynous Women', in *Bharti Kher* (Vancouver: Vancouver Art Gallery, 2016), 32–47.

Brown, Robert L., and Katherine Anne Harper (eds.), *The Roots of Tantra* (Albany: State University of New York Press, 2002).

Bruce, George, *The Stranglers: The Cult of Thuggee and Its Overthrow in British India*, (London: Longmans, 1968).

Bryant, Max, *The Museum by the Park: 14 Queen Anne's Gate from Charles Townley to Axel Johnson* (London: Paul Holberton Publishing, 2017).

Buhler, G. (trans.), *The Laws of Manu* (Delhi: Motilal Banarsidass, 1964).

Bühnemann, Gudrun (ed.), *Mandalas and Yantras in the Hindu Traditions* (Leiden, Boston: Brill, 2003).

Burke, Joseph, 'The Eidetic and the Borrowed Image', in Robert N. Essick (ed.), *The Visionary Hand: Essays for the Study of William Blake's Art and Aesthetics* (Los Angeles: Hennessey & Ingalls, 1973), 253–302.

Calza, Gian Carlo (ed.), *Akbar: The Great Emperor of India* (Milan: Skira, 2012).

Campbell, Colin, *Narrative of the Indian Revolt from Its Outbreak to the Capture of Lucknow* (London: G. Vickers, 1858).

Cantwell, Cathy, 'The Medicinal Accomplishment (Sman Sgrub) Practice in the Dudjom Meteoric Iron Razor (Gnam Lcags Spu Gri) Tradition: Reflections on the Ritual and Meditative Practice at a Monastery in Southern Bhutan', in *Journal of the Oxford Centre for Buddhist Studies*, 8 (2015), 49–95.

Cantwell, Cathy, 'Reflections on Pema Lingpa's Key to the Eight Principal Tantric Medicines, and its Relevance Today', in Dasho Karma Ura, Dorji Penjore, and Chhimi Dem (eds.), *Mandala of 21st Century Perspectives: Proceedings of the International Conference on Tradition and Innovation in Vajrayana Buddhism* (Thimphu: Centre for Bhutan Studies, 2017), 163–75.

Chakravarty, Gautam, *The Indian Mutiny and the British Imagination* (Cambridge: Cambridge University Press, 2005).

Chakravorty, Pallabi, and Scott Alan Kugle (eds.), *Performing Ecstasy: The Poetics and Politics of Religion in India* (New Delhi: Manohar Publishers & Distributors, 2009).

Chambers, Eddie, *Black Artists in British Art: A History Since the 1950s* (London: I. B. Tauris, 2014).

Chandrasekhar, Chaya, 'Vajrayana', in Jackie Menzies, *Goddess: Divine Energy* (Sydney, London: Thames & Hudson, 2006), 226–27.

Chang, Garma C. C. (trans.), *The Hundred Thousand Songs of Milarepa, Abridged Edition* (New York: Harper & Row, 1970).

Chatterjee, Partha, *The Nation and its Fragments: Colonial and Postcolonial Histories* (Princeton: Princeton University Press, 1993).

Chatterji, Bankimcandra, trans. Julius J. Lipner, *Anandamath, or the Sacred Brotherhood* (Oxford: Oxford University Press, 2005).

Chaudhury, J., 'The Theory of Rasa', *The Journal of Aesthetics and Art Criticism*, 11 (1952), 146.

Chittick, William C., *The Sufi Path of Love: The Spiritual Teachings of Rumi* (Albany: State University of New York Press, 1983).

Choudhuri, Keshab, *The Mother and Passionate Politics* (Kolkata: Vidyodaya Library, 1979).

Chowdhury Sengupta, Indira, 'Colonialism and Cultural Identity: The Making of a Hindu Discourse, Bengal 1867–1905', unpublished PhD thesis, SOAS, University of London (1993).

Clark, Steve, and Masashi Suzuki (eds.), *The Reception of Blake in the Orient* (New York, London: Continuum, 2006).

Clark, Timothy T., Osamu Ueda, Donald Jenkins, and Naomi Noble Richard (eds.), *The Actor's Image: Print Makers of the Katsukawa School* (Chicago: Art Institute of Chicago in Association with Princeton University Press, 1994).

Clements, Carl, 'John Coltrane and the Integration of Indian Concepts in Jazz Improvisation', in *Jazz Research Journal*, 2/2 (2009), 155–75.

Coburn, Thomas B., *Encountering the Goddess: A Translation of the Devi-Mahatmya and a Study of Its Interpretation* (Albany: State University of New York Press, 1991).

Colquhoun, Ithell, 'The Night Side of Nature', in Richard Shillitoe and Mark Morrisson (eds.), *I Saw Water: An Occult Novel and Other Selected Writings* (Pennsylvania: Penn State University Press, 2014), 167–71.

Colquhoun, Ithell, *Sword of Wisdom: MacGregor Mathers and 'the Golden Dawn'* (London: Spearman, 1975).

Coltrane, A., and P. Rivelli, 'Alice Coltrane Interviewed by Pauline Rivelli', in Pauline Rivelli and Robert Levin (eds.), *Black Giants* (New York: World Publishing Co., 1970).

Cox, Robert, 'Remarks on the Skulls and Character of the Thugs', in *Phrenological Journal and Miscellany*, 8 (1834), 524–30.

Craddock, Elaine, 'The Anatomy of Devotion: The Life and Poetry of Karaikkal Ammaiyar', in Tracy Pintchman (ed.), *Women's Lives, Women's Rituals in the Hindu Tradition* (New York and Oxford: Oxford University Press, 2007), 131–48.

Custodi, Andrea, 'Review of "The Kiss of the Yogini: 'Tantric Sex' in its South Asian Context" by David Gordon White' in *Anthropological Quarterly*, 76/3 (2003), 539–44.

Dallapiccola, Anna L., *Hindu Visions of the Sacred* (London: British Museum Press, 2004).

Dallapiccola, Anna L., *South Indian Paintings: A Catalogue of the British Museum's Collections* (London: British Museum Press, 2010).

Dalton, Jacob, 2014, 'Padmasambhava', in *The Treasury of Lives: A Biographical Encyclopedia of Tibet, Inner Asia and the Himalaya* online. Online resource: https://treasuryoflives.org/biographies/view/Padmasambhava/7442

Daly, Françâis Charles, *First Rebels: Strictly Confidential Note on the Growth of the Revolutionary Movement in Bengal* (Kolkata: Riddhi-India, 1911).

David-Néel, Alexandra, *Magic and Mystery in Tibet* (London: Souvenir Press, 1967).

Davidson, Ronald M., *Indian Esoteric Buddhism: A Social History of the Tantric Movement* (New York: Columbia University Press, 2002).

Davidson, Ronald M., *Tibetan Renaissance: Tantric Buddhism in the Rebirth of Tibetan Culture* (New York: Columbia University Press, 2005).

Davis, Richard H., *Lives of Indian Images* (Princeton, Chichester: Princeton University Press, 1997).

Ded, Lal, *I, Lalla: The Poems of Lal Ded* (London: Penguin, 2013).

Dehejia, Vidya (ed.), *The Sensuous and the Sacred: Chola Bronzes from South India* (Seattle: University of Washington Press, 2002).

Dehejia, Vidya, *Yogini Cult and Temples: A Tantric Tradition* (New Delhi: National Museum, 1986).

Dehejia, Vidya and Thomas B. Coburn, *Devi: the Great Goddess – Female Divinity in South Asian Art* (Washington: Arthur M. Sackler Gallery, Smithsonian Institution in Association with Mapin Publishing, 1999).

Desai, Vishakha N., *Life at Court: Art for India's Rulers, 16th–19th Centuries* (Boston: Museum of Fine Arts, 1985).

Diamond, Debra, David Gordon White, Tamara I. Sears, Carl W. Ernst, and James Mallinson, *Yoga: The Art of Transformation* (Washington: The Freer Gallery of Art and the Arthur M. Sackler Gallery, 2013).

Diamond, Debra, and Catherine Glynn, *Garden and Cosmos: The Royal Paintings of Jodhpur* (London: Thames & Hudson, 2008).

Digby, Simon, *Wonder-Tales of South Asia: Translated from Hindi, Urdu, Nepali and Persian* (Jersey: Orient Monographs, 2000).

Diksit, R., *Tara Tantra Shastra* (Agra: 1987).

Donaldson, Thomas E., *Hindu Temple Art of Orissa* (Leiden: Brill, 1985).

Donaldson, Thomas E., 'Orissan Images of Varahi, Oddiyana Marici, and Related Sow-Faced Goddesses', *Artibus Asiae*, 55, no.1/2 (1995), 155–82.

Donaldson, Thomas E., 'Propitious-Apotropaic Eroticism in the Art of Orissa', *Artibus Asiae*, 37, no. 1/2 (1975), 75–100.

Donaldson, Thomas E., 'The Sava-Vahana as Purusa in Orissan Images: Camunda to Kali/Tara', *Artibus Asiae*, 51, no. 1/2 (1991), 107–41.

Donaldson, Thomas E., *Tantra and Sakta Art of Orissa* (New Delhi: D. K. Printworld, 2002).

Doniger, Wendy (trans.), *Kamasutra: A New Complete English Translation of the Sanskrit Text* (Oxford: Oxford University Press, 2002).

Doniger, Wendy, *The Origins of Evil in Hindu Mythology* (Berkeley: University of California Press, 1976).

Doniger, Wendy, *Redeeming the Kamasutra* (Oxford, New York: Oxford University Press, 2016).

Doniger, Wendy, *Siva: The Erotic Ascetic* (Oxford, New York: Oxford University Press, 1981).

Dowman, Keith, *Masters of Mahamudra: Songs and Histories of the Eighty-Four Buddhist Siddhas, Translation and Commentary* (Albany: State University of New York Press, 1985).

Duff, Alexander, *India and India Missions: Including Sketches of the Gigantic System of Hinduism, Both in Theory and Practice* (1839; reprint, Delhi: Swati Publications, 1988).

Dupuche, John R., *Abhinavagupta: The Kula Ritual as Elaborated in Chapter 29 of the Tantraloka* (New Delhi: Motilal Banarsidass, 2003).

Dvivedi, Vrajvallabha (ed.), *Guptasadhana Tantra* (Varanasi: Sampurnanand Sanskrit University, 1996).

Ebeling, Klaus, *Ragamala Painting* (Basel: Ravi Kumar, 1973).

Eck, Diana L., *Darsan: Seeing the Divine Image in India* (New York, Anima Books, 1981).

Eck, Diana L., *India: A Sacred Geography* (New York: Harmony, 2012).

Egan, Sean, *The Rough Guide to The Rolling Stones* (London: Rough Guides, 2006).

English, Elizabeth, *Vajrayogini: A Study of Her Visualizations, Rituals & Forms* (Boston: Wisdom Publications, 2002).

English, Michael, *3D Eye* (Paper Tiger Books, 1980).

Ernst, Carl W., 'Accounts of Yogis in Arabic and Persian Historical and Travel Texts', in *Jerusalem Studies in Arabic and Islam*, 33 (2007), 409–26.

Ernst, Carl W., 'Being Careful with the Goddess: Yoginis in Persian and Arabic', in Pallabi Chakravorty and Scott Alan (eds.), *Performing Ecstasy: the Poetics and Politics of Religion in India* (New Delhi: Manohar Publishers, 2009), 189–203.

Ernst, Carl W., 'The Islamization of Yoga in the Amrtakunda Translations', *Journal of the Royal Asiatic Society*, 13/2 (2003), 199–226.

Ernst, Carl W., *The Shambhala Guide to Sufism* (Boston: Shambhala Publications, 1997).

Ernst, Carl W., 'Situating Sufism and Yoga', *Journal of the Royal Asiatic Society*, 15/1 (2005), 15–43.

Ernst, Carl W., *Sufism: An Introduction to the Mystical Tradition of Islam* (Boston, London: Shambhala Publications, 2011).

Ernst, Carl W., 'Sufism and Yoga According to Muhammad Ghawth', *Sufi*, 29 (1996), 9–13.

Ernst, Carl W., 2013, 'Translation of Chapter 4 of the *Bahr al-Hayat*, by Muhammad Ghawth Gwaliyari, translated from the Persian', *Smithsonian Institute Research Online*.

Ferentinou, Victoria, 'The Iconography of Coniunctio Oppositorum: Visual and Verbal Dialogues in Ithell Colquhoun's Oeuvre', in Peter J. Forshaw (ed.), *Lux in Tenebris: The Visual and the Symbolic in Western Esotericism* (Leiden and Boston: Brill, 2016), 393–96.

Ferentinou, Victoria, 'Ithell Colquhoun: Surrealism and the Occult', *Papers of Surrealism*, 9 (2011), 1–24.

Fisch, J., 'A Solitary Vindicator of the Hindus: The Life and Writings of General Charles Stuart', *Journal of the Royal Asiatic Society*, 117/1 (1985), 35–57.

Flood, Gavin D. (ed.), *The Blackwell Companion to Hinduism* (Oxford: Blackwell, 2003).

Flood, Gavin D., *An Introduction to Hinduism* (Cambridge: Cambridge University Press, 1996).

Flood, Gavin D., *The Tantric Body: The Secret Tradition of Hindu Religion* (London, New York: I. B. Tauris, distributed in the USA by Palgrave Macmillan, 2006).

Forbes, Alexander Kinloch, with historical notes by H. G. Rawlinson, *Ras-mala: Hindu Annals of Western India, with Particular Reference to Gujarat* (London: Richardson, 1878; reprint, New Delhi: Heritage Publishers, 1973).

Forbes-Mitchell, William, *Reminiscences of the Great Mutiny 1857–59: Including the Relief, Siege, and Capture of Lucknow, and the Campaigns in Rohilcund and Oude* (London, New York: Macmillan, 1893).

Forshaw, Peter J. (ed.), *Lux in Tenebris: The Visual and the Symbolic in Western Esotericism* (Leiden, Boston: Brill, 2016).

Forte, Robert (ed.), *Timothy Leary: Outside Looking In* (Rochester: Park Street Press, 1999).

Fowler, David, 'Brahmanical Hinduism', in Mark Juergensmeyer and Wade Clark Roof (eds.), *Encyclopedia of Global Religion*, Vol. 1 (Thousand Oaks, CA: SAGE Publications, 2012), 156–57.

Frost, Stuart, 'The Warren Cup: Highlighting Hidden Histories', in *International Journal of Art & Design Education*, 26/1 (2007), 63–72.

Fuentes, Ayesha, 'On the Use of Human Remains in Tibetan Ritual Objects', unpublished PhD thesis, SOAS, University of London (forthcoming).

Gaimster, David, 'Sex and Sensibility at the British Museum', *History Today*, 50/9 (2000), 10–15.

Gallo, Riccarda, 'The Image of Maheshvara: An Early Example of the Integration of Hindu Deities in the Chinese and Central Asian Buddhist Pantheon', unpublished MA Dissertation, SOAS, University of London (2013).

Gangoly, Ordhendra Coomar, *Ragas and Raginis: A Pictorial and Iconographic Study of Indian Musical Modes Based on Original Sources* (Kolkata: Clive Press, 1934).

Gangopadhyay, B. K., *Mahapith Tarapith* (Kolkata, Jaytara Publishers, 2010).

Gardiner, David L., 'Tantric Buddhism in Japan: Shingon, Tendai, and the Esotericization of Japanese Buddhisms', in *Oxford Research Encyclopedia of Religion* (Oxford, New York: Oxford University Press, 2018). Online resource: https://oxfordre.com/religion/view/10.1093/acrefore/9780199340378.001.0001/acrefore-9780199340378-e-619

Gardner, Alexander, 2018, 'Yeshe Tsogyel', in *The Treasury of Lives: A Biographical Encyclopedia of Tibet, Inner Asia and the Himalayan Region Online*. Online resource: https://treasuryoflives.org/biographies/view/Yeshe-Tsogyel/10373

Garrett, F., 'The Alchemy of Accomplishing Medicine (Sman Sgrub): Situating the Yuthok Heart Essence in Literature and History', *Journal of Indian Philosophy*, 37/3 (2009), 207–30.

George, Christopher S. (trans.), *The Candamaharosana-tantra, Chapters 1–8: A Critical Edition and English Translation* (New Haven: American Oriental Society, 1974).

Ghose, Aurobindo, *Bande Mataram: Early Political Writings 1890–1908* (Puducherry: Sri Aurobindo Ashram, 1973).

Ginsberg, Allen, *Collected Poems 1947–1980* (New York: Harper & Row, 1984).

Ginsberg, Allen, *Indian Journals, March 1962–May 1963* (San Francisco: City Lights, 1970).

Ginsberg, Allen, 'Reflections on the Mantra', in *International Tunes* (13–26 February 1967).

Glassé, Cyril, *The New Encyclopedia of Islam* (London: Horizons Editions, 2013).

Godfrey, Emelyne, *Masculinity, Crime and Self-Defence in Victorian Literature: Duelling with Danger* (Basingstoke: Palgrave Macmillan, 2011).

Goodall, Dominic, and Harunaga Isaacson, 'Tantric Traditions', in Jessica Frazier (ed.), *The Continuum Companion to Hindu Studies* (London, New York: Continuum, 2011), 122–37.

Goswami, J., *Charankavi Mukunda Das* (Kolkata: 1972).

Goswamy, B. N., *Essence of Indian Art* (Paris, San Francisco: Asian Art Museum of San Francisco, 1986).

Goswamy, B. N., and E. Fischer, *Pahari Masters: Court Painters of Northern India* (Zürich: Artibus Asiae Publishers, 1992).

Goswamy B. N., and J. S. Grewal, *The Mughals and the Jogis of Akhbar: Some Madad-i-Ma'ash and Other Documents* (Shimla: Indian Institute of Advanced Study, 1967).

Goudriaan, Teun, and Sanjukta Gupta, *Hindu Tantric and Sakta Literature* (Wiesbaden: Harrassowitz, 1981).

Grapard, Allan G., 'Of Emperors and Foxy Ladies', *Cahiers d'Extrême-Asie*, 13/1 (2002), 127–49.

Grautoff, Beatrice M. W., *Glimpses of a Land of Sun and Sadness* (London: Bible Churchmen's Missionary Society, 1928).

Gray, David B., *The Cakrasamvara Tantra (The Discourse of Sri Heruka): A Study and Annotated Translation* (Boston: Wisdom Publications, 2019).

Gray, David B., 'Tantra and the Tantric Traditions of Hinduism and Buddhism', in *Oxford Research Encyclopedia of Religion* (Oxford: Oxford University Press, 2016). Online resource: https://oxfordre.com/religion/view/10.1093/acrefore/9780199340378.001.0001/acrefore-9780199340378-e-59

Gray, David B. and Ryan Richard Overbey (eds.), *Tantric Traditions in Transmission and Translation* (New York: Oxford University Press, 2016).

Greaves, Laxshmi R., 'Brick Foundations: North Indian Brick Temple Architecture and Terracotta Art of the Fourth to Sixth Centuries CE', unpublished PhD thesis, Cardiff University and The British Museum (2015).

Greenstein, Jane, 'A View of India's Modern Tantric Art', in *The Los Angeles Times*, (25 December 1985).

Grunenberg, Christoph (ed.), *Summer of Love: Art of the Psychedelic Era* (London: Tate, 2005).

Guha-Thakurta, T., *The Making of a New 'Indian' Art: Artists, Aesthetics and Nationalism in Bengal, c. 1850–1920* (Cambridge: Cambridge University Press, 1992)

Gupta, Mahandranath, trans. Swami Nikhilananda, *Ramakrsna Kathamrta (Translated as The Gospel of Sri Ramakrishna)* (Mylapore: Sri Ramakrishna Math, 1980).

Gupta, Sanjukta, Jan Hoens Dirk, and Teun Goudriaan, *Hindu Tantrism* (Leiden: Brill, 1979).

Guy, John, and Michael Willis, *L' Escultura en els Temples Indis: L'Art de la Devoció* (Barcelona: La Fundació 'La Caixa', 2007).

Haidar, Navina Najat and Marika Sardar, et al., *Sultans of Deccan India, 1500–1700: Opulence and Fantasy* (New York: Metropolitan Museum of Art, 2015).

Halder, Epsita, 'Singing Is Like My Personal Prayer', in *Kindlemag* (13 February 2017).

Hancarville, Pierre d', *Recherches sur l'origine, l'esprit et les progrés des arts de la Grèce* (London: B. Appleyard, 1985).

Harper, Katherine Anne, and Robert L. Brown (eds.), *The Roots of Tantra* (New York: State University of New York Press, 2002).

Harrison-Hall, Jessica, *China: A History in Objects* (London: Thames & Hudson, 2017).

Hartsuiker, Dolf, *Sadhus: Holy Men of India* (London: Thames & Hudson, 1993).

Harvey, Peter, *An Introduction to Buddhism: Teachings, History and Practices* (Cambridge: Cambridge University Press, 1990).

Hatley, Shaman, 'Converting the Dakini: Goddess Cults and Tantras of the Yoginis between Buddhism and Saivism', in David B. Gray and Ryan Richard Overbey (eds.), *Tantric Traditions in Transmission and Translation* (New York: Oxford University Press, 2016), 37–86.

Hatley, Shaman, 'From Matr to Yogini: Continuity and Transformation in the South Asian Cults of the Mother Goddesses', in István Keul (ed.), *Transformations and Transfer of Tantra in Asia and Beyond* (Berlin: Walter de Gruyter, 2012), 99–129.

Hatley, Shaman, 'Goddesses in Text and Stone: Temples of the Yoginis in Light of Tantric and Puranic Literature', in Benjamin Fleming and Richard Mann (eds.), *Material Culture and Asian Religions: Text, Image, Object* (Abingdon: Routledge, 2014).

Hatley, Shaman, 'Kundalini', in Arvind Sharma (ed.), *Encyclopedia of Indian Religions* (Dordrecht: Springer, 2020), forthcoming.

Hatley, Shaman, 'Mapping the Esoteric Body in the Islamic Yoga of Bengal', *History of Religions*, 46/4 (2007), 351–68.

Hatley, Shaman, 'Tantric Saivism in Early Medieval India: Recent Research and Future Directions', in *Religion Compass*, 4 (2010), 615–28.

Hatley, Shaman and Kiss, Csaba, *The Brahmayamalatantra or Picumata*, Vol. 2 (Puducherry, Paris, Hamburg: Institut français de Pondichéry, 2015).

Heller, Amy, *Tibetan Art: Tracing the Development of Spiritual Ideals and Art in Tibet, 600–2000 AD* (Milan, Woodbridge and Wappingers' Falls: Antique Collectors' Club, 1999).

Henke, James and Parke Puterbaugh (eds.), *I Want to Take You Higher: The Psychedelic Era, 1965–1969* (San Francisco: Chronicle Books, 1997).

Higgins, Kathleen Mary, 'An Alchemy of Emotion: Rasa and Aesthetic Breakthroughs', *The Journal of Aesthetics and Art Criticism*, 65/1 (2007), 43–54.

Hiltebeitel, Alf (ed.), *Criminal Gods and Demon Devotees: Essays on the Guardians of Popular Hinduism* (Albany: State University of New York Press, 1989).

Hiltebeitel, Alf, and Kathleen M. Erndl (eds.), *Is the Goddess a Feminist?: The Politics of South Asian Goddesses* (New York: New York University Press, 2000).

Houben, Jan E. M. and K. R. van Kooij (eds.), *Violence Denied: Violence, Non-Violence and the Rationalization of Violence in South Asian Cultural History* (Leiden, Boston: Brill, 1999).

Hunter, William Wilson, *Annals of Rural Bengal by W. W. Hunter, B.A., M.R.A.S. of the Bengal Civil Service* (London: Smith, Elder, 1868).

Huntington, John C. and Dina Bangdel, *The Circle of Bliss: Buddhist Meditational Art* (Chicago: Serindia Publications, 2003).

Huntington, Susan L. and John C. Huntington (eds.), *Leaves from the Bodhi Tree: The Art of Pala India (8th–12th Centuries) and Its International Legacy* (Washington: Dayton Art Institute in Association with the University of Washington Press, 1990).

Hutton, Deborah S., *Art of the Court of Bijapur* (Bloomington: Indiana University Press, 2006).

Isaacson, Harunaga and Francesco Sferra, 'Tantric Literature: Overview', in Jonathan A. Silk, Oskar von Hinüber, and Vincent Eltschinger (eds.), Brill*'s Encyclopedia of Buddhism*, Vol. 1 (Leiden: Brill, 2015), 307–20.

Iyanaga Nobumi, 'Daijizaiten (Siva/Mahesvara)', in *Hobogirin*, 6 (1983), 761–63.

Iyer, Usha, 'Nevla as Dracula: Figurations of the Tantric as Monster in the Hindi Horror Film', in Meheli Sen and Anustup Basu, *Figurations in Indian Film* (London: Palgrave Macmillan, 2013), 101–15.

Jaffrelot, Christophe, 'The Other Saffron', in *The Indian Express* (6 October 2014).

Jaffrelot, Christophe, 'The Story of Indian Politicians and Tantrics', in *The Indian Express* (7 November 2015).

Jain, Jyotindra, *Kalighat Painting: Images from a Changing World* (Ahmedabad: Mapin Publishing, 1999).

Jain, Kajri, *Gods in the Bazaar: The Economies of Indian Calendar Art* (Durham, London: Duke University Press, 2007).

'Jam mgon Kong sprul Blo gros mtha' yas (ed.), *Gdams ngag mdzod: A Treasury of Instructions and Techniques for Spiritual Realization*, Vol. 9 (Delhi: N. Lungtok and N. Gyaltsan, 1971), 456–66.

Jones, William, *The Works of Sir William Jones*, Vol. 4 (Delhi: Agam Prakasham, 1977 [1799]).

Jung, Carl Gustav, *The Psychology of Kundalini Yoga: Notes of the Seminar Given in 1932*, ed. Sonu Shamdasani (London: Routledge, 1996).

Kaimal, Padma, *Scattered Goddesses: Travels with the Yoginis* (Ann Arbor: Association for Asian Studies, 2012).

Kajiyama, Yuichi, 'Women in Buddhism', in *Eastern Buddhist*, 15/2 (1982), 53–70.

Kalff, Martin, 'Selected Chapters from the Abhidhanottaratantra: The Union of Female and Male Deities', 2 vols, unpublished PhD thesis, Columbia University (1979).

Kandel, Lenore, *The Love Book* (San Francisco: Stolen Paper Review, 1966).

Kaul, Madhusudan (ed.), *Brhannilatantra* (Delhi: Chaukhamba Sanskrit Pratishthan, 1995).

Kaul, R. N., *Kashmir's Mystic: Poetess Lalla Ded Alias Lalla Arifa* (Delhi: S. Chand, 1999).

Kaur, Raminder, and William Mazzarella (eds.), *Censorship in South Asia: Cultural Regulation from Sedition to Seduction* (Bloomington: Indiana University Press, 2009).

Ker, James Campbell, *Political Trouble in India, 1907–1917* (Kolkata: Superintendent Government Printing, 1917).

Kerouac, Jack, *The Dharma Bums* (1958; reprint, London: Penguin, 2016).

Keul, István (ed.), *'Yogini' in South Asia: Interdisciplinary Approaches* (London, New York: Routledge, 2013).

Khare, Meera, 'The Wine-Cup in Mughal Court Culture: From Hedonism to Kingship', *The Medieval History Journal*, 8 (2005), 143–88.

Kilty, Gavin, 'Brief Presentation of Channels, Winds, and Drops according to Kalacakra Tradition by Changkya Rölpa Dorje', in Edward A. Arnold, *As Long as Space Endures: Essays on the Kalacakra Tantra* (Ithaca, NY: Snow Lion Publications, 2009), 145–50.

Kinsley, David R., *Hindu Goddesses: Visions of the Divine Feminine in the Hindu Religious Tradition* (Berkeley: University of California Press, 1986).

Kinsley, David R., *Tantric Visions of the Divine Feminine: The Ten Mahavidyas* (Berkeley: University of California Press, 1997).

Kiss, Csaba, *The Brahmayamala Tantra or Picumata: The Religious Observances and Sexual Ritual of the Tantric Practitioner Chapter 3, 21 and 45* (Puducherry: Institut français de Pondichéry, 2015).

Kokoli, Alexandra M., *The Feminist Uncanny in Theory and Art Practice* (London, New York: Bloomsbury Academic, 2016).

Kooij, Karel R. van, 'Iconography of the Battlefield: The Case of Chinnamasta', in Jan E. M. Houben and K. R. van Kooij (eds.), *Violence Denied: Violence, Non-Violence and the Rationalization of Violence in South Asian Cultural History* (Leiden, Boston: Brill, 1999), 249–74.

Kragh, Ulrich Timme, 'Appropriation and Assertion of the Female Self: Materials for the Study of the Female Tantric Master Laksmi of Uddiyana', *Journal of Feminist Studies in Religion*, 27/2 (2011), 85–108.

Kramrisch, Stella, *Manifestations of Shiva* (Philadelphia: Philadelphia Museum of Art, 1981).

Kripal, Jeffrey J., *Kali's Child: The Mystical and the Erotic in the Life and Teachings of Ramakrishna* (Chicago: University of Chicago Press, 1995).

Kripal, Jeffrey J., *Secret Body: Erotic and Esoteric Currents in the History of Religions* (Chicago: University of Chicago Press, 2017).

Krishna, Brajesh, *Art Under the Gurjara-Pratiharas* (New Delhi: Harman Pub. House, 1989).

Kulkarni, Sadasiv Balwant (ed.), *Rasaratnasamucchaya of Vagbhatta*, 2 vols (Kolhapur: Sivaji University, 1970, 1972).

Kulke, Hermann, 'Jagannatha as the State Deity under the Gajapatis of Orissa', in Anncharlott Eschmann, Hermann Kulke, and Gaya Charan Tripathi, *The Cult of Jagannath and the Regional Tradition of Orissa* (New Delhi: Manohar, 1978), 199–208.

Lamb, Ramdas, 'Sadhus, Samnyasis, and Yogis', in Knut A. Jacobsen, Helene Basu, Angelika Malinar, and Vasudha Narayanan (eds.), *Brill's Encyclopedia of Hinduism*, Vol. 3 (Leiden, Boston: Brill, 2011), 262–78.

LaRocca, Donald J., *Warriors of the Himalayas: Rediscovering the Arms and Armor of Tibet* (New York: Metropolitan Museum of Art; New Haven, Yale University Press, 2006).

Laufer, Berthold, 'Use of Human Skulls and Bones in Tibet', in *Field Museum of Natural History Leaflet No. 10* (1923), 1–16.

Lavezzoli, Peter, *The Dawn of Indian Music in the West* (London: Continuum, 2006).

Lawlor, William T. (ed.), *Beat Culture: Lifestyles, Icons, and Impact* (Santa Barbara, Oxford: ABC-CLIO, 2005).

Leach, Linda York, *Mughal and Other Indian Paintings from the Chester Beatty Library* (London: Scorpion Cavendish, 1995).

Leary, Timothy, *Flashbacks: An Autobiography* (New York: G. P. Putnam's Sons, 1983).

Leary, Timothy, Ralph Metzner and Richard Alpert, *The Psychedelic Experience: A Manual Based on the Tibetan Book of the Dead* (New York: University Books, 1966).

Li, Fang Kuei, and W. South Coblin, *A Study of the Old Tibetan Inscriptions* (Taipei: Zhong yang yan jiu yuan li shi yu yan yan jiu suo, 1987).

Liechty, Mark, 'Building the Road to Kathmandu: Notes on the History of Tourism in Nepal',

*Himalaya, the Journal of the Association for Nepal and Himalayan Studies*, 25/1 (2005). Online resource: http://digitalcommons.macalester.edu/himalaya/vol25/iss1/6

Liechty, Mark, *Far Out: Countercultural Seekers and the Tourist Encounter in Nepal* (Chicago: University of Chicago Press, 2017).

Lin, Lina, trans. Silin Chen, 'Gifts of Good Fortune and Praise-Songs for Peace: Images of Auspicious Portents and Panegyrics from the Yongle Period', in Craig Clunas, Jessica Harrison-Hall, and Yu Ping Luk (eds.), *Ming China: Courts and Contacts, 1400–1450* (London: The British Museum, 2016), 122–33.

Linrothe, Robert N. (ed.), *Holy Madness: Portraits of Tantric Siddhas* (Chicago, Serindia and Enfield: Publishers Group UK, 2006).

Linrothe, Robert N., *Ruthless Compassion: Wrathful Deities in Early Indo-Tibetan Esoteric Buddhist Art* (Boston: Shambhala, 1999).

Linrothe, Robert N., and Jeff Watt, *Demonic Divine: Himalayan Art and Beyond* (New York, Chicago: Rubin Museum of Art and Serindia Publications, 2004).

Lipner, Julius, *Hindus: Their Religious Beliefs and Practices* (London: Routledge, 1994).

Lipner, Julius, 'Samsara', in Knut A. Jacobsen, Helene Basu, Angelika Malinar, and Vasudha Narayanan (eds.), *Brill's Encyclopedia of Hinduism*, Vol. 2 (Leiden, Boston: Brill, 2010), 848–54.

Lorenzen, David N., *The Kapalikas and Kalamukhas: Two Lost Saivite Sects* (New Delhi: Thomson Press India, 1972).

Lorenzen, David N., 'Religious Identity in Gorakhnath and Kabir: Hindus, Muslims, Yogis and Sants', in David N. Lorenzen and Adrian Munoz (eds.), *Yogi Heroes and Poets: History and Legends of the Naths* (Albany: State University of New York Press, 2011), 19–50.

Losty, Jeremiah P. and Malini Roy, *Mughal India: Art, Culture and Empire: Manuscripts and Paintings in the British Library* (London: British Library, 2012).

Luczanits, Christian, 'The Eight Great Siddhas in Early Tibetan Painting', in Linrothe, Robert N. (ed.), *Holy Madness: Portraits of Tantric Siddhas* (Chicago, Serindia and Enfield: Publishers Group UK, 2006), 77–91.

McCormick, Seth, 'Incarnating Duality: Jasper Johns and Tantric Art', in Katherine Markoski (ed.), *In Focus: Dancers on a Plane 1980–1 by Jasper Johns, Tate Research Publication Online* (2017). Online resource: https://www.tate.org.uk/research/publications/in-focus/dancers-on-a-plane/incarnating-duality

McDaniel, June, 'Kali', in Knut A. Jacobsen, Helene Basu, Angelika Malinar, and Vasudha Narayanan (eds.), *Brill's Encyclopedia of Hinduism*, Vol. 1 (Leiden, Boston: Brill, 2009), 587–604.

McDaniel, June, *The Madness of the Saints: Ecstatic Religion in Bengal* (Chicago: University of Chicago Press, 1989).

McDaniel, June, 'Sacred Space in the Temples of West Bengal: Folk, Bhakti, and Tantric Origins', *Pacific World Journal*, 3/8 (2006), 73–88.

McDermott, Rachel Fell, *Mother of My Heart, Daughter of My Dreams: Kali and Uma in the Devotional Poetry of Bengal* (Oxford: Oxford University Press, 2001).

McDermott, Rachel Fell, and Jeffrey John Kripal (eds.), *Encountering Kali: In the Margins, at the Center, in the West* (Berkeley, London: University of California Press, 2003).

McGovern, Nathan, 'Esoteric Buddhism in Southeast Asia', in *Oxford Research Encyclopedia of Religion* (Oxford: Oxford University Press, 2017). Online resource: https://oxfordre.com/religion/view/10.1093/acrefore/9780199340378.001.0001/acrefore-9780199340378-e-617

McLean, Malcolm, 'Eating Corpses and Raising the Dead: The Tantric Madness of Bamaksepa', in Hugh B. Urban et al. (eds.), *In the Flesh: Eros, Secrecy and Power in the Vernacular Tantric Traditions of India* (Albany: University of New York Press, forthcoming).

Malik, Muhammad Latif (ed.), comp. Hasan 'Ala Sijzi, *Fawa'id al-fu'ad by Nizam al-Din Awliya' Bada'oni* (Lahore: Malik Siraj al-Din and Sons, 1966).

Mallinson, James, 'The *Amrtasiddhi*: Hathayoga's Tantric Buddhist Source Text', in Dominic Goodall, Shaman Hatley, and Harunaga Isaacson (eds.), *Saivism and the Tantric Traditions: A Festschrift for Professor Alexis Sanderson* (Leiden: Brill, forthcoming).

Mallinson, James, 'Hatha Yoga', in Knut A. Jacobsen, Helene Basu, Angelika Malinar, and Vasudha Narayanan (eds.), *Brill's Encyclopedia of Hinduism*, Vol. 3 (Leiden, Boston: Brill, 2011), 770–81.

Mallinson, James, 'Nath Sampradaya', in Knut A. Jacobsen, Helene Basu, Angelika Malinar, and Vasudha Narayanan (eds.), *Brill's Encyclopedia of Hinduism*, Vol. 3 (Leiden, Boston: Brill, 2011), 409–28.

Mallinson, James, 'Saktism and Hathayoga', in Bjarne Wernicke Olesen (ed.), *Goddess Traditions in Tantric Hinduism, History, Practice and Doctrine* (Oxford: Routledge, 2016), 109–40.

Mallinson, James, 'Siddhi and Mahasiddhi in Early *Hathayoga*', in K. A. Jacobsen (ed.), *Yoga Powers* (Leiden: Brill, 2012), 327–44.

Mallinson, James, *Translation of the Dattatreyayogasastra, the Earliest Text to Teach Hathayoga* (forthcoming).

Mallinson, James, 'Yoga and Sex: What is the Purpose of Vajrolimudra?', in Karl Baier, Philipp A. Maas, and Karin Preisendanz (eds.), *Yoga in Transformation: Historical and Contemporary Perspectives* (Vienna, Vienna University Press, 2018), 181–222.

Mallinson, James, 'Yogi Insignia in Mughal Painting and Avadhi Romances', in Francesca Orsini (ed.), *Objects, Images, Stories: Simon Digby's Historical Method* (Oxford: Oxford University Press, forthcoming).

Mallinson, James, 2013, 'Yogic Identities: Tradition and Transformation', *Smithsonian Institute Research Online*. Online resource, available from: https://eprints.soas.ac.uk/17966/

Mallinson, James and Mark Singleton, *Roots of Yoga* (London: Penguin Books, 2017).

Menzies, Jackie, *Goddess: Divine Energy* (Sydney, London: Thames & Hudson, 2006).

Miller, B. S. (ed. and trans.), *Love Song of the Dark Lord: Jayadeva's Gitagovinda* (New York: Columbia University Press, 1977).

Mimaki, Katsumi and Toru Tomabechi (eds.), *Pancakrama* (Vol. 8 of *Bibliotheca codicum Asiaticorum*) (Tokyo: Centre for East Asian Cultural Studies for UNESCO, 1994).

Misra, Siddhinandan (ed.), *Rasendracudamani of Somadeva* (Varanasi: Chowkhambha Orientalia, 1984).

Mitter, Partha, *Indian Art* (Oxford: Oxford University Press, 2001).

Mitter, Partha, 'Mechanical Reproduction and the World of the Colonial Artist', in *Contributions to Indian Sociology*, 36/1–2 (2002), 1–32.

Mitter, Partha, *Much Maligned Monsters: A History of European Reactions to Indian Art* (New Delhi: Oxford University Press, 2013).

Mitter, Partha, *The Triumph of Modernism: India's Artists and the Avant-garde, 1922–47* (London: Reaktion, 2007).

Mohanti, Prafulla, *Shunya: Prafulla Mohanti, Paintings* (London: Pimlico Books, 2012).

Mojaddedi, Jawid A. 'Getting Drunk with Abu Yazid or Staying Sober with Junayd: The Creation of a Popular Typology of Sufism', *Bulletin of the School of Oriental and African Studies, University of London*, 66/1 (2003), 1–13.

Monier-Williams, M., *Brahmanism and Hinduism* (London: J. Murray, 1894).

Mookerjee, Ajit, *Tantra Art: Its Philosophy and Physics* (New Delhi: Ravi Kumar, 1966).

Mookerjee, Ajit, *Tantra Asana: A Way to Self-Realization* (Basel: Ravi Kumar, 1971).

Mookerjee, Ajit, and Madhu Khanna *The Tantric Way: Art, Science, Ritual* (London: Thames & Hudson, 1977).

Moor, Edward, *The Hindu Pantheon* (London: T. Bensley, 1810).

Morgan, Jessica and Flavia Frigeri (eds.), *The World Goes Pop: The EY Exhibition* (London: Tate Publishing, 2015).

Morinis, E., *Pilgrimage in the Hindu Tradition: A Case Study of West Bengal* (Oxford: Oxford University Press, 1984).

Morrow, John Andrew (ed.), *Islamic Images and Ideas: Essays on Sacred Symbolism* (Jefferson, London: McFarland, 2014).

Nag, Kalidas (ed.), *Akshay Sahitya-Sambhar*, Vol. 1: *Collected Works of Akshay Chandra Sarkar* (Kolkata: 1967).

Narayanan, Vasudha, 'Auspiciousness and Inauspiciousness', in Knut A. Jacobsen, Helene Basu, Angelika Malinar, and Vasudha Narayanan (eds.), *Brill's Encyclopedia of Hinduism*, Vol. 2 (Leiden, Boston: Brill, 2010), 693–701.

Nebesky-Wojkowitz, René de, *Tibetan Religious Dances: Tibetan Text and Annotated Translation of the 'Chams Yig*, ed. Christoph von Fürer-Haimendorf (Berlin: Walter de Gruyter, 1976).

Neevel, Walter, 'The Transformation of Sri Ramakrishna', in Bardwell L. Smith (ed.), *Hinduism: New Essays in the History of Religions* (Leiden, Brill, 1976), 53–97.

Nikhilananda, Swami, *The Gospel of Sri Ramakrishna* (New York, Ramakrishna-Vivekananda Center, 1952).

Olivelle, Patrick, *Dharmasutras: The Law Codes of Ancient India* (New York: Oxford University Press, 1999).

Oliver, Paul, *Hinduism and the 1960s: The Rise of a Counter-Culture* (London: Bloomsbury Academic, 2014).

Openshaw, Jeanne, 'Bauls', in Knut A. Jacobsen, Helene Basu, Angelika Malinar, and Vasudha Narayanan (eds.), *Brill's Encyclopedia of Hinduism*, Vol. 3 (Leiden, Boston: Brill, 2011), 285–94.

Orzech, Charles D., Henrik H. Sorensen, and Richard K. Payne (eds.), *Esoteric Buddhism and the Tantras in East Asia* (Leiden: Brill, 2011).

Owen, Ted, and Denise Dickson, *High Art: A History of the Psychedelic Poster* (London: Sanctuary Publishing, 1999).

Padoux, André, *The Heart of the Yogini: The Yoginihrdaya, a Sanskrit Tantric Treatise* (New York: Oxford University Press, 2013).

Padoux, André, *The Hindu Tantric World* (Chicago: University of Chicago Press, 2017).

Pal, Pratapadiya, 'Arhats and Mahasiddhas in Himalayan Art', *Arts of Asia* 20 (1990), 143–47.

Pal, Pratapaditya (ed.), *The Art of Tibet* (New York: Asia Society, distributed by New York Graphic Society, 1969).

Pal, Pratapaditya, *The Arts of Kashmir* (New York: Asia Society, 2007).

Pal, Pratapaditya, *The Arts of Nepal* (Leiden: Brill, 1974).

Pal, Pratapaditya (ed.), *Himalayas: An Aesthetic Adventure* (Chicago: Art Institute of Chicago in association with University of California Press and Mapin Publishing, 2003).

Pal, Pratapaditya (ed.), *Hindu Religion and Iconology According to the Tantrasara* (Los Angeles: Vichitra Press, 1981).

Pal, Pratapaditya, *Indian Sculpture*, Vol. 1 (Los Angeles: University of California Press, 1986).

Pal, Pratapaditya, *The Sensuous Immortals: A Selection of Sculptures from the Pan-Asian Collection* (Los Angeles: Los Angeles County Museum of Art, 1977).

Pal, Pratapaditya, *Tibet: Tradition and Change* (Albuquerque: Albuquerque Museum, 1997).

Panthey, Saroj, *Iconography of Siva in Pahari Paintings* (Delhi: Mittal Publications, 1987).

Patel, Alka, and Karen Leonard (eds.), *Indo-Muslim Cultures in Transition* (Leiden, Boston: Brill, 2012).

Paul, Diana, *Women in Buddhism: Images of the Feminine in Mahayana Tradition* (Berkeley: University of California Press, 1985).

Payne, Richard K., 'Homa: Tantric Fire Ritual', in *Oxford Research Encyclopedia of Religion* (Oxford: Oxford University Press, 2016). Online resource: https://oxfordre.com/religion/view/10.1093/acrefore/9780199340378.001.0001/acrefore-9780199340378-e-82?mediaType=Article DOI: 10.1093/acrefore/9780199340378.013.82

Payne Knight, Richard, *A Discourse on the Worship of Priapus* (London, Printed by T. Spilsbury, 1786).

Petersen, Anne Ring, *Migration into Art: Transcultural Identities and Art-Making in a Globalised World* (Manchester: Manchester University Press, 2017).

Pinney, Christopher, *Photos of the Gods: The Printed Image and Political Struggle in India* (London: Reaktion, 2004).

Pintchman, Tracy (ed.), *Women's Lives, Women's Rituals in the Hindu Tradition* (New York, Oxford: Oxford University Press, 2007).

Pollock, Grisselda, 'Tracing Figures of Presence, Naming Ciphers of Absence: Feminism, Imperialism and Postmodernity in the Work of Sutapa Biswas', in Lisa E. Bloom, *With Other Eyes: Looking at Race and Gender in Visual Culture* (Minneapolis: University of Minnesota Press, 1999), 213–36.

Porter, Lewis, *John Coltrane: His Life and Music* (Ann Arbor: University of Michigan Press, 2000).

Postel, M., A. Neven, and K. Mankodi, *Antiquities of Himachal* (Bombay: Franco-Indian Pharmaceuticals, 1985).

Ramaswamy, Sumathi, *The Goddess and the Nation: Mapping Mother India* (Durham, NC: Duke University Press, 2010).

Ramos, Imma, 'A Garland of Melodies: *Ragamala* Paintings for the Rajput, Mughal and Sultanate Courts', in *Orientations*, 48/5 (2017), 61–69.

Ramos, Imma, *Pilgrimage and Politics in Colonial Bengal: The Myth of the Goddess Sati* (London: Routledge, 2017).

Ramos, Imma, '"Private Pleasures" of the Mughal Empire', *Art History*, 37/3 (2014), 408–27.

Ramos, Imma, 'The Visual Politics of Menstruation, Birth and Devotion at Kamakhya Temple in Assam', in A. Motrescu-Mayes and M. Banks (eds), *Visual Histories of South Asia* (Primus Books, 2018), 52–68.

Rawson, Philip S., *Tantra: Catalogue of an Exhibition Organized by Philip S. Rawson and Held at the Hayward Gallery, London, 30 September–14 November 1971* (London: Arts Council of Great Britain, 1972).

Ray, P. C., and Hariscandra Kaviratna (eds.), *Rasarnava Rasaitiava* (Kolkata: Baptist Mission Press, 1910).

Reynolds, Valrae, *From the Sacred Realm: Treasures of Tibetan Art from the Newark Museum* (Munich, London: Prestel, 1999).

Rhie, Marylin M., and Robert Thurman, *Wisdom and Compassion: The Sacred Art of Tibet* (New York: Harry N. Abrams, 2000).

Roberts, Michelle Voss, 'Power, Gender, and the Classification of a Kashmir Saiva "Mystic"', *The Journal of Hindu Studies*, 3/3 (2010), 279–97.

Rorabaugh, W. J., *American Hippies* (New York: Cambridge University Press, 2015).

Saeidi, Ali, and Tim Unwin, 'Persian Wine Tradition and Symbolism: Evidence from the Medieval Poetry of Hafiz', *Journal of Wine Research*, 15/2 (2004), 97–114.

Sahai, Rashmi, 'Poetess and Minstrel, Parvathy Baul Lives and Dances in her Beloved's Divine Heart', in *Hinduism Today* (16 February 2013).

Sakaki, Kazuyo, 'Yogico-tantric Traditions in the Hawd al-Hayat', *Journal of the Japanese Association for South Asian Studies*, 7 (2005), 135–56.

Samanta, Suchitra, 'The "Self-Animal" and Divine Digestion: Goat Sacrifice to the Goddess Kali in Bengal', in *The Journal of Asian Studies*, 53/3 (1994), 779–803.

Samuel, Geoffrey, and Ann R. David, 'The Multiple Meanings and Uses of Tibetan Ritual Dance: "Cham" in Context', in *Journal of Ritual Studies*, 30/1 (2016), 7–24.

Sanderson, Alexis, 'The Saiva Age: The Rise and Dominance of Saivism during the Early Medieval Period' in Shingo Einoo, (ed.), *Genesis and Development of Tantrism* (Tokyo: University of Tokyo, Institute of Oriental Culture, 2009), 41–349.

Sanderson, Alexis, 'The Saiva Religion among the Khmers: Part I', *Bulletin de l'École française d'Extrême-Orient* 90 (2003), 349–462.

Sanderson, Alexis, 'Saiva Texts', in Knut A. Jacobsen, Helene Basu, Angelika Malinar, and Vasudha Narayanan (eds.), *Brill's Encyclopedia of Hinduism*, Vol. 4 (Leiden, Boston: Brill, 2015), 10–42.

Sanderson, Alexis, 'Saivism and the Tantric Traditions', in S. Sutherland, et. al., *The World's Religions* (London: Routledge and Kegan Paul, 1988), 660–704.

Sanderson, Alexis, 'Vajrayana: Origin and Function', in *Buddhism into the Year 2000, International Conference Proceedings from Bangkok and Los Angeles* (Dhammakaya Foundation, 1995), 89–102.

Saradananda, Swami, *Sri Ramakrishna the Great Master* (Mylapore: Sri Ramakrishna Math, 1952).

Sareen, Hemant, 'Biren De (1926–2011)', in *Art Asia Pacific Magazine Online* (12 April 2011). Online resource: http://artasiapacific.com/News/BirenDe19262011

Sarkar, Sumit, '"Kaliyuga", "Chakri" and "Bhakti": Ramakrishna and his Times', in *Economic and Political Weekly*, 27/29 (1992), 1543–66.

Sarkar, Sumit, *Modern India: 1885–1947* (Basingstoke: Macmillan, 1989).

Sarkar, Sumit, *The Swadeshi Movement in Bengal, 1093–1908* (Delhi: People's Publishing House, 1973).

Sarkar, Tanika, *Rebels, Wives, Saints: Designing Selves and Nations in Colonial Times* (Ranikhet: Permanent Black, 2009).

Sastri, Jagadish Lal (ed.), *Kathasaritsagarah kasmirapradesavasina Sriramabhattanudbhavena mahakavi Sri Somadevabhattena viracitah [Kathasaritsagara of Somadeva]* (Delhi: Motilal Banarsidass, 1970).

Sastri, Madhusudan Kaul (ed.), *Netratantra with the Commentary (Netroddyota) of Rajanaka Ksemaraja* (Bombay: KSTS 46 and 59, 1926 and 1939).

Sastri, Madhusudan Kaul (ed.), *Svacchandatantra with the Commentary (Svacchandoddyota) of Rajanaka Ksemaraja* (Bombay: KSTS 31, 38, 44, 48, 51, 53, 56, 1921–35).

Sastri, Radhakrishna S. V. (ed.), *Anandakanda* (Tanjore: TMSSM Library, 1952).

Sastri, Visvanarayana (ed.), *Kalikapuranam* (Varanasi: Caukhamba Sanskrit Series, 1972).

Satpathy, Sarbeswar, *Dasa Mahavidya and Tantra Sastra* (Kolkata: Punthi Pustak, 1992).

Schaeffer, Kurtis R., *Dreaming the Great Brahmin: Tibetan Traditions of the Buddhist Poet-Saint Saraha* (Oxford: Oxford University Press, 2005).

Schaeffer, Kurtis R., Matthew T. Kapstein, and Gray Tuttle (eds.), *Sources of Tibetan Tradition* (New York: Columbia University Press, 2013).

Schelling, Andrew (ed.), *Love and the Turning Seasons: India's Poetry of Spiritual and Erotic Longing* (Berkeley: Counterpoint Press, 2014).

Sherer, Moyle, *Sketches of India, Written by an Officer for Fire-Side Travellers at Home* (London: Longman, Hurst, Rees, Orme, Brown, and Green, 1825).

Schimmel, Annemarie, *As Through a Veil: Mystical Poetry in Islam* (New York, Guildford: Columbia University Press, 1982).

Schoterman, J. A. (ed.), *The Yoni Tantra* (Delhi: Manohar, 1980).

Schrempf, Mona, 'Tibetan Ritual Dances and the Transformation of Space', in *The Tibet Journal*, 19/2 (1994), 95–120.

Sears, Tamara, 'Encountering Ascetics on and Beyond the Indian Temple Wall', in Benjamin Fleming and Richard Mann (eds.), *Material Culture and Asian Religions: Text, Image, Object* (Abingdon: Routledge, 2014), 172–94.

Seligman, Isabel, '"A Wordless, Thoughtless Vacuum": Ithell Colquhoun's Drawing Practices', in *Seeking The Marvellous: Ithell Colquhoun, British Women and Surrealism* (Lopen: Fulgur Press, forthcoming).

Sen, Nilratan, *Caryagitikosa Facsimile Edition* (Shimla: Indian Institute of Advanced Study, 1977).

Sen, Ramprasad, *Grace and Mercy in Her Wild Hair: Selected Poems to the Mother Goddess*, trans. Leonard Nathan and Clinton Seely (Boulder: Great Eastern, 1982).

Sen-Gupta, Achinto, 'Neo-Tantric 20th Century Indian Painting', *Arts of Asia*, 31/3 (2001), 104–15.

Settar, Shadaksharappa, *Hoysala Sculptures in the National Museum, Copenhagen* (Copenhagen: National Museum of Denmark, 1975).

Seyller, John, and Jagdish Mittal, *Pahari Paintings in the Jagdish and Kamla Mittal Museum of Indian Art* (Hyderabad: Jagdish and Kamla Mittal Museum of Indian Art, 2014).

Sferra, Francesco, 'A Fragment of the Vajramritamahatantra: A Critical Edition of the Leaves Contained in Cambridge UL Or.158.1', in Vincenzo Vergiani, Daniele Cuneo, and Camillo Alessio Formigatti (eds.), *Indic Manuscript Cultures through the Ages: Material, Textual, and Historical Investigations* (Berlin, Boston: De Gruyter, 2017), 409–48.

Shah, Mobad, trans. David Shea and Anthony Troyer, *The Dabistan, or School of Manners* (Washington: M. Walter Dunne, 1901).

Shah, Sneha, 'Sexuality on Display: A Case Study of Townley's "Erotic" fragment from India', unpublished MA paper, University College London, 2018.

Sharma, Sunil, 'Representation of Social Groups in Mughal Art: Ethnography or Trope?', in

Alka Patel and Karen Leonard (eds.), *Indo-Muslim Cultures in Transition* (Leiden: Brill, 2012), 17–36.

Shaw, Miranda, *Passionate Enlightenment: Women in Tantric Buddhism* (Princeton, Chichester: Princeton University Press, 1994).

Sheehy, Michael R., 'Severing the Source of Fear: Contemplative Dynamics of the Tibetan Buddhist GCod Tradition', in *Contemporary Buddhism*, 6/1 (2005), 37–52.

Shillitoe, Richard, *Ithell Colquhoun: Magician Born of Nature* (lulu.com: 2009).

Siklos, Bulcsu, 'Vajrabhairava Tantras: Tibetan and Mongolian Texts with Introduction, Translation and Notes', unpublished PhD thesis, University of London (1990).

Singh, Kishore (ed.), *Awakening: A Retrospective of G. R. Santosh* (New Delhi: Delhi Art Gallery, 2011).

Sinha, Gayatri, 'Bharti Kher: A Bearer of Intimate Signs', in Ziba Ardalan (ed.), *Bharti Kher* (London: Parasol Unit, 2012), 122–32.

Sircar, D. C., 'Murti Siva's Bangarh Prasasti of the Time of Nayapala', in *Journal of Ancient Indian History*, 13/1–2 (1980–82), 34–56.

Sleeman, William Henry, *The Thugs or Phansigars of India: Comprising a History of the Rise and Progress of that Extraordinary Fraternity of Assassins* (Philadelphia: Carey & Hart, 1839).

Smyers, Karen Ann, *The Fox and the Jewel: Shared and Private Meanings in Contemporary Japanese Inari Worship* (Honolulu: University of Hawaii Press, 1999).

Snellgrove, David, *The Hevajra Tantra* (London: Oxford University Press, 1959).

Snellgrove, David, *Indo-Tibetan Buddhism: Indian Buddhists and their Tibetan Successors* (London: Serindia, 1987).

Snellgrove, David, 'The Tantras', in Edward Conze (ed.), *Buddhist Texts through the Ages* (Oxford: Bruno Cassirer, 1954), 219–68.

Somadeva, Vasudeva, *The Yoga of the Malinivijayottaratantra* (Puducherry: Institut français de Pondichéry, 2004).

Somerville, Augustus, *Crime and Religious Beliefs in India* (Kolkata: The Criminologist, 1929).

Sopa, Lhundub, Roger Reid Jackson, John Newman and Beth Simon (eds.), *The Wheel of Time: The Kalachakra in Context* (New York: Snow Lion Publications, 1985).

Sponberg, Alan, 'Attitudes toward Women and the Feminine in Early Buddhism', in José Ignacio Cabezón (ed.), *Buddhism, Sexuality, and Gender*

(Albany: State University of New York Press, 1992), 3–36.

Storm, Mary, *Head and Heart: Valour and Self-Sacrifice in the Art of India* (London: Routledge, 2015).

Stuart, Charles, *Vindication of the Hindoos … By a Bengal Officer* (London: R. and J. Rodwell, 1808).

Sullivan, Bruce M. 'Tantroid Phenomena in Early Indic Literature: An Essay in Honor of Jim Sanford', *Pacific World, Journal of the Institute of Buddhist Studies*, 8 (2006), 9–20.

Suru, N. G. (ed.), *Karpura-Manjari by Kaviraja Rajasekhara* (Bombay: 1960).

Taylor, Kathleen, *Sir John Woodroffe, Tantra and Bengal: 'An Indian Soul in a European Body?'* (London: Routledge, 2012).

Teiser, Stephen F., 'The Spirits of Chinese Religion', in Donald Lopez (ed.), *Religions of China in Practice* (Princeton: Princeton University Press, 1996), 3–37.

Thurman, Robert A. F., and David Weldon, *Sacred Symbols: The Ritual Art of Tibet* (London: Sotheby's, 1999).

Tonelli, Edith A. (ed.), *Neo-Tantra: Contemporary Indian Painting Inspired by Tradition* (Los Angeles: The Gallery, 1985).

Topsfield, Andrew (ed.), *In the Realm of Gods and Kings: Arts of India* (London: Philip Wilson, 2004).

Törzsök, Judit, 'Kapalikas', in Knut A. Jacobsen, Helene Basu, Angelika Malinar, and Vasudha Narayanan (eds.), *Brill's Encyclopedia of Hinduism*, Vol. 3 (Leiden, Boston: Brill, 2011), 355–61.

Törzsök, Judit, 'Women in Early Sakta Tantras: Duti, Yogini and Sadhaki', *Cracow Indological Studies*, 16 (2014), 339–67.

Trigilio, T., '"Will You Please Stop Playing with the Mantra?": The Embodied Poetics of Ginsberg's Later Career', in J. Skerl (ed.), *Reconstructing the Beats* (New York: Palgrave Macmillan, 2004), 187–202.

Trungpa, Chogyam, and Francesca Fremantle (trans.), *The Tibetan Book of the Dead: The Great Liberation Through Hearing in the Bardo* (Boulder: Shambhala Publications, 2000).

Tucci, Giuseppe, *The Theory and Practice of the Mandala: With Special Reference to the Modern Psychology of the Subconscious* (London: Rider & Company, 1961).

Urban, Hugh B., 'The Cult of Ecstasy: Tantrism, the New Age, and the Spiritual Logic of Late Capitalism', *History of Religions*, 39/3 (2000), 268–304.

Urban, Hugh B., 'Desire, Blood, and Power', in Jeremy Biles and Kent Brintnall (eds.), *Negative Ecstasies: Georges Bataille and the Study of Religion* (New York: Fordham University Press, 2015), 68–80.

Urban, Hugh B., 'The Extreme Orient: The Construction of "Tantrism" as a Category in the Orientalist Imagination', *Religion: A Journal of Religion and Religions*, 29/2 (1999), 123–46.

Urban, Hugh B., 'The Omnipotent Oom: Tantra and Its Impact on Modern Western Esotericism', *Esoterica* 3 (2001), 218 (www.esoteric. msu.edu/VolumeIII/HTML/Oom.html).

Urban, Hugh B., 'The Path of Power: Impurity, Kingship, and Sacrifice in Assamese Tantra', in *Journal of the American Academy of Religion*, 69/4 (2001), 777–816.

Urban, Hugh B., 'The Politics of Madness: The Construction and Manipulation of the "Baul" Image in Modern Bengal', in *South Asia: Journal of South Asian Studies* 22/1 (1999), 13–46.

Urban, Hugh B., 'The Power of the Impure: Transgression, Violence and Secrecy in Bengali Sakta Tantra and Modern Western Magic', in *Numen*, 50/3 (2003), 269–308.

Urban, Hugh B., *The Power of Tantra: Religion, Sexuality, and the Politics of South Asian Studies* (London, New York: I. B. Tauris, distributed in the USA by Palgrave Macmillan, 2010).

Urban, Hugh B., *Tantra: Sex, Secrecy, Politics, and Power in the Study of Religion* (Berkeley, London: University of California Press, 2003).

Valentine, Chirol, *Indian Unrest* (London: Macmillan, 1910).

Vergiani, Vincenzo, Daniele Cuneo, and Camillo Alessio Formigatti, *Indic Manuscript Cultures through the Ages: Material, Textual, and Historical Investigations* (Berlin: De Gruyter, 2017).

Wachsberger, Ken (ed.), *Insider Histories of the Vietnam Era Underground Press* (East Lansing: Michigan State University Press, 2011).

Wadley, Susan S., 'Women and the Hindu Tradition', in *Signs: Journal of Women in Culture and Society*, 3/1 (1977), 113–25.

Wagner, Kim A., 'Confessions of a Skull: Phrenology and Colonial Knowledge in Early Nineteenth-Century India' in *History Workshop Journal*, 69/1 (2010), 27–51.

Wagner, Kim A., 'The Deconstructed Stranglers: A Reassessment of Thuggee', *Modern Asian Studies*, 38/4 (2004), 931–63.

Wagner, K. A., 'Thuggee and Social Banditry Reconsidered', *Historical Journal*, 50/2 (2007), 353–76.

Wagner, Kim A., *Thuggee: Banditry and the British in Early Nineteenth-Century India* (Basingstoke: Palgrave Macmillan, 2007).

Ward, William, *A View of the History, Literature and Religion of the Hindoos*, Vol. 1 (London: Kinsbury, Parbury and Allen, 1817).

Watt, James C. Y., and Denise Patry Leidy, *Defining Yongle: Imperial Art in Early Fifteenth-Century China* (New York: Metropolitan Museum of Art, 2005).

Watt, Jeff, 2001, 'Mandala of Hevajra', *Himalayan Art Resources Online*. Online resource: https://www.himalayanart.org/items/68874

Watts, Alan, 'Tantra', in *Loka: A Journal from Naropa Institute*, Vol. 1 (Garden City: Anchor Press/Doubleday, 1975), 55–57.

Wayman, Alex, *The Buddhist Tantras. Light on Indo-Tibetan Esotericism* (London: Routledge & Kegan Paul, 1974).

Wayman, Alex, *Yoga of the Guhyasamajatantra: The Arcane Lore of Forty Verses: A Buddhist Tantra Commentary* (Delhi: Motilal Banarsidass, 1977).

Wedemeyer, Christian K., *Making Sense of Tantric Buddhism: History, Semiology and Transgression in the Indian Traditions* (New York: Columbia University Press, 2013).

Whitsel, Brad, 'Walter Siegmeister's Inner-Earth Utopia', in *Utopian Studies*, 12/2 (2001), 82–102.

White, David Gordon, *The Alchemical Body: Siddha Traditions in Medieval India* (Chicago, London: University of Chicago Press, 1996).

White, David Gordon, 'At the Mandala's Dark Fringe: Possession and Protection in Tantric Bhairava Cults', in David Haberman and Laurie Patton (eds.), *Notes from a Mandala: Essays in Honor of Wendy Doniger* (Newark: University of Delaware Press: 2009), 200–15.

White, David Gordon, 'Bhairava', in Knut A. Jacobsen, Helene Basu, Angelika Malinar, and Vasudha Narayanan (eds.), *Brill's Encyclopedia of Hinduism*, Vol. 1 (Leiden, Boston: Brill, 2009), 485–90.

White, David Gordon, *Kiss of the Yogini: 'Tantric Sex' in Its South Asian Contexts* (Chicago: University of Chicago Press, 2003).

White, David Gordon, *Sinister Yogis* (Chicago, London: University of Chicago Press, 2009).

White, David Gordon, 'Tantra', in Knut A. Jacobsen, Helene Basu, Angelika Malinar, and Vasudha Narayanan (eds.), *Brill's Encyclopedia of Hinduism*, Vol. 3 (Leiden, Boston: Brill, 2011), 574–87.

White, David Gordon (ed.), *Tantra in Practice* (Princeton, Oxford: Princeton University Press, 2000).

White, David Gordon, 'Yogini', in Knut A. Jacobsen, Helene Basu, Angelika Malinar, and Vasudha Narayanan (eds.), *Brill's Encyclopedia of Hinduism*, Vol. 1 (Leiden, Boston: Brill, 2009), 823–27.

White, John Claude, *Sikhim & Bhutan: Twenty-one Years on the North-east Frontier, 1887–1908* (London: E. Arnold, 1909).

Whitfield, Susan, *Silk, Slaves and Stupas: Material Culture of the Silk Road* (Oakland, CA: University of California Press, 2018).

Williams, Joanna, 'The Iconography of Khotanese Painting', in *East and West*, 23/1–2 (1973), 109–54.

Willis, Jan, 'Nuns and Benefactresses: The Role of Women in the Development of Buddhism', in Yvonne Haddad and Ellison Banks Findly (eds.), *Women, Religion, and Social Change* (Albany: State University of New York Press, 1985), 59–85.

Willis, Michael D. *The Archaeology of Hindu Ritual: Temples and the Establishment of the Gods* (Cambridge: Cambridge University Press, 2009).

Willis, Michael D., *Tibet: Life, Myth and Art* (London: Duncan Baird, 1999).

Willson, Martin and Martin Brauen (eds.), *Deities of Tibetan Buddhism* (Boston: Wisdom Publications, 2000).

Wolfers, Alex, 'Born like Krishna in the Prison-House: Revolutionary Asceticism in the Political Ashram of Aurobindo Ghose', in *South Asia: Journal of South Asian Studies*, 39/3 (2016), 525–45.

Wolfers, Alex, 'Empire of Spirit: The Political Theology of Aurobindo Ghose', unpublished PhD thesis, University of Cambridge (forthcoming).

Wolfers, Alex, 'The Making of an Avatar: Reading Sri Aurobindo Ghose (1872–1950)', in *Religions of South Asia*, 11 (2018), 274–341.

Woodroffe, John, *Principles of Tantra* (Madras: Ganesh, 1986).

Woodroffe, John, *Shakti and Shakta* (New York: Dover Press, 1978).

Woodroffe, John, *Tantra of the Great Liberation (Mahanirvana Tantra): A Translation from the Sanskrit, with Introduction and Commentary*, Arthur Avalon (pseud.) (London: Luzac & Co, 1913).

Woodroffe, John, *The World as Power* (Madras: Ganesh, 1974).

Woodward, Hiram, 'Esoteric Buddhism in Southeast Asia in the Light of Recent Scholarship', *Journal of Southeast Asian Studies*, 35/2 (2004), 329–54.

Woodward, Hiram, 'Tantric Buddhism at Angkor Thom', *Ars Orientalis*, 12 (1981), 57–67.

Zeiler, Xenia, 'Yantras as Objects of Worship in Hindu and Tantric Traditions: Materiality, Aesthetics, and Practice', in Knut A. Jacobsen, Mikael Aktor, and Kristina Myrvold (eds.), *Objects of Worship in South Asian Religions: Forms, Practices, and Meanings* (London, New York: Routledge, 2015), 67–84.

Zwalf, Wladimir (ed.), *Buddhism: Art and Faith* (London: British Museum Publications, 1985).

Zwalf, Wladimir, *Heritage of Tibet* (London: British Museum Publications, 1981).

# GLOSSARY

**Aghori** – 'non-terrible', a sect whose transgressive and deliberately provocative practices, centring around the Tantric god Bhairava, are often compared to those of the earlier, infamous **Kapalikas**.

*amrita* – 'non-death', the nectar of immortality. In Tantric yoga (see **Hatha yoga** and **Devata yoga**), *amrita* is conceived as residing in the skull.

*asana* – yogic posture. **Hatha yoga** introduced a range of complex *asanas*, to be carried out along with breath control (*pranayama*) and 'body locks' (*bandha*).

*asura* – demonic being.

*bandha* – 'body locks' in **Hatha yoga**, muscular contractions used to direct the flow of breath (*prana*) throughout the body.

*Baul* – connoting 'madman' or religious ecstatic, the term defines a sect of wandering bards famous for their mystical songs, performed with simple stringed instruments. Their syncretic beliefs combine Tantric, **Bhakti** and **Sufi** ideas.

**Bhakti** – connoting 'love' and 'devotion', Bhakti stresses the efficacy of a direct and intimate relationship with a personal deity or guru as a means to achieve *moksha* (freedom from the cycle of death and rebirth).

*bhang* – a hallucinogenic and edible preparation created from the leaves and flowers of the cannabis plant.

*bindu* – 'drop' or 'dot', understood as a symbol of the cosmos and as an expression of cosmic creation as well as seminal fluid at the microcosmic level of **Hatha yoga** practice.

*bodhichitta* – understood as the 'will to enlightenment' in Tantric Buddhism (see **Vajrayana**).

**Brahman** – the transcendent principle binding the universe according to Hindu belief.

*chakra* – 'wheel'; *chakras* are energy centres within the **yogic body** of the individual that are meditated on during yogic practice (see **Hatha yoga**).

*chakrapuja* – also known as a *ganachakra*, a sacramental Tantric ritual gathering common to both Hindu and Buddhist traditions. Initiated

**Tantrikas** gather to consume foods and substances which are then offered to a deity. These substances might either be literal or symbolic versions of the *panchamakara* or the *panchamrita* and *panchamamsa*. Sexual rites might also be carried out.

*chakravartin* – 'wheel-turner', or universal ruler or conqueror.

**Cham** – a Tibetan masked dance during which the performers (typically monks and **lamas**) meditate on and transform themselves into deities. Cham dances, performed at monasteries across Tibet and the Himalayas for lay audiences, re-enact dramatic stories such as the arrival of Tantric Buddhism in Tibet from India and the defeat of demonic forces by **Mahasiddhas** and deities.

**Chandali** – also known as Tummo in Tibetan, Chandali is a flame-like goddess (the Buddhist equivalent of **Kundalini**), who resides at the navel and blazes upwards towards the crown of the head when released during **Devata yoga** (see also **yogic body**).

**Chöd** – 'cutting off', a Tantric meditation practice which entails the visualization of one's body being dissected and offered to deities and demonic spirits, thereby severing all attachments to the ego.

*dakshinachara* – the 'right-hand path' of Tantra (*dakshina* means 'right-hand') which follows certain orthodox (Vedic) codes of conduct. Transgressive acts and substances are interpreted symbolically through visualization or the use of substitutes.

*damaru* – a two-headed drum played by Tantric practitioners and an attribute of Tantric deities.

*darshan* – 'sacred viewing', involving seeing and being seen by a deity or holy person in a reciprocal act of auspicious visual communion.

**Devata yoga** – 'Deity yoga', a Tantric Buddhist practice (see **Vajrayana**) during which a practitioner internalizes deities in union and recognizes both the female (wisdom; see *prajna*) and male (compassion; see *karuna*) principles. This involves the manipulation of the **yogic body** through visualizations and breathing techniques. There are two key stages, referred to as the 'generation' (*utpattikrama*) and 'completion' (*sampannakrama*) stages.

*dharma* – 'path of action' or 'duty'; in Buddhism, *dharma* refers to the teachings of the Buddha.

*dharma-kaya* – '*dharma* body', one of the states or bodies of Buddhahood. A Buddha's transcendent, boundless body, which embodies the ultimate truth of Buddhist teachings (see also **sambhoga-kaya** and **nirmana-kaya**).

*dhikr* – a **Sufi** practice involving the remembrance of God through the recitation of His many names in Arabic as found in the Qur'an, containing the divine revelations made to the Prophet Muhammad.

*diksha* – 'initiation'.

*duti* – 'messenger', a term used in Tantric texts to describe female **Tantrikas** who are partners in sexual rites as well as objects of devotion.

*fana* – 'annihilation [of the self]'; the obliteration of the inhibited self or ego according to **Sufi** teachings.

*garbhagriha* – the 'womb chamber' or inner sanctum of a Hindu temple, enshrining the central deity (*murti*).

*ghanta* – 'bell', a Tantric Buddhist ritual implement (see **Vajrayana**), often paired with a *vajra*.

*granthi* – 'knot', a blockage preventing the proper flow of the breath (*prana*), located within the **yogic body** according to **Hatha yoga** practice.

**guru** – a spiritual master and teacher. Tantra was initiatory, and practices and teachings were accessible only via an experienced guru.

**Hatha yoga** – 'yoga of force'. Hatha yoga drew on earlier Tantric conceptions of the body and methods for internalizing divinity. It introduced a range of complex postures (*asanas*) accompanied by breath control (*pranayama*) and 'body locks' (*bandha*), which were muscular contractions used to direct the flow of breath or life force (*prana*) throughout the body.

*homa* – a votive ritual sacrifice involving the immolation of offerings into a fire. Originally an ancient Vedic ritual centring on the propitiation of invoked gods, it remained an important part of Tantric ritual in which a practitioner could visualize their own chosen deity at the heart of the fire.

*'ishq* – fervent, divine love, directed towards God in the **Sufi** tradition.

*jata* – dreadlocks.

**Kalamukha** – 'black face', Tantric ascetics who were particularly dominant in Karnataka between the 11th and 13th centuries, attracting royal patronage for the founding of monastic centres and temples. Like the **Kapalikas**, the Kalamukhas emulated the deity Bhairava. Their name may refer to the black streaks that marked their foreheads, differentiating them from other sects.

*kama* – 'pleasure' or 'desire', one of the key goals of a fulfilling and righteous life according to orthodox Hindu scriptures, along with duty (***dharma***), prosperity (*artha*) and spiritual liberation (***moksha***). In Tantra, desire can be harnessed to achieve power and enlightenment.

*kangling* – a trumpet made from a human thighbone.

*kapala* – 'skull-cup', used by Tantric practitioners as a ritual drinking vessel and alms bowl, and an attribute of Tantric deities.

**Kapalika** – 'skull-bearer', Tantric ascetic. Kapalikas emulated the deity Bhairava by smearing their bodies with ashes, carrying a ***kapala*** as a begging bowl, consuming and making offerings of taboo substances, and residing in charnel grounds.

*karttrika* – a ritual flaying knife, typically with a curved blade. In Tantric Buddhism (see **Vajrayana**) it is wielded by Tantric deities and practitioners to cut through demonic forces and obstacles, including pride, jealousy, desire and aversion.

*karuna* – 'compassion'; the masculine aspect of a Buddha or Buddhist deity, often paired with wisdom (***prajna***). Together they define the two qualities to be cultivated on the path to enlightenment or Buddhahood.

**Kashmir Shaivism** – a Tantric tradition closely associated with the Kashmiri Tantric master Abhinavagupta (*c.* 975–1025), who described all phenomena as an expression of Shiva, including the self and the body.

*khatvanga* – a skull-topped staff, club or sceptre; an attribute of Tantric deities and practitioners. In a Buddhist context, it was conceived as a ceremonial weapon for conquering one's inner obstacles.

*kila* – 'stake', (*phurbu* in Tibetan) a ritual dagger used in Tantric Buddhist practice, with a protective function. The *kila* is wielded to destroy or to neutralize obstacles that might obstruct practice, whether internal or external.

**Kundalini** – 'she who is coiled', an individual's **Shakti**, located at the base of the spine and visualized as a serpent. The goal of **Hatha yoga** is to enable Kundalini to rise through the *chakras* of the body and reach the cranial vault where she unites with Shiva.

**lama** – a Tibetan Tantric Buddhist master or guru (see **Vajrayana**).

*latifa* (plural *lata'if*) – one of the yogic centres within the body of the individual according to **Sufi** tradition. Like the *chakras* according to **Hatha yoga**, the aim of Sufi practice is to meditate on these centres through breathing techniques and recitations.

*linga* – a symbolic, cylindrical representation of Shiva's erect phallus; an abstract expression of his virility and power.

**Mahasiddha** – 'great accomplished one', mainly used to refer to the eighty-four Tantric Buddhist masters who lived between the 7th and 12th centuries, whose hagiographies are preserved in various lists in Tibet.

**Mahayana** – 'Great Vehicle', a Buddhist tradition and school of thought that emerged between around 150 BCE and 100 CE, and which emphasized cultivating compassion towards all living beings and devotion to a number of Buddhist deities and Bodhisattvas (enlightened saviour beings).

*maithuna* – sexual union; the fifth of the Tantric 'Five Ms' (*panchamakara*).

**mandala** – sacred 'circle'; a circular diagram depicting deities and their surrounding celestial environments and entourages, using geometric forms to capture their cosmic, indefinable qualities. Originating in India, mandalas are also conceived as sacred ritual spaces, and may be traced on the ground to consecrate an area and to invoke deities before an important ritual, such as a Tantric initiation.

**mantra** – Sanskrit syllable sembodying the nature of a god or goddess, which can be ritually used as a tool to invoke their presence. Mantras play a fundamental role as 'power-words' in Tantric practice.

*maqam* – in Sufism (see **Sufi**), one of the internal, ascending 'stations' or stages along the spiritual path to unity with God.

*maya* – cosmic illusion; the creative force made up of the elements of the manifested world. In Hindu belief *maya* is a veil masking the divine oneness of reality, resulting in ignorance of one's own divine nature.

*mithuna* – 'couple'; *mithuna* figures often embellish the exterior façades of Hindu and Buddhist monuments, both to generate prosperity and to protect the inner sanctum.

*moksha* – 'emancipation' or 'liberation' from the continuous cycle of reincarnation (see *samsara*) through the realization of one's unity with **Brahman**.

*mudra* – 'seal', a symbolic gesture made with one or both hands.

*murti* – an image, statue, or icon of a deity.

*nadi* – 'tube' or channel within the **yogic body** through which the breath or life force flows (see *prana*). In Tantric forms of yoga (see **Hatha yoga** and **Devata yoga**) there are three main *nadis* that run through the centre and along the right and left sides of the spine.

**Nath** – member of a Tantric order mainly based in northern India and founded by Gorakhnath around the 12th century. The Naths popularized the integration of methods for raising **Kundalini** with **Hatha yoga** practices.

**Nayanars** – 'hounds of Shiva', a group of sixty-three poet-saints from Tamil Nadu who were devotees of Shiva in the 6th–8th centuries. Their songs combined Tantric and **Bhakti** images and ideas.

*nirmana-kaya* – 'transformation body', one of the states or bodies of Buddhahood. A Buddha's mortal, perishable body that manifests in the earthly realm (see also *dharma-kaya* and *sambhoga-kaya*).

*nirvana* – 'blowing out'; from the Buddhist perspective this implies a complete extinction of the self and release from the cycle of reincarnation (*samsara*).

*panchamakara* – the 'Five Ms' described in some Tantric texts: wine (*madya*), fish (*matsya*), meat (*mamsa*), sexual fluids generated from ritual intercourse (*maithuna*) and parched grain (*mudra*).

*panchamamsa* – 'Five Meats' described in some Tantric Buddhist texts (see **Vajrayana**): human flesh, beef, horse, dog and elephant.

*panchamrita* – 'Five Ambrosias' described in some Tantric Buddhist texts (see **Vajrayana**): urine, excrement, semen, menstrual blood and brains.

*pandal* – a temporary shrine, constructed to venerate a god or goddess.

*pandit* – a scholar or teacher.

*paramitas* – the six Buddhist perfections necessary for attaining Buddhahood: patience, charity, meditation, mental discipline, perseverance and transcendent insight.

*pir* – a Sufi master or teacher, also known as *shaykh*.

*prajna* – 'wisdom'; the feminine aspect of a Buddha or Buddhist deity, often paired with compassion (**karuna**). Together they define the two qualities to be cultivated on the path to enlightenment or Buddhahood.

*prakriti* – 'creative force', 'nature', 'materiality', 'feminine matter'; associated with **Shakti**.

*prana* – breath or life force (see also **Hatha yoga**).

*pranayama* – breath control, employed in **Hatha yoga** to direct the breath or life force (**prana**).

*puja* – the act of worship, through offerings and devotional behaviour.

*purusha* – 'consciousness', associated with Shiva. Also, 'cosmic man'.

*rajapana* – the ritual drinking of female sexual fluids, believed to be imbued with **Shakti**.

*rajas* – female menstrual or generative fluid, associated with **Kundalini**.

*ramdao* – a ceremonial sword used for animal sacrifice, with a curved blade to ensure decapitation in a single stroke. The goddess Kali is often depicted wielding one to slay ignorance in order to replace it with wisdom.

*rasa* – 'essence' or 'taste', an emotional, transcendent state inspired or evoked by an art form through *bhavas* (moods or emotions).

*rus gyan* – a Tibetan net-like skirt or apron, made predominantly of intricately carved human bone (occasionally also animal bone).

*sadhana* – 'practice'; the term can refer to a Tantric practice for attaining spiritual, worldly and/or supernatural goals.

*sahasrara* – 'thousand-petalled', a **chakra** located at the crown of the head (see also **yogic body**).

*samadhi* – a mindful state of blissful awareness in which the individual fully identifies with the object of their meditation.

*sambhoga-kaya* – 'bliss body', one of the states or bodies of Buddhahood. A Buddha's heavenly body located in paradise (see also *dharma-kaya* and *nirmana-kaya*).

*sampannakrama* – the 'completion' stage of **Devata yoga**, during which practitioners draw on advanced techniques for fully identifying their body, speech and mind with a chosen meditational deity. These techniques involve working with the **yogic body** and its network of *chakras* and *nadis*.

*samsara* – the cycle of death and rebirth according to Hindu and Buddhist belief systems.

*satkarman* – 'six actions'; a set of Tantric rites: pacification (*shanti*), subjugation (*vashikarana*), immobilization (*stambhana*), creation of hostility (*vidvesana*), driving away (*ucchatana*) and killing (*marana*).

*sgrub chen* – 'major practice session', a communal Tantric Buddhist practice performed by a group of **lamas** over several days.

**Shaiva Siddhanta** – a 'right-hand path' or *dakshinachara* Tantric tradition centring on a five-faced form of Shiva known as Sadashiva; consisting of public rituals performed by Hindu priests following certain orthodox (Vedic) codes of conduct, including the adherence to pure/impure distinctions and the use of generally vegetarian offerings.

**Shakti** – divine feminine power.

**Shakti Pitha** – 'Seat of Power', a shrine or temple dedicated to **Shakti**. These are located across South Asia. There are numerous myths about their origins and significance, the most famous being that they represent the locations where various parts of the goddess Sati's body landed on Earth following her dismemberment.

*shava sadhana* – 'corpse practice', meditation conducted whilst seated on a corpse, carried out by initiated and experienced **Tantrikas** in cremation- and charnel-ground settings.

**Shingon** – the 'true word' (i.e., **mantra**) tradition of Tantric Buddhism in Japan, founded by Kukai (774–835).

*shunyata* – 'emptiness', a concept outlined by the Buddha, and developed by Buddhist philosopher Nagarjuna (*c.* 150–250 CE), that all phenomena are temporary, unfixed and therefore essentially empty. This does not imply that they do not exist, but rather that all living and inanimate things lack autonomy in and of themselves and are instead characterized by their divine interdependence and interconnectedness.

**Siddha** – 'accomplished one', Tantric practitioner (see also **Mahasiddha**).

*siddhi* – 'attainment' or power (spiritual, worldly and supernatural) that a Tantric practitioner seeks to achieve.

**Sufi** – a follower of Sufism (Islamic mysticism). Sufis seek close, direct and personal experience of God (Allah), which can be achieved through methods designed to obliterate the inhibited self or ego (*fana*).

*Tantrashastra* – 'the teachings of the *Tantras*'.

**Tantrika** – a practitioner of Tantra.

*thangka* – a Tibetan or Nepalese painting on cloth.

**Theravada** – 'Teaching of the Elders', the first major school of thought that emerged after the Buddha's death, and the one that remained closest to the early Buddhist scriptures, revolving around the attainment of spiritual liberation through one's own efforts.

*trishula* – 'trident', an attribute of Shiva.

*utpattikrama* – the 'generation' stage of **Devata yoga**, during which practitioners visualize and identify with their chosen meditational deities.

*vahana* – 'vehicle', the mount of a god or goddess, typically an animal or mythical being.

*vajra* – 'thunderbolt', a Tantric Buddhist symbol of the unbreakable force of the enlightened state which has obliterated all obstacles. Some Tantric texts also refer to the *vajra* as a signifier for a god's phallus.

*vajracharya* – '**Vajrayana** master'. General title for teaching masters of Tantric Buddhism.

**Vajrayana** – 'Thunderbolt Vehicle', also known as Tantric Buddhism. Vajrayana drew on and retained the core philosophical teachings of Gautama Buddha and the **Mahayana** ('Great Vehicle') but promised more powerful, practical methods for attaining the same goal of enlightenment.

*vamachara* – the 'left-hand path' of Tantra (*vama* means 'left-hand'), in which practitioners engage with taboo or transgressive acts and substances.

*varna* – class; the hierarchical social order within orthodox or Brahmanical Hinduism was divided into four classes, each conforming to prescribed roles and rules of behaviour: the Brahmins (priests and teachers), Kshatriyas (warriors and rulers), Vaishyas (farmers, traders and merchants) and Shudras (labourers). There was an excluded fifth *varna*, or *avarna* (literally *varna*-less or outcasts), members of whom were prohibited from participating in Vedic ritual.

*viparita-rata* – the 'inverse' sexual position in which the woman is on top of the man, reflecting Tantra's overturning of hierarchical norms.

*vira* – 'hero'; those brave enough to risk the spiritual 'perils' of Tantric practice.

*yab-yum* – 'father-mother', expressing the union of conceptual polarities or the combination of 'feminine' wisdom (***prajna***) and 'masculine' compassion (***karuna***) through the depiction or visualization of deities in sexual union.

*yantra* – a geometric ritual diagram used as an instrument to invoke deities during Tantric practice and as an aid to stimulate visualizations. It is also used for rites designed to fulfil worldly or supernatural ambitions.

**yogic body** – the network of the 'yogic body' described in Tantric and **Hatha yoga** texts as made up of energy centres called ***chakras***. The *chakras* are linked to the three main channels of the yogic body called ***nadis***, which allow the body's life-force (***prana***) to flow.

*yoni* – 'vulva', a symbol of divine creation associated with **Shakti**, divine feminine power.

*yoni-puja* – 'veneration of the vulva', centred on the belief that mortal women were embodiments of **Shakti**, divine feminine power.

# PICTURE CREDITS

The publisher would like to thank the copyright holders for granting permission to reproduce the images illustrated. Every attempt has been made to trace accurate ownership of copyrighted images in this book. Any errors or omissions will be corrected in subsequent editions provided that notification is sent to the publishers.

Registration numbers for British Museum objects are included in the image captions. Further information about the museum and its collection can be found at britishmuseum.org. Unless otherwise stated below, copyright in photographs belongs to the institution mentioned in the caption.

British Museum objects are © The Trustees of the British Museum, courtesy the Department of Photography and Imaging.

Maps by Paul Goodhead, British Museum

**p. 9 (fig. 2)** Photography by Michael Runkel; robertharding / Alamy Stock Photo

**p. 10 (fig. 3)** Reproduced by permission of the author

**p. 11 (fig. 4)** Reproduced by permission of the author

**p. 15 (fig. 5)** Folio from the *Yoginihridaya* (MS Or.722.6; 1v), reproduced by kind permission of the Syndics of Cambridge University Library

**p. 16 (fig. 6)** Folio from the *Vajramrita Tantra* (MS Or.158.1; 12r), reproduced by kind permission of the Syndics of Cambridge University Library

**p. 18 (fig. 7)** Folio from the *Vajramrita Tantra* (MS Or.158.1; 1v), reproduced by kind permission of the Syndics of Cambridge University Library

**p. 23 (fig. 8)** Reproduced by permission of the artist

**p. 27 (fig. 10)** Photo © Museum Associates / LACMA

**p. 28 (fig. 11)** Photo: Laxshmi Rose Greaves

**p. 30 (fig. 13)** ID 97595107 © Praveen Indramohan | Dreamstime.com

**p. 32 (fig. 16)** The Metropolitan Museum of Art, New York, Purchase, Edward J. Gallagher Jr. Bequest, in memory of his father, Edward Joseph Gallagher, his mother, Ann Hay Gallagher, and his son, Edward Joseph Gallagher III, 1982; www.metmuseum.org

**p. 38 (fig. 19)** The Metropolitan Museum of Art, New York, Gift of Samuel Eilenberg, in memory of Anthony Gardner, 1996; www.metmuseum.org

**p. 41 (fig. 21)** Folio from the *Devi Mahatmya* (MS Add.1588.3; 22v), reproduced by kind permission of the Syndics of Cambridge University Library

**p. 43 (fig. 23)** Photo by De Agostini / G. Nimatallah via Getty Images

**p. 50 (fig. 27)** Folio from the *Vajramrita Tantra* (MS Or.158.1; 11v), reproduced by kind permission of the Syndics of Cambridge University Library

**p. 55 (fig. 32)** Detroit Institute of Arts, Founders Society Purchase, L. A. Young Fund, 57.88

**p. 56 (fig. 33)** Map by Paul Goodhead, British Museum, based on Dehejia, Vidya, *Yogini Cult and Temples: A Tantric Tradition* (New Delhi: National Museum, 1986)

**p. 58 (fig. 34)** Hemis / Alamy Stock Photo

**p. 73 (fig. 41)** National Museum, New Delhi

**p. 75 (fig. 42)** National Museum, New Delhi

**p. 76 (figs. 43, 44)** National Museum, New Delhi

**p. 77 (figs. 45, 46)** National Museum, New Delhi

**p. 78 (figs. 47, 48)** National Museum, New Delhi

**p. 79 (fig. 49)** National Museum, New Delhi

**p. 80 (fig. 50)** Courtesy of The Cleveland Museum of Art

**p. 84 (fig. 52)** © The Trustees of the Chester Beatty Library, Dublin, In 44.3

**p. 88 (fig. 54)** © The Trustees of the Chester Beatty Library, Dublin, In 37 f.44r

**p. 89 (fig. 56)** © The Trustees of the Chester Beatty Library, Dublin, In 16.24r

**p. 89 (fig. 57)** © The Trustees of the Chester Beatty Library, Dublin, In 16.18r

**p. 98 (fig. 66)** The Metropolitan Museum of Art, New York, Purchase, Lila Acheson Wallace Gift, 2011; www.metmuseum.org

**p. 101 (fig. 68)** Photo © 2020 Museum of Fine Arts, Boston

**p. 101 (fig. 69)** Photo © Museum Associates / LACMA

**p. 107 (fig. 72)** © The Trustees of the Chester Beatty Library, Dublin, In 02 f.240v

**p. 107 (fig. 73)** © The Trustees of the Chester Beatty Library, Dublin, In 02 f.241r

**p. 109 (fig. 76)** © The Trustees of the Chester Beatty Library, Dublin, In 11a.31

**p. 125 (fig. 86)** Photography by Gavin Ashworth; image courtesy of the Rubin Museum of Art

**p. 134 (figs. 94, 95)** Tibet Museum, Lhasa

**p. 141 (fig. 101)** Folio from the *Hevajra Tantra* (MS Add.1697.2; 18r), reproduced by kind permission of the Syndics of Cambridge University Library

**p. 143 (fig. 102)** Courtesy of The Cleveland Museum of Art

**p. 152 (fig. 109)** The Metropolitan Museum of Art, New York, Purchase, Friends of Asian Art Gifts, in honor of Wen C. Fong, 2000; www.metmuseum.org

**p. 163 (fig. 119)** Photography by David De Armas; image courtesy of the Rubin Museum of Art

**p. 166 (fig. 122)** Reproduced by permission of the artist

**p. 166 (fig. 123)** Photography by Bryan Mulvihill; reproduced by permission of the artist

**p. 168 (fig. 125)** © Mark Overgaard

**p. 170 (fig. 127)** National Geographic Image Collection / Alamy Stock Photo

**p. 175 (fig. 129)** Map by Paul Goodhead, British Museum, based on Bayly, Christopher Alan, et al., *The Raj: India and the British, 1600–1947* (London: National Portrait Gallery Publications, 1990)

**p. 179 (figs. 132, 133)** Rights reserved

**p. 185 (fig. 137)** Photo: National Gallery of Victoria, Melbourne; Felton Bequest, 1920. This digital record has been made available on NGV Collection Online through the generous support of the Joe White Bequest.

**p. 188 (fig. 139)** Purchase, Gift of Mrs. William J. Calhoun, by exchange, 2013 (2013.17); The Metropolitan Museum of Art, New York © 2019; image © The Metropolitan Museum of Art / Art Resource / Scala, Florence

**p. 194 (fig. 145)** Dinodia Photos / Alamy Stock Photo

**p. 201 (fig. 150)** © The British Library Board, T.21492 opp. title page

**p. 201 (fig. 151)** © The British Library Board, T.21492, foldout opposite p. 382

**p. 206 (fig. 155)** Priya Paul Collection @ Tasveer Ghar

**p. 208 (fig. 156)** Reproduced by permission of the author

**p. 208 (fig. 157)** Rights reserved

**p. 210 (fig. 158)** Rights reserved

**p. 211 (fig. 159)** Rights reserved

**p. 213 (fig. 160)** Rights reserved

**p. 214** Reproduced by permission of the artist's estate

**p. 218 (fig. 161)** © Samaritans, © Noise Abatement Society & © Spire Healthcare

# ACKNOWLEDGMENTS

There are many people to whom I am grateful for their guidance, assistance and expertise. Firstly to Alex Wolfers, for inspiring me every step of the way and for patiently reading early drafts of the book. To Lynne Taggart, Guillem Ramos-Poqui, Qamar Maclean, Nicolas Maclean and Jean Michel Massing for their indefatigable support and feedback. To Christian Luczanits, James Mallinson, Yu-Ping Luk, Jessica Harrison-Hall, Ayesha Fuentes, Alfred Haft and Richard Shillitoe for kindly reading and providing invaluable comments on individual chapters and sections. To my brilliant colleague Tom Young for all his help with the compilation of the bibliography, glossary, captions and endnotes, and for his proofreading skills.

To the British Museum's Head of Publishing (Claudia Bloch), Editorial Assistant (Bethany Holmes), and our colleagues at Thames & Hudson (Flora Spiegel, Susanna Ingram and Susannah Lawson) and Grade Design (Peter Dawson and Amy Shortis) for all their hard work in creating the finished product.

To friends and colleagues who have helped with their guidance and expertise: Varun Khanna, Vincenzo Vergiani, Francesco Sferra, Koel Chakraborty, Laxshmi Greaves, Emma Martin, Thupten Kelsang, Susan Bean, Amrita Jhaveri, Shabir Hussain Santosh, Ian Baker, Isabel Seligman, Peyvand Firouzeh, Zeina Klink-Hoppe, Nadia Jamil and Zoe Sperling.

To my colleagues in the British Museum who, in one way or another, have made this book possible and have encouraged me throughout: Jane Portal, Jill Maggs, Hartwig Fischer, Jonathan Williams, Richard Blurton, Michael Willis, JD Hill, Claire Edwards, Stuart Frost, Jonathan Ould and Mary Linkins.

To British Museum photographers Kevin Lovelock and John Williams for their many hours spent photographing material for the book, and to graphic designer Paul Goodhead for creating the maps. To the following conservators, scientists, collection managers and exhibition assistants for preparing material for photography as well as for the exhibition: Matthias Sotiras, Alice Derham, Valentina Marabini, Monique Pullan, Teresa Heady, Alex Owen, Barbara Wills, Helene Delaunay, Rachel Weatherall, Denise Ling, Rachel Berridge, Michelle Hercules, Tracey Sweek, Keeley Wilson, Joanne Dyer, Carl Heron, Lucy Romeril, Simon Prentice, Georgia Goldsmith, Daryl Tappin, Stephanie Vasiliou, Hannah Scully and Joseph Borges.

And finally to Alka Bagri and the Bagri Foundation, the lead supporter of the accompanying exhibition.

Imma Ramos

# INDEX

Page numbers in *italic* refer to illustrations.

## AUTHOR BIOGRAPHY

Imma Ramos is the curator of the medieval to modern South Asia collections at the British Museum. Her research interests revolve around the relationship between religion, politics and gender in South Asian visual culture. She completed her PhD at the University of Cambridge. Her first book *Pilgrimage and Politics in Colonial Bengal: The Myth of the Goddess Sati* (2017), examined a network of sacred sites dedicated to Sati that provided the basis for an emergent territorial consciousness during the late 19th century.